LISTS OF INHABITANTS OF COLONIAL NEW YORK

Excerpted from The Documentary History of the State of New-York

By
EDMUND BAILEY O'CALLAGHAN

Indexed by
Rosanne Conway

Baltimore
GENEALOGICAL PUBLISHING CO., INC.

Excerpted and reprinted from:
The Documentary History of the State of New-York
Albany, New York, 1849-1851
Genealogical Publishing Co., Inc.
Baltimore, 1979, 1989
© 1979
Genealogical Publishing Co., Inc.
Baltimore, Maryland
All Rights Reserved
International Standard Book Number 0-8063-0847-8
Made in the United States of America

PUBLISHER'S PREFACE

DMUND BAILEY O'CALLAGHAN'S *Documentary History of the State of New-York*, published in four bulky volumes between 1849 and 1851, is one of the key source-books for genealogical and historical research in New York State. Interspersed throughout its more than 4,350 pages are copies of important genealogical records of the seventeenth and eighteenth centuries, among which are census records, rate lists, lists of early settlers, and rolls of militia companies. For the genealogist, unfortunately, these volumes are difficult to use, chiefly because they lack an index to the names of persons mentioned in the records. As the data is classified under various section headings, and is thereunder innocent of system, the location of a name is laborious and time-consuming. This present volume, however, an extract of all the important genealogical records in the O'Callaghan work, brought together in just under 300 pages, contains a complete index of names, and overcomes, for individuals unfamiliar with Dutch or German nomenclature, the confusion caused by variant spellings of family names.

The records are arranged in this work in the same sequence in which they appear in the *Documentary History*. As is customary, the running head at the top of each page serves as a guide to the text. In some instances, however, as in the heading "Administration of Lieut. Gov. Leisler," where the heading identifies an extensive section of the original work, the running head might confuse the reader, who is advised to refer to the table of contents for clarification.

CONTENTS

NAMES

𝕸𝖆𝖑𝖊 𝕴𝖓𝖍𝖆𝖇𝖎𝖙𝖆𝖓𝖙𝖘 𝖔𝖋 𝖀𝖑𝖘𝖙𝖊𝖗 𝕮𝖔𝖚𝖓𝖙𝖞, 1689.

A ROOL OF THE NAMES AND SURNAMES

OF THEM THAT HAUE TAKIN THE OATH OF ALLEGIANCE IN Y^e COUNTY OF VLST^r, BY ORD^r OF HIS EXCELY : Y^c GOUERNOR ; Y^e FFIRST DAY OF SEPTEMB^r ANNO Q^e: DOMINI 1689—

Cap^n: Hennery Beekman

Cap^n Matthis Matthison

Left: Abraham Haesbrock

Lowies Bouier

John Hendricks

Albart Johnson V: Steenwicke

Marten Hoffeman

William Van ffredingborch

Lowranc. Van der Bush

Wessell Tenbrock

John Boorehanc

John Willianson Hogetilen

Gerritt Arsin

Tunis Elison

John ffocken

William DeMy^{r}s:

Johanas Schencke

William De Lamontanij

John Johnson Van Osterenhoudt

Jochijam Hendricks

Harrama Hendricks

John Haesbrock

Cornelis Sweitts

Burgar Mind^{r}son

Hendrick Albertsa

Abraham ffranckford

William: Danswick

Moses Depuis

William Hoogtilin

Gerritt Wincoop

Symon Cool

Isack Dibois

Benj^a: Provorist

Jesely Valleij

Andries Laffever

Pett^r: Dovo

Abraham Deboijs

Moses Laconta

Petter Hellibrandts

Symon Laffever

Sander Roesinkranc

Cornelis Cool

Pett^r: Johnson
Claes Claes Sluitt^r
Powlas Powlas
Thomas Quick
Nicolas Anthony
Johanas Wincop
Jost Jansin
Jacob Arsin
Matthies Slecht
John Middag
Hendrick Cornelis Bogard
Gisbort Albortsa
Gerrit Van ffleitt
Cornelis Slecht
Jacob Cool
Abraham Rutton
Abl Westfalin
Abraham Lamiater
Pett^r: Jacobs
Isack Van ffredingborch
Gerrit Cornelis
Jacob Lamiater
Arrian Tunis
Claes Westfalin
John Cottin
Johanas Westfalin
Thomas Johnson
Hendrick Johnson Van Bush
Andries Petters
Gerritt Jansa Decker
Lendart Cool
Cornelis ffinehoudt
Tunis Jacobs
Jacob Schutt
Leury Jacobs
John Elting
Rollof Swartwout

Arrie ffrance
John Osternhoudt Juno^r:
Hendrick Traphager
Jacob Decker
Rolloff Hendrickes
Cornelis VerNoij
Hendrick Van Wien
Hiuge ffreri Senior
Hiuge ffreri Junior
Pett^r: Cornelis
Gerritt Johnson
Anthony Criupill
Abraham Carrmar
Pett^e: Winniy
John Pett^{r}son
John Josten
Wallraven DeMont Junio^r
Johanas Traphager
Hendrick in the ffeelt
Petter Criupill
Gerrit Gisborts
Hendrick Hendricks
John Gerrittsa of new Church
Hendrick Arreyn
John Van ffleitt
Claes Tunis
Andries Dewitt
Jacob Van Etta
John Schutt
John Dewitt
Hendrick Johnson
Thomas Swardtwout
John Van Etta
Anthony Swartwoudt
John Jacosa Stoll
Heybert Lambertsa
William Jacobs

Dirrick Westbrock
Agbert Hendricks
Saml: Berrey
Lambert Heybertsin
Hendrick Claes
Brown Hendricks
Harrama Pier
John David
John Blanchard
Cornelis Gerritts
John Smedis
Barrant Cuinst
Hellebrandt Lazer
Johanas Bush
Pietter Lhommedien
August Jay
John Rulland
William Traphager Juno^r
Jochyam Van Ama
Aimi canchi
Jacob Besteyansa
Abraham Larew
Matthis Blanzan Junio^r
John Lazier
James Bonamiz
Dirrick Hendricks
John Gerrittsa
James Cordaback
Powlas Powlason Juno^r
John Williamson ye Duitcher
William Schutt
Cornelis Tacke
John Johnson Poast
Petter Demarr
Privie go Doon
Lowies Deboyes Senior
Jacob Deboyes

David Deboyes
Sallomon Deboyes
Evert Wincoope
Johanas Westbrock
John Peteet
Rutt Jores
Heibort Sealand
Jury Tunies
John Broerson Decker
Roulof Johnson
John Matthies
Heymon Roos
John Roos
Arrie Roos
Petter Pettersin
Gerritt Agbortsin
Claes Roosinffelt
Jno: Evedin
Cornelis Lambertsin
Thomas Harramansa
Johanas Dehogos
Moses Cantine
Isack Deboyes
Cornelis Mastin
John Euertsa
Coinradt Elvendorop
Cornelis Petterson
Barrant Jacobs
Marinos Van Acar
Claes Lazier
Barrant Coll
Symon Westfallin
Arrent Jacobs
Artt martenson Doorn
Cornelis Bogardos
Arrent Van Dick

These ffowing persons were present when yᵉ Oath was A givin. but Did Reffeues to taike it Vizᵗ

Antony Tilba	Joseph ffocker
Thomas Van der Marrick	Jacob Horne

These ffollowing persons Did nott appeare Vizᵗ

John Archer	Hellebrandt Lodtman
Livie Larrow	Jacob Brown Alis yᵉ Noorman
Maghell DeMott	Warnar Hornebeak
Euert Pelce	John Lowrance
Symon Pelce	Symon Larow
Terrick Claes Dewitt	Cornelis Hogoboom
Wallraven Demont Senior	Cornelis yᵉ Duitcher
Dirrick Schepmous	Gombart Powlasin
Matthis Tennick	Jnᵒ: Meueson. Alis Jn De pape
Claes Tunis	William Wallaffish
Gisbert Crum	Jnᵒ Pollin
Arre Gerritt Van ffleitt	Antony Bussalin
Dirrick Van ffleitt	Gerritt Aylberts
Jnᵒ: Lodtman	Dirrick Keizer
Jury Lodtman	THOMAS CHAMBERS

New-York Army List, 1700.

LIST OF THE OFFICERS OF THE MILITIA OF THE PROVINCE OF NEW YORKE, 1700.

[Lond. Doc. XIII.]

A Table of the Number of the severall Regiments in yᵉ Province of New York.

County of Suffolk	614
Queen's County	601
King's County	280
Richmond County 2 Compᵃˢ . . .	152
City & County of New York . . .	684
County of West Chester	155
Ulster and Dutchess County . . .	325
City & County of Albany	371
Totall .	3182 men

Province of New York

List of yᵉ present officers of yᵉ Militia in his Maᵗʸˢ Province of New York in America commissionated by his Excel. Richᵈ Earle of Bellomont, Capt Generall & Govʳ in Chief in & over his Maᵗʸˢ said Province &c. vizᵗ

Of yᵉ Regiment of Militia of yᵉ County of Suffolk on yᵉ Island Nassaw

Isaac Arnold . . .	Colonel	⎫
Henry Pierson . .	Lieuᵗ Col	⎬ Field Officers
Matthew Howel . .	Majʳ	⎭

The several Comp^{as} in ye said Regim^t

The Foot Comp^a in the town of Brookhaven

Sam. Smith	. . .	Captain ⎫
Richd Floyd	. . .	Lieut ⎬ Com^{on} Officers
Joseph Tucker	. . .	Ensigne ⎭

Of the Foot Comp^a in ye town of Huntington

Thos Wicks	. . . .	Capt ⎫
Joⁿ Woods	. . . .	Lieu^t ⎬ C. O.
Epenetus Plat	. . . .	Lieu^t ⎭

Of ye Foot Comp^a in ye town of Southampton

Abra. Howell	. . . .	Capt ⎫
Joseph Fordham	. . .	Lieu^t ⎬ C. O.
Isaac Halsey	. . . .	Ensigne ⎭

Of another Comp^a in ye said Town

	. . . .	Capt. ⎫
Joⁿ Lupton	. . . .	Lieut. ⎬ C. O.
Joseph Moore	. . .	Ensigne. ⎭

Of another Comp^a in ye said Town

Tho. Stephens	. . .	Capt. ⎫
Joseph Pierson	. . .	Lieut. ⎬ C. O.
Jerem. Scot	. . . .	Ensigne. ⎭

Of ye Foot Comp^a in ye Town of Southold

Tho Young	. . . .	Capt. ⎫
Sam. Glover	. . .	Lieut. ⎬ C. O.
Rich. Brown	. . .	Ensigne. ⎭

Of another Foot Comp^a in ye said Town

Jonathan Harlon Capt —— Griffin Lieu^t

—— Emens Ensign

Of another Foot Comp^a in ye said Town

Thos Mapas Capt   Joshua Harlow Lieu^t

Joⁿ Booth Ensigne.

Of another Foot Comp^a in ye town of East Hampton

—— Capt ;   —— Lieut ;   —— Ensigne ;

Of another Foot Comp^a in ye said Town

John Wheeler Capt,   Enoch Fitchen Lieut,

Corn. Conchling Ensigne

This Regiment consists of six hundred and fourteen men

Of the Regim^t of Militia in Queens County on ye said Island

		Colonel	
John Jackson	. . .	Lieut. Col	} Field Officers
		Maj^r	

Of the Foot comp^a in the town of Jamaica

Hope Carpenter	. . .	Capt.	
Benjⁿ Thurston	. . .	Leiut.	} Com^{on} Officers
Richd Oldfield	. . .	Ensigne	

Of another Foot Comp^a in ye said Town

Sam. Carpenter	. . .	Capt.	
Joseph Smith	. . .	Leiut.	} C. O.
Dan. Smith	. . .	Ensigne.	

Of the Foot Comp^a in ye town of New Town

Content Titus	. . .	Capt.	
Sam. Kecham	. . .	Lieut.	} C. O.
Sam. Morrell	. . .	Ensigne	

Of another Foot Comp^a in ye said Town

Robt Coe	. . . .	Capt.	
Joⁿ Berian	. . . .	Leiut.	} C. O.
Jonathan Coe	. . .	Ensigne	

Of the Foot Comp^a in ye Town of Hampstead

Jerem. Smith	. . .	Capt.
Richd Hubbs	. . .	Leiut.
Isaac Smith	. . . .	Ensigne,

Cf another Foot Comp^a in ye said Town

Joseph Smith	. . .	Capt.
	. . .	Leiut
Thos Gildersleive	. .	Ensigne.

Of another Foot Comp^a in ye said Town

Tho. Tredwell	. . .	Capt,
Jon. Pine	. . . .	Leiut,
Joⁿ Forster	. . . .	Ensigne,

Of the Foot Comp^a in ye Town of Flushing

Robert Hinchman	. .	Capt,
—— Harrington	. . .	Leiut,
Daniel Wright	. . .	Ensigne

Of the Foot Comp^a in ye town of Oysterbay

Robt Coles . . . . Capt,
Josia Latten . . . Leiut
Nath : Coles Junr . . . Ensigne

Of the Troope of Horse in ye said Regim^t

John Lawrence . . . Capt.
Jonath : Smith . . . Leiut
Daniel Lawrence . . . Cornet
Joⁿ Finne . . . . Quartermaster

The Regiment consists of six hundred & one men,

Of the Regiment of Militia in King's County on ye said Island,

Stephen Cortlandt . . Colonel ⎫
Gerrardus Beekman . . Leiu^t Col· ⎬ Feild Officers
Corn : Van Brunt . . Maj^r ⎭

Of the Foot Comp^a in the town of Amersfort,

Joⁿ Terhermon . . . Capt,
Peter Mansford . . . Leiut,
Corn Van Voorhuyen . . Ensigne.

Of the Foot Comp^a in ye Town of Gravesend.

John Lake . . . . Capt,
Chr : Bemoyn . . . Leiut,
Albert Coerten . . . Ensigne,

Of the Foot Comp^a in the town of Brookland,

Joris Hansen . . . Capt,
Daniel Repalie . . . Leiut,
Teunis Repalie . . . Ensigne.

Of the Foot Comp^a in ye town of New Uytregt.

John Van Dyke . . . Capt.
Joost Van Brunt . . . Leiut.
Matys Smake . . . Ensigne.

Of the Foot Comp^a in ye town of Midwout

Arie Van de Bilt . . . Capt,
Symon Hansen . . . Leiut,
Isaac Hegeman . . . Ensigne.

Of the Foot Comp^a in ye town of Boswick

Peter Pra . . . . Capt,
Michill Parmyter . . . Leiut,
Jochem Vouchnewen . . Ensigne.

Of the Troop of Horse in ye said Regiment

Dan. Polhemius	. . .	Capt.
Roeloft Verkirk	. . .	Leiut,
Jerominus Remse	. . .	Cornet
Gysbert Bayard	. . .	Quarter Master

This Regiment consists of two hundred & eighty men.

Of the Militia in the County of Richmond.

Of the Foot Comp^a in the said County

Tho. Stilwell . . . Capt,

Tho. Morgane ⎱
Nice Teunisse ⎰ . . . Leiuts^a

Of another Comp^e in ye said County

Andrew Carmon . . . Capt

John Stilwell ⎱
Jaque Poilton ⎰ . . . Leiut^s

The said two Comp^{as} in the said County consists of one hundred & fifty two men.

Of the Regim^t of Militia in ye City & County of New York

Abra : De Peyster . . Colonel ⎱
Wm Mervet . . . Leiut Col. ⎬ Field Officers
Jo^n Henry De Bruyn . Maj^r ⎰

Of a Foot Comp^a in ye said City

Robt. Walters . . . Capt, ⎱
Andrew Teller . . . Leiut ⎬ Com^{on} Officers
Jo^n Hardinbrooke . . Ensigne, ⎰

Of another Foot Comp^a in ye said City

David Provost . . . Capt, ⎱
Wm Churcher . . . Leiut, ⎬ C. O.
Absa : Brasier . . . Ensigne, ⎰

Of one other Foot Comp^a in ye said City.

Leonard Lewis . . . Capt, ⎱
Jacob Vander Speigle . . Leiut, ⎬ C. O.
Isaac Governeur . . . Ensigne, ⎰

Of one other Troop Comp^a in ye said City.

Isaac De Keimer	. . .	Capt
Steph Richards	. . .	Leiut
Nicho. Blank,	. . .	Ensigne

Of one other Foot Comp^a in ye said Citty

Cornelius De Peyster	.	.	Capt,
Roger Baker	.	.	.	Leiut
Corn : Lodge	.	.	.	Ensigne

Of one other Foot Comp^a in ye said Citty

John Theobalds	.	.	.	Capt
Peter de Melt	.	.	.	Leiut
Isaac Brasier	.	.	.	Ensigne

Of another Foot Comp^a in ye said Citty

Evert Byvanck	.	.	.	Capt,
John Vander Speigel	.	.	Leiut,
Jo^n Tiebout	.	.	.	Ensigne.

Of one other Foot Comp^a in ye said City

Martin Clock	.	.	.	Capt,
Tho Fornuier	.	.	.	Leiut,
Hend : Breevort	.	.	.	Ensigne,

Of the Troop of Horse in ye said Regim^t

| John De Peyster Capt, | Jo^n Outman | Cornet |
| Jo^n Hoghland Leiut, | Evert Van deWater Quarter master |

This Regiment consists of six hundred & eighty five men.

Of the Regiment of Militia in ye County of West Chester.

	.	.	Colonel ⎫
	.	.	Lieut. Col. ⎬ Field Officers
Augt Graham	.	.	Maj^r ⎭

Of a Foot Comp^a in the town of East Chester.

John Drake	.	.	.	Capt, ⎫
Joseph Drake	.	.	.	Leiut, ⎬ C. O.
Henry Tower	.	.	.	Ensigne ⎭

Of a Foot Comp^a in ye town of New Rochell,

Oliver Besley	.	.	.	Capt,
Isaac Merier	.	.	.	Leiut,
Pierre Vasleau	.	.	.	Ensigne

Of a Foot Comp^a in ye town of Mamarioneck

James Mott	.	.	.	.	Captain
Robert Lauting	.	.	.	Leiut,
Tho : Ives	.	.	.	.	Ensigne

This Regiment consists of one hundred fifty five men.

Of the Regiment of Militia in yᵉ Counties of Ulster & Dutchess.

. . .	Colonel	⎫	
Jacob Rutsen . . .	Lieut Col.	⎬ Field Officers
. . .	Majʳ	⎭

Of a Foot Compᵃ in yᵉ said Countys.

Matthias Mattyson   .   .   Captain ⎫
Evert Bogardus   .   .   .   Leiut.   ⎬ Comᵒⁿ Officers
Tennis Tappen   .   .   .   Ensigne, ⎭

Of an other Foot Compᵃ in yᵉ sᵈ Countys.

Abso : Hasbrooke   .   .   Captain
Moses Quantain   .   .   .   Leiut,
Lewis Bavea   .   .   .   Ensigne.

Of an other Foot Compᵃ in yᵉ said Countys.

George Middagh   .   .   .   Capt,
Gysbert Kroom   .   .   .   Leiut,
Alex. Rosebrans   .   .   .   Ensigne.

Of another Foot Compᵃ in yᵉ said Countys,

Aria Rose   .   .   .   .   Captain
John Rose   .   .   .   .   Leiut.
Aria Gerrutse   .   .   .   .   Ensigne

Of another Foot Compᵃ in yᵉ said Countys.

Jocham Schoonmaker   .   .   Captain
John Van Camp   .   .   .   Leiut
Jacob Decker   .   .   .   .   Ensigne

Of another Foot Compᵃ in yᵉ said Countys

Coenrod Elmendorp   .   .   Captain
Mattyse Sleight   .   .   .   Leiut
Garret Wyncoop   .   .   .   Ensigne

Of another Foot Compᵃ in yᵉ said Countys

Baltus Van Cleet   .   .   .   Captain
Hendrick Kipp   .   .   .   Leiut
John Ter Bus   .   .   .   .   Ensigne

Of the Troop of Horse in yᵉ said Regiment

Egbert Schoonmaker Captain   Abra: Gasbert   Cornet
Corn: Decker   Leiut.   Mattyse Jansen Quartermaster
This Regiment consists of Three hundred five & twenty men.

Of the Regiment of Militia in yᵉ City & County of Albany.

Peter Schuyler   .   .   .   Colonel ⎫

.   .   .   Leiut. Col ⎬ Field Officers

Dyrck Wcssells   .   .   .   Majʳ ⎭

Of a Foot Company in the city of Albany

Johannes Bleeker   .   .   Captain ⎫

Johannes Roseboome   .   .   Leiut ⎬ Comⁿ Officers

Abra: Cuyler   .   .   .   Ensigne ⎭

Of another Foote Compᵃ in yᵉ said city

Albert Rykman   .   .   .   Captain

Wessel ten Broek   .   ,   .   Leiut.

Johannes Thomasse   .   .   .   Ensigne.

Of another Foot Compᵃ in the said County

Martin Cornelisse   .   .   .   Captain

Andris Douw   .   .   .   Leiut.

Andris Koyman   .   .   .   Ensigne.

Of another Foot Compᵃ in the said County

Gerrit Teunisse   .   .   .   Captain

Jonas Douw   ⎫

Jochem Lamerse ⎭   .   .   Leiutˢ

Volckart V. Hoesem ⎫

Abra: Hanse   ⎭   .   .   Ensignes

Of a Foot Compᵃ in yᵉ town of Schenectady

Johannes Sanderse Glen   .   .   Captain

Adam Woman [Vrooman?] ,   .   Leiut.

Harman V. Slyke   .   .   .   Ensigne.

Of the Troope of Horse in yᵉ said Regiment

Kilian van Renslaer   .   .   .   Captain

Johannes Schuyler   .   .   .   Leiut.

Bennone V. Corlaer   .   .   Cornet

Anthony Bries   .   .   .   Qnartermaster

This Regiment consists of Three hundred seaventy one men.

(Indorsed)   " No 13. New Yorke. List of the Officers of the
" Militia in the Province of New Yorke Referred
" to in yᵉ E of Bellomonts lrê of yᵉ 28 Novʳ
" 1700   Recd 18 Feb   Read   1700⸰

CENSUS

OF THE

Counties of Orange, Dutches & Albany.

———————◆———————

1702, 1714, 1720.

LIST OF THE INHABITANTS IN THE COUNTY OF ORANGE. 1702.

Males from 16 To 60.	Males men Above 60:	Females women	Males Childeren	Females chil-dren	Males Negros	Females Negros	Males negros Childeren	Females Negro Children
Daniel D. Clercqe	William Merritt	Margry His Wijff	1 Child	1 Mayd	4 Men.	1 Women	1 Child.	2 Gerls.
Jacob d Clercqe		Geretje His Wijff			1 Men.	1 Women	1 Child.	1 Gerl
Abram Hearingh								
Thonis Van Howtten		Trijntje His Wiffe	1 Child	6 Mayds		1 Woman	1 Child.	
Roloff Van Howtten								
Claes Van Howtten								
Hendrick Geritssen		Mary His Wijfe	3 Children					
John Hendrickssen								
Herman Hendrickssen								
Geridt Hendriessen								
Lambert Ariaussen		Margrit His Wiffe	2 Childeren	4 gerells				
Geridt Lambertzen								
Lowe Reynerssen		Lysbeth His Wijffe	1 Child	1 gerell				1 gerell
Thonis Taelman	Reyn Janzen	Brechtie His Wyffe	3 Childeren.	3 gerells	2 Men	1 Women		1 gerrell
		Dirckje A Widow						
Casper Janssen		May His Wyffe		3 gerells			1 Child.	
Johan Classen		Trijntje His Wyffe		2 gerells				
Johanns Gerissen		Cathrin His Wiffe	6 Childeren	1 gerell				
Jacob Cool		Barbara His Wiffe	2 Childeren	1 gerell				
Coenrat Hanssen		Leuntje His Wiffe	1 Child	1 gerell				
Reijnier Mijnerssen		Mary His Wiffe		4 gerls	4		1 Child.	
Dirck Straat		Tryntje His Wiffe	1 Child				1 Child.	
Cornelis Hearingh		Cathe His Wiffe	1 Child	1 gerll				
Cosyn Hearingh		Mary His Wiffe	2 Children		1 Men	1 Women		
Jacob Flierboom		Marij His Wiffe			1 Men			
Samuel Conklijn		Hanna His Wiffe	1 Child	3 gerels				
Abram Blauvelt		Gritje His Wiffe	4 Childeren	3 gerlls				
John: Waard		Gritje His Wiffe						

		Wiffe	Children	Gerlls	Men	Women	Childes	Gerels
Isaac Gerissen		Mary His Wiffe	1 Child	5 Gerlls				
Pieter Hearingh		Gritje His Wiffe	1 Child	3 Gerlls	1 men			
Jeremiah Ceniff		Anna His Wiffe	3 Children	3 Gerlls				
John D'puy		Janneke His Wiffe	3 Childeren	3 Gerlls				
John: d'fries		Ariantje His Wiffe	2 Children	2 Gerlls				
Gerritt Huijbrechtz								1 Gerll.
John: Meijer		Antje A Wedow	2 Children.	3 Gerlls	1 Men			
Poulus Tjurckssen								
John: Hey		Trijntje A Wedow		2 Gerlls				
Melchert Casperssen		Gertruyt His Wife.	2 Children.	2 Gerlls				
Jeurian Melgerissen								
John: Perre		Sara His Wiffe	1 Child:	3 Gerlls				
Jemes Weller		Bethe His Wiffe	3 Children.					
Isaac Brett		Magdalen His Wyffe		1 Gerlls				
Will: Juell		Sara His Wiffe	2 Children.	4 Gerlls				
Will: Juell Juner	floris Crom							
Willem Crom		Lyne His Wiffe	1 Child:	2 Gerells				
Arian Crom		Geritje His Wiffe	1 Child:					
Gysbert Crom							1 Child..	
Albert Mimelay		Meenske His Wiffe	4 Children.	5 Gerlls	1 Men	2 Women		
Cornlis Coeper		Altje His Wiffe	2 Children.	7 Gerlls	1 Men			
Edward Mek	frans Wey	Sara Crab Widow		1 Gerll				
	Direk Storm	Indian W: His Wyffe						
		Mery His Wiffe						
Coms to 49 men	Coms to 5 men	Coms to 40 Wiffe	Coms to 57 C'ildr:	Coms to 84 gerlls	Coms to 13 men	Coms to 7 Women	Coms to 7 Childes	Coms to 6 gerels

In the Countij Orange the 16th Day of Junij 1702.   This js a Trew ACount off all the Males and ffemales of Men Women and Childeren

WITNESS OUWER HAND   WILL MERRETT
                                       DANIEL DE KLERCK

Pr: Order of the Justices

the paes

D. STORM Cl:

Dit is **R** het marck van } Justices

THEUNIS ROELOFFZEN VAN HOWTEN
CORNELIS CLASEN

[Endorsed]   This is a Trieuw Acount of the County Orange.

A LIST OF THE INHABITANTS AND SLAVES IN THE COUNTY OF DUTCHES. 1714.

The Severall places or Districts in the County where Inhabiting.	Numbers of Male persons above sixty years of age	Numbers of male persons from sixteen to sixty years of age	Numbers of male persons under sixteene	Numbers of ffemales above sixty	Numbers of ffemales from sixty to sixteen	Numbers of ffemales under sixteen	Numbers of male slaves from sixteen and above	Numbers of male slaves under sixteen	Numbers of female slaves from sixteen and above	Numbers of female slaves under sixteen
Jacob Kip		2	4			4			1	
Jacob Plowgh		1			1	2				
Matieis Slegt		1	1		1	1				
Evert Van Wagenen		1	3			2	1			
Whilliam Ostrander		1	1		1	2				
Lowrans Ostrout		1	2		1	2				
Peter Palmater		1	2		1	3				
Maghell Pallmatir	1	2	1		1	2	1		1	
William Tetsort	1	2			2	1				
Hendrick Pells		1	2		2	1				
Peter Vely		1	1		1	2				
John Kip		1	5		1	1				
Elena Van De Bogart		4	1		4	1				
John De Grave		1	2		1	2				
Lenar Lewis		3	3		5	2	1			
Bartolumus Hoogenboom		1	1		1					
Baltus Van Kleek	1	2	1		1				2	1
Frans Le Roy		1	3		2	2		1	1	1
Barent Van Kleck		2	3		1	1				
John Ostrom	2	3	2		2	1				
Harmen Rinders		1	3		1	1				
Meindert Van Den Bogart		1	3		1	1				
Johanes Van Kleck		1	2		2	1				
Lenar Le Roy		1	2		1	2				
Swart Van Wagenen		1	3		1	1				
Henry Van Der Burgh		1			2	3	2	1	1	
Elias Van Bunchoten		1	2		2	1				
Thomas Sanders		1	2		2	2				
Catrine Lasink Wedo:	1	1	2			1				
Peter Lasink		1	4		1					
——ey Scouten		3	3		2	1				
Mellen Springsteen	1		2		1	2				1
Johnes Terbots		2	2		1	3				
John Beuys		1	1		3	2				
Abram Beuys		1			1					
Garatt Van Vleit		2	1		4	1				
William Outen	1									
Andreis Daivedes		1	3		1	2				
Frans De Langen		1	4		1	1				
Aret Masten		1	1		1	3				
James Husey		2	2		3	1	1	1	1	
Roger Brett		1	3		1	1		1	1	1

The severall places or Districts in the County where Inhabiting.	Numbers of Male persons above sixty years of age.	Numbers of male persons from sixteen to sixty years of age	Numbers of male persons under sixteene	Numbers of ffemales above sixty	Numbers of ffemales from sixty to sixteen	Numbers of ffemales under sixteen	Numbers of male slaves from sixteen and above	Numbers of male slaves under sixteen	Numbers of female slaves from sixteen and above	Numbers of female slaves under sixteen
Peter De Boyes	....	1	5	....	2	1				
Isack Hendricks	....	1	1	....	1	1				
John Breines	....	1	....	....	1	1				
Jeurey Sprinsten	....	1	4	....	1	1				
Peck De Wit..................	....	1	2	....	2	3	1			
Adaam Van alsted	....	1	1	....	2					
Cellitie kool	....	1	2	....	2					
Harmen knickerbacker........	1	1	2	....	2					
Johanis Dyckman Sienjer......	....	1	....	....	1	1	1			
Jacob Hoghtelingh.............	....	1	2	....	1	3				
Dirck Wesselse	1	2	....	1	2	....	2	1	2	
Willem Schot	....	1	....	....	3	3				
Jacob Vosburgh................	....	5	....	....	3	1	1			
Tunis Pieterse	....	2	2	....	3	2				
henderick bretsiert.............	....	1								
Roelif Duijtser	....	1	3	....	2	1	1			
Johannis Spoor Junjoor........	1	1	5	....	1	1				
Abraham Vosburgh	....	1	3	....	1	2				
Abraham Van Dusen	....	1	2	....	1	4				
Willem Wijt...................	....	1	1	....	1	3				
Louwerens knickerbacker	....	1	2	....	1					
henderck Sissum	....	1	....	....	1	1				
Aenderis Gerdener	....	2	1	....	1	1				
Gysbert oosterhout.............	....	1	....	....	1	6				
Johannis Dyckman Junjor	....	1	....	....	1	1				
	11	89	120	1	97	98	12	6	7	4

[Total Nº. of souls, 445.]

A LIST OF THE FFREEHOLDERS OF THE CITY AND COUNTY
OF ALBANY. 1720.

first ward

Evert Wendell
Jno Dunbar
Harmanis Wendell
Peter Van Brugh
Johannis Schuyler
Antoney Van Schaick
Mindert Schuyler
Antoney Vanschaick Snor
Robert Livingston Junr
Tho: Williams
Coonrodt Tennyck
Joseph Yates Junr
Jacob Roseboom
Jacob Staats
John Rosie
Wm: Hogan
Johannis Van Alen
Jacob Lansen
Baltis Van Bentheusen
Harmanis Ryckman
Fred. Mindertsen
Daniell Kelly
Johannis Vandenbergh
Joseph Vansante
Joseph Yeats Snor
Winant Vanderpoel
John Kidney
Mindert Lansen
Obediah Cooper
Johannis Vansante
Matthews Flantsburgh
Tobias Ryckman
Peter Ryckman
Wm. Hilton
Johannis De Garmoe
Claes Van Woort
Henry Holland
John Collins
Hend: Halenbeek
Peter Gramoe
Johannis Ratclif
Luykas Hooghkirck
Hendrick Oothout
Nicolas Winegaert
Cornelis Vandyke
Johannis Lansen
Luykas Winegaert
Ryert Gerritse
Gose Van Schaick
Barent Egbertsen
Bastian Visser
Antoney Bregardes
Thomas Wendell
Johannis Tenbroeck
Antoney Coster
Danl Flantsburgh
Johannis Beekman
Johannis Wendell Junr

Antoney Van Schaick Junr
Phillip Livingston
Jacob Beekman
Revr'nd Thomas Barclay
David Grewsbeck
Stephanjs Grewsbeck

2d Ward

Johannis Cuyler
Nicos: Bleeker
Abram: Cuyler
Warner Van Ivera
Reyner Mindertsen
Barent Sanders
Wm: Grewsbeck
Guisbert Marselis
Herpert Jacobsen
Arent Pruyn
Johannis Mingaell
Johannis Hansen
Seibolet Brigardes
David Van Dyke
Johannis Vinhagen
Abram Kip
Cornelis Schermerhorn
Hendrick Tennyck
Johannis Beekman Snor
Gerrit Lansen
Issack Kip
Nanning Visser
Hendrick Roseboom
Mindert Roseboom
Andries Nach
Jan: Janse Bleeker
Johannis Bleeker
Christofell Yeats
Phillip Wendell
Jan Lansen
Gerrit Roseboom
Cornelis Van Scherline
Johans: Evertse Wendell
Abram: Lansen
Johannis Roseboom
John Hogan
Johannis Visser
Benj. Egbertsen
Johannis Grewsbeck
Claes Funda
Wm: Jacobsen

3d Ward

Isaac Funda
Samuell Babington
Gerrit Van Ness
Albert Ryckman
Cornelis Borghaert
Jacob Borghaert
Johannis Hun
Phillip Van Vechten
Lenord Gansivoort

Jan: Evertsen
Evert Janse
Jacob Evertse
Jno: Solomonse
Hendrick Hansen
Abram: Schuyler
Derrick Brat
Johannis Van Ostrande
Johannis Evertsen
Tunis Egbertsen
Derrick Tenbroeck
David Schuyler
Winant Vandenbergh
Takel Derrickse
Johannis Backer
Thomas Long
John Gerritse
Elbert Gerritse
Issac Borghaert
Cornelis Maasse
Jan Maasse
Barnt Brat
Jacob Borghaert Junr
Jacob Visser
Jacobus Luykasse Winegaert
Johannis Pruyn
Wessell Tenbroeck
Peter Winne
Jacob Muller
Johannis Muller
Samll: Pruyn
Reuben Ven Vechten
Cornlis Switzs
Guisbert Vandenbergh
Teirck Harminse Visser
Tunis Brat
Peter Walderom
Rutger Bleeker
Harpert Vandeusen

COUNTY OF ALBANY VIZ.

Schonectady.

Jonathan Stevens
William Coppernoll
Claes Franse
Teirck Franse
Yellous Fonda
Adam Vroman
Phillip Schuyler
David Lewis
Mindert Guisling
Peter Quacumbus
Abram Meebe
Benj. Van Vlack
Marte Powlisse
Harma Van Slyck
Sanders Gelon
Evert Van Eps
Arent Van Petten
John Weemp
Simon Switzs
Jacob Switzs
Mindert Weemp
Arent Brat
Hendrick Vrooman Junr
Harmanis Vedder
Dow Aukus
Johannis Mindertsen
Adam: Smith
Abram Trueax

Rob: Yeats
Abram: Lythall
Assweris Marselis
Abram: Groot
Hendrick Vroman Snor
Wouter Vroman
Jno. Baptist Van Epps
Derrick Brat
Jan Barentse Wemp
Barent Vroman
Jan Vroman
Gerrit Van Brackell
Arent Danilse
Simon Vroman
Lawrence Chase
Cornlis Vander Volgen
Abram De Grave
Daniell Danielse
Cornelis Pootman
Sam: Hagadoring
Guisbert Van Brakell
Volkert Simonse
Jacob Schermerhorn
Jacobus Vandyke
Helmes Vedder
Arnout De Grave
Johannis Teller
Albert Vedder
Derrick Groot
Gerrit Simonse
Yealous Van Vost
Victore Pootman
Jan Delemont
Caleb Beck
Nicolas Schuyler
Johannis Gelen
Jacob Gelen
Jesse De Grave
Carle Hanse Toll
Daniell Toll
William Marrinas
Arent Schermerhorn
Esays Swaert
Johannis Vroman
Andries De Grave
Joseph Clament
John Bumstead
Harma Phillipse
Jereme Thickstone
Jacob Van Olinda
Arent Vedder
Peter Vroman
Daniell Janse
Peter Danielse
Jan Danielse
Jan Meebe
Johannis Peek
Jacobus Peek
Claes Van Petten
Cornelis Van Slyck
Marte Van Slyck
Cornelis Feele
Arnout Brat Juni
Johannis Vedder
Tunis Vander Volgen
Claes Van Petten
Andries Van Petten
Jan Schermerhorn
Wouter Swaert
Arent Pootman

Kenderhook and part Mannor of
Livingston Viz.
Jochim Van Valkenburgh
Isaac Fansborough
Casper Rouse
Peter Van Alen
Lamert Huyck
Burger Huyck
Johannis Huyck
Derrick Gardineer
Peter Van Slyck
Jno: Gardineer
Evert Wieler
Derrick Goes
Peter Fausburgh
Peter Van buren
Jno: Goes
Mattias Goes
Luykas Van Alen
Jacobus Van Alen
Evert Van Alen
Johannis Vandeusen
Cornelis Schermerhorn
Johannis Van Alen
Gerrit Dingmans
Bartlemeus Van Valkenburgh
Thomas Van Alstine
Coonrodt Burgaert
Stephanis Van Alen
John Burgaert
Abram: Van Alstine
Lawrence Van Schauk
Elias Van Schauk
Jurie Klaime
Guisbert Scherp
Lawrence Scherp
Hendrick Clawe
Lamert Valkenburgh
Melgert Vanderpoel
Lenord Conine
The north part of the Mannor of
Livingston:
Robert Livingston **Esqr**
Peter Colle
Killian Winne
Jan Emnerick **Plees**
Hans Sihans
Claes Bruise
Jonat: Rees
Coonrodt Ham
Coonrodt Schureman
Johannis Pulver
Bastian Spikerman
Nicolas Smith
Baltis Auspah
Jno: Wm: Simon
Hanse Jurie Prooper
Abram Luyke
Broer Decker
Jurie Decker
Nicolas Witbeck
Johannis Uldrigh
ffitz: Muzigh
Coonrod Kelder
David Hooper
Gabriell Broose
Solomon Schutt
Jacob Stover
Johanis Roseman
Nicos: Styker

Claverack
Tobias Tenbroeck
Cornelis Mulder
Cornlis Esselstine
Jeremias Mulder
Derrick Hogoboom
Cornelis: Huyck
Isaac Vandusen
Jno: Hoose
George Sidnem
Richard Moor
John Hardyck
Hendr: Van Salsbergen
Jacob Van Hoosem
Kasper Van Hoosem
Jan Van Hoosem
Saml Tenbroeck
Peter Hogoboom
Rob: Van Deusen
Casper Conine
Frank Hardyke
Johannis Van Hoosem
John Bout
Wm: Halenbeck
Johannis Coole
John Rees
Wm: Rees
Johannis Scherp
Andries Rees
Ghondia Lamafire
Hendrick Whitbeck
Jurie Fretts
Hendrick Lodowick
Jacob Eswin
Jurie Jan
Cloude Lamatere
Nicos: Vanduse *Cats Kills*
Coxhacky and Cats Kills
Mindert Schut
Wessell Tenbroeck
Wm: Lefferrese
Helme Janse
Saml Van Vechten
Gerrit Van berghen
Marte Van berghen
Frank Salisbury
Jno Brunk
Minkas Van Schauk
John Albertse
Arent Van Schauk
Michael Collier
Cornelis Van Wormer
Johannis Halenbeek
Casper Halenbeek
Jan Van Loan
Albert Van Loan
Jno: Van Loan Junr
Abram: Provoost
Jacob Halenbeek
Jno: Casperse
Coonrodt Hotlen
Philip Conine
Jno: Vanhoosem
Lenord Brunk
Peter Brunk
Isaac Spoor
Canastigonie
Jno: Quacumbus
Jno: ffoort

Jacob Pearse
Derrick Brat
Maes Rycksen
Evert Rycksen
Gerrit Rycksen
Nicholas Van Vranken
Lapion Kanfort
Cornelis Christianse
Eldert Timonse
Jno: Quakenboes Junr
Peter Ouderkerk
Jacob Cluit
John Cluit
Frederick Cluit
Saml: Creeger
Derrick Takelsen
Mattias Boose Snor
Johannis Christianse

Half Moon.
Jacobus Van Schoonhoven
Evert Van Ness
Daniell Fort
Corn'ls Vanburen
Conelis Van Ness
Isaac Ouderkerk
Lavinus Harminse
Tunis Harminse
Winant Vandenbergh
Roolif Gerritse
Hendrick Roolifse
Jno: De Voe
Daniell Van Olinda
Eldert Ouderkerk
Cornelis Vandenbergh

Schautkooke
Saml Doxie
Curset Fetner
Johannis Knickerbacker
Derrick Van Vechten
Johannis De Wandelaer
Simon Danielse
Martin Delamon
Lewis Fele
Daniell: Ketlyne
Peter Winne
Adrian Quacumbus
Abram Fort

Colloney Renselaers Wyck.
Wouter Barheyt
Johannis Valkenburgh
Jno: Barheyt
Isaac Van Alstine
Jacob Schermerhorn
Jacob Schermerhorn Junr
Johns: Ouderkerk
Claes Gardineer
Andries Gardinier
Hend: Valkenburgh
Jacob Valkenburgn
Andries Huyck
Maes Van Buren
Corn'lis Van Vechten
Jonat: Witbeck
Martin Vanburen

Barent Geritse
Jan Witbeck
Jonas Dow
Andries Dow
Folcort Dow
Jno: Van Vechten
Gerrit Lansen
Volcort Van Vechten
Melgert Vandeuse
Rut Vandeuse
Tho: Witbeek
Luykas Witbeek
Solomon Van Vechten
Cap: Hendrick Van Renselaer
Philip Foreest
Martin Van Alstine
Albert Roolifse
Marte Van Alstine Junr
Jno: Funda
Derrick Vanderhyden
Gerrit Vandenbergh
Albert Brat
Cornelis Van Alstine
Johns: Wendell
Jan: Van Alstyne
Adrian Oothout
Peter Coyeman
Barent Staats
Andries Coyeman
Samuell Coyeman
Jno: Witbeek
Coonrod Hooghteeling
Storm Backer
Jno: Backer
Hendrick Van Wyen
Wm: Van Alen
Daniell Winne
Gerrit Van Wie
Jan Van Wie
Gerrit Vandenbergh
Hendr: Dow
Albert Slingerlant
Evert Banker
Wouter Vanderse
Killian Vanderse
Johannis Appel
Peter Husyele
Derrick Hagodorn
Andries Brat
Storm Brat
Ome Legrange
Johns: Legrange
Johannis Simonse
Nicos: Grewsbeek
Jno: Oothout
Mindert Marselis
Jacob Lansen
Abram Ouderkerk
Peter Schuyler Esqr
Abram Wendell
William Ketlyne
Frans Pryn
Jaac Falkenburgh
Claes Bovie
Phillip Wendell

Pursuant to an Order of Court of Judicature held for the Province of New York on the Eleventh Day of June 1720, Directed to Gerrit Vanschaick high Sherrif of the City and County of Albany; A Returne of the free holders of the said City and County. GERRET VANSCHAIJCK Sheriff

CENSUS OF THE CITY OF NEW-YORK.

[ABOUT THE YEAR 1703.]

EAST WARD.

MASTERS OF FAMILYS	Males from 16 to 60	females	Male Children	female Children	Male Negros	female Negros	Male Negro Children	female Negro Children	all above 60
Ebenezr Wilson	3	4	1	3	1	1	....	....	....
Mr Leuis	....	1	4	2	....	1	....	....	....
Mr Everson	....	2	2	....	1	....	....	....	....
Mrs Vantyle	...	1	1	1	....	....	....	....	....
Mr Haris	2	1	....	1	....	2	3	1	....
Thoms Dyer	1	....	....	....	....	....	....	....	....
Mrs Smith	...	3	4	....	....	....	....	....	....
Garot Haier	2	2	2	....	....	....	....	....	....
Frances Coderos	...	2	1	3	....	1	....	....	....
John Lasly	1	1	....	....	....	....	....	....	....
Thoms Evens	1	1	1	....	....	....	....	....	....
Hendrick	1	3	....	....	....	....	....	....	....
Peter Vantilbry	2	1	1	....	....	1	....	....	....
Frances Wessells	2	2	....	5	5	....	....	....	....
Mrs Basset	....	1	1	2	....	....	....	....	....
Capt Novered	...	1	2	1	....	1	....	....	....
John Morthouse	1	....	....	....	....	....	....	....	....
Beverly Latham	1	1	3	1	....	....	....	....	....
Mrs Rabi	1	2	2	....	....	....	....	....	....
Capt Morris	1	1	....	3	1	2	1	....	....
Peter Mountu	1	3	1	....	....	....	....	....	....
Hendrick Mayr	1	1	2	....	....	....	....	....	....
John Stephens	1	1	2	3	....	....	....	....	....
Capt Tudor	2	5	2	4	....	1	1	....	....
Stuen Valo	1	2	1	3	....	....	....	....	....
Fany ye Doctr	1	3	....	1	....	....	....	....	....
Abraham Brazier	1	1	1	1	....	....	....	....	....
Mr Sinkeler	2	1	0	1	1	1	1	1	....
Mr Lees	2	1	....	....	....	2	....	....	....
Capt Forkell	1	1	1	2	....	1	1	3	....
Peter Thouet	1	2	....	....	....	....	1	1	....
James Spencer	....	1	....	2	....	....	....	....	....
Margrett Briges	...	1	....	....	....	....	....	....	....
Doctr Defany	1	1	....	2	....	....	....	....	....
Mr Sellwood	1	....	....	....	....	....	....	....	....
Widd Brown	...	2	1	....	....	....	....	....	....
Mr Cholwell	1	1	2	1	....	2	1	....	....
John Ledham	1	1	1	1	....	....	....	....	....
Andrew Gravenrod	1	1	2	3	1	1	....	....	....
William Apell	1	1	....	....	....	....	....	....	....
James Blower	1	1	....	....	....	....	....	....	....
John Vanderspeygel	2	1	1	3	....	....	....	1	....
John Bures	1	1	....	1	....	1	....	....	....
Mrs Blackgrove	...	1	3	1	2	2	2	1	....
Mrs Byner	2	2	....	....	1	1	....	1	....
Doctr Peters	1	1	....	1	....	....	....	....	....
John Devi	1	1	2	3	....	1	....	....	....
Mr Burger	2	1	3	2	2	1	....	....	....
John Brockman	1	1	....	1	....	....	....	....	....
John Bason	1	1	1	....	....	....	....	....	....
John Dyer	1	2	1	1	....	....	....	....	....

MASTERS OF FAMILYS	Males from 16 to 60	females	Male Children	female Children	Male Negros	female Negros	Male Negro Children	female Negro Children	all above 60
Capt Borditt	2	1	2	....	1	....	....	....	....
Capt Baker	1	....	....	....	....	....	....	1	....
James Emmett	1	2	3	....	1	1	....	....	....
Samson Boutons	4	....	2	1	....	....	....	....	....
James Bouloro	1	1	....	....	....	....	....	....	....
Evert Pelts	1	1	....	3	....	....	....	....	....
Mr Carter	....	2	....	....	....	....	....	....	....
Joseph Isacks	1	1	1	3	1	....	....	....	....
John Theobalds	1	....	2	3	2	1	....	....	....
Mr Rinderson	1	1	....	1	1	1	....	....	....
Widd Smith	....	1	3	....	1	....	....	....	....
Leend Hewsen	1	....	1	2	1	1	....	....	....
Benj Druelef	3	1	2	....	1	1	1	....	....
Mr Waters	1	1	2	1	....	2	....	....	....
Mr Lysoner	1	....	....	2	....	2	....	....	1
Mr Hardinburg	1	1	3	2	1	1	....	....	....
Paul Myler	1	1	3	....	....	1	....	....	....
Capt Vancrouger	1	1	1	1	....	....	....	1	....
Mrs Clobery	....	1	....	2	....	1	....	1	....
John Marteris	1	....	1	....	....	....	....	....	....
Georg Stanton	2	1	2	2	4	2	2	....	....
Daniel Janden	2	1	3	1	....	....	....	....	....
Abraham Vanhorn	1	1	....	1	1	1	1	....	....
Abraham Abranson	....	2	2	1	....	....	1	....	....
Andries Abrahamse	1	1	....	1	....	....	....	....	....
Derick Adolph	1	1	3	....	....	....	....	....	....
John Manbruitts	1	1	1	1	....	....	....	....	....
Garott Van Caver	1	1	1	1	....	1	....	....	....
Hogland	1	1	1	4	2	1	....	1	....
Mr Read	1	1	1	1	....	1	....	....	....
Mr Monsett	1	2	2	1	....	....	....	....	....
Thoms Caroll	1	2	2	1	....	1	....	....	....
Widd Petersebants	1	2	1	2	....	....	1	....	....
Aaron Bloom	1	2	2	4	....	1	1	....	....
Mr Toy	1	1	1	....	....	....	....	....	....
Georg Maynard	1	1	....	....	....	....	....	....	....
Abraham Wandell	1	2	....	....	....	....	....	....	....
John Tomson	1	2	2	3	....	....	....	....	....
Benj Barns	1	1	....	....	....	....	....	....	....
Capt Cragror	1	2	....	2	....	1	....	....	....
Wm Nasroses	....	1	1	4	....	....	....	....	....
Wm Shickles	....	1	....	3	....	....	....	....	....
Nicholas Dauly	1	1	1	....	....	....	....	....	....
Caston Lusen	1	1	....	1	....	....	....	....	....
Johnas Longstrauts	1	1	2	1	....	....	....	....	....
Abraham Molts	1	1	....	1	....	....	....	....	....
Capt Trevett	1	2	....	....	....	....	....	....	....
Georg Elesworth	1	1	4	2	2	....	....	....	....
Colonl Depyster	1	2	1	3	5	2	....	2	....
Georg Dunken	1	1	1	1	....	2	....	....	....
Widd Decay	....	1	3	2	1	1	1	....	....
Meyer Merett	1	2	....	3	....	....	....	....	....
Capt Shelly	1	2	....	....	1	1	1	....	....
Peter Morrayn	1	1	....	6	1	....	....	....	....
Thoms Adams	1	6	2	1	....	....	....	....	....
Widd Kidd	....	2	....	....	....	....	....	....	....
Widd Vanbroug	....	1	....	....	1	....	....	....	....
Widd Proost	....	1	2	4	2	....	....	....	....
Jacobus Vanderspegle	1	1	4	3	....	1	....	....	....
Doct Stets	1	....	2	7	....	1	....	....	....
Elyes Now	1	3	2	2	1	....	....	....	....

MASTERS OF FAMILYS	Males from 16 to 60	females	Male Children	female Children	Male Negros	female Negros	Male Negro Children	female Negro Children	all above 60
Widd Van Vous	....	1	1	2	1	1	2	....	....
John Davi	1	1	2	....	....	....	1	....	....
Abraham Johns	2	....	....	....	1	1	....	....	....
Simon Bonan	1	1	....	....	....	....	....	....	....
Widd Vanbusing	....	1	....	....	1	....	....	....	....
Widd Adolph	1	3	1	....	....	....	1	....	....
Thoms Child	1	1	1	....	2	1	1	1	....
Saml Phillips	1	1	1	....	1	....	....	....	....
Amon Bonan	1	....	1	....	....	1	....	....	....
Johanes D. Wandler	1	....	1	4	....	....	....	....	....
Joseph Smith	1	2	4	....	....	....	....	....	....
Johanes Dohneare	1	1	1	4	1	1	2	1	....
John Godfry	1	1	1	1	....	1	....	....	....
Barnardus Smith	1	1	1	1	....	0	....	....	....
Elyes Rambert	1	1	4	....	....	....	....	....	....
Jacob Bratt	1	1	....	2	1	....	....	....	....
Peter Rous	1	....	2	1	....	....	....	....	....
Widd Jordan	....	1	2	4	1	1	1	....	....
Thoms Sanderson	1	1	1	1	....	....	1	....	....
Michell	....	....	....	....	....	....	....	....	....
Denes Rishey	1	1	2	....	....	....	....	....	....
Andrew Larrance	1	1	5	1	....	....	....	....	....
Agustous Loukes	1	....	1	....	1	....	....	1	....
Cornelius Joussos	1	1	3	....	....	....	....	....	....
John Poulee	1	2	4	....	....	....	....	....	....
Mr Funnell	1	1	3	....	....	2	1	....	....
Mr D Romer	1	1	2	....	1	....	1	1	....
Capt Peneston	1	1	1	....	1	....	....	....	....
James Turse	1	1	2	1	....	....	....	....	....
James Turse	....	....	....	....	....	....	....	....	....
Michael Slevett	2	2	....	1	....	1	....	....	....
Peter Baunt	1	1	1	1	....	....	....	....	....
Widd Ellworth	....	1	1	2	....	....	....	....	....
Capt Wilson	1	1	3	2	1	....	....	....	....
Boult Leire	1	1	....	....	....	....	....	....	....
Benj Bill	1	1	1	1	....	1	....	....	....
Danl Fargoe	1	....	....	1	....	....	....	....	....
Danl Devous	1	1	2	1	....	....	....	....	....
Arthr Williams	1	1	....	2	....	....	....	....	....
Georg Brass	1	1	4	2	....	....	....	....	....
Wm Eleworth	1	1	1	3	....	....	....	....	...
Joshuah David	1	1	4	1	....	....	....	....	....
Widd Vandewater	....	1	2	1	....	....	....	....	....
Cornelius Bolson	1	1	1	....	....	....	....	....	....
Danl Mynard	1	1	1	1	....	....	....	....	....
John Mambroits	1	1	1	1	....	....	....	....	....
Mr Cromlin	1	....	....	1	....	....	....	....	....
Lucas Tinhoven	1	1	....	2	....	....	....	....	....
Johanes Urielant	1	1	....	1	....	....	....	....	....
Pete Newcurk	1	1	0	5	0	2	....	....	....
Gabriell Ludlow	1	1	1	5	1	1	....	....	....
Canny Flower	1	1	1	2	....	....	....	....	....
Mr Slay	1	1	2	2	....	....	....	....	....
Wm Bikman	0	0	0	1	2	1	....	....	1
James Debross	1	0	0	0	1	....	....	....	....
Wm Anderson	1	1	2	0	2	0	1	....	....
Peter Rightman	1	1	3	2	....	....	....	....	....
Capt Tuder	1	1	1	4	0	1	....	....	....
Wm Fardnandus	1	1	....	....	....	....	....	....	....
Hendrick Carkman	1	1	1	1	0	1	....	....	....
John Lastly	1	1	1	....	....	....	....	....	....

MASTERS OF FAMILYS	Males from 16 to 60	females	Male Children	female Children	Male Negros	female Negros	Male Negro Children	female Negro Children	all above 60
Widd Vontylborough	0	1	1	2	....	....	....	....	....
Wm Pell	1	1	1	3	....	....	....	....	....
Thoms Huck	2	0	0	0	1	....	....	....	....
Widd Peterow	0	1	3	3	1	....	....	....	....
Robert Pudenton	1	2	....	....	....	....	....	....	....
Wm Shackerly	1	1	0	1	1	....	....	....	....
Mr Huddleston	1	1	2	1	0	2	....	....	....
Nichol Debower	1	1	1	1	....	....	....	....	....
Johanes D'payster	1	1	1	3	1	2	0	2	....
Wm White	1	1	1	....	....	....	....	....	....
Widd Nanclaft	0	1	....	3	....	1	1	1	....
Abraham Moll	1	1	....	1	....	....	....	....	....
Levenus Deuind	1	1	....	....	....	....	1	....	....
Richd Sackett	1	1	2	2	3	1	....	....	....
Elener Eleworth	1	....	2	3	2	1	....	....	...
Stoffell Seeworth	....	....	....	....	1	1	....	....	1
Isaac Dinell	1	1	4	1	....	....	....	....	....
Isaac Ferbergin	1	1	4	....	....	....	....	....	....
Johanes Jooston	1	1	2	....	....	....	....	....	....
Widd Lees	....	1	....	1	....	....	....	....	....
Mrs Mussett	1	1	....	....	....	....	....	....	....
Wm Naseros	1	1	1	4	....	....	....	....	....
Loud Leuis	1	1	2	5	1	1	1	....	....
Thoms Roberts	1	....	....	....	....	....	....	....	....
Roger Britt	1	....	....	....	....	....	....	....	....
Thoms Hams	1	1	....	....	....	....	....	....	....
Robt Walls	1	....	....	....	....	....	....	....	....
Giddeon Vergeren	1	0	....	....	....	....	....	1	....
Evert Dicken	....	....	....	....	....	....	....	....	....
John Nanfan	1	....	....	....	1	....	....	....	....
Claud Bouden	....	....	....	....	....	....	....	....	....
Hendrick Vandespegle	1	....	....	....	....	....	....	....	....
Mr Gleencross	1	1	....	....	....	....	....	....	....
Dan Thwaictes	1	1	....	2	....	....	....	....	....
Widd Petrer Bond	....	2	....	2	....	....	1	....	....
Charl Bakeman	1	....	....	....	....	....	....	....	....
Johanes Banker	1	....	....	....	....	....	....	....	....
Harma Louricar	1	1	1	....	....	....	....	....	....
Jos Carlsee	....	....	....	....	....	....	....	....	2
Simeon Shumoine	1	0	2	2	....	....	....	....	....

SOUTH WARD.

Danill Roberts	3	1	....	....	....	....	....	....	....
Mr Ling	2	0	0	0	0	3	....	....	....
John & Elias Petram	2	1	4	2	1	1	0	1	....
Hendrick Kellison	1	1	3	0	0	0	0	0	....
Archibald Morris	1	1	0	1	0	....	....	....	....
Jurian Bush	1	1	1	2	....	....	....	....	....
Victor Bicker	1	2	0	1	....	....	....	....	....
Elizabeth Eliot	0	1	....	....	....	....	....	....	....
Sarah Scouton	1	2	1	4	....	....	....	....	....
Saml Sokane	1	2	1	3	....	....	....	....	....
Jacobus Cornelius	1	1	1	2	0	0	0	1	....
Peter Wesels	1	1	3	1	0	1	....	....	....
Jacobus Morrisgreen	1	1	0	1	1	....	....	....	..
William Syms	1	1	0	3	....	....	....	....	1
John Wattson	0	1	1	1	1	....	....	....	1
William Haywood	2	1	2	2	....	....	....	1	1
John Canoon	2	1	0	1	....	....	1	....	....
Thomas Elison	1	4	1	3	....	....	....	....	....
Widdow Bush	1	2	1	1	....	....	....	....	1

MASTERS OF FAMILYS	Males from 16 to 60	females	Male Children	female Children	Male Negros	female Negros	Male Negro Children	female Negro Children	all above 60
William Kage	1	2	0	....	....	1	....	....	....
Widdow Wessells	2	3	....	....	....	....	....	....	....
William Jackson	4	1	1	1	1	1	....	....	....
Johannes Van Geser	2	3	....	....	....	....	....	....	....
Willelmus Neuenhousen	1	2	....	....	....	....	....	1	....
William Taylor	1	1	3	1	2	1	....	....	....
Michael Hardin	2	3	....	....	....	....	....	1	....
Thomas Hardin	2	1	1	2	0	1	....	....	....
Anna Smith	0	1	1	....	....	1	....	....	....
Mr Shaepass	1	1	0	1	0	1	....	....	1
Capt Debrouts	....	3	....	....	....	1	....	....	3
Madam Duboise	0	3	....	....	....	....	....	....	....
Cornelius Depeyster	1	2	1	3	0	1	1	....	....
Widdow ffrouse	....	2	3	1	....	....	....	....	....
Thomas Roberts	1	1	2	3	3	1	....	....	....
John Elison	2	1	3	0	1	2	1	....	....
Isaac Depeyster	1	1	3	3	....	....	....	3	....
Widdow Howard	....	3	....	1	....	....	....	4	1
Nicholas Tinoven	1	1	....	....	....	1	1	1	....
Mr Davenport	2	1	....	....	....	....	1	....	....
Giles Gaudenoa	....	1	....	....	....	....	....	1	1
Widdow Stokes	1	1	....	1	....	....	2	....	....
Robert Elison	1	2	....	....	....	....	2	....	....
Andreas Maer	2	2	2	1	....	....	1	....	....
Benjamin Winecope	2	1	1	....	....	....	....	....	....
Widdow Stukey	1	2	2	....	....	....	....	....	....
Madm Weaver	....	2	1	2	1	2	....	1	....
Thomas Ives	2	1	....	....	1	1	....	....	....
Derick Ten Eyck	3	1	2	....	12	1	....	....	....
John Peroe	1	3	....	....	....	....	....	....	....
Thos Gleaves	1	1	3	2	2	2	1	....	....
Pasco	1	1	....	....	....	....	1	1	....
Mr Cosens	1	1	2	2	....	2	1	....	....
Andrew Law	2	3	2	....	....	....	....	....	....
Widdow Bassett	....	1	2	1	....	....	....	....	....
William Lloyd	....	1	2	....	....	....	....	....	....
Adrian Man	4	01	3	1	....	....	....	....	....
Widdow Lysenner	0	2	....	1	....	....	....	....	....
Mr Van Dam	2	2	3	2	3	2	1	....	....
Widdow Cloper	2	1	1	1	....	....	....	1	....
John Pitt	1	1	1	1	....	....	....	....	....
Robert Deintant	1	1	....	1	....	....	....	....	....
Widdow Dikey	....	2	1	7	4	1	1	1	....
Widdow van Scarck	....	6	1	2	1	1	1	1	....
Capt Corbutt	3	3	....	2	2	2	....	....	....
Delancena Jew	1	1	1	1	....	1	....	1	....
Anthony Farmer	1	1	1	2	....	1	1	2	....
Gilbert Vanimbrough	1	1	1	3	1	....	....	....	....
Abraham Vanderell	1	1	....	....	....	....	....	....	....
Lawrence Heading	1	2	....	....	....	....	....	1	1
Widdow Symonse Janson	....	1	....	....	....	....	....	....	....
Widdow Hallgrave	0	1	0	1	....	....	....	....	....
Widdow Phillips	....	1	1	....	1	2	2	1	....
Stephen Richards	1	2	1	2	....	1	....	....	....
Mr Rossoll	1	1	2	1	....	1	1	....	....
Widdew Seiler	....	1	1	....	3	1	....	1	....
John Wansart	1	1	....	....	....	....	....	....	....
Herman Rutgese	2	1	....	1	2	....	....	....	....
Widdow Nespot	1	1	....	1	....	....	....	....	....
Widdow Deforest	1	1	2	5	....	....	....	....	....
Justus Jay	1	2	....	3	1	....	....	....	....

MASTERS OF FAMILYS	Males from 16 to 60	females	Male Children	female Children	Male Negros	female Negros	Male Negro Children	female Negro Children	all above 60
Widdow Brown	....	1	1	3	....	....	....	....	....
Peter Myir	1	1	1	4	....	....	....	....	....
Widdow Doweher	1	1	1.	2	....	....	....	....	....
John Kingstone	1	1	....	....	....	....	....	....	....
Nicholas Lorteen	1	1	....	....	....	....	....	....	....
Capt Matthews	....	1	3	2	....	1	1	....	....
Johannes Johnson	1	1	2	2	....	....	....	....	....
John Petraaslot	1	1	1	1	....	....	....	....	....
James Many	1	3	....	....	....	....	....	....	....
Samll Burges	....	1	....	3	....	1	....	....	....
Mr Cooper	1	2	2	2	....	....	1	1	....
Johannes Vanrost	1	1	2	3	....	....	1	....	....
Mr Vangoson	1	2	1	....	....	....	....	....	....
Mr Vangoson	1	2	1	1	....	....	....	....	....
Capt Tinoven	1	1	....	....	....	1	1	1	....
Christophr Hogland	1	1	2	....	....	....	....	....	....
Widdow van plank	....	3	2	3	....	1	....	....	....
Johannes Vanderhield	1	1	1	....	1	1	....	....	....
Widdow Keisted	....	2	5	1	1	....	....	....	....
Andreas Breestad	2	4	4	2	2	1	....	....	....
Widdow Deshamp	1	2	1	....	....	4	....	2	....
Mr Antill	1	1	2	2	....	2	....	2	....
Wilellmus Navensusen	2	2	....	....	....	....	....	1	....
Francis Vincent	2	1	1	2	1	1	1	....	....
Peter Kip	1	1	1	....	....	....	1	....	....
Gre Robertson	....	2	....	....	....	....	....	....	....
Jacob Maurice	2	1	1	....	1	....	....	....	....
Garrett Vesey	1	1	1	3	1	....	....	....	....
Widdow Bush	1	2	....	....	....	....	....	....	....
Johannes Craft	1	1	....	....	....	....	....	....	....
Samll Beckman	1	1	2	4	....	....	....	....	....
Mr Honan	1	2	....	1	....	1	....	....	....
Widdow Cortland	2	2	....	3	5	2	1	1	....
Widdow Keisteed	1	1	....	1	....	....	....	1	....
Hendrick Mester	1	1	....	....	....	....	....	....	....
Abraham Webrana	1	1	2	....	....	....	....	....	....
Edward Blagg	1	....	1	....	....	2	....	....	....
Capt ffinch	1	1	....	2	....	....	....	....	....
NORTH WARD.									
Isaac Stoutenbrough	1	1	2	0	....	....	....	....	1
Lydiah Rose	0	3	1	....	....	....	....	....	....
Johannes Veckden	1	1	1	2	....	....	....	....	....
Gerrard Grans	1	1	4	1	....	....	....	....	....
Jeemz Lie	1	1	....	1	....	....	....	....	....
Freerick Bloom	1	1	2	1	....	....	....	....	....
Wm Ockton	1	1	....	....	....	....	....	....	....
Gerret De Boogh	1	1	1	....	....	....	....	....	....
Mangell Ransen	1	1	2	2	2	....	....	....	1
Danl Domskon	1	1	1	1	....	....	....	....	....
Jacob Van Direse	1	1	1	3	....	....	....	....	....
Eleazer Bogert	1	1	4	....	....	....	....	....	....
Joriz Breger	1	1	2	....	....	....	....	....	....
Jasbuz Boz	1	1	2	....	1	....	....	....	....
Johannes Bogert	1	1	....	0	....	....	....	....	....
Wm Waderson	1	2	....	....	....	....	....	....	....
Johannes Proovoost	1	1	....	1	....	....	....	....	....
Joseph Waderson	1	1	2	3	....	....	....	....	....
Henry Coleman	1	1	....	1	1	....	....	....	....
Philip Bellenz	1	1	....	1	....	....	....	....	....
Joseph Bresser	1	1	....	1	....	....	....	....	....

MASTERS OF FAMILYS	Males from 16 to 60	females	Male Children	female Children	Male Negros	female Negros	Male Negro Children	female Negro Children	all above 60
Ratie Vanderbeeck	....	1	2	....	....	....	....	....	....
Johannes Bant	1	1	2	....	....	....	....	....	....
Jacob Balck	1	1	0	1	....	....	....	....	....
Saml Marten	1	1	....	....	....	....	....	....	....
Jo Dickter	1	1	....	2	....	....	....	....	....
John Terree	1	1	....	1	....	....	....	....	....
Kuijbert Vandenberg	1	1	....	3	....	....	....	....	....
John Bentell	....	3	....	....	....	....	....	....	....
Joseph Paling	1	1	1	3	1	1	....	....	....
Mr Evert	1	1	0	3	0	1	....	....	....
Jacob Swart	1	1	2	1	....	....	....	....	....
Bartholemew Vonol	1	1	1	....	....	....	....	....	....
Edwd Lock	1	1	2	1	....	....	....	....	....
Marre Quick	....	1	1	....	....	....	....	....	....
Isaac Juter	1	1	2	1	....	....	....	....	....
Mr Floran	1	1	0	1	....	....	....	....	....
Danl Travore	1	1	1	....	....	....	....	....	....
Mr Ritvire	1	1	....	....	....	....	....	....	....
Henderick Drimiez	1	1	1	1	....	....	....	....	....
Derick Ritenbogert	1	1	1	1	....	....	....	....	....
Abraham Vanaren	1	1	2	2	1	1	1	1	1
Jan Karelse	1	1	....	1	....	....	....	....	....
Janetie degrau's	....	2	0	1	....	....	....	....	....
Harmen degrau's	1	1	3	2	....	....	....	....	....
Andrew Douwe	1	1	....	2	....	....	....	....	....
Aijs Van Velsen	1	1	2	2	....	....	....	....	....
Yochem Lolyer	1	1	2	1	....	....	....	....	....
Mr Hooper	....	1	0	2	....	....	....	....	....
Hendrick Oostrom	....	....	....	....	....	....	....	....	....
Yan Heslook	1	1	....	1	....	....	....	....	....
Jan Beadre	1	1	2	....	....	....	....	....	....
Christian Lowrier	1	1	2	....	....	....	....	....	....
Annetie Lowrier	....	1	....	....	....	....	....	....	....
Wm Visser	1	1	2	4	1	....	....	....	....
Robt Milre	....	....	....	....	....	....	....	....	2
Stoffel Pelz	1	1	2	2	1	1	1	....	....
Aijme Vandyck	1	1	2	2	....	....	....	....	....
Peter Van Waggele	1	1	....	2	1	....	....	....	....
Susanna Tocter	....	1	....	1	....	....	....	....	....
Evert Bressen	1	1	2	5	....	....	....	....	....
Johannes P Cavice	1	1	....	1	....	....	....	....	....
Hanz Kierstede	1	1	2	1	....	....	....	....	....
Wyburgh Vanbos	....	1	....	1	....	....	....	....	....
Direck Slick	1	1	2	1	....	....	....	....	....
Enoch Kill	1	1	....	....	....	....	....	....	....
Danl Barteloo	1	1	....	2	....	....	....	....	....
Reyere Martese	1	1	2	1	....	....	....	....	....
Abraham Vandurse	1	1	3	2	....	....	....	....	....
Danl Walderon	1	1	....	5	....	....	....	....	....
Morott	....	1	0	2	....	....	....	....	....
Tam Pell	1	1	....	2	....	....	....	....	....
Alexander Lam	1	1	2	4	....	....	....	....	....
Wm Attell	1	1	2	3	....	....	....	....	....
Mrs Ameker	....	....	....	....	....	....	....	....	1
Peter Burger	1	1	2	2	....	....	....	....	....
Wm Mandriese	1	1	1	1	....	....	....	....	....
Onerre Obee	....	5	....	....	....	....	....	....	....
Catherine Fip	....	1	4	4	2	2	....	1	....
Wm Vaneckt	1	1	3	1	....	....	....	....	....
Isaack Kip	1	2	5	1	2	2	....	....	....
Orseltie Vandyck	....	2	1	....	....	....	....	....	....

MASTERS OF FAMILYS	Males from 16 to 60	females	Male Children	female Children	Male Negros	female Negros	Male Negro Children	female Negro Children	all above 60
Jacob Boele	1	1	4	1	0	1	2	1	....
Engletre Mol	....	1	1	2	....	....	....	....	....
Wm Rooseboom	1	1	....	3	....	....	....	....	....
Abraham Vangeldere	1	1	1	3	....	....	....	....	....
Yoost Leyresse	1	1	3	....	....	....	....	....	....
Antre Vanoorstrant	....	1	2	2	1	....	....	....	....
Johannes Kenne	1	....	....	....	....	....	....	....	....
Nicholas Delaplyne	....	....	....	....	....	....	....	....	1
Jacob Carrebill	1	1	....	....	....	....	....	....	....
Wier Boergeran	1	1	1	....	....	....	....	....	....
Abraham Keteltaz	1	1	1	1	....	....	....	....	....
Antiene Yellerton	....	1	2	1	....	....	....	....	....
Benj Proovoost	1	0	5	6	....	....	....	....	....
Denis Sweetman	1	1	1	....	....	....	....	....	....
Hendrick Boz	1	1	3	1	....	....	....	....	....
Garret Lansen	1	1	2	3	....	....	....	....	....
Annetie Henne	....	1	....	1	....	....	....	....	....
Mr Vandrick	....	1	....	1	....	....	....	....	....
Abraham Kip	1	1	1	1	1	1	1	1	....
ffrans Vandyck	1	1	3	....	....	....	....	....	....
Robert Podventon	1	....	....	....	....	....	....	....	....
Aaron Vanvlarden	1	1	4	1	....	....	....	....	....
John Van strijp	1	1	....	....	....	....	....	....	....
Hathman Wessels	1	1	....	1	....	....	....	....	....
Peter Yaaokse	1	1	2	1	1	1	....	....	....
Mattyz Boeckout	1	1	....	....	....	....	....	....	....
Peter Saryo	1	1	1	1	....	....	....	....	....
Yan Sivvere	1	....	....	....	....	....	....	....	....
Yan Hille	1	2	3	3	....	....	....	....	....
Yan Yonz	1	....	....	....	....	....	....	....	....
Stijntie Yoris	....	1	....	....	....	....	....	....	....
Anenez Tiebout	1	1	3	2	....	....	....	....	....
Wm Yorster	1	1	3	2	....	....	....	....	....
Wm Proovoost	1	1	2	2	....	....	....	....	....
Mr Kinning	....	1	7	1	....	....	....	....	....
Catharina Selecoat	....	1	....	....	....	....	....	....	....
Fillet Sweer	1	1	....	....	....	....	....	....	....
Wm Pell	1	1	2	3	....	....	....	....	....
Cornelia Vandervoers	1	1	....	....	....	....	....	....	....
Yan Meet	1	1	4	2	....	....	....	....	....
Barent Vantilburg	1	....	1	1	....	....	....	....	....
Wm Stenton	1	1	0	2	....	....	....	....	....
Loo Witten	1	1	....	2	....	....	....	....	....
Nieste Viene	....	2	1	....	....	1	....	....	....
Yan Devenne	1	1	....	1	1	....	....	....	....
Cornelia Maruz	....	1	2	3	....	....	....	....	....
Doreman Stor	1	1	....	....	1	....	....	....	....
Mrs Lindslee	....	1	....	....	....	....	....	....	....
Swerez Hendricks	1	....	....	1	....	....	....	....	....
David Hoesaert	1	1	2	1	....	....	....	....	....
Ante Burgers	0	1	3	3	....	....	....	....	....
Ysack Brat	1	1	....	2	....	....	....	....	....
Elsie Sippe	....	3	4	....	....	....	....	....	....
Yohanniz Vandewater	1	2	2	....	....	....	....	....	....
Nelte Plaurere	2	2	1	4	....	....	....	....	1
Garret Hallaer	1	1	....	1	1	....	....	....	....
Hardmen Holduz	1	....	....	....	....	....	....	....	....
Solomon Vanderboogh	1	1	3	....	....	....	....	....	....
Allebertuz Ringo	1	1	3	2	....	....	....	....	....
Vansent Tielo	1	1	2	3	....	....	....	....	....
Hester Montaine	....	1	3	1	....	....	....	....	....

MASTERS OF FAMILYS	Males from 16 to 60	females	Male Children	female Children	Male Negros	female Negros	Male Negro Children	female Negro Children	all above 60
David Christeaense	2	1	1	2	....	....	....	....	....
Yan Keoeck	1	1	5	1	1	1	....	....	....
Sarebz Loeter	1	4	1	1	....	....	....	....	....
Mrs Stevez	....	2	....	....	4	1	....	....	2
Anderiez Marschalock	1	2	5	1	....	....	....	....	....
Yacob Bennett	1	2	3	1	....	....	....	....	....
Wm Bogaert	1	1	1	1	....	....	....	....	....
Yan Vanhorn	1	1	....	....	....	....	....	....	....
Aennez Ynick	1	1	2	2	....	1	....	....	....
Garret Wouterse	1	1	1	1	....	....	....	....	....
Hatie Provoost	....	1	2	4	2	....	....	....	....
Martie Vandeheyden	0	1	1	1	....	....	....	....	....
Barent Lool	1	1	2	2	....	....	....	....	....
Yannez Laegerau	1	1	....	1	1	....	....	....	....
Garret Onckelback	1	1	1	2	....	....	....	....	....
Yan Vantilburgh	1	1	....	....	....	....	....	....	....
Saml Lockeriest	1	1	3	....	1	1	....	....	1
Barnarduz Smit	1	1	9	1	....	....	....	....	....
Yan Pieterse Boz	....	....	....	....	....	....	....	....	2
Caterina Bootz	....	....	....	....	....	....	....	....	1
Barnardus Hardebroer	1	....	1	4	1	....	....	....	....
Corneliz Loris	1	1	4	....	1	....	....	....	....
Peter Boz	1	1	1	2	....	....	....	....	....
Mrs Monvel	....	1	1	....	....	....	2	....	....
Garret Burger	1	1	2	2	....	....	....	....	....
Yan Herrick	1	1	0	2	....	....	....	....	....
Garret Wynanse	1	1	....	....	....	....	....	....	....
Lavie Vandmirse	....	1	2	2	....	....	....	....	....
Sijmon Breeste	1	1	2	3	1	....	....	....	....
Yannetre Wande Watee	....	1	....	....	....	....	....	....	....
Am Reijt	1	1	1	1	....	....	....	....	....
Yacob deportee	1	1	2	1	....	....	....	....	....
Yan Narbree	1	1	1	....	....	....	....	....	....
Yohannez Vantiburgh	1	1	2	....	....	....	....	....	....
Yan Konee	1	....	....	....	....	....	....	....	....
Mrs Boseit	....	1	....	....	....	....	....	....	....
Wessell Everse	1	1	2	2	....	....	....	....	....
Bettie Rammesen	....	2	1	....	....	....	....	....	....

WEST WARD.

MASTERS OF FAMILYS	Males from 16 to 60	females	Male Children	female Children	Male Negros	female Negros	Male Negro Children	female Negro Children	all above 60
Peter Bayard	1	1	....	2	....	1	....	....	....
Garret Vantright	0	2	....	1	....	....	....	....	1
Cornelius Lodge	1	1	....	1	....	....	....	....	....
Wm Smith Aldermn	1	1	....	....	2	4	4	2	....
Ball: Bayard	4	1	....	....	1	1	3	1	1
Matt: De Hart	2	2	1	2	....	....	....	....	....
Jacob Vansune	1	2	....	....	....	....	1	....	....
Catherine Rolegome	....	2	....	....	1	....	....	1	....
Charles Denisoe	1	1	....	....	....	1	....	....	....
Robt Darkins	2	2	1	1	1	2	....	....	....
Derus Vandinbrough	1	1	1	1	2	1	....	....	....
Bar: Laroox	2	1	3	3	0	1	....	....	....
John Barbarie	2	1	3	3	0	3	....	....	....
James Colett	1	1	4	....	....	....	....	....	....
John Dublett	....	2	....	....	....	....	....	....	1
Peter Munvill	1	1	....	....	....	1	....	....	....
Isaac De Boogh	1	1	....	....	....	....	....	....	....
Peter Pieret	2	2	1	2	11	1	1	1	....
Mrs Rumboll	....	3	0	....	....	1	0	2	0
Evert Van Howk	1	1	3	2	....	....	....	....	....
Robt White	1	1	1	2	....	....	....	....	....

MASTERS OF FAMILYS	Males from 16 to 60	females	Male Children	female Children	Male Negros	female Negros	Male Negro Children	female Negro Children	all above 60
Margrett Hudson	....	1	1	1	....	....	....	....	....
Catherine White	....	2	....	2	....	....	....	....	....
Wm Walch	1	2	3	....	....	....	....	....	....
Johan: Van Gelder	1	1	5	2	....	....	....	....	....
Isaac Anderson	1	1	3	1	....	1	....	....	....
John Hutchins	1	1	....	....	....	2	1	....	....
Susannah Wells	....	1	1	1	....	....	....	....	....
Deborah Symcom	....	....	....	1	....	....	....	....	1
Cornelius Clopper	1	1	1	2	....	....	....	....	....
And: Faucout	1	1	....	....	....	....	....	....	....
Augustus Grassett	1	1	....	....	....	1	....	....	....
Jacobus Berrey	1	1	1	2	....	....	1	....	....
Coll: Peartree	1	1	1	....	2	2	1	1	....
Urian Blank	1	....	....	....	....	....	....	....	....
Mary Blank	....	1	....	1	....	....	....	....	....
Robt Edwards	1	1	....	2	....	....	....	....	....
Rebekah Adams	....	1	1	1	....	....	....	....	....
George Williams	1	1	....	....	....	....	....	....	....
Wm Stoks	1	1	1	1	....	....	....	....	....
Francis Bocketts	1	1	2	2	....	....	....	....	....
Tobias Stoutenbrough	2	2	4	....	1	1	....	....	....
Agnes Davis	....	1	....	2	....	....	....	....	....
Daniel Ebbetts	2	1	....	....	....	....	....	....	....
Eliz: Plumley	....	2	1	....	....	1	....	....	....
Samp: Shilton Braughton	2	4	....	....	1	....	....	....	....
Han: Tenijck	2	3	1	1	....	....	....	....	....
Robt Anderson	1	1	1	....	....	....	....	....	....
Peter Johnson	1	1	....	....	1	....	....	....	....
Abra: Masiear	1	1	3	2	1	1	....	....	....
John Anen	1	2	....	2	....	....	....	....	....
Wm Arison	1	1	....	2	1	1	....	....	....
David Mackdugell	1	1	1	....	....	....	....	....	....
Isaac Garners	1	1	1	....	....	....	....	....	....
Will: Shullwood	1	1	....	1	....	....	....	....	....
Laynard D Graw	1	3	4	2	....	....	....	....	....
Jores Riersie	1	2	4	4	2	....	1	....	....
John Cure	1	1	....	1	....	....	....	....	....
Archibald Reed	1	1	....	....	....	....	....	....	....
Hanna Tinbrook	2	1	1	....	....	....	....	....	....
Andrew Lamarue	1	1	1	1	....	....	....	....	....
Michael Harring	1	....	....	1	....	....	....	....	....
Edwd Burley	1	1	1	....	....	....	....	....	....
Lieft: Buckley	....	1	....	4	....	....	....	....	....
Rinear Risoe	2	2	1	1	....	....	....	....	....
Walter D Boise	1	1	....	1	....	1	....	....	...
Garret Cosyn	1	1	1	1	....	....	....	....	....
Pietr Parmyter	1	2	1	1	....	....	....	....	...
Alberts Laynderts	....	....	....	....	....	....	....	....	1
Paul Tuk	....	1	....	....	....	....	....	....	1
Peter Marks	1	1	....	....	....	....	....	....	....
Armanus Van Geldr	1	1	2	3	....	....	....	....	....
Phill: Doley	1	1	1	....	....	....	....	....	....
Jno D. Le ffountaine	1	1	3	2	....	....	....	....	....
Jacob Kuwning	1	1	1	2	....	....	....	....	....
Joseph Wright	1	1	....	1	....	....	....	....	....
Peter Willtrans Roome	1	1	4	4	....	....	....	....	....
Wm Moss	1	2	2	2	....	....	....	....	....
Nicholas Blachford	1	1	....	....	....	....	....	....	....
Will: Robinson	1	1	....	....	....	....	....	....	....
Mary Collum	....	1	....	2	1	....	....	....	....
Garret Blank	....	1	2	2	1	....	....	....	....

MASTERS OF FAMILYS	Males from 16 to 60	females	Male Children	female Children	Male Negros	female Negros	Male Negro Children	female Negro Children	all above 60
Margaret Van D: Schuyer	....	1	....	....	....	....	....	....	....
Peter Do	1	1	4	2	....	....	....	....	....
John French	1	2	....	3	....	....	....	....	....
Mary Harks	....	2	....	....	....	....	....	....	....
Edmund Thomas	1	1	1	....	....	....	....	....	....
Francis Cowenhoaf	2	....	....	....	....	....	....	....	....
Margrett Markner	....	4	....	....	....	....	....	....	....
John Swere	1	1	2	1	....	....	....	....	....
Eliz: Collier	....	1	....	....	....	....	....	....	....
Cor: Garretts	1	1	1	1	....	....	....	....	....
John Harris	1	1	1	1	1	....	....	....	....
Alford Suerts	1	1	1	4	1	1	3	....	....
Will: Hagers	1	1	2	....	....	....	....	....	....
Walter Hagers	1	1	....	1	....	....	....	....	....
Johannes Ebon	2	1	2	2	....	....	....	....	....
Garret Ketteltass	....	....	....	....	....	....	....	....	....
James Beard	....	....	....	....	....	....	....	....	....
Cornelius Quick	1	1	4	2	....	1	....	....	....
Jacob Naoms	1	....	1	....	....	1	....	....	....
John Windefort	1	1	2	1	....	....	....	....	....
Bernard Bush	1	1	1	2	....	....	....	....	....
Jocum Robeson	1	1	2	....	....	....	....	....	....
John Vanderbeck	1	1	1	1	....	....	....	....	....
Conradus Do:	1	1	1	1	....	....	....	....	....
William Pearce	1	3	2	3	....	....	....	....	....
Robt Crannell	1	1	2	2	....	....	....	....	....
Anne Marie	....	1	....	1	....	....	....	....	....
John Thorn	1	1	....	....	....	....	....	....	....
Richard Fleming	1	1	....	1	....	....	....	....	....
Margt: ffordiz	....	2	....	....	....	....	....	....	....
John Williams Romiere	1	1	1	1	....	....	....	....	....
ies Dolsie	1	1	1	....	....	....	....	....	....
Jacob Hases	1	1	1	....	....	....	....	....	....
John Peake	1	2	4	3	....	....	....	....	....
John Leathing	1	1	1	....	....	....	....	....	....
Edwd Anderson	1	1	....	1	....	....	....	....	....
Peter Low	2	....	....	....	....	1	....	....	....
Alida Wright	....	1	....	2	....	....	....	....	....
Griffin Jones	1	1	....	....	....	....	....	....	....
Powels Turke Junr	1	1	....	2	....	....	....	....	....
Hendrick Johnson	1	1	....	3	....	....	....	....	1
Eliz: Wackham	....	4	....	....	....	....	....	....	....
Thomas Coburn	1	1	....	....	....	....	....	....	....
Richard Green	1	1	....	1	....	....	....	....	....
John Lucas	1	1	....	1	....	....	....	....	....
Sergeant Smith	1	1	....	....	....	....	....	....	....
John Bowring	1	1	....	1	....	....	....	....	....
Peter Fauconnier	1	3	2	2	1	1	....	....	....

DOCK WARD.

MASTERS OF FAMILYS	Males from 16 to 60	females	Male Children	female Children	Male Negros	female Negros	Male Negro Children	female Negro Children	all above 60
Phillip ffrench	1	1	1	2	3	2	1	1	....
Mrs Mogon	....	1	2	2	....	1	....	....	....
Zacharie Angeum	1	1	....	3	....	....	....	....	....
Anthony Davis	....	1	1	1	....	1	....	1	....
Elias Budinot	1	1	....	1	....	1	....	1	....
Johan: Hardenbrok	1	1	1	2	....	....	....	1	....
John Parmiter	1	1	1	1	....	....	....	....	....
Samuel Bayard	1	1	1	2	1	1	....	....	....
Nicholas Jamin	....	1	....	....	....	5	1	....	1
Jno Casall	1	1	....	....	....	2	....	....	....
Johannes Hoglandt	1	2	1	....	1	1	....	....	....

MASTERS OF FAMILYS	Males from 16 to 60	females	Male Children	female Children	Male Negros	female Negros	Male Negro Children	female Negro Children	all above 60
Widdow Alkfield.....................	....	1	1	1	....	....	....	....	....
Garret Dyking	1	1	2	2	1	1	1	1	....
Catharin Potter	....	1	....	2	....	1	....	....	....
David Jameson.......................	1	1	1	2	1	2	....	....	....
Moses Levey	3	2	1	1	....	1	1	....	....
Robert Lurting......................	2	3	3	3	....	1	1	....	....
Samuel Veach.......................	1	2	....	1	....	....	....	2	....
Widdow Taylor......................	0	1	2	1	1	1	....	2	....
David Villat	1	1	1	1	....	....	....	....	....
Mrs Allie	....	1	2	....	....	1	1	....	....
David Logall	1	1	1	2	....	1	....	....	....
Thos Burrough.......................	1	1	1	2	1	1	....	....	....
Capt Simes.........................	1	2	2	1	1	1	1	....	....
Robt Skelton........................	1	2	....	1	1	....	....	....	....
Charles Wooley	3	....	....	....	1	....	....	....	....
Garret Vanhorne..........	1	1	1	2	2	1	....	....	....
Paul Drulett	1	1	2	4	....	2	....	....	....
Lewis ffarree	1	3	2	2	....	1	1	....	....
Stephen D'lancey	1	1	2	....	3	2	1	1	....
Jno James Vanveale	1	1	....	....	....	1	....	1	....
Widdow ffagett	....	3	....	....	....	....	....	....	....
Hendrick Vand: Hull.................	1	1	1	1	....	....	....	....	....
John Shackmaple.	1	2	....	....	....	....	....	....	....
Peter Hemoims	2	1	....	1	....	....	....	....	....
John Van horne......................	1	1	2	01	3	01	1	....	....
Jacobus vancourtlandt	1	1	2	2	2	2	1	....	....
Jacobus Decay	1	1	2	1	4	3	1	1	....
Mrs Cuylar..........................	1	2	1	....	1	1	....	....	....
Jacob Ten Eyck	2	2	....	1	....	....	1	....	....
Abraham Governere	1	1	1	1	....	....	....	1	....
English Smith	....	2	1	....	....	....	....	....	1
Cornelius Jacobs	....	2	1	5	....	1	....	1	....
David Provost Junr	1	....	2	3	2	1	....	....	....
Widdow Sanders.....................	....	3	....	....	....	1	3	....	....
Affey Tuder.........................	....	1	1	....	....	1	....	....	....
Widdow D Roblus	....	4	3	1	....	1	....	....	....
Widdow Lillies & Nathaniel Masston in Ditto	3	4	1	5	....	1	....	....	1
Widdow Vanhorne...................	1	3	....	....	....	1	....	....	....
Abraham Sanford....................	1	1	3	2	....	....	....	....	....
William Walton......................	1	2	1	....	1	....	1	....	....
Christopher Gillin	1	1	1	2	....	....	....	....	....
William Chambers...................	1	2	3	....	1	....	....	....	....
Johannes outman....................	1	2	1	....	1	....	....	....	....
Isaac D Markeys	1	2	1	1	1	2	....	1	....
Widdow Lawrence	....	1	3	2	....	....	....	....	....
Peter Lakerman	1	1	1	....	1	1	1	....	1
John Gurney.........................	1	1	....	1	1	1	....	....	....
Widdow Sowalls.....................	1	2	....	....	....	....	....	....	....
Coll. Nich: Bayard..................	....	1	1	....	2	....	....	1	....
ffrancis Garrabrant..................	1	2	....	2	2	....	....	....	....
William Barkley.....................	1	3	1	1	....	1	....	....	....
Nicholas ffieldon .;..................	1	1	2	2	....	....	....	....	....
Bartholomew Hart....................	1	1	....	1	2	1	....	....	....
Overin	1	....	....	....	....	....	....	....	....
Thomas Wenham	1	1	1	1	2	3	....	....	....
Hibon	2	1	....	2	1	....	....	....	....
Vandermar.....................	1	2	1	....	....	....	....	....	....
iv Cookers	....	2	....	1	....	....	....	....	....
John Scott	1	2	1	....	....	....	1	....	....
Widdow D. Pyster....................	....	1	....	2	1	1	....	....	....

CENSUS OF NEW-YORK CITY.

MASTERS OF FAMILYS	Males from 16 to 60	females	Male Children	female Children	Male Negros	female Negros	Male Negro Children	female Negro Children	all above 60
John Lorring	1	1	1	1	....	2	....	1	....
Nicholas Garretts	....	3	2	2	1	0	....	1	....
Abraham V : D : waters	1	1	....	....	....	....	....	....	....
Harmanes Burger	1	1	1	1	....	....	....	....	....
Martines Criger	1	1	1	....	....	....	....	....	....
Andris Tenbrook	1	1	1	1	....	....	....	....	....
Rugert Waldron	3	1	1	1	....	....	....	....	....
John Davis	1	1	1	1	2	1	1	2	....
Widdow Buddinot	1	4	2	....	1	2	....	....	....
Richard Willit	2	1	....	....	....	1	1	....	....
• vis Gomas	2	2	3	1	1	1	....	....	....
John Harperding	....	1	....	1	....	....	....	1	1
Avert Elberseye	1	3	4	....	1	....	....	....	....
Roger Jones	2	....	....	....	....	....	....	....	....
Johannes Thiebout	1	1	1	....	....	....	....	....	....
Martin Cloock	1	1	....	1	....	2	....	....	....
Albert Cloock	2	1	3	2	1	1	....	....	....
Lawrence Vanhoock	2	2	2	2	1	....	....	....	....
Cornelius Veilin	2	1	1	2	....	....	....	1	....
Abrahm Mettelares	2	1	5	1	1	1	....	....	....
John Lansing	....	....	....	....	....	....	....	....	....
Evert Van D. watr	1	1	....	1	....	....	....	1	....
William Echeles	1	1	....	1	2	....	....	....	....
Edward Marshall	1	1	1	....	....	1	....	....	....
John Wanshares	1	1	....	1	....	....	....	....	....
John Vansent	2	1	....	....	2	1	....	....	....
William Bradford	2	1	3	2	....	2	....	....	....
Conrad Ten Eyke	4	3	1	....	1	....	....	....	....
• rd Provost Senr	1	2	....	2	....	1	....	....	....
John Everts	1	1	....	1	1	....	....	....	....
Geesje ten Eges	....	1	....	....	....	1	....	....	....
Hugh Crow	1	1	1	....	....	....	....	1	....
Anthony Rutgers	1	1	2	....	....	1	....	....	....
John Whitt	1	0	1	2	....	....	....	....	....
Mr Legrand	1	....	....	....	....	....	....	....	....
Nicholas Materbe	1	1	....	....	....	....	....	....	....
Samll Leveridg	1	3	4	....	2	1	....	....	1
William White Junr	2	1	....	....	....	....	....	....	....
Mary Wakham	....	4	....	....	....	....	1	....	....
Henry Money	2	1	....	....	....	....	....	....	....
John Stephens	2	....	....	....	....	....	....	....	....
Richd Green	1	1	....	....	....	....	....	....	....
• n Varickbookhouse	2	3	1	3	....	....	....	....	....
• rence Vessells	1	1	2	2	3	1	....	....	....
• aham Lawkerman	1	1	1	....	3	2	1	1	....
Everdas Borgadas	1	2	....	....	....	....	....	....	....
William Bickley	2	....	....	....	....	1	1	1	....
Jannetie Van briekelen	....	3	....	....	....	....	....	....	....
Abraham Splinter	2	1	....	2	....	....	....	1	....
Gabrll Thiebod	1	1	2	....	....	....	....	....	....
Widdow Colie	2	....	....	....	....	....	....	....	....
Mrs Mashett	....	1	1	....	....	....	....	....	....
Johannes Burger	1	2	4	....	....	....	....	....	....

• These names cannot be made out on account of the MS. being torn

OUT WARD.

MASTERS OF FAMILYS	Males from 16 to 60	females	Male Children	female Children	Male Negros	female Negros	Male Negro Children	female Negro Children	all above 60
* Ritman	2	2	2	1	1	....	2	....	....
* Kip	2	2	....	1	5	2	1	....	....
* elus Bak	1	1	1	1	....	....	....	....	....
* ids Widd	....	1	2	3	....	....	....	....	....
Peter Bokho	1	1	....	....	....	....	....	....	....
John Barr	2	1	1	3	....	....	....	....	....
—— Solomon	1	2	2	....	....	....	....	....	1
* hn Peter	1	1	1	2	....	....	....	....	....
* nl Carpenter	2	2	1	....	....	....	....	....	1
Abraham Brimer	1	1	4	....	....	....	....	....	....
—— Gunoson	1	1	....	1	....	....	....	....	....
John Dikman	1	1	....	....	....	....	....	....	....
,—— Tunsedes	2	4	....	2	1	....	3	2	1
John Devor	2	....	3	3	....	....	....	....	....
Cornelius Drk	2	1	2	2	....	....	....	....	1
Cornelius Aker	1	1	4	....	....	....	1	....	....
Tuns Cornelius	2	1	3	1	1	....	2	....	....
Oranout Waber	....	1	1	1	....	....	....	....	1
Wolford Waber	1	1	1	1	....	....	....	....	....
—— Solomon	1	1	2	....	....	....	....	....	....
Will Da	1	1	....	1	....	....	....	....	....
Hendrick Bordis	1	1	4	2	1	....	....	....	....
* Moor	2	1	1	2	1	....	....	....	....
* Griggs	1	1	....	2	....	....	....	....	....
* Thomas	1	1	....	3	1	....	....	1	....
* Gracklin	....	....	....	....	....	....	....	....	....
Sam'l Mountaine	1	2	6	2	1	....	....	....	....
Capt Sidmen	2	1	1	1	4	2	2	2	0
John Bronod	1	1	2	1	1	....	1	1	1
Rebeccah Van Scyock	1	1	....	....	2	1	....	....	....
Wases Peterson	1	1	2	2	1	....	....	....	....
Thoms Akerson	1	1	2	1	....	....	....	....	....
Solomon Widdow	1	1	1	2	....	....	....	....	....
Amanuel Franson	2	2	....	1	....	....	....	....	....
Jacob Cornelius	2	1	....	2	....	....	....	0	1
Thoms Sekls	1	1	....	....	....	....	....	....	....
John Clapp	1	1	2	....	2	1	....	....	....
Abraham Bolt	1	1	3	6	....	1	1	....	....
Capt Lock	1	1	....	1	1	....	....	....	1
Hendrick Van Scoyock	....	1	2	....	....	....	....	....	....
Philip Minthorne	1	1	3	....	....	....	....	....	....
* ou	1	1	1	1	1	1	1	....	....
* eabor	....	1	....	....	....	1	....	1	1
* way	1	1	1	1	5	1	1	....	....
*	....	3	1	1	2	....	1	....	....
* noute	1	....	1	2	....	1	....	....	....
* Thomas	2	2	1	1	....	....	....	....	2
Walter Lamas	....	....	....	....	1	....	....	....	1
David Minvel	1	2	1	....	1	1	....	....	....
* lin Pierson	2	1	2	4	1	1	....	....	....
Agar Harman	2	2	1	4	....	....	2	....	....
Jacob Conant	1	1	....	1	....	....	1	....	....

NAMES OF INHABITANTS OF THE TOWN OF HEMPSTEAD 1673.

[Vanderkemp's Transl. of Dutch Rec. XXII.]

John ——
John Smith Blew
Richard Geldersly, Sen
—————
Vrolphert Jacobs
Jan Carman
John Symons jun
Robert Jackson
Symon Tory
John Smith
Peter janse Schol
Richard Gildersly
Robbert Beedill
George Hallet
Samuel Allen
Richard Valentyn
Kaleb Carman
John Williams
Thomas Richmore
John Ellesson
Edward Spry
William Osborne
Edward Remsen
John Fossaker
John Sorram
James Payne
William Fixton
Samuel Denton
Robberd Hobbs
Thomas Sodderd
John Smith jun
Joseph Williams
Ralph Haal
Daniel Beedell
John Jackson
Johnathan Smith
John Champion

John Hobbs
John Langd
Jonathan Semmes
John Bordes
Robbard Marisseu
Mos Hemmery
John Beets carpenter
Samuel Embry
Matthew Beedel
    Comes
Thomas Ellison
Philip Davis
—————— Hopkins
——— ———
Adam View
Edward Titus
Richard Eliison
John Seavin
Thomas Teasay
Thomas Ireland
Thomas Ellison
Joseph Gem
Thomas Champion
Joseph Pettet
Richard Fotter
John Beddell
Thomas Southward
John Beates
Calvet Goullet
Christoffel Yeomans
John Woully
Edward Banbury
Thomas Gowes
John Mavein
Wm Thorne
Joshua Watske
Benjamin Symenson

Jan Roelossen
Elbert Hubssen
Lewis Niot
John Ellison jun
Thomas Seabrook
Samuel Jackson
John Pine
Peter Jansen
William Ware
Solomon Semmar
Teunis Smith
Richard Valentin jun.
Joseph Wood
Herman Flouwer
William Dose
Symon Foster
Henry Mott
Wm Fourmer
Joseph Small
Walter pine
Josia Carman
John Peacock
John Quakerson
Thomas Daniels
John Napper
Richard Osborn
George Robbert
Charles Abram
Thomas Appelbe
Samuel Smith
———— Persell
Adam Mott Junr.
Samuel Jackson
Joseph Truax
Joseph Hoyt &
Nine others whose names
    are lost

THE ROLL

OFF THOSE WHO HAUE TAKEN THE OATH OFF ALLEGIANCE IN THE KINGS COUNTY IN THE PROVINCE OFF NEW YORKE THE 26 : 27 : 28 : 29 AND 30th DAY OFF SEPTEMBER IN THE THIRD YEARE OFF HIS MAYtsh RAIGNE ANNOQue DOMINE 1687.

[MSS. in Sec's. Office.]

off fflackbush

Willem Jacobs Van boerum was in this country 38 Jeare
Christoffel Probasco 33 Jeare
hendrick Rijcken 24 Jeare
Pieter Strycker native off this Province off N : Yorke
Cornelis Pieterse native
Cornelis Peters Luijster native
Dirck Jansn Van Vliet 23 Jeare
gerrit Lubberse native
Ruth Albertse 25 Jeare
gerrardus beakman native
Jacob henk. hafften 23 Jeare
gerrit Dorlant native
Engelbert Lott native
Simon hanssen 48 Jeare
Jacob Willem Van bueren 38 Jeare
Reynier aertsen 34 Jeare
Pieter Lott 35 Jeare
Cornelis barense Van Wyck 27 yeare
Jacob Remsen native
Jan harmenssen Van amesfoort 29 Jeares
Willem hendrickse native
Joseph hegeman 37 yeare
Claes Willkens 25 yeare
Willem guil Janse 47 yeare
Auke Reijnierse native
Jooris Remssen native
Jan Wouterse Van bosch 28 yeare
Lambert Jansen native
Jan Remsen native
Jan Dircks Van Vliet 23 yeare
hendrickus hegeman 36 yeare
Jan Spigelaer 25 yeare
adriaen hend aaten 36 yeare
Lefferd Pieterse 27 Jeare
Isaack hegeman native
Pieter guil Janse 45 Jeare
Pieter Willemsen native
Cornelis Jansse Seeu 27 Jeare
hendrick Lott native
Daniel Polhemius native
Jan Van Ditmaertz native
Denijs theunissen native
Jan Strycker 35 yeare
Isaack Van Cassant 35 Jeare
Jan barense blom native
Adriaen Reyerse 41 Jeare
Aris Vanderbilt native
Auke Janse Van Nuys 36 Jeare
Elbert adriaense native
Daniel Remsen native
Jacob Vandebilt native
Marten adriaense native
Christiaen Snediker native

Abram hegeman native
Jan Cornelissen Vander Veer native
Theodorus Van Wijck native
Thomas aaten native
gerrit Snediker native
hendrick Janse native
Roeloff Verkerck 24 Jeare
barent Janssen native
Jacobus hegeman 36 Jeare
hendrick Willemse 38 Jeare
Dirck Jan hooglant 30 Jeare
Jan Dircks hooglant native
Willem Dircks hooglant native
Jan oake 36 Jeare
gerrit Janse Strijker 35 Jeare
Rem Remssen native

off Breucklijn

Thomas Lamberse 36 Jeare
Jooris hanssen native
hendrick Vechten 27 Jeare
Claes Arense Vechten 27 Jeare
Jan Aertsen 26 Jeare
hendrick Claasen 33 Jeare
Jacob hanssen bergen native
Jooris Martens native
hendrick thyssen 21 Jeare
Mauritius Couverts native
Willem huijcken 24 Jeare
theunis gysbertse bogaert 35 Jeare
Willem bennitt native
hendrick Lamberse native
Jan ffredricks 35 Jeare
Jan Couverts native
Luijcas Couverts 24 Jeare
ffrans abramse native
gerrit aerts middag native
Simon Aertsen 23 Jeare
Matthys Cornelisen 24 yeare
Ephraim hendricks 33 jeare
Claes thomas Van Dyck native
Jeronimus d'Rapale native
Jeronimus Remsen native
Casper Janssen native
Achias Janse Vandijck 36 yeare
Jacob Joorissen native
Jacobus d'beauvois 28 Jeare
harmen Joorissen native
Jacob Willemse bennit native
Jacob brouwer native
bourgon broulaet 12 Jeare
Jan Damen 37 Jeare
Cornelis Subrink native
hendrick Sleght 35 Jeare
Juriaen Vanderbreets native
Pieter Staats native

Abram Remsen native
Machiel hanssen native
theunis tobiassen native
Pieter Corsen native
theunis Janse Couverts 36 Jeare
Aert Simonssen native
Adam brouwer Junior native
Alexander Schaers native
Willem Pos native
Jan gerrise dorland 35 Jeare
Johannis Casperse 35 Jeare
Claes barentse blom native
Pieter brouwer native
Abram brouwer native
Jan bennitt native
barent Sleght native
Jacobus Vande Water 29 Jeare
benjamin VandeWater native
Pieter Weijnants native
joost ffranssen 33 Jeare
hendrick aaten native
Jan Janse Staats native
Claes Simons native
Anthonij Souso 5 Jeare
Joost Casperse 35 Jeare
thijs Lubberse 50 Jeare
Paulus dirckse 36 Jeare
Adam brouwer 45 Jeare
Josias Dreths 26 Jeare
Pieter Van Nesten 40 Jeare
Jan theunisen native
Dirck Janse Woertman 40 Jeare
Daniel d'Rapale native
gijsbert boomgaert native
Volkert Vanderbrats native
Jan buijs 39 Jeare
gerrit Dorlant native
Adriaen bennit native
Thomas Verdon native
Pieter janse Staats native

off New Uijtrecht

Tielman Vandermij 13 Jeare
karel Janse Vandijck 35 Jeare
Jan Janse Vandijck 35 Jeare
thomas tierckse 35 Jaer
Wouter Van Pelt 24 Jeare
Jacob Christiaense native
Lambert Janse 22 Jeare
Jan Van Deventer 25 Jeare
Cornelis Janse Vandeventer native
gijsbert thysen Laenen 24 Jeare
theunis Janse Van Pelt Laenen 24 Jeare
Anthony Van Pelt 24 Jeare
Jan Clement 22 Jeare
Cornelis wijnhart 30 Jeare
kreijn Janse Van Meeteren 24 Jeare
Joost Rutsen Van brent native
Aert theunissen Van Pelt native
Anthonij du Chaine 24 Jeare
Jan thijssen Laenen native
Jacob thijssen Laenen native
Laurens Janse native
Jan Van Cleeff 34 Jeare
Wellem klinckenberg native
Nicolase Vandergrifft native
Jan Van kerck junior native
Jan Van kerck senior 24 Jeare
parent Joosten Ridder 35 Jeare

hendrick Mathysse Smack 33 Jeare
Cornelis Van kleeff native
Dirck Janse Van Sutphen 36 Jeare
Jan kiersen 38 Jeare
Gerrit Courten Van Voorhuys native
Ruth Joosten Van brunt 34 Jeare
Pieter ffransisco native
Jacques Cortejou 35 Jeare
Jacques Corteljou Junior native
Cornelis Corteljou native
Pieter Corteljou native
Willem Corteljouw native
gerrit Cornelis Van Duyn 38 Jeare
Cornelis gerris Vanduyn native
Denijs gerrise Vanduyn native
Laurens Janse de Camp 23 Jaer
Pieter thyssen native
Swaen Janssen 33 Jeare
gerrit Stoffelse 36 Jeare
Jan hanssen bruynenburg 48 Jeare
Stoffel gerritse native
Joost debaene 4 Jeare
hendrick Janse kamminga 9 Jaer
Cornelis Rutsen Van brunt native
barent Verkerck native

off Boswijck

Volkert Dirckse native
Pieter Janse deWitt 35 Jeare
Pieter Daniel 10 Jeare
Adriaen La fforge 15 jeare
Joost kockuyt 27 Jeare
Isaack La ffebre 4 Jeare
Pieter Schamp 15 Jeare
Wouter gysbert Verschier 38 Jaer
Pieter Loyse native
Jacques ffontaine native
Pelgrom klock 31 Jeare
Volkert Witt native
Daniel Waldron 35 Jeare
Simon haecks 16 Jeare
Cornelis Loyse 36 Jeare
Jean Le quie 30 Jeare
Alezander Cockevaer 30 Jeare
Albert hendrickse 25 Jeare
Jean Miseroll junior 20 Jeare
Claes Cornelissen Kat 25 Jeare
Michiel Palmentier 23 Jeare
Vincent bale 4 Jeare
Pieter Para 28 Jeare
Johannis ffontaine native
Jean de Consilie 25 Jeare
Josst durie 12 Jeare
Jan Janse 36 Jeare
Jacob Janse native
Pieter Simonse native
Jacob dirckse Rosekrans native
Jochem VerSchuer native
hendrick Verschuer native
Laurens koeck 26 yeare

off fflackland

Elbert Elbertse 50 Jeare
Roeloff Martense Schenck 37 Jeare
Jan Roeloffs Schenck native
Jan Martense Schenck 37 Jeares
Jan theunis Van dyckhuys 34 Jeare
Court Stevense VanVoorhuys 27 Jeare
Pieter Nevius native

Abram Willemsen 25 Jeare
Marten Roeloffe Schenck native
hans Janssen 47 Jeare
Albert Courten Van Voorhuijs native
Pieter Claasen wijckoff 51 Jaere
Simon Janse Van Aerts Daalen 34 Jeare
Cornelis Simonsen Van Aerts daalen native
gerrit Pieterse wijckoff native
Jan brouwer 30 Jeare
gerrit hanssen native
Evert Janssen Van Wickelen 23 Jeare
Claes Pieterse wijckoff native
Dirck brouwer native
gerrit hendrickse bresse native
Pieter brouwer native
Dirck Janssen Ammerman 37 Jeare
adriaen kume 27 Jeare
gerret Elberts Stoothoff native
Jacob Strijcker 36 Jeare
Dirck Stoffelse 30 Jeare
Stoffel Dirckse native
fferdinandus Van Sichgelen 35 Jeare
hendrick Pieterse wijckoff native
Willem gerritse Van Couwenhooven native
gerrit Willemsen Van Couwenhooven native
Jan Pieterse wijckoff native
Anthony Wanshaer native
Luycas Stevense 27 Jeare

Pieter Cornelis Luyster 31 Jeare
Jan Stevense 27 Jeare
Ruth bruynsen 34 Jeare
Willem Willemse borcklo native
Pieter Pieterse Tull 30 Jaer
hendrick brouwer native
Pieter Monffoort native
theunis Janse Van amach 14 Jeare
Thys Pieterse luyster 31 Jeare
Jan albertse terhuen native
Willem Davies 34 Jeare
Johannis Willemse 25 Jeare

off gravens End

Renier Van Siegelen native
Stoffel Janse Romeyn 34 Jeare
Johannis Machielse native
John boisbidland 2 Jeare
  had Letters off Denisatie
barent Juriaense 29 Jeare
Jan barense Van Zutphen 30 Jeare
Marten Pieterse native
Jochem gulick 34 Jeare
Cornelis buys native
Jan Willemsen Van borcklo native
Rem gerritse native
Adam Machielse Messcher 40 Jeare
Willem Willemse 30 Jeare
Jan Carstense native
Johannis brouwer native

AN EXACT LIST

OF ALL Y[e] INHABITANTS NAMES W[th]IN Y[e] TOWNE OF ffLUSHING AND P'CINCTS OF OLD AND YOUNG ffREEMEN & SERUANTS WHITE & BLACKE &c. 1698.

Coll: Tho Willett and Mtrs
9 { Alena his wife
Elbert
Cornelius } Sones.
Abraham
John
Alena } Daughters
Elizabeth
John Clement: Servt
Negros ffrancis }
Jeffrey Hary Jack } 7
and Dick Mary
9 { Justice Tho: Hukes &
Mrs Mary his wife
Isaac: Benjamin—Charles } Sones
Wm Stephen Charely
Mary ; daugt
Negros: Will Cuffee } 6
Sherry ffreegeft & Jane
Majr. Wm Lawrense
& Deborah his wife
William Richard
11 Obadiah Damell
Samuell John
Adam Debo: Sarah

Negros James Tom } 6
Lew Bess 2 child
Richard Cornell
& Sarah his wife
Sone Richard
6 { Sarah
Elizabeth } Daug
& Mary
Negros Tom }
Lewi Toby } 6
Sarah & Dina
5 { John Esmond &
Elizab: his wife
John & Mary
Wm Jewell serut
Samll: Thorne &
Susana his wife
8 { Benjamin }
Samuell & } Sone
Nathan
Jane Kesia } Da:
& Deborah
Negros Coffe }
Dinah Kate } 5
Charles Tony

James Clement
& Sarah his wife
Thomas ⎫
Jacob ⎬ Sones
Joseph & two ⎭
12 Samll &
Nathan
Mary ⎫
Hannah ⎬ Daug
Margarett ⎬
Bridgett ⎭
Negros Toby

Dutch Inhabitants.

Cornelius Barnion
& Anna his wife
Johannis sone
Alke Anna ⎫
7 Elizabeth & ⎬ Da :
Arante ⎭
Negros Antony ⎫
Jack Corose ⎬ 6
Mary Isabella ⎭
Martin Wiltsee &
6 Maria his wife
Cornelius Hendrick
Johannis & Margrett.
Elbert Arinson &
5 Cataline his wife
Rem & Elbert sones
Anneke—negro Dick'r
Garratt Hanson &
Janneke his wife
10 Hance Rem Jan ⎫ 6
Peter Danll Jores ⎭
Janake Cattaline Dau
Negro Jeffrey 1
Lorus Haff
Canuerte his wife
Jewrin Peter ⎫ Sones
11 Johannis & Jacob ⎭
Stinchee Maria ⎫
Tuntee Margaretta ⎬ Dau
Sauta ⎭
Edec : Van Skyagg &
Ebell his wife
7 Cornelius ffrancis
& Arian
Elizabeth Rebecca
Poulas Amarman
3 and Abiena his wife
Abena : Daughter
Barn Bloome &
4 ffammily his wife
Garratt, Johannis.
Eliz Bloodgood
5 Wm & Elizabeth
one negro Will
Dirick Poules
& Sarah his wife
8 Peter Thynis
Rich'd : Wm Jon
Charles Sarah
one negro Tom
2 John Bloodgood
· & Mary his wife
2 Powell Hoff &
Rachell his wife

2 John Jores &
Maria his wife
Derick Brewer &
3 his wife Hannah
1 child

French Inhabits

John : Genung
3 & Margreta his wife :
John : sone
negros 2
ffrancis Burto &
Mary his wife
5 John ffrancis
Abigal : Daug
Sarah Doughty
4 Benjamin ⎫ Sones
William ⎭
Sarah Seruant
Negros : Okee & Mary
2 Mary Perkins
Abigale Daug
Bess : Robin Maria ⎫ 3
Hanes ⎭
2 Ann Noble
Abigale serut
Negros : Jack Jan 2
3 Mary Bowne
Annis Ruth ; Daug
Negros : James & ⎫ 2
Nell ⎭
Arther powell &
4 Margrett his wife
Richard Arther sones
John Hinchman
& Sarah his wife
7 John James
Mercy Mary &
Sarah
Negroo Hetchtor 1
Richard Chew &
ffrances his wife
7 Rich'd Henry Tho
Hannah Charely
Mary Elizabeth
Thomas Runley &
4 Mary his wife
Thomas sone
Hannah
ffrancis Doughty
& Mary his wife
8 Elias palmer
ffrancis Obadiah
Sarah Charely Mary
Negros Vester Rose 2
John Talman &
Mary his wife
7 John James peter
Mary Elizabeth
Charles Tom
Sarah 2 ch 5
John Thorne Senr &
5 Mary his wife
Hannah & Sarah Wm
Negros Alex wo : 3
William ffowler Carp
and Mary his wife
8 William John
Joseph Benj

Mary Rebeca
Negro Jack 1
John Thorne Jun'r
6 Katherin his wife
John Mary
Eliz: Deborah
Henry Taylor &
5 Mary Sarah his wife
Sarah phebe
Negro Tonny 1
Edward Greffin ju
4 Deborah his wife
Edward Mary
2 William Owen &
Mary his wife
2 Hugh Cowperthawt
Mary Southick
Negro Anthony—1
2 Henry ffranklin
& Sarah his wife
1 negro
3 Patience Cornelius
Elias: Mary—
Tho: ffarrington
& Abigale his wife
Thomas Robert
Benjamin—
8 Elizab: Bridgett
Abigale
Negros—Mingo ⎱ 2
Winnee ⎰
Harman Kinge
6 & Mary his wife
John Joseph
Benj. ffrancis
Toby 1
William ffowler wea
3 & Judeth his wife
William sone
Thomas Willett
3 & Sarah his wife
Sarah—Daughter
Negro Lay—1
Thomas Hinchman
4 & Meriam his wife
Thomas & Sarah—
2 George Langley &
Rebeca his wife
Mary & Sampson—2
Matt ffarrington
5 & Hannah his wife
Matthew Sarah &
Edward
John Mariton
ffrancis John
5 Cornelius
Deborah Ebell—
Thomas Yeates
& Mary his wife
6 Mary ye mother
Wm Benj Jane.
Elias Doughty
Elizabeth his wife
5 Elias Eliz: Thomas
Negro: Jack—1
Charles Doughty
& Elizabeth his wife
6 John Charles—
Sarah Elizabth

1 negro black boy 1
John Harrington
& Elzbth his wife
John Edward Matthew
13 Thomas Sam'll Robert
Mercy Margrett
Dorythy Anna—
Elizabeth
Sam'll Bowne
& Mary his wife
6 Sam'll Thomas
Ellmer Hannah
Negros Simon
Nany mingo 3
Joseph palmer
6 & Sarah his wife
Dani'll Esther
Ric'h pricilla
Tho: Hedger &
Elizabeth his wife
Eliakim Thomas
11 Mary Hannah—
Jane Sarah Deborah
Elizabeth
Joseph Thorne &
Mary his wife—
Joseph William
11 Thomas John—
Benjamin Abraham
Hannah Mary Susan.
1 Negro Tom:—1
Sam'll Haight &
Sarah his wife—
10 Nicholas Jonathan
Dauid John Sarah Mary
Hannah phebe—
and one negro 1
Thomas fford and
3 Sarah his wife—
Thomas Child
2 Esther fford
William
Negro Anthony—1
John Embree and
6 Sarah his wife
Robert John Samll
Sarah
Hatham'll Roe and
3 Elizab'th his wife
Dauid
Charles Morgan
& Elizabeth his wife
7 Charles James Thomas
Sarah Ephraim Sophy
Negros: peter James
John Cornelius &
Mary his wife—
10 John Dani'll Sam'll
Joseph Deborah
Mary phebe Sarah
Negro: Zambo: 1
Jona Wright Senr
and Sarah his wife
9 Sam'll Richard Charles
Job: Mary Hannah
John
Henry Wright and
4 Mary his wife
Hannah Sarah

Jona: Wright Ju
4 & Wine his wife
Jonathan Elizabeth
Dauid Wright and
4 Hannah his wife
Dauid phebe
Joseph Lawrense
4 & Mary his wife
Richard Thomas
1 negro Jack—1
2 John Hopper Peintr
& Christopher
2 John Hopper Jun
& Margarett his wife
John Harrison
& Elizabeth his wife
7 William Edward
Henry Eliz Ann
Negros Hetchtor
Kate $\Big\}$ 2
Margery Smith
3 Judeth Hannah
Samuel Tatem &
Elizabeth his wife
6 Sam'll Eliza patience
Mary—negro 1
Benj Heauileind &
5 Abigaile his wife
Adam Benj John
Abigale Bethia
William Benger &
5 his wife Elizabeth
John Jacob Eliz
John Heauiland &
3 Sarah his wife—
John
Thomas Wildee
& Elizabeth his wife
8 Edward Rich'd
Tho Obadiah
Isaaih Eliz'bth
Edward Greffein Se
3 and Mary his wife
Deborah
Negro: Jack:—1
John Rodman
& Mary his wife
9 John Samuell—
Joseph William
Thomas An Eliz:
Negros—11
John Lawrence &
his wife Elizab'th
7 William Richard
Eliz: Mary Deborah
Negros James Rose
Bess Robin Moll—5
Benj ffeild and
Hannah his wife
6 Benj John Antho
Sam'll
Negros Jo: Betty—2
John Greffin &
Elizabeth his wife

5 John Benj Isaac
Joseph Elizab'th
Rich'd Greffin and
5 Susan his wife
Sam'll Sarah Rich'd
Dauid Roe Mary
3 his wife
Mary: Negro Sam 1
Rebeca Clery
4 Athelana Rebeca
phebe Negro: 1
Philip Odall &
his wife Mary
7 Philip Mary
John Elizab'th
Deborah
Joseph Hedger
& Hannah his
7 wife—Joseph
Margrett—
Uriah Sarah
Hannah
Antnody Badgley
5 Elizabeth his wife
Anthony Georg—
phebe: 1 Negro 1
Dan'll Patrick &
4 Dinah his wife
Sarah James ffeke
One Negro 1
John Ryder & his
wife, John Robert
6 Hartie Wintle
one negro 1
2 Dennis Holdrone
Sarah his wife
Josiah Genning
3 & Martha his wife
one child
Edee Wilday
3 Rebeeca & Mary

ffreemen-men

Tho: Lawrense
James Clement Ju'r
John Clement
John Huker
Jacob Cornell
Thomas ffeild
Joseph ffeild
Derick Areson
John Areson
John Yeates
John Man
James ffeke
Robert Snelhen
Tho: Steuens
John Dewildoe
Abraham Rich
Robert Hinchmen

Inhabitants 530

Negros 113

According to ye best of our Knowledges   JONATHAN WRIGHT
                                                    JAMES CLEMENT

[*Endorsed.*] a trew Lest as it is returned to us by the above Constable and
Clerke this Last of august 1698

THO: HICKS
DAN'LL WHITE
JOHN SMITH
EDWARD WHITE
SAMUEL MOWETT
JOHN TREDWELL
WILLIAM HALLETT

A LIST OF Y^E INHABITANTS

OF Y^e TOWNE OF SOUTHAMPTON OLD AND YONG CHRISTIANS AND
HETHEN FFREEMEN AND SERVANTS WHITE AND BLACK A^{nno} 1698

William Jennings
Samuell Jennings
Benjn Haines
Benjn Haines Jur
John Haines
James Haines Jur
Thomas Shaw
David frances
Frances Shaw
John Shaw
Samuell Clark
Samuell Clark Jur
Elish Clark
Eliphelett Clark
Clark
Clark
Jerhamiah Scott
John Scott
George Haris
George Haris Jur
Joseph Smith
Will Smith
Thomas Smith
Abiell Davis
Balhariah Davis
John Davis Jur
Eldad Davis
John Davis
Thomas Lupton
Joseph Lupton
Richard minthorn
Jeremiah Jager
Jeremiah Jager Jur
John Jager Jur
John Erle
David Erle
Samuell Cooper
James white
Ichabod Cooper
Peeter White
James Cooper
James Cooper Jur
John Cooper
Nathan Cooper
Abraham Cooper
John Reeves
John Reeves Jur
Thomas Reeves

Gershum Culver
Jerimiah Culver
David Culver
Jonathan Culver
Moses: Culver
Nahum Culver
John Bishope Jur
Joseph Poast
Will Mason
John Poastt
Richard Poast
Thomas Sayre
Will ffoster
Charles Topping
ffrancis Sayre
Ichabod Sayre
Caleb Sayre
Caleb Gilbord
Daniell Sayre
Ephraim Sayre
Nathan Sayre
John Bishop
Samuell Bishope
Josiah Bishope
John Bishope
Joshew Barns
Samuell Barns
Robert Wooly
John Wooly
Wooly Joseph
Isaac Bower
Jonah Bower
David Bower
Daniell Bower
John foster
John foster Jur
David ffoster
Jonathan foster
John ffoster Terts
Jermiah foster
Joseph Hildrith
Joseph Hildrith Jur
nathan Hildrith
Isaak Hildrith
Ephraim Hildrith
Daniell Hildrith
Jonathan Hildrith
John Woodrufe

Samll Woodrufe
Joseph woodrufe
Benjn woodrufe
nathanl woodrufe
Jonathan woodrufe
Isaac woodrufe
John Burnat
Samuel Butler
Gidian Butler
nathaniell Butler
Obedia Roggers
obadiah Johnson
Ensn Joseph Peirson
Henry Peirson
Joseph Peirson
Ephraim Peirson
Samll Peirson
Thomas Parvine
Thomas Pervine Jur
Lift Thomas Steephens
Isaack Willman
James Willman
Daniell Davis
and Will Hericke
Will Hericke Jur
John Herick
Herick
Thomas Hericke
Robertt Patin
Ephraim Topping
Thomas Toping
Thomas Toping
Mr. William Barker Esq
Mr. John Wick
Job Wick
Arther Davis
John Carwith
Joseph Howell
Zebulon Howell
Joseph Howell Jur
James Howell
John ware
Jacob ware
John Ware Jur
John Jessup
Isaac Jessup:
Jer: Jessup
Henry Jessup

Thomas Jessup
Mr. Edward Howell
Samuell Howell
Jonah Howell
Edward Howell Jur
Benjn Howell
Tho: Howell
Joseph foster
Christopher ffoster
Joseph foster
Daniell ffoster
nathan ffoster
John Howell
Manassa Kompton
Richard Howell
Richard Howell Jur
Hezeckia Howell
Edward Howell
obadia Howell
Chris: Howell
Joseph Goodale
Jonathan Goodale
Joseph Goodale
Will goodale
Benjn marshall
Jonathan Rayner
Jonathan Rayner Jur
Richard Wood
Isaac Halsey:
Ephraim Halsey
Nathaniell Howell
nehemiah Howell
Henry Howell
Ensn Joseph ffordham
Joseph ffordham Jur
ffellatia ffordham
John Willman
Mr. Jonah fordham
Jonah fordham Jur
Mr. Joseph Whitin
Samuell Whitin
Joseph whitin Jur
Benjn whitin
Will Blyeth
Benjn Hildrith
Job Sayre
Benjn Sayre
John Maltby
Ephrm whit
Stephen white
Charles white
Isaac Halsey
Isaac Halsely Jur
Isaac Halsey Ters
Joshua Halsey
Thomas Halsey
Samuell Halsey
Samell Johnes
Samuell Johnes Jur
nathan Howell
Israell Howell
Ezekiel Howell
John Jager
John Jager Jur
Samuell Jager
Jonathan Jager
Benjn Jagger
Josiah Howell
Daniell Howell

Timoth: Hileyrd
Thomas Hongson
John Mowbry
Anning Mowbry
Samuell Clark
Jermiah Clark
Charles Clark
Will Clark
Richard Rounesfield
Richard Rounesfield
David Howell
John Rayne
Ephraim Howell
Ephraim Howell
Samuell Howell
Isaac Rayner
Daniell Halsey
Richard Halsey
Daniell Hallsey Jur
Lift abraham Howell
Abraham Howell
Charles Howell
Philip Howell
Ebenezer Howell
John Sayre
John Sayre
Thomas Sayre
Lott Burnot
Joseph Burnott
David Burnott
nathan Burnott
Jonathan Burnot
Samiel Burnot
Isaac Burnott
Thomas ffoster
Benjn ffoster
David ffoster
Jonathan ffoster
Isaac ffoster
nathanel Hasey
Jonnathan Howell
Jonathan Howell Jur
Isaa Howell
David Howell
Josiah Halsey
Josiah Halsey Jur
Jonathan Halsey
Benjn ffoster Jur
Henry Ludlom
Will Ludlom
Henry ludlom Jur
Jeremiah ludlom
Aibiell Cook
Abiell Cook Jur
Josiah Cooke
Thomas Rose
Israell Rose
Humphrey Huse
John Parker
abner Huse
William Rose
uriah Huse
John masen
Jedadia Huse
James ffoster
John Huse
David Halsey
abraham Halsey
David Rose

James Rose.
David Rose Jur
Anthony ludlom
James Herick
Aron Burnot
Aaron Burnot Jur
moses Burnat
Jonah Rogers
Jonah Rogers
Rogers
James Haines
Samuell Haines
Ellis Cook
Charles fordham
John Cook
John Cook Jur
Ellias Cook
obadia Cook
Ellijah Cook
Ensn John lupton
Christopher Lupton
Benj lupton
Samuell Loome
mathew Loome
Samuell Loome
Isaac Mills
Isaac mills Jur
Thomas Cooper
Thomas Cooper Jur
Jonathan miles
Richard Cooper
Joseph more
Joseph more
Benjn more
Elisha Howell
Lemuell Howell
martine Rose
Jacob Wood
Lenard Rose
William Tarbill
Will Tarbill Jur
John michill
John michill Jur
Jermiah Halsey
Jere: Halsey Jur
Benony nutton
Benjn nuton
Isaac nuton
Jonathan nuton
John nuton
James Hildrith
James Hildrith Jur
Joshua Hildrith
Ezekill Sanford
Ezekill Sanford Jur
Thomas Sanford
Samuell Barbur
Jonathan Strickling
nathaniell Resco Jur
Josiah hand
natha: Resco
Amij Resco
Peregrin Stanbrough
James Stanbrough
Doct nath. Wade
Simon wade
Alexander Wilmot
Joseph Wickham
Joseph wickham Jur

Thomas Diamond
Capt. Elnathan Topping
Stephen Topping
Sillvanus Topping
Edward Petty
Ellnathan Petty
Edward Pety Jur
Josiah Topping
Josiah Topping Jur
Hezekia Topping
Robert Noris
Robert noris Jur
oliver noris
Mr. Ebenezer white

Elnath white
Lift Coll Henry Peirson
John Peirson
David Peirson
Theophilus Person
Abraham Peirson
Josiah Peirson
Bennony flint
John fflint
John morehouse
John morehouse Jur
Peter noris ———
Lift Theophilus Howell
Theoph: Howell Jur

Cilley Howell
Theoder Peirson
Theoder Peirson
John Stanbrough
John Stanbrough Jur
Daniell Sayre Jur
Daniell Sayre terts
Dan Burnot
Ichabod Burnot
Dan Burnot Jur

The numbr of male }
    Christians   } 389

FFEAMALES.

Ann Peirkins
Hannah Haines
Lidia Haines
mary Haines
mary Shaw
Susanah Shaw
Jeane Shaw
Sarah Clark
mary Clark
Ester Clark
Sarah Clark
mary Scott
Sarah Haris
Eunice Haris
mary Davis
mary Davis
Mary lupton
mary lupton
Hanah luptons
abigaill luptons
Abigaill Rose
Hanah Rose
Abigaile Rose Jur
Sarah Rose:
Hanah Rose
martha Bose
debro Rose
Hanah Jager
Sarah Jager
Hanah Jager.
Elizabeth Davis
mahitable davis
      Jager
mary Erle
Mary Cooper
Sarah Cooper
mary Cooper Jur
Elisabeth Cooper
Elisabeth Cooper Jur
Jerash Cooper
Phebe Cooper
Elisabeth Cooper Jur
Johana Cooper
mahitable Cooper
mary Culver
mary Culver Jur
Rachell Reeves
Lidia Bishop
abigaile Bishop
marey Bishop
Eunis Bishop
Sarah Poast
mary Poast

mary Post Jur
Patience Sayere
mary Davis
Sarah Sayre
mary Sayre
mary Sayre
An Halsey
Abigaile Reeves
Ellisabeth gilbord
Cethia Gilbord
mary gilbord
Hanah Sayre
mary Bishop
Susanah Bishope
Susanah Bishop Jur
Sarah Bishop
mary Bishop
Patience Barns
Sarah Barns
ann Woolly
Ann Woolly
Elisabeth woolly
Hanah woolly
Phebe wooly
mary woolly
Hanah Travely
Susanah Beswik
Ruth bower
mahitabell Bower
Sarah Erle
Sarah ffoster
Phebe foster
Hanah foster
Hanah foster
Hanah foster
Hana ffoster
Hanah Hildrith
Hanah woodrufe
Sarah woodrufe
Hanah Woodrufe
abigaile woodrufe
Elisabeth woodrufe
Ellisabeth Butler
martha Buler
Sarah Butler
Amy Butler
mary butler
mary Rogers
mary Rogers Jur
mary Rogers ter
Sary Roegers
debro Rogers
Patience Rogers

mary Peirson
Rebeika Parvin
Elisabeth Steevens
Phebe Steephens
Susanah Stevens
Susana willman
hanah willmans
Elisbeth willmans
mahitable hericke
Ireniah Hericke
Phebe Hericke
mahitable Herick
Martha Herick
Debro Toping
Hanah Reeves
Temprance wick
Temprance Wick
Lidia Howell
Bothia Howell
ffreelove Howell
Ellisabeth ware
Elisabetb Jesup
mary Jessup
Hanah Jessup
martha Davis
Sarah Jussup
mary Howell
mary Howell
Ireniah Roggers
mindwell Erle
Mrs. mary Howell
Sibell Howell
Elisabeth Simpkins
Johanah Howell
Abigaile ffoster
Sarah ffoster
mahitabell foster
Damary ffoster
Penellopie ffoster
Ellisabeth Howell
Dorkis Howell
Sary Howell
Sarah Howell
abigaile Howell
Elisabeth goodale
mary goodale
Hanah goodale
Sarah Rayner
debrah Rayner
Hanah Rayner
Sarah ffeild
mary Halsey
mahitable Halsey

mary Halsey
Sarah minthorn
Mrs. Susanah Howell
Prudence Howell
Hanah Howell
mahite Howell
martha Howell
mary fordham
mary fordham Jur
mary fordham 3d
Phebe fordham
Allath fordham
Deborah Whiting
Rebecca Whiting
Hanah whiting
Ellisabeth whiting
Susannah Maltbey
Susanah Sayre
Ester fordham
Keziah fordham
Hanah fordham
Ruth White
Sarah white
mary Halsey
Elisabeth Halsey
Pheby Halsey
Hanah Erle
mary Poast
Sarah Poast
Dorithee Post
martha Poast
Deborah Poast
Ester Johnes
Phebe Johnes
Mrs. mary Howell
Eunis Howell
Jerusha Howell
Hanah Jager
Lidia Jagger
Hanah Melvine
margret Hilyard
mary Howell
Mistris anning
Hanah Clark
Pheebe Clark
Hanah Rounsifield
Martha Rounsifield
Abigaill wilson
Hanah Howell
Sarah Howell
Hanah Howell
Judith Howell
Ann Howell
Grisill Howell
Amy Halsey
Hulda Erle
Ellisabeth Halsey
Debro Halsey
mary Ranr
Phebe Raynr
Hanah Raynr
Sarah Sayre
Sarah Sayre
Damorus Sayre

Phebe Burnatt
Lidia foster
Elisabeth white
Debro foster
Zeruiah foster
Annah Halsey
Hanah Howell
Zerusah Howell
mary Howell
Temprance Halsey
Sarah Halsey
Temprance Halsey
abigaile Halsey
martha foster
Bothy foster
martha foster
Sarah foster
Rachell Ludlom
Jane Ludlom
Abigaile ludlom
Rachell Ludlom Jur
ffrances Cooke
ffrances Cooke Jur
Hanah Rose
Hanah Rose
Sarah Hericke
Elisabeth Burnot
Elisabeth Burnott
Hanah Burnot
Mary Parker
Ester Rose
Hanah Halsey
Hanah Halsey
Prudence Halsey
Patience Ludlom
Patience Ludlom
Phebe Rogers
Phebe Rogers
Sarah Haines
Sarah Haines
Sarah nichill
Elisabeth Cook
Susanah Cook
Hanah Shaw
Ellisabeth Cook
martha Cook
Hanah Lupton
Hanah Lupton
Lidia Lupton
mary laughton
Hanah Lome
Abigaile Lome
Hanah Loome
Johanah nuton
Johanah nuton
Ester leeming
Hannah Cooper
Sarah taping
Sarah more
Elisabeth more
Sarah more Jur
mary more
Hanah Sayre
Damones Howell

Elliner Howell
Penellopie Howell
abiecah Howell
mary Tarbill
mary tarbill
mary Haris
mary haris
Deborah Hildrith
Deborah Hildrith
Hanah Sanford
Hanah Sanford
Elisabeth nuton
Phebe nuton
annah Halsey
annah Halsey
Johanah Resco
mary barbur
deliverance priest
mary barbur
mary Strickland
Mary hand
Abigaile wade
Sarah Stanbrough
Ollive Stanbrough
Eunis Stanbrough
Ellisabeth Stanbrough
mary Willmott
Sarah Wickham
mary Topping
mary Baylee
Hannah Topping
Hanah Toping
Temprance Toping
Toping
martha huse
Hanah noris
Hanah noris
mary noris
Sarah noris
hanah leeming
mrs mahitable white
Elisabeth langton
mrs Susanah Peirson
Abigaile toping
Hanah Peirson
Sarah Peirson
mary flint
mary flint
Hanah flintt
Sarah noris
Hanah noris
Elisabeth noris

Debro Howell
Phebee Howell
hanah noris
ffrances Peirson
Ann Peirson
martha Stanbrough
martha Stanbrough
Sarah Sayre
Hanah Sayre
Sarah Sayre
Abigaile burnot
    feamale Christians **34**

NEGRO MALES.

Will	Dick	Jack	Ceaser	Titus	mingo
John	Tom	Jack	Jethro	Jefery	Dick
Peter	Guie	Dick	Jack	Lewis	Tittus

Tom	ffranck	Jehue	Sambo	Peter	brigitt
Will	Ceser	Nero	ned:	Cisto	———
Jack	Samson	George	Tobee		40

[7 names destroyed.]

NEGRO FEMALES.

Ann	Sarah	bety	Rueth	Sarah	Bess
bety	Hanah	Hanah	Rueth	Sarah	mariah
Isabell	Joane	Rachel	Dorekis	Rose	Simony
bety	Sarah	Judith	Smony	margery	———
Elisabeth	bety	Judith	Pegee	hanah	females negro
Perle	Joane	Jinny	Philis	molly	persons 43
Abee	Hager	Simony	hitabell	Dinah	

[6 names destroyed.]

The number of Christian Males is . . . . . 389 } 738 }
The number of Christian ffeemales is . . . . . 349 }   } 821
The number of negro Slaves men is . . . . . 040 } 083 }
The nuber of women negro Slaves is . . . . . 043 }
Indian males that are upwards of fifteen years—The Squas and children few of whom have any nam

Chice	Indian	Coyemow	Indian	Steephen	Indian
Johnson	Indian	ffranck	Indian	nodian	Indian
———	———	Toby	Indian	Judas	Indian
Arther	Indian	macrobow	Indian	Weegon	Indian
Anthony	Indian	nabamacow	Indian	Cough	Indian
Thamanty	Indian	Philip	Indian	Sam	Indian
Johnaquan	Indian	Sam	Indian	William	Indian
queegano	Indian	Tom lenard	Indian	na	Indian
Lenard	Indian	Dick	Indian	Chitty	Indian
Pisacomary	Indian	Plato	Indian	Hary	Indian
Jefery	Indian	Tom-hodge	Indian	Joseph	Indian
Rhichoam	Indian	Denitt	Indian	Tom	Indian
Redhedwill	Indian	obedia	Indian	waynantuck	Indian
Pomquaneo	Indian	Cuttwas	Indian	waneno	Indian
Simon	Indian	Abraham	Indian	Titus	Indian
Canady	Indian	Isaac	Indian		
Tohemon	Indian	Sam	Indian		

The nuber of Indians upwards of 15 years 52
The Indians Informes there is about The same number of woomen } 100
and as many Children . . . . }

152

The hethen are So Scattered To and frow that they can neither be Sumonsed in [Manuscript torn.]
The above listt of the Inhabitants of ye Town of Southampton, Taken p me this 15th day of September 1698

MATHEW HOWELL.

A LIST OF THE NAMES

OF OLD AND YOUNG, CHRISTIANS, AND HEATHENS, FFREMEN, AND SERVANTS ; WHITE ; AND BLACK ; &C. INHABITTEINGE WITHIN THE TOWN-SHIPP OF SOUTHOLD VIZ—

Isaac Arnold	Thomas Mapes	Ebenezer Way
Sarah Arnold	Mary Mapes	Irene Way
Rachel Arnold	Abigall Mapes	Eliezer Way
Sarah Arnold Junjr	Margarett Edwards	Jonathan Horton
Susannah Arnold	Joshua Hobart	Bathia Horton
Susannah Washbourn	Peter Hobart	Jonathan Horton Junjr
John Washbourn	John Hobart	William Horton

James Horton
Mehitobel Horton
Mary Horton
Abigall Horton
Patience Horton
Stephen Bouyer
Jonas Holdsworth
Joshua Horton
Mary Horton
Ephraim Horton
Mary Horton Junjr
Bathia Horton
Elizabeth Horton
Zerviah Horton
Jasper Griffing
Hannah Griffing
Robert Griffing
Susanna Griffing
Edward Griffing
Robert Griffing Junjr
Samuel Griffing
John Griffing
John Youngs
Wm Walter
Theoder Ballens
Mary Griffing
Prudence Smith
John Booth
Hannah Booth
Mehitophel Booth
John Booth Junjr
Obadiah Booth
Daniel Booth
Hannah Booth Junjr
Patience Booth
Thomas Emmons
Mary Emmons,
Obadiah Emmons
Elizth. Emmons
Thomas Paine
John Tutthill
Sarah Tutthill
Daniel Tutthill
Nathaniel Tutthill
Ephraim Youngs
Mary Youngs
Ruth Terry
Thomas Youngs
Mary Youngs
Christopher Bradly
John Edwards
William Barnes
Mary Mayhew
Benjamen Lhommedieu
Patience Lhommedieu
Benjamen Lhommedieu Junjr
Hosea Lhommedieu
Eliza Sylvester
William Booth
Hannah Booth
Wm Booth Junjr
Samuel Booth
George Booth
Hannah Booth Junjr
Thomas Terry
Eliza Terry
Thomas Terry Junjr.
Daniel Terry

Joseph Terry
Abigall Terry
Hannah Martin
John Rogers
John Conckline
Sarah Concklin
Sarah Conckline Junr.
John Conckline Junjr.
Henry Conckline
Rachel Concklin
Thomas Conckline
Mary Concklin
Joseph Concklin
Abigall Concklin
Joseph Concklin Junjr
John Concklin
Phillip Gooding
Sarah Gooding
Amos Gooding
Phillip Gooding Junjr.
ffreeloue Gooding
Christopher Youngs
Mercy Youngs
Abraham Youngs
Nathaniel Youngs
John Youngs
Charity Nashbourne
Thomas Terrell
John Terrell
Richard Terrell
Abigall Terrell
Nicholas Terrell
Catharine Terrell
Peter Hallock
Eliza Hallock
Bathia Hallock
Abigall Hallock
Peter Hallock Junjr
William Hallock
Noah Hallock .
Richard Benjamen
Eliza Benjamen
Anna Benjamen
John Benjamen
Richard Benjamen Junjr.
Jonathan Benjamen
David Benjamen
Joshua Benjamen
Joseph Benjamen
Daniel Terry
Sarah Terry
Daniel Terry Junjr.
Samuel Terry
Eliza Terry
James Terry
Isaac Ouenton
John Ouenton
Thomas Ouenton
Thomas Goldsmith
Bathia Goldsmith
Joshua Goldsmith
Richard Terry
Prudence Terry
Abigall Coleman
Caleb Horton
John Reeue
hannah Reeue
Walter Reeue
John Reeue Junjr

Elisha Reeue
Abigall Reeue
Bathia Reeue
Margarett Giles
Peter Dickerson
Naomy Dickerson
Philemon Dickerson
John Dickerson
Mary Dickerson Junjr
Naomy Dickerson
Thomas Dickerson
Mary Dickerson
Mary Monjoy
Jonathan Reeue
Martha Reeue
Margarett Reeue
Mary Reeue
Martha Reeue Junjr
Mathew Reeue
Jonathan Mapes
Hester Mapes
Benjamen Youngs
Mary Youngs
Grover Youngs
John Bailey
Lott Johnson
Gideon Youngs
Sarah Youngs
Joseph Youngs
Jonathan Youngs
David Youngs
Gidion Youngs
Sarah Youngs
Hannah Youngs
Margarett Youngs
Mary Youngs,
Hannah Wiggin widdow
James Wiggin
Annis Wiggin
Eliza Wiggin
Patience Ryder
Thomas Hallock
Hope Hallock
Thomas Hallock
Kingsland Hallock
Ichabod Hallock
Zerobabel Hallock
Anna Hallock
Patience Hallock
Richard Hallock
Richard Howell
David Howell
Jonathan Howell
Richard Howell Junjr.
Isaac Howell
Jacob Howell
Eliza Howell
Dorathy Howell
Mary Youngs Junjr widdow
Christopher Youngs Junjr
Anna Youngs
Phebe Youngs
Eliza Youngs
John Gattin
Sarah Gattin
Anna Gattin
Jonathan Brown
Eliza Brown
Jonathan Brown Junjr

Eliza Brown junjr
Hannah Brown
Rachel Brown
Mary Giles
Edward Gattin
Mary Youngs widdow
Daniel Youngs
William Youngs
Joshua Youngs
Samuel Turner
Mary Wiggans
Nathan Langdon
Hannah Langdon
Eliza Langdon
Nathan Langdon Junjr
James Langdon
Samuel Youngs
Joseph Sweazy
Mary Sweazy
Johanna Sweazy
Joseph Sweazy Junjr
Mary Swazy
Sarah Swazy
Samuel Swazy
Richard Swazy
Stephen Swazy
Bathia Swazy
Thomas Moor junjr
Jean Moor
Mary Moor
Rachel Moor
Isaac Osmond
Chaterine Osmond
Martha Osmond
Prudence Osmond
Isaac Osmond
William Downs
Abigall Downs
Abijah Downs Junjr.
Samuel King Junjr.
Hannah King
Samuel King
Zacharias King
John Swazy
Mary Swazy
Jno. Swazy Junjr
Susana. Swazy
Mary Swazy Junjr
Joshua & Phebe Swazy
Jacob Conckline
Mary Conckline
Jacob Conckline Junjr
Samuel Conckline
John Concklioe
Gideon Conckline
Mary Conckline Junjr
Joseph Conckline
Joseph Conckline Junjr
Mary Baily
Theophilus Corwin
John Harwood
William Brown
Catharine Brown
Wm Brown junjr
John Brown
Walter Brown
Silvanus Brown
David Brown
Mary Brown

Sarah Martin
John Corwin
Matthias Corwin
Samuel Corwin
Anna Corwin
Abigall Corwin
John Corwin Junjr
Sarah Corwin
Sarah Corwin Junjr
Eliza Corwin
Hester Corwin
Jacob Ozmond
Sarah Ozmond
Mary Ozmond
Sarah Ozmond Junjr
Eliza Ozmond
Hester Ozmond
Pinnina Ozmond
Hannah Ozmond
Martha Ozmond widdw
Sarah Ozmond
Dinah Blyth
Jno. Howel
Thomas Clark
Mary Clark
Thomas Clark Junjr
Elizabeth Clark
Mary Ozmond widdow
Deborah Ozmond
Phebe Ozmond
Johanna Ozmond
Mercy Ozmond
Samuel Ozmond
William King
Abigall King
Wm King Junjr
Hannah King
David King
Sarah Youngs
Daniel King
Robert Labe
Caleb Curtjes
Eliza Curtjes
Joshua Curtjes
Mary Curtjes
Samuel Curtjes
Sarah Curtjes
Hannah Curtjes
Richard Curtjes
Stephen Baily
Mary Baily
Hannah Bailey
Israel Baily
Temperance Baily
Jonathan Baily
Christian Baily
David Gardiner
Martha Gardiner
Mary Gardiner
Mehitobel Corwin
Samuel King
Abigall King
Theophilus Case
hannah Case
William Case
Icabod Case
John Case
Eliza Robertson
Jasper Griffing Junjr

Ruth Griffing
Jasper Griffing
Ruth Griffing
Abraham Corey
Margarett Corey
Mary Corey
Abraham Corey Junjr
Jno Corey
Dorathy Corey
Patience Mayhew
Isaac Corey
Sarah Corey
Isaac Corey Junjr
David Corey
Jonathan Corey
Sarah Corey Junjr
Phebe Corey
Deborah Corey
Peter Aldridge
Annis Reeue widdow
Walter Brown
Joseph Brown
Daniel Brown
Gersham Aldridge
James Pattay
Experience Pattay
James Pattay Junjr
Mary Pattay
nymon Pattay
Experience Pattay
Thomas Ryder
Joseph Ryder
Providence Ryder
Jeremiah Ryder
Hester Ryder
Mehitobel Ryder
John Budd
Hester Budd
John Budd Junjr
Joseph Budd
Susannah Budd
Mary Budd
Martha Moor widdow
John Trusteen
Jonathan Moor
William Moor
Mary Trusteen
John Pain Junjr
Sarah Pain
Nathaniel Pain
John Pain
Samuel Crook
Joseph Crook
Sussannah Crook
John ffrancklin
Philla: ffrancklin
Jno ffrancklin Junjr
Mary ffrancklin
Samuel ffrancklin
Martha ffrancklin
ffrancis Noise
Perrsha Noice
Catharine Noise
Eliza Lewis
Mary Reeue widdow
Wm Reeue
Abigall Reeue
Margaret Reeue
Sarah Reeue

Thomas Reeue
Henry Tutthill
Batthia Tutthill
Henry Tutthill Junjr
Jonathan Tutthill
Nathaniel Tutthill
Barnabas Tutthill
Abigall Martin
Hester Hoaman widdow
Hester Hoaman Junjr
John Joanes
Thomas Hunter
Eliza hunter
Eliza hunter Junjr
Zervia Hunter
Hannah Hunter
Sarah Horton Widdw
Peanellope Horton
John Pattay
Mary Pattay
Edward Pattay
David Pattay
Mary Pattay
Joshua Wells
Hannah Wells
William Wells
Jno. Wells
Joshua Wells
Deliuerance Wells
Abigall Wells
Ann Wells
Mary Martin
John Owen
Thomas Booth
Mary Booth
John Booth
Thomas Booth Junjr
James Booth
Giles Booth
Mary Booth Junjr
Abraham Ozmond
Rebecca Ozmond
Joseph Ozmond
John Ozmond
Damarass Terrell
John Allowbin
hannah Allowbin Junjr
Mary Allowbin
Tabitha Allowbin
John Goldsmith
Eliza Goldsmith
John Goldsmith Junjr
Thomas Goldsmith
Richard Goldsmith
Nathaniel Goldsmith
Mary Goldsmith
Henry Wells
Mary Wells
Martha Carr
Samuel Glouer
Sarah Glouer
Samuel Glouer junjr
Martha Glouer
hanna. Glouer
Hester Glouer
William Glouer
Charles Glouer
Martha Glouer
Euan Davis

Mary Davis
Mordecai hoaman
William Coleman
Mary Coleman
Sarah Coleman
William Coleman Junjr
Mary Coleman Junjr
Sarah Coleman Junjr
Charles Booth
Abigall Booth
Mary Horton widdow
Jean Mappon
Charles Booth Junjr
Abigall Booth Junjr
David Booth
Jacob Aldridge
Caleb Horton
Jonathan Horton
David Horton
Barnabas Horton
Phebe Horton
Samuel Windes
Mary Windes
Wm Coe
Charley Edwards
Lott Johnson
Joseph Pattay
Mary Pattay
Daniel Pattay
James Reeue
Deborah Reeue
Mary Reeue
Isaac Reeue
Thomas Reeue
Mary Reeue
Richard Brown
Dorithy Brown
Richard Brown Junjr
Samuel Brown
Dorathy Brown
Abigall Brown
Mehitobel Brown
Henry Brown
Samuel Hutcheson
Elizabeth Hutcheson
Samuel Hutcheson Junjr
Gersham Terry
Deborah Terry
Gersham Terry Junjr
Deborah Terry Junjr
Abigall Terry
Richard Terry
Barsheba Terry
Mehitobel Terry
Eliza Cleaues
Jerediah Cleaues
John Cleaues
Eliza Cleaues Junjr
Mary Cleaues
Hannah Cleaues
John Cleaues Junjr
Abigall Cleaues
Thomas Tusten
Priscilla Tuston, Widdow
Eliza Tusten
Mereiam Tusten
Grace Tusten
Carterett Gillam
Mary Gillam

Anna Gilliam
Arnold Gillam
James Gillam
John Wiggam
James Pershall
Margaret Pershall
Mary Pershall
Israel Pershall
David Pershall
Benjamen Pershall
Margarett Pershall Junjr
Thomas Terrell Junjr
Sarah Terrell
Thomas Terrell
Sarah Terrell Junjr
Joshua Horton Junjr
Eliza Horton
Eliza Horton Junjr
Patience Horton
Deborah Horton
Martha Horton
Henry Case
Tabitha Case
Henry Case Junjr
Samuel Case
Benjamn Case
Tabitha Case Junjr
Mary Case
John Bond
Sarah Rodman
John Barnes
Joseph Reeue
Abigall Reeue
Joseph Reeue Junjr
Benjamen Reeue
David Reeue
Ezikias Reeue
Solomon Reeue
Abigall Reeue
Mary Reeue
Margarett Hallock widdow
Dorathy Ozmon
Barnabas Windes
Mary Windes
Barnabas Windes Junjr
Samuel Windes
Bathia Windes
Peanellope Windes
Sussanna Willman
Bathia Horton
Susanna Windes
Martha Hutcheson widdow
Thomas Hutcheson
Mathias Hutcheson
Martha Hutcheson Junjr
Hanna. Case
John Terry
Hannah Terry
John Terry Junjr
Nathaniel Moor
Jacob Cory
Ann Cory
Jacob Corey Junjr
Ann Corey Junjr
Abigall Cory
Jehoada Corey
John Corey
Benjamn Corey
Christopher Merrick

Hannah Merrick
Jeremiah Veale
Anne Veale
Thomas Veale
Jeremiah Veale Junjr
Mary Veale
Mary Moor
Joshua Sylvester
Joseph Moor
Martha Moor
Joseph Moor Junjr
Sarah Solmon widdow
William Solmon
Sarah Solomn Junjr
Mary Solmon
Amy Solmon
Elizabeth Youngs widdow
John Youngs
Benjamen Youngs Junr
Eliza Youngs Junjr
Christian Youngs
Jno. Coleman
Mary Harwood
William Allobon
Andrew Miller
Margarett Miller
David Miller
Eliza Miller
Margarett Miller Junjr
Hannah Miller
Gersham Tincker
Samuel Youngs
Mary Youngs
Margarett Youngs
Nathan Youngs
Zerobabel Youngs
Bathia Corwin
Joseph Youngs
Eliza Youngs
Mary Youngs
Thomas Youngs
Abigall Pain widdow
Abigall Pain Junjr
Mary Pain
Sarah Pain
John Daines
Sarah Moor, widdow
Abigall Moor
Patience Moor
Deborah Moor

Thomas Moor
John Moor
Nathaniel Moor
Martha Moor
Eliza Moor
Symon Grouer
Eliza Grouer
Martha Veale
Benjamin Barns
Barnabas Horton
Samuel Bodman
Benjamen Moor
Abigall Moor
John Hutson
Mary Hutson
John Pain
Jemima Pain
Mary Pain
Martha Pain
Jemima Pain
Eliza Pain
John Pain Junjr
John Corwin
Benjamen Bedwell
Thomas Longworth
Deborah Longworth
Joshiah Youngs
Mary Youngs
Mary Youngs Junjr
Daniel Corwin
William Hallocke
Mary Hallock
William Hallock Junjr
Ruth Howell
Prudence Hallock
Zebulon Hallock
Mary Hallock Jun'r
Mary Corwin
Jabez Mapes
Eliza Mapes
Sarah Mapes
Eliza Mapes Junjr
Hannah Mapes
Ealse Mapes
John Carter
Ann Carter
Gesia Carter
Hester Carter
Eliza Rackett
John Rackett

Ann Carter Junjr
Mary Carter
Joseph Mapes
Ruth Mapes
Joseph Mapes Junjr
William Mapes
Hannah Mapes
David Youngs
Mary Youngs
John Loring
Richard Loring
Samuel Loring
Jno Loring Junjr
Wm Loring
Thomas Loring
John Veale
Grace Veale
John Veale Junjr
Daniel Veale
Samuel Veale
Obadiah Veale
Mary Veale
Abigall Veale
Irene Veale
Tabitha Veale
Joyce Veale
Mercy Pattay widdow
Ralph Pattay
Lucas Pattay
Moses Pattay
Margery Pattay
Ann Pattay
Symon Rumsey
Mary Rumsey
Mary Rumsey Junjr
Peter Symons
    Symons
    Symons
    Symons
John Tutthill Junjr
Mehitobell Tutthill
Waite Benjamen widdow
William Benjamen
Waite Benjamen Junjr
Anna Benjamen
hannah Benjamen
John Benjamen
William Rosebash
Ann Rosebash

The Names of the Slaves, Men Weomen and Children

Tony	Prissilla	Peter	Bristol	Dorrad	Jack
Maria	Adrea	Nager	Grace	Sarah	Betty
Semony	Abigall	John	Cato	Jenny a Girl	Rose
Mobsey	Grace	Santo	Semony	Jenny	huson
Titus	Liddy	hope	Rose	Judah	Titus
Sombo	Jack	Pegge	Tomm	Cate	Sambo
Tom	Betty	Jack	Robbin	James	In all 41

Indians ffreemen, Servants, men wemen and Children in number - 40
Whose Names Cannot be known because not Contant To any Name &c
One hundred thirty and two ffamelyes; Consisting of Christians, old, and
    young; - - - - - - - - - - 800
Indians, old, & young. - - - - - - - - - 040
Slaves, old & young,— - - - - - - - - - 41

In all - - - 881

Pr. ISA. ARNOTS
THOMAS MAPES

LIST OF THE COMMISSIONS ISSUED BY Lᵀ GOVᴿ LEISLER.

No.	Name.	Office	Place.	Date.
3	Obadia Holmes	Justice of the Peace	Richmond	12 Dec 1689
4	John Coe	High Sheriff	Queens	13 "
5	Gerardus Beekman	Justice	Kings	12 "
6	John Howell	Justice	Suffolk	12 "
7	Roelof Martense	Justice	Kings	12 "
8	Jeronimes Rapallie	Justice	Kings	12 "
10	Nicholas Stilwell	Justice	Kings	13 "
11	Johannes Jansen	Highsheriffe	New York	14 "
12	John Tredwell	Justice	Queens	13 "
13	Nathaniel Cole	Justice	Queens	13 "
14	Myndert Coerte	High Sheriffe	Kings	13 "
15	Matthias Harvey	Justice	Queens	13 "
16	Samuel Edsall	Justice	Queens	13 "
17	Nathaniel Denton	Justice	Queens	13 "
18	Richard Smith	Justice	Suffolk	14 "
19	Thomas Statham	High Sheriff	Westchester	14 "
20	Joseph Pudway	Justice	Westchester	14 "
21	Richᵈ Ponton	Justice	Westchester	14 "
22	Andrew Tauvet	Justice	Westchester	14 "
23	Samuel Molferd	Justice	Suffolk	14 "¹
24	Edward Waters	Justice	Westchester	14 "
25	Thomas Mapes	Justice	Suffolk	14 "
26	Ebnezer Platt	Justice	Suffolk	14 "

1 Renewed 28th May 1690.

LIST OF THE COMMISSIONS ISSUED—Continued.

No.	Name.	Office.	Place.	Date.
27	Thomas Williams	Justice	Westchester	14 Dec 1689
28	Jaques Poullion	Justice	Richmond	14 " "
29	William Lawrence	Justice	Orange	14 " "
30	Theunis Roelofzen	Justice	Orange	14 " "
31	Ely Crosson	High Sheriff	Richmond	14 " "
32	Matthew Howell	High Sheriff	Suffolk	14 " "
33	Daniel deClercq	Justice	Orange	14 " "
34	Thomas Morgan	Justice	Richmond	14 " "
35	Jacob Gerritse	Justice	Richmond	14 " "
36	Henry Cuyler	Major of foot	New York	16 " "
37	Robert Walter	Capt "	South ward N York	16 " "
38	Isaac de Riemer	Lieut "	Walters comp. N York	16 " "
39	Jacobus vander Spiegell	Ensign "	same N York	16 " "
40	Sivert Olphertse	Capt "	west ward N York	16 " "
41	Paulus Turck	Lieut "	same N York	16 " "
42	Peter White	Ensigne "	same N York	17 " "
43	Abraham de Peyster	Captain "	Dock Ward N York	13 " "
45	Johannes de Peyster	Lieut "	same N York	13 " "
46	Peter de Mill	Ensigne "	same N York	13 " "
47	Gerrit Duyckingk	Captain "	North Ward N York	16 " "
48	Hendrick Ten Eyck	Lieut "	same N York	17 " "
49	Joannes Beeckman	Ensign "	same N York	17 " "
50	John de Browne	Captain "	East ward N York	17 " "
51	Jaques Puillion	Captain "	Richmond	18 " "
52	Peter Verbrugh	Lieutent "	de Brown's Co. N. York	17 " "

No.	Name	Office	Place			
53	Abm Brasher	Ensigne "	same New York	17	"	"
54	Adriaen Cornelisn Van Schayck	Captain "	out Ward N. Y.	16	"	"
55	Peter D'Lanoy	Collector	N York	11	"	"
77	same	Mayor	N York	12	"	"
57	Daniel ter Neur	Lieutenant	Van Schayck's Co.	18	"	"
58	John Slott	Ensign	V S's Comp.	18	"	"
59	Thomas Morgan	Lieutenant	Richmond	18	"	"
60	Seger Gerritsen	Ensign	Richmond	18	"	"
61	William Bogardus	Notary Pub.	New York	18	"	"
	Ebenezer Platt	Justice&DedimusPotest.	L: I & Westch.	17	"	"
62	Roelof Swartwout	same	Ulster	13	"	"
	Jochem Staas	same	Albany	26	"	"
	John Howell	same	Suffolk		"	"
63	same	Clerk	"	18	"	"
64	same	Collector	"	19	"	"
66,7	Cornelis Corsen	Justice & Capt.	Richmond	19	"	"
68	Cornelis Nevius	Ensign	"	19	"	"
70	Edward Collier	Clerk	Westchester	20	"	"
71	Jacobus Van de Water	Clerk	Kings	20	"	"
73	James Evetts	Searcher & Waiter	N York	17	"	"
75	Gerret Cornelisse	Justice	Kings	19	"	"
76	Abrah: Gouverneur	Clerk	N York	20	"	"
78	Daniel Danton	Clerk	Queens	20	"	"
79	Hendricus Beeckman	Justice	Ulster	24	"	"
80	Willm Haynes	Justice	Ulster	24	"	"
81	Jacob Aertse	Justice	Ulster	24	"	"
82	Gysbert Crom	Justice	Ulster	24	"	"

LIST OF THE COMMISSIONS ISSUED—CONTINUED.

No.	Name.	Office.	Place.	Date.
83 91	Abrah^m Haesbrooc	Justice & Capt	the Paltz Ulster	24 Dec 1689
84 98	Roelof Swartwout	Justice & Collect^r	Ulster	24 "
85	Wm de Lamontagne	High Sheriff	Ulster	24 "
86	Nicolaes Anthony	Clerk	Ulster	24 "
87	Thomas Chamber	Major	Ulster	24 "
88	Matthys Matthyssen	Captain	Kingtown	24 "
89	Johannes de Hooges	Capt	Hurley	24 "
90	Thomas Teunis Quick	Capt.	Marble	24 "
94,5	Richd Pretty	Collect^r & Sheriff	Albany	28 "
97	Johannes Cuyler	Clerk	Albany	28 "
99	David Christoffelse	Justice	Schanectade	28 "
100	Reyer Jacobse	Justice	"	28 "
101	Myndert Wemp	Justice	"	28 "
102	Reynier Schaets	Justice	"	28 "
103	Douwe Auckus	Justice	"	28 "
108	John Townsend	Justice	Queens	13 "
109	John Simmons Junr	Justice	Queens	13 "
110	Thomas Lawrence	Major of Horse	Queens	30 "
111	Joseph Smith	Capt foot	Hemstead	30 "
112	Content Titus	Capt. "	Newtown	30 "
113	Gerardus Beeckman	Major of Horse	Queens	
114	Pieter Strycker	Capt foot	Flackbush	27 "
115	Symon Janse	Lieut	Flackbush	27 "
116	Isaac Hegeman	Ensign	Flackbush	27 "
117	Jost Koockuyt	Capt of foot	Bushwick	27 "

No.	Name	Rank	Place	Date
118	Nicolaes Stilwell	Capt	Gravesandt	27 "
119	Michell Hanse	Capt foot	Breukelen	27 "
120	Coort Stevense	"	fflatlands	27 "
121	Jan Hanse	"	N: Utrecht	27 "
122	James Evetts	Collector excise	New York	17 "
123	Thomas Lammerse	Lieut	Breuckelen	27 "
124	Volkert Hendrickse	Ensign	"	27 "
125	Jan Janse Van Dyke	Lieut	N: Utrecht	27 "
126	Joost V. Brunt	Ensign	"	27 "
127	Jan Teuniss van Dyckhuyse	Lieut	fflatlands	27 "
132	Dirck Jansen	Ensign	"	27 "
133	Michiel Palmiter	Lieut	Buswick	27 "
134	Dirck Volkertse	Ens.	"	27 "
135	Daniell Leeck	Lieut	Gravesand	27 "
136	Joghem Gulick	Ens.	"	27 "
137	Jeremiah Borrowes	Lieut	Newtown	27 "
138	Jeremiah Smith	Ensign	Hampstead	27 "
139	Robert Coe	"	Newtown	2 Jany 1690
140	Richard Gildersleef	Lieut.	Hemsteed	2 Jany "
141	John Lawrence	Capt of Horse	Queens	10 "
142	Jonathan Smith	Lieut	"	10 "
143	Daniel Lawrence	Cornet	"	10 "
144	Charles Morgan	Quarter Mastr	"	10 "
145	John Theunis Van Pelt	Lieut	"	10 "
146	Jacob Corbet	Clerk	Richmond	19 dec. 89
149	Hope Carpenter	Ensign	Richmond	18 dec
150	Jonah Wood	Liev	Jamaico	10 Jany 90
			Jamaico	10 "

LIST OF THE COMMISSIONS ISSUED—CONTINUED

No.	Name.	Office.	Place.	Date.
151	John Bayly	Capt	Jamaico	10 Jany 90
152	Richard Osbourne	Capt	Madnansneck	10 "
153	John Hobs	Lievt	"	10 "
154	Joseph Sutton Junr	Ensign		10 "
155	Roelof Martense Schenk	Capt of Horse	Kings	13d "
156	Gerrit Elbertse Stoothof	Lieut	"	13 "
157	Joseph Hegeman	Cornet	"	13 "
158	Gerrit Stryker	Quarter Master	"	13 "
169	Leonard Beckett	Land Surveyor	N York	14 feb "
176	Cornelis Claessen Cuyper	Captn & Justice	Orange	18 feb 1690
177	Johannes Gerritsen	Lieut.	"	18 "
178	Theunis Douw	Ensign	"	18 "
179	Edwd Harrington	Captain	flushing	19 "
180	John Harrison	Lieut	"	19 "
181	Robert Hunksman	Ens.	"	19 "
182	Samuel Moore	Capt.	Newtown	19 "
183	Joseph Sucket	Lieut.	"	19 "
184	Gersham More	Ensigne	"	19 "
185	Robert Coles	Capt.	Oisterbay	19 "
186	Moses Modge	Lieut	"	19 "
187	James Weekes	Ens.		19 "
188	floris Willemse Crom	High Sheriff	Orange	19 "
189	James Evett	Adjutant	New York	18 "
190	Richard Penton	Major	Westchester	21 "
191	Barnard Lewis	Captain	Canada Expedition	26 "

No.	Name	Rank	Place	Date
193	Marten Clock	Lieut	"	26 "
194	Jacobus de Warm	Ens.	"	26 "
196	James Mott	Justice	Westchester	10 "
	Peter Johnson	Coroner	Kings	18 "
201	John Willet	Capt.	Easthampton	24 Mch 1690
205	Thomas Wicks	Capt	Huntington	16 Apr.
	John Wood	Lieut	"	16 "
	Thomas Hickly	Ens.	"	16 "
	Johannes Hardenbrock	High Sheriff	Ulster	30 July 1690
	Pieter Jansen	Lieut of Horse	Kings	29 "
	Daniel Polhemius	Cornet	Kings	29 "
	Humphrey Davenport	Clerk	Ulster Co	6 Oct
	Joseph Smith	Justice	Queens	6 "
	Johannes Wendel	Mayor	Albany	8 "
	Laurens Van Aelen	Justice	"	" "
	Reyer Jacobse Schermerhoorn	"	"	" "
	Barent Pietersen Koeymans	"	"	" "
	John Thyssen	"	"	" "
	Claas Van Potten	"	"	" "
	Myndert Harmensen	"	"	" "
	Harmen Gansevoort	"	"	" "
	Jacob Staas	"	"	" "
	John Naill	"	"	" "
	Jan Finagel	"	"	" "
	Jan Janse Bleeker	"	"	" "
	Barent Wemp	Captain	"	" "
	Isaac Cornelis Switz	Lieut	"	" "

LIST OF THE COMMISSIONS ISSUED—Continued.

Name.	Office.	Place.	Date.
Douwe Aukus	Ensigne	Albany	8 Oct 1690
Pieter Wogolem	Capt	"	" " "
Hans Hendricx	"	"	" " "
James Campbell	Town Mayor		19 Oct "
John Bates	Lieut	fort Orange	15 " "
John Pell	Justice	Westchester	30 " "
John Lansing	Captain	Albany	11 Nov "
Reynier Barents	Lieut	"	" " "
Abrahᵐ Coyler	Ensign	"	" " "
Jan Hendrix de Bruyn	Major	N. York	Dec. 20. 1690
Abraham Brasher	Sheriff	N. York	Jan 8. 1691
John Lawrence	Sheriff	Queens	" 19. 1691
Dirck Jans Amermen	Capt	Kings	" 20 "
John Albertsen	Lieut	Kings	" 20 "
Albert Courten	Ens	Kings	Jany 20 1691
Christopher Johnson Romeyn	Lieut	Gravesend	" 20 "

RATE LISTS

OF

Long Island.

---------◆---------

1675, 1676 & 1683.

THE LIST OF EAST HAMPTON AUGUST Yᴱ 24ᵀᴴ: 1675.

	£	s	d
Jeremiah Conchling	193—10	—0	
Stephen Hodges	243—10		
Joshua garlich sen:	104—13	4	
Tho: Hand	097—	3—4	
Wm: Mulford	164—	3—4	
Tho: Edwards	091—	3—4	
Mʳ Tho Chatfeild	238—16	—8	
Tho: Osborne sen	166—10		
John Corte	100—10		
Wm Miller	090—13	4	
John Hoping	169—00		
Robert Daiton	205—00		
Philip Leckie	043—	6—8	
Hand	11—	0	
Joshua garlich Ju:	056—	0	
Rich: Shaw	146—13	4	
Rich: Brooke	142—	6—8	
Wm fithian	180—	3—4	
Samuel Parsons	085—	0	
Arthur Croasy	048—	0	
Tho: Osborne Ju:	175—	0	
John Parsons	126—	0	
Abraham Hauke	033—10		
John Miller	103—	0	
James Bird	028—	0	
John Theller	173—	3—4	
Benjamin Osborne	067—	0	
	138	0	
[*MS. destroyed.*]	223—	0	
	146—	6—8	
	318—	0	
John Richeson	027—10		
Capt. Tho Talmag	255—10		
John Stretton Sen:	291	06	8
John Stretton Jun:	090	00	
Misses Codnon	025	00	

	£	s	d
Reneck garison	042	00	
Nath: Bushop	177	3	4
James Hand	058	10	
James Loper	076	00	
Samuel Mulford	083	00	
Joseph Osborne	044	00	
Richard Stretton	264	13	4
Tho diment	225	00	
Ebeneser Leek	034	00	
Natha. dorrony	091	00	
Samuel Brooke	066	6	8
Wm Perkins	230	0	
John Miller Junior	030	0	
John Osborne	196	13	4
Enoch fithian	067	00	
Benia: Conckling	103	00	
John feild	040	00	
Joanah Hodges	045	00	
Tho: dimont Jun:	030	00	
Tho: Chatfield	018	00	
Edward •	018	00	
The totall Summe	6842	16	8

Oyster Bay the 27th Augt 1675.

S^{r}—Your Warrant wee haue receued, dated ye 7th Augt for y^e
sending in to ye Office ye Sum of our Townes Estate ye w^{ch}
wee haue dun & ye Estate of our Townes is 4900£. now sent
by this bearrer Mr Shakerly.   not Elce to acquaint your Worship
wth but desiering your welfare I rest yours to Comand—

          12   NATHANIELL COLE
          4900)408–4

          20–8–4

Endorsed   To ye Worship^l Matthias
                    Nichols Mayor these
                         p^{r}sents
                         In New Yorke

A LIST OF Yᵉ ESTATE OF Yᵉ TOWNE OF HUNTINGTON FOR THE YEARE 1675.

	Land & Meadow	Vessells	Swine	Sheepe	Yearlings	2 yeares	3 yeares	Cowes	Oxen	Yearlings	2 years	3 yeares	Horses
Capᵗ Fleet	21	40	08	00	02	02	02	01	00	00	00	00	01
Tho: Fleet Junʳ	00	00	00	00	00	00	00	00	00	00	00	00	00
Steph Jarvis	16	05	05	00	01	01	03	03	02	00	01	02	00
Robᵗ Cranfeild	18	00	00	00	04	02	02	02	04	01	00	00	01
Tho: Scudder	28	00	28	06	05	05	05	04	06	00	01	03	04
Isaak Scudder	00	00	00	00	00	00	00	00	00	00	00	00	00
Jnᵒ Scudder	00	00	00	00	00	00	00	00	00	01	00	00	00
Ja: Chichister Sen	27	00	03	12	04	02	01	04	06	01	00	01	02
Ja: Chichister Junʳ	00	00	00	00	00	00	00	00	00	00	00	02	02
Nathˡˡ Foster	19	05	05	00	02	04	01	02	04	01	00	00	02
Jnᵒ Finch Senʳ	26	00	05	00	02	00	02	02	02	00	00	00	03
Jnᵒ Finch Junʳ	00	00	00	00	00	00	00	00	00	00	02	00	00
Joseph Baily	25	00	05	02	02	03	02	04	00	00	00	00	02
Tho: Whitson	20	00	01	03	02	02	02	03	00	01	00	00	02
Jnᵒ Weekes	18	00	09	08	00	03	01	05	04	02	00	00	03
Mʳ Jonas Wood Senʳ	48	00	10	17	03	04	04	07	06	00	00	00	04
Jnᵒ Wood	00	00	00	00	00	00	00	00	00	00	00	00	00
Isaak Platt	25	00	19	10	04	02	06	06	05	00	00	00	01
Tho: Powers	30	00	09	06	05	04	04	09	05	00	00	01	02

A LIST &c.—(CONTINUED.)

	Land & Meadow	Vessells	Swine	Sheepe	Yearlings	2 yeares	3 yeares	Cows	Oxen	Yearlings	2 years	3 yeares	Horses
Caleb Wood	08	00	00	02	03	01	04	03	05	00	00	00	04
Joseph Wood	07	00	00	00	00	02	01	01	00	00	00	01	02
Sam'l Wood	24	00	16	06	02	00	02	05	06	00	00	00	02
Jno Green	12	00	01	00	00	00	07	01	00	01	00	00	01
Tho Weekes	28	00	06	07	01	01	02	04	04	00	00	00	02
Jno Carye	12	00	06	06	01	02	00	03	02	00	00	00	00
Epen Platt	39	00	20	07	04	04	03	03	02	00	00	00	03
Walter Nokes	08	00	12	00	01	00	00	01	00	00	00	00	01
Rich'd Brush	16	00	05	02	04	00	00	03	02	01	00	00	01
Jonas Wood Jun'r	20	00	09	06	02	02	02	05	04	01	00	00	01
Joseph Whitman	27	00	16	13	00	01	01	06	04	00	00	00	01
Thomas Brush	36	00	17	22	02	04	00	06	06	00	00	00	03
Jno Brush	00	00	00	00	00	00	03	00	00	00	00	00	00
Abigail Titus	18	00	07	04	03	02	04	04	02	00	00	00	02
Sam'l Ketchman	16	00	15	05	00	04	00	04	04	00	00	00	03
Rich: Williams	11	00	10	00	01	06	00	06	00	01	00	00	00
Sam'l Titus	34	00	03	03	02	02	00	05	04	00	00	00	02
Jothan Scudder	00	00	00	00	00	00	00	00	00	00	00	00	00
David Scudder	00	00	00	00	00	00	00	00	00	00	00	00	00

Moses Scudder	00	00	00	00	00	00	00	00	00	00	00	00	00
John Tedd	16	00	04	00	02	00	02	01	02	01	00	00	01
Tomᵒ Conklyn	18	00	11	06	01	00	03	04	02	00	00	01	03
Samˡ Messenger	12	00	00	00	01	02	00	02	02	00	00	00	01
Jnᵒ Samwayes	18	00	05	07	04	01	04	02	04	00	00	00	02
The Land of Jacob Walker	18	00	08	00	00	00	00	00	00	00	00	00	00
Henry Sooper	14	00	00	14	02	02	01	03	02	00	01	00	01
Jona: Rogers	45	00	20	40	02	05	03	04	07	00	00	03	03
George Baldwin	00	00	01	00	00	00	00	00	00	00	00	00	01
Edwᵈ Bunce	18	00	08	00	02	02	02	06	04	00	00	00	01
John Page	09	00	00	00	01	00	00	02	00	00	00	00	00
Tho: Martin	09	00	02	00	02	00	00	02	00	00	00	00	01
Jnᵒ Inkerson	16	00	08	00	02	04	00	06	04	00	00	00	02
Adam Whithead	00	00	00	00	00	00	00	00	00	00	00	00	00
Tho: Scidmore Sen	21	00	02	00	02	00	00	07	04	00	00	00	02
Tho: Scidmore Junʳ	00	00	00	00	00	00	00	00	00	00	00	00	00
Philip Udale	10	00	01	00	01	00	00	03	00	00	00	00	01
Jnᵒ Goulden	00	00	02	00	02	00	00	04	00	00	00	00	01
Peeter Floid	06	00	00	00	00	00	00	00	00	00	00	00	01
Wᵐ Brothᵋton	07	00	00	00	00	00	00	03	00	00	00	00	01
Benj: Jones	11	00	00	00	03	00	00	05	00	00	02	00	02
Jonath Heind	00	00	00	00	00	01	00	02	00	00	00	01	00
Jnᵒ Everit	00	00	00	00	00	00	00	00	00	00	00	00	00
Roger Quint	00	00	00	00	00	00	00	00	00	00	00	00	00
Richard White	00	00	00	00	00	00	00	00	00	00	00	00	00
Widow Jones	48	00	14	10	06	04	00	08	04	00	00	00	06

A LIST, &c.—(CONTINUED.)

	Horses	3 years	2 years	Yearling	Oxen	Cowes	3 years	2 years	Yearling	Sheep	Swine	Vessells	Land & Meadow
Jnᵒ Jones	01	00	00	00	00	02	01	00	01	00	00	00	13
Jnᵒ Ketcham	02	00	00	00	04	03	01	00	00	06	02	00	09
Johannes Race	01	00	00	00	00	00	00	00	00	00	00	00	00
Mr Bryans Estate	00	01	00	00	04	10	00	00	00	00	00	00	00
Mr Kane	00	00	00	00	00	00	01	00	00	00	00	00	00

Memorandum Mr bryan and Mr Wakers parsons are not heir

SOUTHHOULDS ESTIMATE THE 16TH SEPTEMBR 1675.

John Paine

1 heade	18	— —
10 acres land	10	— —
2 oxen	12	— —
5 Cows 1: 3 Yr old	29	— —
3: 2 Yr old	07	10 —
2: Yerlings	03	— —
3 horses	36	— —
10 gotes	04	— —
	119.	10 —

Wm Robinson

1 heade 1 horse	30	— —
12 acors land	12	— —
3 oxen	18	— —
3 cows	15	— —
2: 3 Yr old	08	— —
3: 2 Yr old	05	— —
3: Yerlings	04	10 —
	92	10 —

John Greete

1 heade	18	— —
30 acors land	30	— —
2 oxen	12	— —
6 cows	30	— —
1: 3 Yr old	04	— —
2: 2 Yr olds	05	— —
4: Yerlings	06	— —
2 horses	12	— —
1 Yerling horse	03	— —
4 Swine	04	— —
	124	— —

Caleb Curtis

1 heade 12 acors of land	30	— —

2: oxen: 5 Cows ...	37	— —
1: 3 yr old: 2 2 yr old	09	— —
4 Yerl	06	— —
1 horse: 1: 3 yr old	20	— —
4 Swine	04	— —
	106	— —

Walter Jones

1 heade	18	— —
12 acors land	12	— —
1 ox 3 cows	21	— —
$\frac{1}{2}$ a horse	06	— —
2: 2 yr olds 4 yerlings	11	— —
	68	— —

Giddion Yongs

1 heade	18	— —
35 acors land	35	— —
2 oxen: 5 cows	37	— —
1: 3 yr 3: 2 yr olds	11	10 —
4 yerlings	06	— —
2 horses 1 yerling	27	— —
7 Swine	07	— —
	141	10 —

Abrahâ Whithere

1 heade 25 acors land	43	— —
1 ox 5 cows	31	— —
3: 3 yr old	12	— —
2:2 yr old 2 yerlings	08	— —
4$\frac{1}{2}$ horses	54	— —
1 yerling horse	03	— —
8 Swine	08	— —
	159	— ·

Tho: Terry

1 heade	18 — —
8 acors land	08 — —
2: oxen 4 cows ...	32 — —
2: 3 yr olds	08 — —
3: 2 yer old 2 yer-	
lings	10 10 —
3 horses 1: 3 yer old	44 — —
1: 2 yr 1 yerling horse	08 — —
1 Swine	01 — —
	129 10 —

John Tuthill

2 heads	36 — —
40 acors land	40 — —
2 oxen 7 cows	47 — —
5: 3 yr olde	20 — —
7: 2 yr olde 2 yer-	
lings	20 10 —
3 horses & 1 yerling	39 — —
9 Shepe	03 — —
1 Swine	01 — —
	206 10 —

Richard Browne

4 heads	72 — —
50 acors land......	50 — —
8 oxen	48 — —
10 Cows	50 — —
6: 3 y^r old	24 — —
7 2 yr old	17 10 —
5 yerlings.........	07 10 —
6 horses..........	72 — —
1: 3 yr old 1 yerling	11 — —
24 Shepe	08 — —
10 Swine	10 — —
	370 — —

Samll King

1 heade	18 — —
40 acors land......	40 — —
5 oxen............	30 — —
6 cows	30 — —
2: 3 yr olds.......	08 — —
5: 2 yr olds......	12 10 —
4 yerlings	06 — —
2 horses 1 Swine ...	25 — —
	169 10 —

Joseph Maps

1 heade 1: yr old...	20 10 —
	20 10 —

Samll Grouer

1 heade	18 — —
2 acors land.......	2 — —
1 horse 1 Cow.....	17 — —
	37 — —

Tho: Moore Junr

1 heade	18 — —
40 acors land......	40 — —
4 oxen	24 — —
9 Cows...........	45 — —
2 Yerlings	03 — —
4 horses..........	48 — —
18 shepe	06 — —
2 Swine..........	02 — —
	186 — —

Jonathan Moore

1 heade	18 — —
40 acors land......	40 — —
2 oxen 6 cows....	42 — —
1: 3 yrold 1: 2 yrold	06 10 —
4 yerlings	06 — —

2 horses 1: 2 yrold. 29 — —
6 Swine.......... 06 — —

147 10 —

Capt John Yongs
3 heads 10 acres land 64 — —
2 oxen 4 cows..... 32 — —
4: 3 yr 2: 2 yrold ... 21 — —
4 yerlings......... 06 — —
8 horses.......... 96 — —
9 Shepe 6 Swine ... 09 — —

228 — —

Mr John Yongs Jur
1 heade .... 18 — —
24 acors land ...... 24 — —
4 oxen: 7 Cows.... 59 — —
6 Yrlings......... 09 — —
2 horses.......... 24 — —
2 Yrlings......... 06 — —
15 Shepe .... 05 — —
3 Swine.......... 03 — —

148 — —

Peter Simons
1 heade.......... 18 — —

Mr John Conklin
1 head 80 acors land 98 — —
8 oxen........... 48 — —
9 Cows........... 45 — —
5: 3 yrolds........ 20 — —
9: 2 yr olds .... 22 10 —
6 yerling.......... 09 — —
5 horses .... 60 — —
3: 2 yrold horses ... 15 — —
21 shepe .... 07 — —
20 Swine.......... 20 — —

1: 3 yrold Bull.... 04 — —

348-10 | 358l-10s- 358 10 —
Jacob Conklin
1 heade .... 18 — —
14 acors land....... 14 — —
2 oxen 4 cows..... 32 — —
4: 3 yr 5: 2 yr: 3 yer-
lings........... 33 — —
2 horses .... 24 — —
3 Shepe 8 Swine ... 09 — —

130 — —

John Cory
1 heade .... 18 — —
1 ox............. 06 — —
1 horse 1 3 yrold .. 20 — —

44 — —

Thomas Rider
2 heads .... 36 — —
30 acors land .... 30 — —
4 oxen 8 cows..... 64 — —
1: 2 yrold 1: 3 yrold 06 10 —
4 yerlings......... 06 — —
24 shepe 10 Swine .. 18 — —

160 10 —

John Franklin and John Wigins
2 heads 40 acors land 76 — —
4 oxen: 6 cows...... 54 — —
1 2 yrold 5 yerlings 10 — —
2 horses 1: 2 yrold . 29 — —
9 shepe .... 03 — —
4 Swine.......... 04 — —

176 — —

Jeremy Valle

3 heads	54	— —
10 acors land 2 oxen	22	— —
6 cows 3: 3 yrolds..	42	— —
1: 2 yrold 3 yrlings.	07	— —
1 horse 12 Shepe...	16	— —
11 Swine	11	— —
	152	— —

Edward Petty

2 heads	36	— —
10 acors land	10	— —
2 oxen 5 cows	37	— —
1 horse	12	— —
	95	— —

Simon Grover

2 heads 5 acors land	41	— —
2 cows	10	— —
1: 2 yrold 1 yerling	04	— —
1 horse 3 Swine....	15	— —
	70	— —

Nathall Moore

1 head	18	— —
4 acors land 2 cows	14	— —
	32	— —

Mr Thomas Moore Senr

1 head 10 acors land	28	— —
6 oxen 5 cows	61	— —
2: 3 yr 2 yerlings ..	11	— —
2 horses 3 Swine...	27	— —
	27	— —

Joseph Yongs

1 head 12 acors land	30	— —
2 oxen 5 cows	37	— —

2: 3 yrold 2 Swine .	11	— —
	78	— —

Isack Reeues

1 head 1 horse	30	— —

Samll Yongs

1 heade 8 acors land	26	— —
2 Cows	10	— —
2: 3 yr 2: 2 yr olds	13	— —
1 horse	12	— —
1: 3 yr 1 yerling ...	11	— —
	72	— —

Stephen Bayly

1 heade	18	— —
13 acors land.......	13	— —
2 Cows 3: 3 yerolds	22	— —
1 horse 1 yerling ...	15	— —
3 Shepe	01	— —
	69	— —

Mr John Yongs marinr

1 heade 2 acors land	20	— —
4 Cows	20	— —
1 horse 1 swine....	13	— —
	53	— —

Samll Glouer

1 heade 1 ox	24	— —
3 Cows	15	— —
4:3 yerold 3:3 yerold	23	10 —
1 horse 1 swine	13	— —
	75	10 —

Beniam Yongs

2 heads	36	— —
18 acors land.......	18	— —

6 oxen 3 cows..... 51 — —
2:3 yrolds 2:2 yerold 13 — —
1 horse: 1 yerling hors 15 — —
21 shepe: 2 Swine... 09 — —

142 — —

Christop^r Yongs Senr
1 heade 12 acors land 30 — —
2 oxen 4 cows..... 32 — —
1: 2 yr old.......... 02 10 —
4 horses.......... 48 — —
12 shepe 1 swine.... 08 — —

120 10 —

Richd Clark
1 head............ 18 — —
4 acors land 1 Cow. 09 — —
3:3 yrold 2 yerlings . 15 — —
1 horse........... 12 — —
6 shepe 6 swine.... 08 — —

62 — —

John Booth
2 heads........... 36 — —
17 acors land....... 17 — —
3 oxen .... 18 — —
4 cows........... 20 — —
2:2 yrolds 2 yerlings 08 — —
3 horses 1: 2 yrold. 41 — —
3 Shepe.......... 01 — —
6 Swine.......... 06 — —

147 — —

John Curwin
2 heads 21 acors land 57 — —
6 oxen 6 cows..... 66 — —
3: 3 yrold .... 12 — —
1: 2 yrold .... 02 10 —

5 horses.......... 60 — —
2: 3 yrold .... 16 — —
1: 2 yrold 1 yerling 08 — —
5 Swine.......... 05 — —
6 shepe .... 02 — —

228 10 —

Barnab^s Horton
2 heads .... 36 — —
37 acors land....... 37 — —
9 oxen .... 54 — —
8 cows........... 40 — —
4: 3 yrold .... 16 — —
4: 2 yrold .... 10 — —
4 yerlings .... 06 — —
69 shepe .... 23 — —
6 horses.......... 72 — —
1 yerling.......... 03 — —
8 swine........... 08 — —

305 — —

Jonathan Horton
1 heade .... 18 — —
36 acors land....... 36 — —
2 oxen 6 cows .... 42 — —
3: 3 yrolds .... 12 — —
5: 2 yrolds .... 12 10 —
2 yerlings .... 03 — —
3 horses 1 yerling.. 39 — —
9 shepe 6 swine ... 09 — —

171 10 —

Richd Beniamin
2 heads .... 36 — —
39 acors land....... 39 — —
8 oxen 6 cows..... 78 — —
2: 3 yrold: 6:2 yrold 23 — —
4: yerlings........ 06 — —

4 horses.......... 48 — —
2: 2 yr: 1: yerling.. 13 — —
4 swine .... 04 — —
                   ——————
                   247 — —

Beniam Moore

1 heade .... 18 — —
14 acors land....... 14 — —
4 cows: 2: 3 yrolds 28 — —
2: 2 yr: 2 yerlings.. 08 — —
4 horses .... 48 — —
2 Swine .... 02 — —
                   ——————
                   118 — —

Mr John Bud not being at home
  is lumpt at by ye last years
  accopt at....... £ s d
                   300 — —

Abraham Cory

1 heade 4 acors land 22 — —
2 oxen........... 12 — —
2: 3 yrold 1: 2 yrold 10 10 —
1 horse: 1 yerling.. 15 — —
5 swine .... 05 — —
                   ——————
                   64 10 —

Joshua Horton

1 heade 20 acres land 38 — —
8 oxen 4 Cows.... 68 — —
7: 3 yr 3: 2 yr 3
  yerlings........ 40 — —
3 horses: 1 2 yrold. 41 — —
10 swine .... 10 — —
                   ——————
                   197 — —

Baranb^s Wines

1 heade 15 acors land 53 — —
2 oxen 9 cows..... 57 — —
5: 3 yr olds....... 20 — —

2: 2 yrolds 6 yrlings. 14   —
6 sheep 6 swine.... 08   —
                   ——————
                   152 - —

Isaac Ouenton

2 heades 24 acors land 60
5 oxen: 6 cows.... 60
4: 3 yr olds....... 16
8: 2 yer 6 yerlings 29
4: horses 1 yerling 51
20 shepe 9 swine.... 16
              £ ——————
              232 -233 — —

Mr Tho Hucisson

1 heade 14 acors lan 32 — —
5 oxen 5 cows.... 55 — —
4: 3 y^r 3: 2 yr 2
  yerlings........ 22 10 —
4 horses 19 swine.. 67 — —
                   ——————
                   176 10 —

Jacob Cory

1 heade 10 acors land 28 — —
4 oxen 2 cows..... 34 — —
3: 3 yr 2 yerlings.. 15 — —
1 horse 4 swine.... 16 — —
                   ——————
                   93 — —

Tho Reeues

1 heade 23 acors land 41 — —
4 oxen 5 cows..... 49 — —
2: 3 yr 3: 2 yr 2 yer-
  lings.......... 18 10 -
2 horses 5 swine.... 29 — —
                   ——————
                   137 10 —

John Reeues

1 heade 1 ox...... 24 — —
1: 3 yr 1 yerling.... 05 10 —

1 horse 1: 3 yr old
horse.......... 20 — —
5 Swine.......... 05 — —
_____
54 10 —

Peeter Paine
1 heade 6 acors land 24 — —
2 cows............ 10 — —
2: 2 yrold: 2 yerlings 08 — —
1 horse 4 swine.... 16 — —
_____
58 — —

Dainell Terry
1 heade 12 acors land 30 — —
4 oxen 5 cows .... 49 — —
3: 3 yr: 3: 2 yr 3 yer-
lings.......... 24 — —
1 horse 1 yerling... 15 — —
8 swine.......... 08 — —
_____
126 — —

Peeter Dicisson
2 heads 20 acors land 56 — —
8 oxen .... 48 — —
12 cows .... 60 — —
3: 3 yrolds........ 12 — —
6: 2 yrolds 3 yerlings 19 10 —
1 horse .... 12 — —
1: 3 yr 1: 2 yrold.. 13 — —
40 gotes .... 16 — —
14 Swine.......... 14 — —
_____
250 10 —

Richard Cozens
1 heade.......... 18
4 acres land 4
_____
22 — —

Nathall Terry
2 heads 20 acors land 56 — —

7 oxen 8 cows..... 82 — —
2: 3 yrold......... 08 — —
5: 2 yr 5 yrlings... 20 — —
2 horses.......... 24 — —
1: 3 yr 1 yrling.... 11 — —
18 Swine.......... 18 — —
_____
219 — —

Samˡˡ Wines
1 head 9 acors land 27 — —
2 oxen............ 12 — —
4 cows 3 yrlings.... 24 10 —
1 horse 3 Swine.... 15 — —
_____
78 10—

Mʳˢ Mary Welles
26 acors land...... 26 — —
4: oxen 6 cows.... 54 — —
5: 3 yrolds........ 20 — —
7: 2 yr 2 yrlings.... 20 10 —
27 Shepe.......... 09 — —
5 horses.......... 60 — —
1: 3 yr 1: 2 yr 1 yer-
ling horse...... 16 — —
12 Swine.......... 12 — —
_____
217 10 —

Simieon Beinam
1 heade 10 acors land 28 — —
2 oxen 3 cows..... 27 — —
4 3 yrold 1 yerling.. 19 — —
2 horses 1 yr...... 27 — —
3 shepe 4 swine.... 05 — —
_____
106 — —

Will Colleman
1 heade 4 acors land 22 — —
2 cows............ 10 — —
2: 2 yrolds........ 05 — —

2 yerlings .... 03 — —
1 horse 1: 2 yrold.. 17 — —
2 Swine.. .... 02 — —
_____
59 — —

Calib Horton
1 heade 80 acors land 96 — —
6 oxen .... 36 — —
12 Cows .... 60 — —
5: 3 yr olds ...... 20 — —
7: 2 yr olds ...... 17 10 —
7 yerlings .... 10 10 —
2 horses 1: 3 yr old
horse .... 32 — —
1: 2 yr old 1 yerling
horse .... 08 — —
2 Swine .... 02 — —
_____
282 — —

Tho Maps Junr
1 heade 15 acors land 33 — —
1 ox: 3 Cows ..... 21 — —
2: 3 yr 4: 2 yr 2
yerlings ...... 21 — —
1 horse 12 Swine... 24 — —
_____
99 — —

Thomas Tusteene
1 heade 6 acors land 24 — —
2 oxen 1 Cow .... 17 — —
1: 3 yr 2: 2 yr: 1
yerling........ 08 — —
1 hors 3 Swine.... 15 — —
_____
64 — —

Thoms Maps Senr
2 heads 24 acors land 60 — —
6 oxen 6 cows .... 76 — —
3: 3 yr olds....... 12 — —
4: 2 yr old 5 ycrlings 17 10 —

3 horses 2 yrlings
horse .... 42 — —
20 Swine .... 20 — —
_____
227 10 —

Thoms Terrill
1 heade 14 acors land 32 — —
2 oxen 3 cows .... 27 — —
3: 3 yr old .... 12 — —
2: 2 yr old 2 yerlings 08 — —
2 horses 6 Swine ... 30 — —
_____
109 — —

James Reeues
1 heade 24 acors land 42 — —
10 oxen 7 cows .... 95 — —
6: 3 yr olds ...... 24 — —
5: 2 yr 2 ycrlings.. 15 10 —
3 horses .... 36 — —
1: 3 yr old 1 yerling 11 — —
3 Shepe 20 Swine.. 21 — —
_____
244 10 —

Will Reeues
1 heade 5 acors land 23 — —
3 cows 1: 3 yr old 19 — —
2: 2 yr 3 yerlings .. 09 10 —
1 horse 6 swine.... 18 — —
_____
69 10 —

John Swasie Senr
2 heads .... 36 — —
12 acors land ...... 12 — —
6 oxen 6 cows..... 66 — —
1: 3 yr old bull.... 04 — —
5: 2 yr old 1 ycrling 14 — —
4 horses.......... 48 — —
20 Swine.......... 20 — —
_____
200 — —

John Swasie Jun[r]

1 heade 10 acors land	28	— —
2 oxen 2 cows	22	— —
1: 2 yr old 4 yerlings	08	10 —
4 Swine	04	— —
	62	10 —

Joseph Swasie

1 heade 8 acors land	26	— —
2 oxen 2 cows	22	— —
1: 2 yr 1 yerling	04	— —
1 horse	12	— —
2 Swine	02	— —
	66	— —

Will Halloke

3 heads	54	— —
70 acors land	70	— —
8 oxen	48	— —
14 cows	70	— —
4: 3 yr old	16	— —
10: 2 yr old	25	— —
9 yerlings	13	10 —
2 horses	24	— —
4: 2 yr old 1 yrling	11	— —
30 Swine	30	— —
	361	10 —

John Hallok

1 heade	18	— —
4 acors land	04	— —
2 oxen 2 cows	22	— —
2 yrlings	03	— —
2 horses 1: 2 yr old	29	— —
6 Swine	06	— —
	82	— —

Richard Howell

1 heade 6 acors land	24	— —

2 oxen 1 cow	17	— —
1: 3 yr old	04	— —
2: 2 yr 2 yerlings	08	— —
1 horse 1 yrling	15	— —
5 Gotes 7 swine	09	— —
	77	— —

Thoms Osman

2 heads 8 acors land	44	— —
4 oxen 4 cows	44	— —
5: 3 yr olds	20	— —
6: 2 yr	15	— —
6 yerlings	09	— —
4 horses	48	— —
1: 2 yr old horse	05	— —
9 swine	09	— —
	194	— —

Will Poole

2 heads 7 acors land	25	— —
2 oxen 8 cows	52	— —
1: 3 yr old 1: 2 yr old	06	10 —
7 yerlings	10	10 —
1 horse 8 swine	20	— —
	114	— —

Christopher Yongs Jun[r]

1 heade 1 horse	30	— —
2: 3 yr olds 2: 2 yr olds	26	— —
	56	— —

John Sallmon

1 heade	18	— —
1: 3 yr old horse	08	— —
	26	— —

James Lee

1 heade	18	— —

Beni[n] Horton

1 heade	18 — —
70 acors land	70 — —
4 oxen	24 — —
8 cows	40 — —
4: 3 yr olds	16 — —
5: 2 yr old	12 10 —
4 horses	48 — —
4 Swine	04 — —
	232 10 —

Sarah Yongs

8 acors land	08
2 oxen 4 cows	32

4: 3 yr old	16
1: 2 yr old	02 10
1 horse	12 — —
2 Swine	02 — —
	72 10 —

The totall Summe is

£.   s.   d

10935: 10: 00

Endorsed

Southhold Valuacôns

past Octo[b] 25 1675

10935—10—0

45—11—3½

To the wors[l] his ever hon[rd] & much esteemed friend Cap[t] Matthias Nicolls Secretary at N: Yorke theise p[r]sent—

Southampton Sept: 28: 1675.

WORTHY S[R]—Wee the subscribed p[e]sent our best respects to you hopeing of & much Desireing your good health &c: Wee re[cd] your order or warrant for y[e] makeing up and sending to you the estimate or waluation of our towne And at length with care and trouble wee have effected it: And it exactly amounts to twelve thousand five hundred and fourty one poundes xvi[s] viii[d]: Wee have dilligently accompted every mans estate vp, & that is the just totall according to our best inspection ; Wee herein send you not the pticulers, for wee conceive that would bee but lost labour to vs, and noe advantage, nor more satisfaction, but rather a cumber to you: And therefore according to our former maner to y[e] High Shereife wee Send you the Sume in gross, which wee hope will be Sufficient, & fully answer your expectation: Wee crave yo[r] favour & pdon that wee could not procure it Sooner into your hand ; But hope it will come So Seasonably, that wee haveing your Order by the bearer our loveing friend and much respected, Justice Topping at his returne, may make paym[t]: in the most Suitable maner wee can to the Cu[n]tries

occations ; But corne is but Scarce with most of yᵉ Inhabitants &
wee desire that Specie may not bee enjoyned in your warrant.
Sʳ wee have presumed to write to the Governʳ respecting our
estimate, and therein what we have Sett yᵉ horse-kinde at, & have
made request to him touching that Subject. If his honʳ bee not
well pleased, Wee desire yoʳ worᴘᴘ: to bee Instrumentall as you
can to excuse our goeing beside that old law or order (which wee
can not but thinke now to follow is excessive hard and oppressive)
that rates horses and mares one with another at 12ˡᵇ a peece.
Sʳ there are so many people everywhere, besides ours, doe Soe
exceedingly complaine that mares Should be rated at 12ˡᵇ ps, when
hardly the best will give 4ˡᵇ and many of them not 40ˢ a peece,
emboldened us now to accompt them at 4ˡᵇ a peece one with
another which is more than any one will give — Yet least it should
fall out (contrary to our expectation and beleif) that his honʳ the
Governʳ Should be dissatisfyed, and that wee may deale uprightly,
discharge our Conscience for the towne and Duty towards yᵉ
Cuntry wee have as afforesaid Sumd up the horses and mares at
4ˡᵇ 3 year olds at 3 ˡᵇ two year'l: at 40ˢ and year'l at 20ˢ ps: And
withall we have collected out of all the bills men pticulorly brought
in, the just numbers of horses & mares — 3 year olds 2 year olds
& yearlings: that Soe, if not witestanding our honᵉᵇˡ Governʳ
Shall See cause, & it be his pleasure to continue them Still at yᵉ
old rate of 12ˡᵇ a ps: &c. We crave yoʳ favour to view the
inclosed acctᵗ and ad the difference on yᵗ which remaines (according
to yᵉ Sᵈ acct) unto our waluation. And yeⁿ yᵉ estimate will bee
compleated: Sʳ ift is Desired yᵗ at yᵉ Court you will promove
the alteration of valuation of yᵉ horse kind:

Sʳ Wee are yoʳˢ to Comand to our power

Wee are greived to heare of yᵉ loss   THOMAS TOPPING Consᵗ
of English blood by yᵉ cruell dam-   HENRY PEIRSON
ned pagans and very many are   THOMAS COOPER
Sorry the Indians here have theire   FRANCIS SAWYER
guns returned to them.   JOHN FAYGAN

(Enclosed)	lb.	s.	d.
250 horses & mares at 4^{lb}: ps:	1000	00	00
19 of three year old at 3^{lb}: ps:	0057	00	00
35 of 2 yeare old at 2^{lb}: ps:	0070	00	00
29 yearlings at 20^s: ps:..............	0029	00	00
	1156	00	00
250 —— at 12^{lb}: ps:.................	3000	00	00
19 —— at 8^{lb}: ps:	0152	00	00
35 —— at 5^{lb}: ps:	0175	00	00
29 —— at 3^{lb}: ps:	0087	00	00
	3414	00	00
Substracted........	1156	00	00
Remaines.........	2258	00	00

Endorsed

Southton Valuacons brought in Octr 2^{cd} 1675   (Note by the Gov.)
    13667–16–8   Rate 56–18–11¾   The 1156 added.
          Past

VALUATIONS OF ESTATES AT FLUSHING 1675.

	shepe	swine	yerlinges	to yere oldes	thra yer oldes	Cowes	oxen and boles	yerlinges	to yere oldes	three yer oldes	horses mares	madoes	Landes	negeres
Charles bridgs	00	06	04	04	10	12	12	00	02	00	07	60	50	08
John Furbosh	30	00	03	03	03	08	06	00	00	00	04	40	18	03
Alias douty	40	04	00	03	00	12	00	00	00	00	00	20	12	01
John Thorn	06	03	02	02	00	08	02	00	00	00	01	10	06	00
william noble	12	03	01	01	02	04	02	00	00	00	01	20	05	01
Daniell patrek	00	00	01	02	02	00	00	00	00	00	01	00	04	00
dorothy farington	30	16	05	00	03	08	02	00	00	00	03	30	12	00
James Clamenes	00	02	01	01	00	03	00	00	00	00	00	00	04	00
anthony fellde	00	00	00	01	00	05	02	01	00	00	02	20	07	00
Thomas stilles	00	07	03	02	00	04	02	00	00	00	00	10	12	00
richard tew	00	00	00	00	00	01	00	00	00	00	01	00	04	00
william danfard	10	00	00	00	00	02	00	00	00	00	01	05	04	00
John tere	08	04	01	01	02	02	00	00	00	00	01	10	04	01
Rich'd willde	10	00	02	02	04	03	00	00	00	00	01	05	07	00
adward grifen Jun	00	05	04	01	00	07	02	00	00	00	01	10	12	01
richard stockton	00	00	04	01	00	04	04	00	00	00	01	00	12	00
Jonethan wright	00	00	00	04	00	04	00	00	00	00	01	00	06	01
Denis Holdren	00	00	00	00	00	04	00	00	00	00	01	00	00	00
Derek Arason	00	00	00	00	02	01	00	00	00	00	00	00	00	00

VALUATIONS &c.—(CONTINUED.)

	negeres	Landes	madoes	horses mares	three yer olds	to yere oldes	yerlinges	oxen and boles	Cowes	thre yer oldes	to yere oldes	yerlinges	swine	shepe
John Adames	00	08	00	01	00	00	00	01	04	00	01	02	01	00
John depre	00	06	00	01	00	00	00	02	03	02	02	01	00	12
moses browne	00	08	00	01	00	00	00	00	02	01	01	01	06	00
william yates	00	02	05	01	00	00	00	02	00	00	02	00	00	00
Thomas Whittiker	00	08	00	02	00	00	00	00	02	00	00	01	03	00
John emere	00	04	00	00	00	00	00	02	03	00	00	00	00	00
Nicholas Parson	01	14	15	00	00	00	00	02	08	00	05	02	01	25
Thomas Cimse	00	04	00	01	00	00	00	00	02	00	00	00	00	00
Thomas ford	00	01	00	01	00	00	00	00	02	00	00	00	01	00
Arien Cornelus	00	06	05	02	00	00	00	00	03	00	00	00	00	08
samuel Thorn	00	04	10	01	01	02	02	02	00	03	01	00	04	00
henry teyler	00	20	30	02	00	00	00	00	04	00	00	04	01	20
John bowne	00	20	10	04	00	00	00	04	07	07	03	00	10	50
mary smith	00	14	15	02	00	00	00	02	04	04	00	02	08	11
John hinchman	01	10	10	02	00	00	00	04	04	04	00	00	04	40
william haverland	00	15	30	06	00	00	00	04	05	07	00	00	01	00
Thomas lawrance	01	02	10	01	00	00	00	02	04	02	00	00	02	00
Frances bloodgood	00	03	06	01	00	00	00	02	04	00	04	02	05	40
david Row	00	16	00	00	00	00	00	02	06	01	02	01	06	16

william Chadderton	00	04	05	00	00	00	00	00	01	00	02	00	00	00
simon thewall	00	03	00	00	00	30	00	02	03	00	02	00	04	12
John gelime	00	03	00	01	00	00	00	00	02	00	00	00	03	00
Nicholus Snathan	00	02	10	01	00	00	00	02	03	00	02	02	00	00
John hoper	00	01	00	00	00	00	00	00	02	02	01	00	00	00
minderd Corto	00	00	10	01	00	00	00	00	02	00	00	00	00	00
gerret hendrekes	00	00	00	00	00	00	00	00	03	00	00	00	00	00
Thomas williames	01	00	00	00	00	00	00	00	00	02	00	00	00	00
william begen	00	02	00	00	00	00	00	02	00	00	00	00	00	00
Joseph Thorn	00	03	10	00	00	00	00	00	04	01	02	02	01	14

Endorsed.

Valuacons of Estates
at Flushng
brought in
Oct. 9. 1675

Ex^d *lb s d*

Rate   18.3.10

hed mone for singel men

Elias purrington
John farrington
Edward farrington
Jonethon fillepes
Andres depre
pole denorman
Edward grifen Junyer
richerd tendoll
Thomos mam
John tayler
Joseph haverland
John fellde

flushing
september 29
1675

Cap Thoms hikes hath not
yet prought in a list
of his estate

This to Secretarie Nicolls att: N: Yorke Lett bee deliuered

———

The Accoumpts from GRAUESEND this 14th of the 7th Moth Anno 1675 of all personns Rateable according to ye Law, as allso of there Lands both vpland and meadow Ground, With the number of there cattle namely: Oxen; Cows; horses, Mares, and Sheepe as follows

Impris:

of: personns the troopers excepted 30
of: oxen there is............................. 26
of: Cows there is to ye number off 107
of: Cattle of three yeres ould there is 20
of: Cattle of twoe yeares ould there is........... 32
of: Cattle of one yeare ould there is............. 55
of: Horses and Mares there is 62
of: Horses of three yeares ould................. 05
of: Horses of twoe years ould 08

of: Horses of one yeare ould................... 16
of: Sheepe to the number of 60
of: Acors of vpland & Meadow ground 932

        By mee nicholas Stilwell Constable £ s d

        and the Ourseers................ 13. 14. 3

Endorsed

    Gravesend Valuacons Brought in Septr 20th 1675

        Ex^d   L.   s.   d

        Rate — 13 — 14. 3

To Mr Mathias Nicoles Secretary at New Yorke this deliver

RESPECTED SIR—According to your order i have herein Sent you the valvation of our townes estate, in the paper inclosed, So with my Service to you I rest yovrs to comand Hempsted Sept: 7th 1675.

                        SIMON SARING

ENCLOSURE :—The totall Sume of our townds Esteats doth amount to : 11532–19–4 this yere deated at Hempsted this 28 day of Agust in the yere of our Lord 1675

              NATHANIELL PEARSALE Clar

Endorsed

    The Returne of ye valuacons from Hempsteed

      brought in Sept 9th 1675. Octo^r 25. past

              11532. 19. 4

    48–1–1

To the hon^ed Capt Nicoles at New Yorke

HON^RD S^R—We haue prent^d to your uew the hole esteate of our towne as it is giuen in to us the ualewation where of doe amount to 5700l the troopers with their horsis being includid which deduct if you please

Jemaica Sep^tr th 8 1675   By order of the Constable and

                        Ouerseer

                      BENIEMIN COE

Endorsed

    Jamaica Valuacons Brought in Sept 11th 1675.

      past Ocr 25 —   5700 —

            23–15–0 —

A LIST OFF THE ESTATE OF NEWTOWNE, SEPTᴿ 1675.

	Males	Vp land & Meadow	Horses	3 yer oulds	2 yer oulds	Yearlings	Oxen	Cowes.	3 yer oulds	2 yer oulds	Yer. Oulds	Shep	Swine
Jonathan Hazard	1	16	1	0	0	0	0	6	0	0	0	0	1
John ffarman	0	16	0	0	0	1	2	3	0	0	5	2	4
Gershom hazard	1	3	1	0	0	0	2	2	0	0	0	0	0
Samuell Gray	0	12	2	0	0	0	0	2	0	1	2	2	2
Jacob Reder	2	26	2	0	0	1	2	5	2	2	2	2	3
Lambert Woodward	1	8	1	0	0	0	2	3	0	2	2	6	7
Elaser Leaueridg	1	0	0	0	0	0	0	0	0	0	0	9	4
John Burrougs	2	40	1	0	0	0	4	4	0	0	4	24	6
Nath: Pettet	1	08	1	0	0	1	0	1	2	0	0	2	4
James Way	1	20	1	0	0	0	2	4	6	6	3	20	0
Jerimiʰ Burrouges	1	6	2	0	0	0	2	3	0	1	2	00	1
Joseph Reder	1	15	1	0	0	0	2	3	0	1	3	00	2
Calib Leueridg	2	29	1	0	0	0	2	4	0	2	1	14	1
Content titus	1	20	1	0	0	0	2	3	1	2	2	10	1
Dannell Blomf	1	30	1	0	0	0	4	4	2	2	1	4	3
Joseph Sackett	1	03	1	0	0	0	0	1	2	2	2	3	1
Isack Reeder	1	13	1	0	0	0	2	3	0	2	4	12	1
John Scudder	1	36	1	0	0	0	4	5	4	4	0	18	4
Robart Colwell	1	03	0	0	0	0	0	1	0	0	0	00	0
Richard Owen	1	14	1	0	0	0	2	5	0	0	0	4	3

Thomas Robarts	1	09	1	0	0	0	0	3	1	2	1	1	4
Tho: Morrell	1	09	0	0	0	0	0	0	2	0	0	0	0
James Way Junor	1	10	1	0	0	0	4	0	1	0	2	3	1
John Denman	1	12	1	1	1	0	0	1	0	0	0	0	2
abram ffrost	1	07	1	0	0	0	0	2	1	1	0	0	0
John alburtis	1	20	0	0	0	1	4	4	4	1	0	12	3
arthor alburtis	1	8	1	0	0	0	0	1	1	0	0	00	2
Thomas pettit	1	15	1	0	0	0	2	3	2	0	0	5	4
John Scudder Jur	1	12	1	0	0	1	2	4	4	1	1	5	4
Hendrick Jonson	1	03	1	0	0	0	0	0	3	1	0	0	1
John Reder	2	16	1	0	0	0	2	3	0	2	2	6	3
Theophi: phillips	4	6	1	0	0	0	2	2	0	0	0	2	6
John Ramsden	1	30	1	0	0	0	4	5	3	4	3	8	3
John Coe	1	22	2	0	0	0	2	4	0	1	0	6	9
Joseph phillips	1	12	1	0	1	0	0	3	1	0	1	2	1
Thom: Wandall	1	93	1	0	0	0	8	5	6	5	5	81	6
Georg Steauenson	1	45	2	0	0	1	4	6	4	3	3	10	
James Lawrason	1	10	1	0	0	0	2	1	2	0	0	11	00
Thomas Etherington	1	04	0	0	0	0	0	1	0	0	0	20	00
Nathan ffish		8	0	0	0	0	0	1	0	0	0	0	3
Nath: Baly	0	5	0	0	0	0	0	0	0	0	0	0	
John pettit	1	8	1	0	0	0	2	2	0	0	0	2	2
Georg Wood	1	20	0	0	0	0	2	2	1	0	2	10	0
Joshua hazard		9	1	0	0	0	0	0	0	3	0	0	0
Thomas Larence	3	40	2	0	0	0	4	8	4	2	5	00	14
John Kitcham		45	1	0	0	0	4	5	3	3	3	30	00
William Graues	0	16	1	0	0	1	0	2	2	3	0	10	5

A LIST, &c.—(CONTINUED.)

	Males	Vp Land & Meadow	Horses	3 yer oulds	2 yer oulds	Yerlings	Oxen	Cowes.	3 yer. oulds	2 yer. oulds	Yer. oulds.	Shep	Swine
harrik Sibartson..........	0	30	2	2	0	0	2	4	0	0	0	00	1
Sibart harrickson........	1	24	1	0	0	0	2	3	0	0	0	00	1
Hendrik Marteaceson.....	1	16	2	0	0	1	2	2	0	1	0	2	0
Cornelus Mateace........	1	10	0	0	0	0	2	4	0	0	2	0	0
John Smith	2	29	1	0	0	0	1	5	4	3	2	15	
Jeri: Reader............	1	14	1	0	0	0	0	1	0	0	1	02	1
Samuell Scudder	1	1	0	0	0	0	0	0	0	0	0	00	0
William Burtis..........	1	0	0	0	1	0	0	0	0	0	0	00	0
Thom: Case.............	1	20	1	0	0	0	2	4	0	0	2	20	3
John parsell	2	40	2	0	0	0	2	4	2	2	4	10	4
Johanes Lorus	1	10	0	0	0	0	0	1	1	4	1	0	1
John Woodstoncraft......	1	10	1	0	0	0	0	2	4	2			1
—— Buckhood	1	5	0	0	9	0	0	1	1	0	0	0	0
John Lorus.............	0	12	0	0	0	0	2	2	0	1	1	0	3
Lores Peterson.........	1	8	0	0	0	0	2	2	0	1	0	0	0
Gershom More.........	2	20	1	0	0	0	2	2	2	3	0	30	3
Joseph Redde	1	00	0	0	0	1	2	0	0	0	0	00	0
Edwa: Steuenson	0	30	0	0	0	0	2	4	0	0	1		
William hallit..........	1	25	4	0	0	3	2	5	2	2	0	14	3
Will: hallet Junor......	0	13	1	0	0	1	2	3	2	2	3	3	2

peter Roulsson	1	12	1	0	0	0	2	4	0	2	2	0	0
Tho: Riders bore	1	15	2	0	0	0	2	2	0	0	2	0	3
Jona: Strickland	1	15	1	0	0	1	2	4	1	2	2	4	2
John Copstafe	0	00	0	0	0	0	0	0	0	0	0	0	—
Josiah ffarman	2	15	1	0	0	0	2	4	0	0	2	4	—
Robart ffeelde	1	30	1	0	0	0	2	5	3	2	1	20	2
ffrances Hendrick	1	10	2	0	0	0	0	3	0	2	2	00	1
Tho: Steuenson	1	34	0	0	0	0	4	7	3	2	1	9	5
peter pangburn	1	00	0	0	0	0	0	0	0	0	0	0	0
Joseph burrougs	1	00	0	0	0	0	0	1	0	0	0	0	0
John Bull	1	4	0	0	0	0	0	0	1	0	0	0	0
Samuel More	0	14	1	0	0	0	2	3	0	2	1	5	3
John Graues	1	00	0	0	0	0	0	2	3	0	2	6	4
Richard ffidoe	1	18	1	1	0	0	0	3	0	1	1	3	3
Ralph Hunt	2	30	1	1	1	1	4	4	4	3	2	16	2

Newtowne Valuations brought in Sepr Beginning
Ex —— 1675.

Rate—26—6—8.

A VALLUATION FOR THE CONTRY PARTE OF BROOKHAVEN IN THE YERE OF OUR LORD GOD 1675.

parsons	Heads	Oxen	Cows	1 yere	2 yere	3 yere	Horses	1 yere	2 yere	3 yere	Swine	Meadow Lands	Sheepe	
Thomas ward	1	2	1	2	2	2	1				9	10		0-91- 0
John Thomas	1		1								4	4		0-31- 0
Nath Norten	1	2	2	2	2	2	1				4	11	4	0-84- 6-8
Saml Daiton	2	4	5	2		3	2				6	11		1-17- 0
Andr Miller	1	4	3	3		2	4	1			6	14		1-37-10
hen Rogers	3	3	5	3	1	2	1				8	18		1-55- 0
John Roe	1	4	4	4	2	3	2		2		5	7		1-12-10
Rich Ffloyd	1	4	4	2	1	2	3				16	28	15	1-63- 0
Thomas Thorp	1	4	3	4	1	2	1				3	11		0-99-10
Luk hawkens	1	4	3	1	1		2				5	8		0-98- 0
peter Whirtheare	1	3	3	1		2	1				2	10		0-83- 0
Rich Ffarr	2		2		1		1				2			0-42- 0
will Satterly	2	3	2	1	1	3	3				6	10	15	1-24- 0
John Tooker	1	6	7	3		5	1				18	20		1-89- 0
Sargent Bigs	1	4	2	2			3				2	12		1-02- 0
Robert Akerly	1	2	2		6							7		0-47- 0
Sam Akerly	2	0	3	4	1							3		0-42- 0
Mr longbothem	1	6	7	5	1	3	5			1	20	15		2-36-10
John Daves	1		1									3		0-28-10
Widow Smith	1	2	7	4		2	2				11	16		1-40-10

Name													£ s d
Robart Smith	1	2	2	2	1	3	1				5	4	0–54–10
Will Salyer	1		3				1					3	0–60– 0
Joseph Daves	1	2	3	1	1		1	2		2	2	4	0–72– 0
Abr Daiton	1	2	2				5			1	1	3	1–04– 0
Obed Seward	1	3	3			2	2					5	0–67–10
Thomas Bigs	1	4	3	3	2	5	1			5	5	5	1–20–10
John Bigs	1			4	2		2						0–39– 0
Tho Smith	1	2	3	2		1	2	1	1	7		6	0–85– 0
Rich Waring	1		2		1		2				4	3	0–49–10
John Jeners	3	3	4	1	1	1	5			5		13	1–70–10
John Tomson	2			1			2					6	0–66– 0

Octr 25t past 3065–16–8

£ s d

12–15–5¾

Endorsed. Seatalcotts Valuacón of the Estates, brought in the 22d Day of Sept. 75

ASSESSMENT ROLLS

Of the Five Dutch Towns [in King's County] Long Island;

PRIMO OCTOBER, ANNO

1676.

[Translated from the Dutch.]

ASSESSMENT ROLL OF MIDDELWOUT[1] MADE UP 20 SEPT[R] 1676.

£   s   d

No. 1. BAERTELT CLAESSEN
        1 poll 2 horses 1 ditto of 3 yrs 2
        cows 1 hog.................. £61.
        1 morgen of valley............. 2.
                                 £63

  2. GERRIT SNEDEGER
        1 poll 2 horses 2 do. of 3 yrs, 6
        cows 4 ditto of 2 year 3 do. of
        1 yr. 3 hogs .... £105.10.
        20 morg. land and valley........ 40.
                                 145 10

  3. AUWKE JANSE
        1 poll 4 horses, 4 cows 6 sheep.. £88.10.
        18 morg of land................ 36.
                                 124 10

  4. GERRIT LUBBERTSE
        1 poll 4 horses 5 cows 3 do. of 2
        yrs 4 hogs.................. £96.10
        20 morg. land and valley .... 40.
                                 136 10

1 Now, Flatbush.

5. REYN AERSEN
    1 poll 2 horses 4 cows 3 do. of 1
    year 66 10
6. STOFFEL JANSEN
    1 poll 4 horses.................   30
7. CORNELIS JANSEN ZEUW
    6 cows 4 do of 1 year............ £99
    valley 60
                        159
8. [Paper utterly destroyed.]
9. JAN BAERENTSEN
    1 poll 2 horses 2 cows 1 ditto of 1 yr
    1 hog 54 10
10. JAN COERTEN
    4 polls 4 cows 3 hogs   95
11. ARIE LAMBERTSE
    1 poll 4 horses 5 cows, 2 do of one
    year 4 hogs................. £103
    22 morg. land and valley......... 44
                        147
12. JAN JANSEN VAN DITMERSEN
    1 poll 4 horses 4 oxen 8 cows 2 do.
    of 2 yrs 3 do. of 1 yr.......... £139.10
    30 morg. land and valley......... 60.
                        199 10
13. HANS CRISTOFFEL
    1 poll 2 horses 5 cows 2 do of 1 yr
    3 hogs.....................   73
14. ARIE RYERSE
    1 poll 2 horses 3 do of 1 yr 5 cows
    1 do of 3 yrs 2 do of 2 yrs 2 do of
    1 yr 2 hogs................. £90
    20 morg. land.................. 40
                        130
15. AERS JANSEN
    1 poll 3   cows 2 do 3 yr 3 do
    of 2 yr   of 1 yr 1 hog........ £88.10
    20 morg. land & valley........... 40
                        128 10

16. JAN JANSEN
    1 poll 2 oxen 2 cows £45
    7 morg. land & valley.......... 14
                                           59

17 PIETER LOOTT
    2 polls 2 horses 10 cows 2 do. of 2
      y^r 2 do of 1 y^r 2 hogs........ £120.
    16 morg. land & valley... .... 32.
                                           152

18 JAN STREYCKER
    3 polls 4 horses 2   2 horses....
    – cows, 3 d^o of 3 year, 4 d^o of 1 yr 1 hog £196
    30 morg. of land & valley 60
                                           256

19. HENDRICK STREYCKER
    1 poll, 2 horses 1 sheep £43.14
    12 morg of land and valley .... 24.
                                           67 14

20 WILLEM GUILLIAMSEN
    1 poll 2 horses 2 oxen 7 cows, 2 d^o of
    3 yrs. 2 do of 2 yrs. 2 hogs .... £104.
    19 morg land & valley .... 38.
                                           142

21 HENDRICK CORN: SLECHT
    1 poll 2 Cows 1 hog.............. [MS. destroyed.]
    3 morg land.....................

22 HARMEN KEY
                horses.............. [MS. destroyed.]

23 JACOB HENDRICKS
    1 poll, 4 horses 3 cows...........
    2 d^o of 1 yr. 1 hog .... [MS. destroyed.]
    20 morg land & valley 40
                                           1

24 STOFFEL PROBASKY
    1 poll 2 horses 1 d^o of 2 yr 5 cows..
    1 d^o of 2 yr. 2 d^o of 1 yr £78
    12 morg. land & valley 24
                                           102

25 Corn: Jansen Berry
    1 poll 4 horses 1 ditto of 1 yʳ 8 cows
    2 dᵒ of 2 yʳ 3 do of 1 yʳ 2 sheep... £119.7
    23 morg. land & valley............ 46
                               ———— 165 7

26. Lambert Jansen
    1 poll........................... 18

27 Ruth Albertse
    1 poll........................... 18

28 Seymen Hansen
    1 poll 4 horses 3 cows 2 dᵒ of 3 yr..
    3 dᵒ of 2 yʳ 1 dᵒ of 1 yʳ 1 hog..... £99
    14 morg. of land & valey 28
                               ——— 127

29 Claes Willems
    1 poll........................... 18

30 Willem Jacobsen
    2 polls 2 horses, 1 dᵒ of 3 yrs 1 dᵒ of 2 yrs
    2 oxen 7 cows 2 dᵒ of dᵒ of yʳ 6 hogs £137
    24 morg. of land................. 48
                                ——— 185

31 Hendrick Willemsen
    1 poll 2 horses 5 cows. £67
    20 morg. land 40
                                ——— 107

32 Jan Harmense
    1 poll........................... 18

33 Arie Hendrickse
    1 poll   [Remʳ destroyed.] 43

34. Gysbert Jansen
    1 poll........................... 18

35. Jobecq Jansen van de Bildtt
    1 poll........................... 18

36 Floores Croom
    1 poll 2 horses 3 cows 1 dᵒ of 2 yrs
    1 dᵒ of 1 yr. 1 hog............... £62
    16 morg. land & valley........... 32
                                ——— 94

37. DIRECK JANSEN HOGLANT
    1 poll 3 horses 1 d° of 1 y^r 6 cows
    1 hog.......................... £89
    13 morg. land & valley 26
                                              ̈115

38 CORN^s SEBRINGH
    1 poll   horses 1 do of 4 yr. 3 cows 3 d°
                2 d° of 1 yr...........
            land & valley........... [MS. destroyed.]
39   JANSEN
    1 poll......................... 18
40 MINNE JOHANNES
    3 polls 1 horse 1 cow............. £71
    16 morg. land & valley 32
                                              103

41 CATERINNE HEGEMANS
    3 polls 4 horses 1 d° of 1 y^r 4 oxen
    11 cows 4 d° of 3 y^r 2 d° of 2 y^r
    4 d° of 1 y^r..................
    4 hogs......................... £215
    36 morgen land & valley 72
                                              287

42 CORNELIS BAERENTSE
    1 poll 4 horses 1 d° of 2 y^{rs} 7 cows
    3 d° of 3 yrs 3 do of 2 yrs 2 do of
    1 y^r 1 hog.................... £129.10
    18 morg. of land & valley.......... 36
                                         ——— 165 10

43 DIERCK JANSEN VAN DER VLIETT
    1 poll 3 horses 5 cows 3 d° of 2 yrs.
    2 d° of 1 yr.................... £89.10
    14 morg. land & valley 28
                                         ——— 117 10

44 ELDERT LUYKERSE
    1 poll 4 horses 4 cows   hog....... £87
    16 morg. land & valley 32
                                              119

45. LEFFERIT PIETERSE
    1 poll 2 horses   cows 1 dᵒ of 3 yʳ..
    4 do. of 2 yʳ   dᵒ of 1 yʳ. .... £70.
    17 morg. land & valley 34
                                104

46 TITUS STRIX
    1 poll 1 horse 2 do. of 2 yʳ 4 cows..
    6 do. of 3 yr. 3 do of 2 yʳ 5 do of
    1 yr 4 hogs £103
    25 morg. of land & valley.......... 50
                                153

47 PIETER GUILLIAMSEN
    1 poll 6 oxen 5 cows 2 do. of 2 yr.
    3 hogs...................... £87
    19 morg. land & valley............ 36
                                123

The whole Property of Midwout amounts to   £4872 11

Taxed @ 1d. in the pound Sterlg
  should amount to 20 pound 6 shgˢ.
               Your obedient Servant

                       MICHIL HAINELLE.

ASSESSMENT ROLL OF BREUCKELEN MADE UP SEPTEMBᴿ 1676.

1 CLAES AERENSE
    3 polls 1 horse 5 cows   2 of 2
    yʳˢ 2 do. of 1 yr. £96.10
    14 morg. land & vally............ 28
                            124 10

2 JAN DE SWEDE
    1 poll 1 horse 1 do of 1 yʳ 4 cows
    1 do. of 1 yʳ 1 hog £55.10
    2 morg. land 4
                         59 10

3 BAERENT HEGBERTSE
    1 poll   1 cow............. £62.
    3 morg. land .... 6.
                       68

4 Joost Fransen
    1 poll 2 horses 1 do of 1 y^r 5 cows
    1 do of 2 y^r 3 do of 1 y^r 2 hogs   £79.
    19 morg. land & valley...........   38.
                                 —— 117

5 Andries Juriaense
    1 poll 2 horses 2 do of 3 y^r 8 cows
    1 do of 2 year 2 do of 1 y^r.... £103.10
    28 morg. land & valley...........   56.
                                   —— 159 10

6 Lambert Jansen Dortlant
    1 poll 3 cows..................   £33
    8 morg. land & valley..........   16
                                   —— 49

7   Hendrickse
    1 poll.......................   18
8 [MS destroyed.]
9 Wouter Geisse[?]
    1 poll.......................   18
10 Seimen Aersen
    1 poll 2 oxen 4 cows 1 do of 2 y^r
    1 hog £56
    8 morg. of land & valley........   16
                                   —— 72

11 Jean Piettersen Mackenzie [?]
    1 poll 4 cows..................   £38
    8 morg. land..................   16
                                   —— 54

12 Jean Frederickse
    1 poll 2 horses 2 cows..........   £52
    7 morg land...................   14
                                   —— 66

13 Johannes Christoffel
    1 poll 2 oxen 2 cows do of 2 y^{rs}... £42.10
    7 morg. land   14
                                   —— 56 10

14 Mr Paulus van der Beeck
    2 poll 3 horses 4 cows 2 do of 2 yrs
    2 do of 1 yr.................   £100.
    20 morg. land & valley..........   40
                                   —— 140

15 THEUNES GISBERTTSE [BOGAERT]
    3 poll 4 horses 1 do of 2 yrs 5 oxen
    .. Cows 5 do of 3 yrs 10 do of 2
    yrs 8 do of 1 yr 9 hogs........ £251.
    40 morg. land & valley........... 80.
                             ————— 331

16 SEIMEN CLAES
    1 poll 1 horse .. Cows 1 do of 2
    yrs 2 do of 1 yr 1 hog........ £46. 10
    7 morg. land & valley.......... 14
                             ————— 60 10

17 JUFFROUW POTTERS
    1 horse 1 do of 3 yrs. 4 cows 1 do
    of 2 yrs 3 hogs 45

18 JEAN AERSEN
    1 poll 3 horses 2 Cows 1 do of 3 yr
    2 do of 2 yr 1 do of 1 yr........ £74.10.
    18 morg. land & valley 36
                             ————— 110 10

19 THOMAS JANSEN VAN D[UYN?]
    1 poll 2 horses 3 cows £57
    1 morg. land................. 2
                             ————— 59

20 ACHEYS JANSEN VAN DEICK
    1 poll 2 oxen 2 cows 1 do of 1 yr £41.10
    1 morg. land 2
                             ————— 43 10

21 DIERCK HATTUM
    1 poll 2 oxen 2 cows do of 3 yrs 1
    do of 2 yrs................. £50.10
    1 morg. land................. 4
                             ————— 54 10

22 JURIAN BLANCKE
    2 horses 1 cow 2 do of 1 yr...... £32
    6 morg. of land.............. 12
                             ————— 44

23 DANIEL DE RAPPALLIE
    1 poll 1 hors cows .... [Valuation destroyed.]

24 JERM. DE RAPPALLIE
     2 polls 2 horses   cows ....
     8 morg of land ....   [Val: destroyed.]

25 PIETER JANSEN
     1 poll, 2 horses 2 oxen 6 cows 4 of
       2 yrs 3 do. of 1 yr...........   £98.10.
     25 morg. land & valley   50
                                     ——— 148 10

26 JAN JANSEN
     1 poll 2 oxen .. Cows 1 do of 2 yrs
       3 do of 1 yr ....   £45.10.
     2 morg. of land...............   4
                                     ——— 49 10

27 HENDRICK CORSEN
     1 poll 3 horses 2 cows 1 do of 2 yrs   £66.10
     12 morg. land & valley..........   24
                                     ——— 90 10

28 PIETTER CORSEN
     1 poll......................   18
29 CASPER CORNELISE
     1 poll......................   18
30 WILLEM WILLEMSE BENNETT
     1 poll 2 horses 2 do of 1 yr 2 oxen
       5 cows 4 do of 2 yr. 3 do of 1 yr   £99.10
     13½ morg land and valley.........   27 —
                                     ——— 126 10

31 RHEM JANSEN
     3 poll 4 horses .. cows 5 do of 3 yrs
       2 do of 2 yrs   do of 1 yr 2 hogs £184.10
     19 morg. land & valley   38
                                     ——— 222 10

32 TIERCK STOORM
     1 poll 1 horse.................   £30.
     11 morg. land & valley..........   22.
                                     ——— 52

33 MAERTE RYERSE
     1 poll 4 horses 8 cows   of 2 yrs 3
       of 1 yr 2 hogs...............   £117.10
     31½ morg. land & valley...........   63
                                     ——— 180 10

34 ABRENT ISAACK
    1 poll   18
35 SUSANNE DUBELS
    2 oxen 6 cows 3 d⁰ of 2 yrs 3 d⁰ of
      1 yʳ......................   £62.10
    18 morg. land ....   36 —
                             ———— 98 10
36 THEUNIS JANSEN
    3 poll 3 horses   do. of 2 yr. 2 oxen
    4 cows 4 do of 3 yr 4 do of 1 yʳ 2 hogs £151
    23 morg. land & valley 46
                             ———— 197
37 JAN HANSEN
    1 poll 2 horses 4 cows 1 do of 3 yʳ..
    1 do. of 2 yʳ 1 hog..............£69.10
    18 morg. land & valley .... 36.
                            ———— 105 10
38 DIERCK PAULUSE
    1 poll 2 horses 4 cows 4 do of 2 yrs
    3 do. of 1 yʳ...................£76.10
    12 morg. land & valley .... 24.
                            ———— 100 1ᴸ
39 THOMAS LAMBERTSE
    1 poll 2 horses 1 do of 3 yʳ 4 oxen 8 cows
        year 2 do. of 1 yʳ 4 sheep...
      [MS. destroyed.] 147.4
    23 morg. land & valley............ 46
                            ———— 193 4
40 [Name destroyed.]
    1 poll 1 horse of 1 yʳ 1 ox 4 cows 1
      do of 2 yrs .. sheep............£51
    15 morg. land & valley 30
                          ———— 81
41 PAULUS DIERCKSE
    2 polls 2 horses 2 oxen 5 cows.....
    2 do. of 3 yrs 5 do. of 2 yrs 3 do. of
      1 yr. 5 hogs.................£127
    12 morg. land & valley......... .. 24
                          ———— 151

42 JEAN GERRITTSE
    1 poll 2 horses 2 cows 2 do of 3 yrs
    2 do. of 2 yrs 2 do. of 1 yr 2 sheep,
    1 hog...................... £70.
    11½ morg. land & valley 23
                                   ——   93

43 BOURGON BROUCHAERT
    1 poll 2 cows ....₃ £28
    11½ morg. land & valley 23
                                   ——   51

44 ADAM BROUWER
    1 poll 3 cows 4 sheep & 1½ morg.
    valley......................... 37 14

45 WILLEM BROUWER
    1 poll 18

46 JABECQ BROUWER
    1 poll........................ 18

47 CONRADUS VANDER
    1 poll 2 oxen 2 cows 1 do. of 1 year £43
    14 morg. of land.................. 28
                                   ——   71

48 Captⁿ CORNELIS
    1 poll 3 horses   cows 2 do of 3 yrs
    1 do. of 2 yrs   do. of 1 yʳ £84
    22 morg. of land and valley........ 44
                                   ——   28

49 WEYNANT PIETTERSE
    1 poll 2 horses 3 cows............ £57
    5 morg. land................... 10
                                   ——   67

50 PAULUS MICHILSE VANDER VOORT
    1 poll 2 oxen 3 cows 1 do. of 2 yrs
    1 do. of 1 yʳ.................... £49
    12 morg. land & valley 24
                                   ——   73

51 PIETTER VAN NEST
    3 poll 4 cows 1 do. of   yr.   hog.. £80
    5½ morg. land & valley 11
                                   ——   91

52 MICHIL HANSEN
    1 poll: 2 horses 5 cows 1 do. of 3 yrs
      2 do. of 1 y^r.................. £74
    20 morg. land & valley........... 40
                                     —— 114

53 HENDRICK THEUNESE
    1 poll 1 horse 2 cows 1 do. of 2 yrs £42.10
    4 morg. land.................... 8
                                     —— 50 10

54 JORES JACOBSE
    3 polls 4 horses 3 do. of 2 y^r 2 oxen
    3 cows 2 do. of 3 y^r 4 do of 2 yr
      do. of 1 yr. 2 hogs 3 sheep..... £–6
    30 morg. land.................... 60
                                   ——

55 DIERCK CORNELISSE
    1 poll 2 horses 3 cows........... [MS. destroyed.]
    15 morg. land ....

56 JAN CORNELISE BUIS
    1 poll 2 horses 3 cows 1 do. of
    2 hogs 12 sheep.................. [MS. destroyed.]
    8 morg. land & valley............

57 GERRIT CROES
    1 poll 2 oxen   cows 3 do. of 3 y^r..
    2 do. of 2 y^r 3 do. of 1 y^r........ £76.10
    14 morgen land & valley.......... 28.
                                    —— 94 10

The whole Property of Breuckelen amounts to   £5067 18

    Taxed at 1^d in the pound stg
    should amount to £21.2.4d

                Your obedient servant
                     MICHIL HAINELLE

ASSESSMENT ROLL OF BOSWYCK MADE UP 23 SEPTEMB. 1676.

1 GISBERT THEUNISSE
  2 polls 3 horses 2 do of   yrs 5 cows
    2 do of 3 yrs 4 do of 2 yrs   do
    of 1 yr 1 hog 8 sheep £138.8
  22 morg. land & valley...........   44
                                     ———   182 8

2 WOUTER GISBERTTSE
  1 poll 3 horses 8 cows 2 do of 3 yrs
    4 do of 1 y^r 4 sheep..........   £109.14
  18 morg. land & valley..........   36
                                     ———   145 14

3 VOLKERT DIERCKSE
  2 polls 3 horses 1 do of 2 yrs. 8
    cows 2 do of 3 yrs 3 do of 2 yrs
    4 do of 1 yr 8 sheep 2 hogs....   £143.18
  25 morg. land & valley...........   50
                                     ———   193 18

4 CHARLES HOUSMAN
  1 poll 2 horses 6 cows 2 do of 1 yr
    2 sheep.....................   £75.18
  11 morg. land & valley..........   22
                                     ———   97 18

5 CORNELIS JANSEN
  1 poll 2 cows 1 do of 3 yrs 1 sheep   £32.8
  4 morg. land   8
                                     ———   40

6 PIETTER JANSEN
  1 poll 2 horses 1 cow............   47

7 CLAES CORNELISE
  1 poll & 5 morg. land...........   28

8   DE LA FORGE
  1 poll 1 horse 2 cows   40

9 [MS. destroyed.]

10 [Name illegible.]
  1 poll 1 horse 4 oxen 11 cows 4 do
    of 3 yrs 1 do of 2 yrs 3 do of 1
    y^r 4 hogs £136
  40 morg. land & valley...........   80
                                     ———   216

11 ALBERT HENDRICKSE
 1 poll.... 18
12 JAN CAERLESE
 1 poll........................ 18
13 AMADOR FOUPIER
 1 poll........................ 18
14 JAN CORNELISE ZEUW
 1 poll 2 horses 2 cows 5 sheep.... 54.2
 17 morg. land & valley 34
           88 2
15 EVERTT HEDEMAN
 1 poll 2 oxen 2 cows 7 sheep 3 hogs 46
 13½ morg. land & valley......... 27
           73
16 JAN KOROM
 1 poll 2 horses 1 do of 1 yr 3 cows
  1 do of 1 yr 2 hogs 2 sheep.... £64.8
 3 morg land................... 6
           70 8
17 ALEXANDER COQUER
 1 poll 1 hog 2 sheep............ £19.18
 2 morg. land................. 4
           23 18
18 JAN LESQUIER
 2 polls 2 horses 5 cows 2 do of 3
  yrs 1 do of 1 yr 1 sheep £103
 28 morg. land................. 56
           159
19 Capt. PIETTER JANSEN WITT
 3 polls 4 horses 2 do of 2 yrs 1 do
  of 1 yrs 9 cows 4 do of 3 yrs 2
  do of 2 yrs 7 do of 1 yr 18 sheep
  7 hogs...................... £206. 3
 50 morg. Land & Valley.......... 100
          306 3
20 JABECQ DIERCKSE
 1 poll 2 horses 1 do of 1 yr 2 sheep £45.18
 10 morg. land.................. 20.
           65 18

21 PIETTER SCHAMP
 1 poll 3 cows 1 do of 1 y^r £34.10
 9 morgen of land .... 18.
           52 10

22 JOOST COECKWYTT
 1 poll 2 horses 7 cows 2 do of 2 yrs
  1 do of 1 yr. 7 sheep 1 hog.... £90.10
 15 morg. of land & Valley .... 30.
          120 10

23 SEIMEN HAECKX
 1 poll 18

24 METTIE JANSEN
 2 cows 1 ditto of 2 yrs 3 sheep 2
  hogs .... [MS. destroyed]

25 JAN JANSEN
 2 polls 1 horse 2 cows ....

26 HENDRICK BAERENTSE
 1 poll 3 horses, 3 ditto of 3 year 5
  cows, 2 do of 3 yr. 4 do of 1 y^r
  5 sheep 3 hogs.............. £141
 20 morg. land & valley 40
          181

27 JAN CORNELIS DAMEN
 1 poll 3 horses 1 do of 1 year 6
  cows 1 do of 3 yr 3 do of 2 y^r 4
  do of 1 y^r 16 sheep 3 hogs...... £113. 3
 28 morg. land & valley 56
          169 3

28 JAN ARIAENSE
 1 poll 3 cows 1 do of 1 y^r 4 sheep £37. 4
 3 morg. land................ 6
          43 4

29 CORNELIS HARMENSE VOGEL
 2 polls 3 sheep 37 5

30 PIETTER PARMENTIE
 2 polls 3 horses 2 oxen 5 cows 2 do
  of 3 yer 2 do of 2 y^r 3 do of 1 y^r
  4 hogs £130.10
 20 morg. Land & Valley......... 40
          170 10

31 JACOB LAROILLE
    1 poll 2 horses   [MS. destroyed]

32 PHILIP BERCKELO
    1 poll........................   18

33 MATTHEIS JANSEN
    1 poll.........................   18

34 THEUNIS GISBERTTSE BOGAERT
    8 morgen Valley...............   16

35 OUFIE CLEY
    2 polls 2 horses 6 cows 3 ditto of 2
    y^r 3 ditto of 1 y^r............. £102
    12 morg. Land & Valley.......... 24
                                                   126

The assessment roll of Boswyck amounts to.. £2960 14
    Rated at 1d. in the pound Stg
        should amount to £12.6.9d.
                Your obt Servant
                        MICHIL HAINELLE.

ASSESMENT ROLL OF NEW UTRECHT MADE UP 29 SEPT^R
1676.

1 HANS HARMENSE
    1 poll 3 horses 4 cows   of 3 y^{rs} 4
    do of 2 yrs 2 do of 1 yr....... £97.2
    24 morgen land................. 48
                                            145 2

2 JAN VAN DEUENTER
    2 polls 1 horse of 2 yrs 3 cows 1
    do of 3 yrs 1 do of 2 yrs...... £62.10
    12 morg. land.................. 24
                                          86.10

3 JAN VERCKERCKE
    3 polls 6 horses 2 do of 2 yrs 4 cows
    20 sheep.................... £164.10
    95 morg. land & valley.......... 192
                                        356 10

4 GISBERTT THEYSE
   1 poll 2 horses 1 cow 1 ditto of 2
     yrs 1 ditto of 1 year.......... £51
   18 morg land 36
                             ——— 87

5 HENDRICK MATHEISE
   1 poll 4 horses 3 cows 3 do of 3 yrs
     3 do of 2 yrs 3 do of 1 year ... £105
   30 morg. land.................. 60
                             ——— 165

6 LAURENS JANSEN
   1 poll 2 horses 2 cows.......... £52
   12 morg. land.................. 24
                             ——— 76

7   JOOSTEN
   1 poll 3 horses 6 cows.......... £84
   20 morg. land.................. 40
                             ——— 124

8 [MS. destroyed.]
                6 cows........ £104
   20 morg. land.................. 40
                             ——— 144

9   RHEIN
   1 poll   horses 3 do of 2 yrs 2 do
     of 1 yr £46
   20 morg. land.................. 40
                             ——— 86

10 JAN JANSEN VAN DEYCK
•   1 poll 2 horses 2 cows of 3 yrs 1 do
     of 2 yrs £52.10
   16 morg. land.................. 32
                             ——— 84 10

11 CAREL JANSEN VAN DEYCK
   1 poll 2 horses 3 cows.......... £57
   24 morg. land.................. 48
                             ——— 105

12 RUTGER JOOSTEN
   2 polls 4 horses 6 cows 2 oxen 2
   ditto of 3 yrs 3 do of 2 yrs 4 do
     of 1 yr 12 sheep............. £152.12
   100 morgen land................ 200
                           ——— 352 12

13 Jean Clement
    1 poll 1 horse 2 cows 1 do of 3 yrs
    1 do of 2 yrs 46 10
14 Jacob Bastiansen
    1 poll 1 cow   23
15 Theys Jansen
    1 poll 1 horse 2 oxen   cows 1 ditto
    of 3 yrs 1 hog ....   £80.
    15 morg. land..................   30
                                     ———— 110
16 Theys Lubbertse
    1 poll 2 horses   cows of 2 yrs...   £44.10
    12 morg. land..................   24
                                      ———— 68 10
17 Jean Van
    1 poll 2 horses 4 cows 4 ditto of 2 yrs   £72
    40 morg. land..................   80
                                      ———— 152
18 Crein Jansen
    2 polls 2 horses and 1 do of 2 yrs..   £65
    24 morg. land..................   48
                                      ———— 113
19 Arie Willemse
    1 poll 3 horses 5 cows, 2 do of 2
    year, 3 do of 1 year..........   £88.10.
    24 morg. land..................   48
                                      ———— 136 10
20 Pietter Jacobse
    1 poll 2 cows..................   28
21 Theunis Jansen Van Peltt
    2 polls 3 horses 5 cows 1 do of 1
    year 4 Sheep................   £100. 4
    24 morg. land   48
                                      ———— 148 4
22 Huibert Stoock
    1 poll......................   18

23 LUYCKES MOYERSE
    1 poll 3 horses 5 cows 1 dᵒ of 3 yrs
      2 dᵒ of 1 yr .... £74.
    20 morg. of land   40
                    ———— 114

24 ANTHONY VANDER EYCKE
    1 poll 2 horses 3 cows ....
    12 morg. land .... [MS. destroyed]
25 JORES BOURIER
    1 poll 2 cows 2 oxen ....
    12 morg. land...................
26 ZEGERTT GERRITTSE
    1 poll.......................   18
27 HENDRICK JANSEN VAN DEYCK
    1 poll.......................   18
28 JEAN MUSEROL
    1 poll 2 oxen 4 cows............ £50
    12 morg. land.................   24
                    ———— 74
      assessment roll

The Property of N. Utrecht amounts to... £3024 18
      Rated @ 1d per pound Stg
          should amount to £12.12.1d.
               Your obt Servant
                  MICHIL HAINELLE

VALUATION OF AMSFORTT[1] MADE UP SEPTEMBR 1676.

1 CLAES PIETTERSE
    1 poll 2 horses 1 do of yrs 6 cows £75.
    7 morg. land.................   14
                    ———— 89

2 GILLES JANSEN
    3 polls 3 horses 2 oxen cows.... £105
    10 morgen land & valley   20
                    ———— 125

1 Now, Flatlands.

3 GERRITT REINERSE
   2 polls 4 horses 7 cows 2 ditto of
     1 yr 1 hog.................. £125.
   23 morg. land & valley.......... 46
                           ——— 171

4 WM VAN BERCKELO
   1 poll 2 horses 1 cow............ 47

5 DIERCKIE WILLEMSE
   1 horse 2 cows 1 do of 2 yrs 4 morg
     land...................... 32 10

6 WILLEM WILLEMSE
   1 poll 2 horses 4 cows 1 do of 3 yrs
     1 ditto of 1 year............. £67.10
   11 morg. land & valley.......... 22 —
                           ——— 89 10

7 HANS JANSEN
   1 poll 2 oxen 5 cows 1 ditto of 2 yrs £57.10
   17 morg. land & valley.......... 34
                           ——— 91 10

8 ALBERT ALBERTSE
   2 polls 4 horses 1 do of 1 y^r 7 cows
     do of 2 yr. 2 hogs............ £129.
   29 morg. land & valley.......... 58
                           ——— 187

9 STEUENSE
   1 poll   horses 1 ditto of 2 yrs
     4 cows   ditto of 1 yr....... £84.10
   20 morg. land & valley.......... 40
                          ——— 124 10

10 [Name destroyed]
   1 poll 1 horse 1 cow............ 47

11 ALBERT ALBERTSE the younger
   1 poll 1 horse 3 cows............ 45

12 DIERCK JANSEN
   1 poll 1 horse 3 cows............. 45

13 PIETTER CLAESSEN
   2 polls 5 horses 13 cows 3 do of 3
     yrs 2 oxen 2 sheep £186.5
   59 morg. & valley.............. 118
                        ——— 304 5

14 LAURENS CORNELISE
    1 poll 1 horse....................   30

15 FERNANDES VAN CICKEL
    1 poll 2 horses 2 cows   52

16 JAN BROUWER
    1 poll 2 horses 4 cows 3 hogs   65

17 ABRAHAM JOORESE
    1 poll 2 horses 1 do of 2 yrs 14
    cows 2 do of 3 yrs 4 do of 2 yrs
    4 do of 1 yr.................. £141
    35 morg. land & valley.......... 70
                                  ——   211

18 ROELOFF MAERTENSE
    2 polls 4 horses 1 do of   yrs 10
    cows 2 do of 2 yrs 4 ditto of 1
    yr 3 hogs................... £152.14
    52 morg. land & valley 104
                                  —— 256 14

19 STEUEN COERTTEN
    2 polls 4 horses   cows 5 ditto of 2
    yrs £129
    55 morg. land 110
                                  ——   239

20 JAN KIERSEN
    2 polls 2 horses   cows 2 do of 1
    year £103
    31 morg. land & valley.......... 62
                                  ——   165

21 WILLEM GERRITTSE
    1 poll 4 horses 2 do of 1 yr 1 ox,
    7 cows 3 do of 3 yr 2 do of 2 yr
    1 do of 1 year............... £131.10
    28 morg. land & valley.......... 56
                                  —— 187 10

22 PIETTER MONFORTT
    1 poll 1 horse 2 cows............   40

23 JAN MONFORTT
    1 poll.......................   18

24 ARIAEN PIETTERSE
    1 poll, 2 horses 2 cows.......... £52
    8 morg. land and valley......... 16
                                  —— 68

25 PIETTER HENDRICKSE
    1 poll, 1 horse................. 30

26 SEIMAN JANSEN
    2 polls, 4 horses 8 cows, 3 do of 3
      yrs 1 do of 2 yrs 2 do of 1 yr 4
      sheep 1 hog................. £144.4
    32 morg. of land & valley 64
                                    —— 208 4

27. PIETER CORNELISE
    2 polls, 5 horses 1 do of 3 yrs   cows
    2 do of 3 yrs. 3 do of 2 yrs   do of
    1 yr. 4 hogs...................
    24 morg. land & valley............ [MS. destroyed.]

28 SWAEN JANSEN
    1 poll, 2 horses 1 cow 2 hogs...... £49
    5 morg. land & valley 10
                                    —— 59

29 HENDRICK PIETERSE
    1 poll 3 horses 2 oxen 5 cows 1 do.
      of 1 yr. 1 hog........ .... £93.10
    19 morg. land & valley 38
                                  ——— 131 10

30 COERTT STEUENSE
    1 poll 4 horses 1 do. of 2 yrs 2 oxen
    6 cows 4 do. of 2 yrs 4 do. of 1 yr.. £127.
    44 morgens land & valley.......... 88
                                    —— 215

31 JACOB & GERRITT STREYCKER
    3 polls 2 horses 7 cows 2 hogs £115
    1½ morg. land.................. 3
                                    —— 118

32 JAN MARTENSE
    1 poll 3 horses 1 do. of 2 yrs 1 do.
    of 2 yrs 2 do of 1 yr. 3 cows 2 do
    of 1 yr...................... £83
    10 morg. land & valley 30
                              103

33 WILLEM HULETT
    1 poll 1 horse 2 cows 40

34 WILLEM
    1 poll 2 horses 1 do of   yrs 5 cows
    2 do of 1 yr. 2 hogs............ £77
    12 morg. land & valley............ 24
                              101

The Whole Valuation of Amsfortt amounts to   £3966 13

PROPERTY RATE.

The property is rated as follows
    Each Poll   @   .... £18.
    Each horse over 4 yrs old .... 12.
            between 3 & 4 yrs .... 8.
            between 2 & 3 yrs........... 5.
            between 1 & 2 yrs .... 3.
    Each Ox above 4 yrs old.............. 6.
    Each Cow above 4 yrs old .... 5.
            between 3 & 4 yrs old......... 4.
            between 2 & 3 yrs old......... 2.10
            between 1 & 2 yrs old 1.10
    Each hog above a year old.............. 1.
    Each sheep above a year old 8.6
    Each morgen of land.................. 2.

The property above mentioned of 3966 pounds 13 shillings
@ 1d per pound Stg should amount to 16 pounds 10 sh 6½ pence.
Your Ob^t Servant
MICHIL HAINELLE

RATE BILLS OF THE FIVE DUTCH TOWNS; 1ST OCTOBER 1676.

£4872.11	Rate Bill of Middelwout	£20. 6.-
5067.18	Rate Bill of Breukelen	21. 2.4
2960.14	Rate Bill of Boswyck	12. 6.9
3024.18	Rate Bill of N. Utrecht	12.12.1
3966.13	Rate Bill of Amsfort	16.10.6½

£19892.14   Assessment of the 5 Towns @ 1d per pound £82.17.8½

RATE LIST OF BUSHWYCK, 8 SEPTᴿ Aᴼ 1683.

Constable Wouter Ghysberts Verscheur;
1 poll, 4 horses 2 of 2 yrs, 8 cows, 5 of 3
yrs, 1 of 2 yrs 3 of 1 yr. 1 hog ...... £114.
22 morgens of land & valley 44
        ——— £188.-

Jacob Jansen; 2 polls, 2 horses, 1 of 3 yrs,
5 cows, 4 of 3 yrs. 2 of 2 yrs, 2 of 1
yr. 1 hog £118
18 morg. of land 36
        —— 154 -

Pieter Jansen Meet; 1 poll 18.-
Albert Hendrickzen; 1 poll, 1 horse 30.-
Joost Kockuyt; 1 poll, 2 horses, 8 cows 3 of
3 yrs 4 of 2 yrs, 3 of 1 yr. 9 sheep ... £112.6.6
22 morgens of land & valley 44.-.-
        —— 156.6.6

Charel Fonteyn; 2 polls, 2 horses, 1 of 3 yrs,
1 of 2 yrs, 15 cows, 2 of 3 yrs, 4 of 2
yrs, 4 of 1 yr. 7 sheep, 1 hog £175.-.-
61 morgens of land and valley 122.-.-
        —— 297.-.-

Pieter Jansen Wit; 2 polls, 7 horses, 1 of 3
yrs, 1 of 2 yrs, 2 oxen 12 cows, 3 of 3 yrs
3 of 2 yrs 7 of 1 yr. 15 sheep, 2 hogs.. £243.7.6
50 morgens of land & valley 100.-.-
        —— 343.7.6

1 So in orig. Ought to be £154.

Jacques Cossart ; 1 poll, 2 horses, 1 of 2 yrs,
    5 cows, 1 of 2 yrs, 2 of 1 yr. 1 hog ..   £78.-.-
    18 morgens of land.................   36
                                    ————— 114.-.-

Pieter Jans Loy ; 1 poll, 1 horse, 2 of 2 yrs,
    1 cow, 1 of 1 yr..................   46.10.-
Onvre Klay ; 1 poll, 1 horse, 5 cows, 2 of 2
    yrs £60.-.-
    18 morgens of land & valley 36.-.-
                                    ————— 96.—.-

Claes Cornelis Kat ; 1 poll, 1 horse, 1 of 1
    yr. 1 cow, 2 of 3 yrs, 2 of 2 yrs......   £51.-.-
    13 morgens of land..................   26.-.-
                                    ————— 77.—.-

Jan Cornelis Zeeu ; 1 poll, 2 cows   28
Cornelis Jansen Loy ; 1 poll, 3 horses, 5
    cows, 2 of 2 yrs. 2 of 1 yr. 3 sheep ..   £88.5.6
    10½ morgens of land & valley.........   21.
                                    ————— 109. 5.6

Adriaen Laforse ; 1 poll, 2 horses, 3 cows, 1
    of 3 yrs. 2 of 1 yr. 1 hog, 3 sheep ...   £68.5.6
    8½ morgens of land & valley 17.-.-
                                    ————— 85. 5.6

Jacob Dirckx ; 1 poll, 1 horse, 7 morgens of
    land.............................   44.—.
Symon Haecx ; 1 poll..................   18.—
Joost Dury ; 1 poll, 2 horses, 1 of 2 yrs, 5
    cows, 1 of 3 yrs 2 of 2 yrs 2 of 1 yr..   £84.-.-
    16 morgens of land & valley   32
                                    ————— 116.—

Pieter Parmentier ; 1 poll, 1 cow, 1 hog....   £24.-.-
    4 morgens of land..................   8.-.-
    1 mill estimated @ 50.-.-
                                    ————— 82.—

Pieter Jacobsen ; 1 poll, 1 cow, 13 morgens
    of land ....   49.—
Volckert Dircksen ; 1 poll, 1 horse, 1 of 3
    yrs, 1 of 1 yr. 6 cows, 3 of 3 yrs, 4 of
    2 yrs, 4 of 1 yr. 4 sheep............   £100.14.
    50 morgens of land & valley   100
                                    ————— 200.14.-

Jan Miserol; 1 poll, 3 oxen, 6 cows, 4 of 3
  yrs 1 of 1 yr. 3 hogs .... £86.10.
32 morgens of land & valley 64
                            —— 150.—.-

Jan Miserol the younger; 1 poll, 3 cows, 2
  of 1 yr .... £36.-.-.
4 morgens of land 8
                            —— 44.—.-

Jan Loquier; 1 poll, 2 horses, 7 cows, 4 of
  3 yrs 5 of 2 yrs, 4 of 1 yr £111.-.-
28 morgens of land & valley 56.-.-
                            —— 167.—.-

Neeltje Jans; 2 cows, 1 of 1 yr 11.10.-
Theunis Ghysberts; 8 morgens of valley ... 16.—.-
Hendrick Barents Smit; 16 morgens of land
  & valley .... 32.—.-
Joost Adriaens' widow; 1 horse, 1 of 2 yrs.
  5 cows, 5 of 1 yr £49.-.-
25 morgens of land & valley 50.-.-
                            —— 99.10.-

Jannitje Schamp; 1 cow, 2 of 3 yrs .... 13.—.-
Michel Parmentier; 1 poll, 2 horses, 1 of 3
  yrs, 5 cows, 2 of 3 yrs, 2 of 2 yrs, 2 of
  1 yr £85.-.-
30 morgens of land & valley 60.-.-
                            —— 145.—.-

The rate is 12 pounds, 4 shil. 3 pence.   Pounds 2931.—.-

By order of the Constable & overseers of Bushwyck

P. Clocq, Clerk.

RATE LIST OF AMESFORT [FLATLANDS] 25 SEPT^R 1683.

Roelof Martens; 2 men, 2 negroes, 4 horses, 1 of 2 yrs,
  1 of 1 yr. 2 oxen, 8 cows, 3 of 3 yrs., 6 of 2 yrs
  6 of 1 yr 60 morg. of land £1. 7.10
Gerrit Strycker; 2 men & one negro, 3 horses, 7 cows,
  1 of 2 yrs. 1 of 1 year & 2 morgens of land ..... .11.—

Albert Albertsen the younger ; 1 poll, 1 ox, 2 cows, 2
    of 3 years 1 of 1 year......................   3. 6
Aryaen Pieters : one man, 2 horses, 5 cows, 2 of 1 year
    & 12 morg land...........................   7. 9
Stoffel Jansen ; 1 poll, 1 horse, 4 cows, 2 of 1 y^r 3
    morg. land...............................   4.10
Clas Pieters ; 1 poll, 1 negro, 2 horses, 6 cows, 2 of 3
    & 2 of 2 yrs. 2 of 1 year and 23 morgens of land   12. 7
Abraham Jores ; 2 men, 4 horses, 2 oxen, 10 cows, 6 of
    3 yrs, 6 of 2 yrs. 4 of 1 yr. 8 Sheep, & 46 morgens
    of land..................................   1. 4.—
Jan Martens ; one man, one negro, 2 horses, 1 of 3 yrs.
    5 cows 2 of 3 yrs. 2 of 2 yrs. 2 of 1 yr. & 28
    morgens land..............................   11. 9
Jan Teunise ; 2 men, 3 horses, 2 cows, 10 morg: land—   8. 6
Pieter Maffoort ; 1 man, 2 horses, 1 of 2 yrs. 5 cows, 2
    of 3 yrs. 1 of 2 yrs. 2 of 1 yr. & 12 morgens of
    land.....................................   7. 1
Jan Maffoort ; 1 man, one horse...................   2. 6
Dirck Jansen ; 1 man, 2 horses, 3 cows, & 1 of 2 yrs &
    20 morg land..............................   8. 6
Albert Albertsen ; 1 man, 2 horses, 7 cows, 3 of 2 yrs.
    & 2 of 1 y^r & 35 morgens of land..............   13. 1
Jan Alberts ; 1 man, 1 horse, 2 cows & 1 of 3 years...   2.11
Fernandes ; 2 men, 2 horses, 2 cows, & 4 morgens....   6. 6
Willem Jansen ; 1 man, 2 horses, 2 cows, & 3 morg.
    land.....................................   4.10
Hendrick Agasuerus ; 1 man, 1 horse...............   2. 6
Jan Brouwer ; 2 men, 2 horses, 4 cows, 1 ox, 1 of 1 y^r
    & 2 morg. land.............................   7. 7
Symen Jansen ; 2 men, 2 horses, 8 cows, 4 of 3 yrs, 4
    of 2 yrs. 4 of 1 y^r & 42 morg: of land..........   17.10
Jacop Verdon ; 1 man, 1 horse, 3 cows.............   3. 9
Dirckye Roelffsen ; 1 man, 2 horses, 2 cows, 2 of 3 yrs.
    2 of 1 yr. & 4 morg. land 5. 6
Hendrick Pieters ; 1 man, 1 horse, 1 ox, 4 cows, 1 of 2
    yrs. 1 of 1 yr. & 12 morgens of land 6.11

Pieter Hendricksen ; 1 man, 3 cows, 1 horse, 1 of 2 years 3.11

Pieter Cornelis ; 2 men & 1 negro, 4 horses, 2 of 3 yrs. 6 cows, 5 of 3 yrs. 5 of 2 yrs. 3 of 1 y^r & 28 morgens land............................... 1. 1.—

Coert Stevens ; 2 men, 4 horses, 1 of 2 yrs. 4 oxen, 6 cows, 3 of 3 yrs. 7 of 2 yrs. 6 of 1 y^r & 60 morg. land. .... 1. 5.—

Pieter Classen ; 3 men, 5 horses, 2 oxen, 11 cows, 5 of 3 yrs 4 of 2 yrs. 5 of 1 year, 49 morgens of land 1. 6. 2

Albert Stevens ; 1 man 3 horses, 4 cows, 1 of 3 years, 5 of 1 year.................................... . 7.—

Steven Coerten ; 1 man, 4 cows, 5 of 3 yrs. 4 of 2 yrs. & 55 morgen of land 14. 8

Jan Stevens ; 1 man, 2 horses, 4 cows, 1 of 2 yrs. 1 of 1 yr. & 9 morg. land......................... 6.11

Rutgert Bruynsen ; 1 man, 3 horses, 2 cows, 6 morg. land 6. 4

Marten Pieters ; 1 man, 3 cows,.................... 2. 9

William Davidts ; 1 man, 2 horses, 5 cows, 3 of 3 yrs. 1 ox, 2 of 2 yrs, 2 of 1 yr. & 25 morg: land. 11. 9

Luyckas ; 1 man, 2 horses, & 1 of 2 yrs. 7 cows, 4 of 3 yrs. 2 of 2 yrs. 2 of 1 yr. & 34 morgens land.... 14. 5

Jans Jansen ; 3 men, 3 horses, 2 oxen, 6 cows, 3 of 3 yrs. 2 of 2 yrs., 2 of 1 yr. & 26 morgen land.... 16.10

Willem Gerrits ; 2 men, 5 horses, 2 of 1 y^r 9 cows, & 8 of 3 yrs. & 4 of 2 yrs. & 5 of 1 yr. & 30 morg. land.. 1. 1. 1.

Teunis Jansen ; 1 man............................ 1. 6

Pieter Nefyes.................................... 1. 6

Pieter Tul 1. 6

The list of Amesfort amounts to........ Pounds 19. 8. 1

VALUATION OF BREUCKELEN TAKEN 26 SEPT 1683.

Jeronimus Jorisen:—

1 poll	£18.—	
1 horse	12	
6 cows	30	
2 do of 2 yrs	5	
1 do of 1 yr.	1.10	
2 Hogs	2.—	
8 morg. land	16	
		84.10

Jan Cornelis Damen:—

2 horses	£24.	
5 cows	25.	
4 do of 2 yrs	10.	
3 do of 1 yr	4.10	
10 morg. land	20.	
		83.10

Teunis Jansen :—

2 horses	24	
5 cows	25	
6 do of 2 yrs	15.	
3 do of 1 yr	4.10	
4 sheep	4.—	
1 poll	18	
20 morg. land	40	
		130.10

Willm Huicke :—

2 horses	£24	
1 do of 1 yr	3.	
3 cows	15.	
3 do of 2 yr	7.10	
2 do of 1 yr	3.10	
8 morg. land	16.—	
		69.—

Daniel Rapalie

5 horses	£60.
6 cows	30.
4 do 2@3 yrs	10.
3 do 2 yrs	7.10

2 do 1 yr	3.—	
24 morg. land	48.—	
		158.10

Jan Aersen :—

3 horses	£36.	
5 cows	25	
2 do of 2 yrs	5.	
4 sheep	4.	
27 morg. land	54.	
		124.—

Thomas Vardon :—

2 horses	£24 —	
3 cows	15.	
1 do 2@3 yrs	2.10	
4 do 1 yr	6.—	
1 poll	18.—	
8 morg: land	16.—	
		81.10

Jacob Jansen Bergen :—

2 horses	£24.	
1 poll	18.	
3 cows	15.	
1 do of 1 yr	1.10	
3 do of 3 yrs	7.10	
1 do of 1 yr	1.10	
24 morg land & valley	48.—	
		115.10

Joris Hansen:—

1 poll	18	
2 horses	24	
3 cows	25	
2 do of 3 yrs	4	
1 do of 2 yr	2.10	
2 do of 1 yr	3.—	
12 morg. land	24.—	
		110.10

Cornelis Sibbings :—

1 poll	18.

2 horses.... 24.
2 cows..... 10.
3 do of 3 yrs 12.
17 morg. land
  & valley.. 34.
             98.—

Tryntie Korssen :—
3 cows..... 15.—
2 do 2 yr... 5.—
2 do 3 yrs.. 8.—
2 morg. land
  & vly .... 4.—
             32.—

Pieter Korssen:—
1 poll...... 18.—
2 horses.... 24.—
4 cows..... 20.—
10 morg. land
  & vly..... 20.
             82.

Hendrick Korssen:—
10 morg. land   20.—

Jacob Brouwer:—
2 cows..... 10.—
1 do of 2 yrs 2.10
6 morg. land
  & valley.. 12.—
             42.10

Pieter Jansen
1 poll...... 18.—
3 horses.... 36.—
18 morg. land
  & vly.... 36.—
6 Cows .... 30.—
2 do of 3 yrs 8.—
1 do of 2 yrs 2.10
3 do of 1 yr. 4.10
             135.—

Klaes Arentse:—
2 polls..... £36.—
4 cows..... 20 —
2 do of 2 yrs 5 —
2 do of 1 yr 3.—
12 morg. land 24.—
             88.—

Poulus Dirckse
1 poll...... £18.—
3 horses.... 36.
5 cows .... 25.—
2 do of 3 yrs 8.—
4 do of 2 yrs 10.—
2 do of 1 yr 3.—
1 do of 6 yr 6.—
25 morg. land 50.—
             156.—

Liesbet Pouse:—
1 cow. .... £5.—
1 do of 3 yrs 4.—
1 do of 5 yrs 6.—
1 do of 2 yrs 2.10
1 do of 1 yr 1.10
             19.—

Mattys Brouwer:—
1 poll...... £18.
1 cow...... 5.
1 do of 3 yrs 4
             27.—

Jan Frederickse
1 poll...... £18
3 horses.... 36
6 cows 30
2 do of 2 yrs 5
1 do of 1 yr 1.10
14 morg. land 28
             118.10

Joost Franse:—
1 poll...... £18.—

2 horses.... 24.—
3 cows .... 15.—
1 do of 3 yrs 4.—
2 do of 2 yrs 5.—
1 do of 1 yr 1.10
16 mor. land
  & vly 32.10
                 99.10

Ariaen van Laer:—
1 poll...... £18.
2 cows .... 10.
1 horse .... 12.
1 yearling.. 1.10
1 morg. land 2.—
                 43.10

Abraham Ackerman:-
1 poll £18
1 cow...... 5
                 23.—

Thomas Lammerse:—
2 polls...... £36.
3 horses.... 36.
1 do of 2 yrs 5.
7 cows .... 35.
1 do of 3 yrs 4
4 do of 2 yrs 10.—
4 do of 1 yr 6.—
4 sheep.... 4.—
18 morg. land 36
                 172.—

Willem Joresen:—
1 poll...... 18.—
5 cows .... 25.
2 do of 2 yrs 5.
2 horses.... 24.
12 morg. land 24.
                 96.—

Folckert Hendrickse:—
1 poll...... £18.
2 horses.... 24.

6 cows .... 30.—
2 do of 2 yrs 5.—
2 do of 1 yr 3.—
14 morg. land 28.—
                 108.—

Jacob Joresen:—
1 poll ...... £18.
3 horses.... 36.—
5 cows .... 25.—
2 do of 2 yrs 5.—
1 do of 1 yr 1.10
2 sheep .... 2.—
12 morg. land 24.
                 111.10

Joris Jacobsen:—
3 horses.... £36.
6 cows..... 30.—
2 do of 2 yrs 5.—
16 morg. land 32
                 103.-

Cornelis Nevies:—
1 poll...... £18.
3 cows .... 15.
1 do 2 yrs.. 2.10
1 do 1 yr .. 1.10
                 37.—

Adam Brouwer:—
1 poll...... £18.
1 mill...... 100.
3 cows .... 15.
1 do of 2 yrs 2.10
2 do ...... 5.—
3 sheep .... 3.—
3 morg. land 6.
                 149.10

Hendrickse Sleght:-
2 horses.... £24.
4 cows .... 20.—
21 morg. land 42
                 86 -

Rendel Evans:—
2 horses.... 24.
1 poll...... 18.
————— 42.

Jacobus vande Water:—
1 poll...... £18.
1 horse .... 12.
4 cows .. 20.—
1 do of 2 yrs 2.10
2 do of 1 yr 3.—
4 sheep.... 4.—
12 morg. land 24
————— 83.10

Machiel Hansen:—
1 poll...... £18.—
2 horses.... 24.—
6 cows .... 30.—
4 do of 3 yrs 16.—
5 do of 2 yrs 12.10
5 do of 1 yr 7.10
20 morg. land 40.—
————— 148.—

Thomas Jansen:—
1 poll...... £18.
2 oxen..... 12.
1 horse 12
2 cows .... 10.
2 do of 3 yrs 8.
3 do of 2 yrs 7.10
11 morg. land 22.
————— 89.10

Hendrick Tysen:—
1 poll...... £18.—
2 oxen..... 12.—
2 cows .... 10.—
3 do 2 yrs.. 7.10
1 horse 1 yr 3.—
12 morg. land 24.—
————— 74.10

Jesies Dregz:—
1 poll...... £18.—
1 horse .... 12.—
————— 30.—

Evert Hendrickse:—
1 poll...... £18.—
1 cow ..... 5.—
1 do yearling 1.18
————— 24.10

Akus Jansen
1 poll...... £18.
2 oxen .... 12.—
3 cows .... 15.—
1 do 2 yrs.. 2.10
2 do 1 yr .. 3.
8 morg. land 16.
————— 66.10

Ariaen Willemse:—
1 poll...... £18.—
3 horses.... 36.—
6 cows .... 30.—
1 ox of 4 yrs 6.—
4 do 4 yrs.. 16.—
3 do 1 yr .. 3.
25 morg. land 50
————— 159.–

Jan Gerritse Dorlant :—
1 poll ...... £18.
2 horses.... 24.
1 do 2 yrs.. 5.
1 do 1 yr... 3.
5 cows..... 25.
2 do 2 yrs.. 5.
2 do 1 yr... 3.
20 morg. land 40.
————— 123.—

Simen Aersen :—
1 poll ...... £18.
4 oxen..... 24
4 cows..... 20
4 do of 2 yrs 10.

1 do of 1 yr	1.10	
1 horse.....	8.	
24 morg. land	48.—	
		129.10

Jan Teunisen

1 poll	£18.	
2 horses....	24.	
4 cows.	20.	
2 do 2 yrs..	5.	
21 morg. land	42	
		109.—

Jan Jansen:—

1 poll......	£18.	
2 horses....	24.	
2 oxen.....	12.	
7 cows	35.	
2 do 3 yrs..	8.	
5 do 1 yr...	7.10	
21 morg. land	42.—	
		146.10

Luickes Teunise:—

1 poll......	£18.	
3 horses....	36.	
1 do 1 yr...	3.	
2 cows	10.	
10 morg. land	20.	
		87.—

Frans Abrahamse:—

1 poll.......	£18.	
2 horses....	24.	
1 cow......	5.	
4 morg. land	8	
		55.—

Hendrick Jansen:—

1 poll	£18.	
2 horses....	24	
2 cows	10.	
1 do 4 yrs..	4.	
		56.—

Johanes Kosperse:—

1 poll......	£18.	

2 horses....	24.	
4 cows.....	20.	
2 do 2 yrs..	5.	
5 morg. land	10.—	
		77.—

Casper Jansen:—

2 polls.....	36.	
3 horses....	36.	
1 do 2 yrs..	5.	
2 cows.....	10.	
2 do 2 yrs..	5.	
11 morg. land	22	
		114.

Juraen Blanck:—

1 poll	£18.	
1 horse.....	12.	
2 cows.....	10.	
		40.

Winant Pietersen:—

2 polls.....	£36.	
1 cow......	5.	
1 do 3 yrs..	4.	
1 do 2 yrs..	2.10	
1 do 1 yr...	1.10	
		49.—

Hendricka Sprokels:—

1 horse 4 yrs £	8.	
1 do of 2 yrs	5.	
4 cows.....	20.	
2 do 3 yrs..	8.	
3 do 2 yrs..	7.10	
4 sheep....	4.—	
10 morg. land	20.—	
		72.10

Jan Smit:—

1 poll......	£18.	
1 horse.....	12.	
		30 —

Tuenes Giesbertse Bogert:—

4 horses....	£18.—	

1 do 3 yrs..	8.—	
10 cows	50.—	
6 do 2 yrs..	15.—	
6 do 1 yr ..	9.—	
2 polls	36.—	
40 morg. land	80.	
		246.—

Marten Reisen:—

1 poll......	£18.	
2 horses....	24.	
2 do 1 yr ..	6.	
5 cows	25.	
3 do 2 yrs..	7.10	
1 do 1 yr ..	4.—	
19 morg. land	38.—	
		122.10

The widow of Rem Jansen:—

3 polls	£54	
6 horses....	72.	
12 cows	60.	
1 do of 4 yrs	4.	
4 do 3 yrs..	16.	
6 do 2 yrs..	15.	
6 do 1 yr...	7.10	
22 morg. land		
& vly	44—	
		272.10

Johanes Cristoffelse:—

1 poll......	£18.	
3 horses	36.	
2 cows	10.	
2 do 2 yrs..	5.	
9 morg. land	18.	
		87.—

Willem Bennings:—

1 poll......	£18.	
2 horses....	24.	
1 do 3 yrs..	8.	
1 do 2 yrs..	5.	

6 cows	30.	
3 oxen	18.	
1 do 2 yrs..	2.10	
1 do 1 yr...	1.10	
21 morg. land	42.—	
		149.—

Rissiert Gibs:—

1 poll......	£18.	
1 horse.....	12	
		30.—

Thomas Jansen op Brackelen:—

1 poll......	£18.	
2 horses....	24	
		42

Pieter Van Nest:—

2 polls.....	£36	
3 cows.	15.	
1 yearling..	1.10	
		52.10

Jan Buys:—

1 poll	£18.	
2 horses....	24 —	
2 cows.....	10 –	
		52.—

Dirck Jansen:—

1 poll	£18.	
3 cows.....	15.	
1 do 3 yrs..	4.	
1 do 1 yr...	1.10	
2 horses....	24.	
1 do 3 yrs..	8.	
30 morg. land	60.	
		130.10

£5793.10

+ Jan Cornelise Damen
Jan Gerritse van Couwenhoven
                    as Clerk

RATE LIST OF MIDWOUT [FLATBUSH] 1683.

Names	Polls 18 lb	Horses 12 lb	3 years 8 lb	2 years 5 lb	Yearlings 3 lb	Oxen 6 lb	Cows 5 lb	3 years 4 lb	2 years 50 sh	yearlings 30 sh	Hogs 1 lb	acres 1 lb	Total
Nys Teunisen	1	1				2	4	3	6	3		50	100
Loffert Pietersen	1	2					7	2	2	7		54	174 10
Cornelis Berryen	1	3				3	10		3	1		152	279 10
Laurens Cornelis	1	2					2	1	3	5		36	97
Reynier Arens	2	3					7		2	2		40	166
Pieter Guilliams	1	4					7	1	2	2		160	287
Theodorus Polhemius	1	2			1		5	3	7	9			79
Jan van Ditmersen	2	3					12			2		120	295
Dirck Hooglant	2	2		1			1	1	1	1		52	120
Jacop Hendrickx	1	4		1			4	1		5		46	140
Willem Guilliams	2	4					6	7	6	4		144	277
Pieter Lot	2	4					6		2	1	1	140	308
Harmen Key	1	1			1		3	1	1	1		44	95 10
Lowys Jans	1	1					2	3		1			44
Jan Auke	1	2		1			4		4	3		46	114 10
Adrian Reyerse	2	2	1	1			5		3	2		70	197
Titus Zirachz	1	3					8	2	2	3		50	159 10
Jan Rems	2	2	2				4	3	3	3		38	135 10
Hendrick Rycke	1	2					4			3		38	140

Name										Acres	Total
Dirck van der Vlier	2	2	2	1	3					36	130
Hendrick Willems	1	4	2	2	7					100	217
Jan Vlier	1	2			2					60	117
Cornelis van der Veer	2	4	4	4	11					100	257 10
Cornelis Barents	1	4	5	2	8					100	240
Willem Jacops	2	3	3	2	9					60	197
Gerrit Lubbers	1	3	2	1	8					60	165
Auke Jans van Nuys	2	3	3	2	5					48	153 10
Rem Remse	1	3	4	1	5					60	157 10
Gerrit Snedeker	2	3	2		10	4				90	236
Jacop Larzilier	1	3	1		6					60	160
Pieter Cornelissen										60	54
Cornilis Pieterse	1	2	2	3	4					54	156 10
Gerrit Strycker	1	2		1	3					84	127 10
Stoffel Probasco	1	2	3	4	6					60	146 10
Lymen Hanse	2	3	1	3	5						125
Jan Barensen	1	1	1		2	2				60	101 10
Joost Casperse	1	2			3					30	89 10
Claes Barens	1	2		3	2					30	82
Jan Strycker	1	2	2		7					72	176 10
Mr. Tomes Barker	1	3			2					40	111
Mr. Maris	3	3	6		6					110	210 10
Catryna Hegemans	1	3	4	3	9					132	300 10
Jacop Janse	1	1			5					32	87
Hendrick Hegeman	2	2								60	102
Adriaen Hendricks	1	2	2		4					28	117
Pieter Strycker		3	5	1	8					50	156 10

RATE. LIST, &c.—(Continued.)

Names	Polls 18 lb	Horses 12 lb	3 years 8 lb	2 years 5 lb	yearlings 3 lb	Oxen 6 lb	Cows 5 lb	3 years 4 lb	2 years 50 sh	yearlings 30 sh	Hogs 1 lb	acres 1 lb	
Adriaen Andriessen	2	4				3	3	4	1			30	131
Aris Janse	1	3					6		5	3		108	243
													£7757 10

RATE LIST OF NEW UTRECHT; 28th Sept. 1683.

Names	Polls	Acres of land	Horses	Horses 3 years	Horses 2 years	Horses 1 year	Oxen	Cows	Cows 4 years	Cows 3 years	Cows 2 years	Cows 1 year
Jan Jansen van Dyck	1	60	3					6		1	3	3
Baerent Joosten	1	40	5					8		2	2	5
Louris Janssen	1	40	2					3		1	2	2
Antony van Peelt	1	20	1	1				2		2		2
Thys Lubbers	2	20	3					4	1	1		2
Heinderyck van Peelt	2	50	4					4				1
Lambert Janse	1	0						1				
Gerret Stoffelsen	1	18	2					3			3	
Heind'k Kamgo	1											

Antoony Duseen	1	20	3			1	4		1		2
Herreman Smyt,	1						1			2	3
Derck van Sutfon.	1	12	1				3				
Jan Klement.	1						4		3		1
Tomas Farckx.	1	20	1		1		1		1		2
Cornelis Wynhat	2	30	2		2		3	6	6	6	6
Ruthgret Joosten	2	200	6		1		2		1	4	4
Henderyck Matyssen	2	100	4				12				5
Jan Verkercke,	2	155	6			1	5				4
Toonis van Peelt.	3	48	3				10		3		
Gerret Cornelissen.	3	20	2				6	1			
Kryn Janse van Meetsen	2	40	2				5		2	2	4
Gysbert Tyssen,	1	60	2	1			2		3	3	
Tylman Jacopsen	1			1			3				
Jan Kiersen,	1	70	4				1				3
Jan vandeNeuter.	3	20	2				5				2
Jan van Kleef.	1	80	4		1		4		1	1	
Karel Jansen van Dyck	1	60	3		1		8				4
Jan Hansen.	2	40	2				3			4	1
Meindert Koerte.	1	40	4				8				5
Roelof verkercke.	1		2				5				
Hendryck Toonissen.	1	16					3				
	43	1279	73	2	6	2	131	9	35	35	61

By order of the Constable and overseers

GESUP STYTEWEERDE

CLAESE VANDER WERSSEN

AN ACCO^T FROM GRAUESEND OF Y^E PERSONS LANDS AND CATTLES RATEABLE ACCORDING TO Y^E LAW.

Anno Domo 1683.

Raphe Cardall ;	£	s.	d.
7 Cowes	0	2	11
1 " of 2 yrs ould	0	0	2½
3 " 1 yeare ould	0	0	4½
80 Acors of land....	0	6	8
4 horses	0	4	0
1 " 1 yeare	0	0	3
	0	14	5

Joseph Goulding			
3 Cowes...........	0	1	3
1 " of 3 yeares...	0	0	4
2 " of 2 yeare....	0	0	5
2 " of 1 yeare....	0	0	3
3 Horses	0	3	0
41 Acors of land.....	0	3	5
1 head............	0	1	6
	0	10	2

Peter Sympson ;			
3 Cowes	0	1	3
1 " 3 yeares.....	0	0	4
1 " 2 yeares.....	0	0	2½
1 " 1 yeare	0	0	1½
2 horses...........	0	2	0
44 Acors of land.....	0	3	8
	0	7	7

John Briggs,			
4 Cowes...........	0	1	8
2 " 3 years	0	0	8
1 " 1 yeare......	0	0	1½
3 horses.	0	3	0
1 " 1 year ould..	0	0	3

	£	s.	d.
84 Acors of land.....	0	7	0
1 head............		1	6
	14		2½

John Emauns			
7 Cowes	0	2	11
1 " 3 yeares.....	0	0	4
3 " 2 yeares.....	0	0	7½
2 " 1 yeare	0	0	3
5 horses...........	0	5	0
88 acors land........	0	7	4
1 head............	0	1	6
	0	17	11½

Barnes Jurissonn			
6 Cowes	0	2	6
5 " 2 years oulds	0	1	0½
1 " 1 yeare	0	0	1½
2 horses...........	0	2	0
88 acors of land.....	0	7	4
1 head............	0	1	6
	0	14	6

William Goulding			
6 Cowes...........	0	2	6
3 " 3 yeares.....	0	1	0
3 " 1 yeare......	0	0	4½
1 horse............	0	1	0
20 acors land........	0	1	8
	0	6	6½

Yawcum Goijcliffe			
5 Cowes...........	0	2	1
1 " of 3 yeares..	0	0	4
4 " of 2 yeares..	0	0	10

	£	s.	d.
3 " of 1 yeare....	0	0	4½
1 horse	0	1	0
25 acors of land	0	2	1
1 person	0	1	6
	0	8	2½

John Lake sen[r]

7 Cowes	0	2	11
5 " of 2 yeares...	0	1	0½
4 " of 1 yeare ...	0	0	6
4 horses	0	4	0
88 acors land	0	7	4
1 personn	0	1	6
	0	17	3½

Clause Johnsonn

5 Cowes	0	2	1
2 " of 3 yeares..	0	0	8
1 " 2 yeares..	0	0	2½
2 horses	0	2	0
1 " of 1 yeare....	0	0	3
44 acors land	0	3	8
1 person.	0	1	6
	0	10	4½

John Lake Jun[r]

1 Mare	0	1	0
1 head	0	1	6
	0	2	6

Martha Wilkins

6 cowes	0	2	6
1 " 3 yeares	0	0	4
2 " 2 yeares.	0	0	5
3 " 1 yeare	0	0	4½
2 horses	0	2	0
88 acors of land	0	7	4
	0	12	11½

William Stillwell

	£	s.	d.
3 Cowes.	0	1	3
1 " 3 yeares	0	0	4
1 " 2 yeares	0	0	2½
1 " 1 yeare	0	0	1½
1 horse	0	1	0
44 acors of land	0	3	8
	0	6	7

John Barnes

3 cowes	0	1	3
1 " 3 yeares	0	0	4
2 " 2 yeares	0	0	5
2 " 1 yeare	0	0	3
2 horses	0	2	0
60 acors of land	0	5	0
1 person	0	1	6
	0	10	9

John Briggs Jun[r]

1 person	0	1	6

Cornelius Boyce

2 cowes	0	0	10
1 horse	0	1	0
1 person	0	1	6
	0	3	4

William Williamson

5 cowes	0	2	1
1 " 2 years	0	0	2½
2 " 1 yeare	0	0	3
1 horse	0	1	0
44 acors land	0	3	8
1 personn	0	1	6
	0	8	8½

Jeremie Stillwell

16 acors land	0	1	4

Carson Johnson	£	s.	d.
10 cowes	0	4	2
3 " of 2 yeares	0	0	7½
4 " of 1 yeare	0	0	6
1 " of 4 yeares	0	0	5
4 horses	0	4	0
1 " 3 ycares	0	0	8
44 acors land	0	3	8
2 persons	0	3	0
	17	0½	

Nicholas Stillwell			
6 cowes	0	2	6
2 " 3 yeares ould	0	0	8
3 " 2 ycares	0	0	7½
2 " 1 yeare	0	0	3
2 horses	0	2	0
44 acors land	0	3	8
	0	9	8½

Johannus Michaelson			
4 cowes	0	0	8
1 " of 3 yeares	0	0	4
1 Mare	0	1	0
44 acors land	0	3	8
1 personn	0	1	6
	0	8	2

John Poling			
3 cowes	0	1	3
1 " of 1 yeare	0	0	1½
2 horses	0	2	0
17 acoˢ land	0	1	5
44 " more of land	0	3	8
1 heade	0	1	6
	0	9	11½

Sammˡˡ Spicer			
9 cowes	0	3	9

3 " 3 yeares	0	1	0
5 " 2 yeares	0	1	0½
6 " 1 yeare	0	0	9
3 horses	0	3	0
1 " 2 yeares	0	0	5
1 " 1 yeare	0	0	3
100 acors land	0	8	4
1 heade	0	1	6
5 sheepe	0	0	1½
	1	0	2

Danniell Lake	0	1	6

John Tilton Juʳ			
7 cowes	0	2	11
3 " 3 years	0	1	0
3 " 1 yeare	0	0	4½
3 horses	0	3	0
1 " 3 yeares	0	0	8
1 " 2 yeares	0	0	5
2 " 1 yeare	0	0	6
60 acors land	0	5	0
1 heade	0	1	6
	0	15	4½

Jo: Tilton Senʳ			
5 cowes	0	2	1
1 horse	0	1	0
9 Sheepe	0	0	3
2 hoggs	0	0	3
29 acors land	0	2	5
	0	6	0

Alse Osborne			
10 cowes	0	4	2
5 " 3 yeares	0	1	8
2 " 2 yeares	0	0	5
5 " 1 yeare	0	0	7½
5 horses	0	5	0

115 acors land 0 9 7

1 1 5

John Carsonsonn
2 cowes 0 0 10
1 Mare 0 1 0
1 heade 0 1 6

0 3 4

Lawrence Haft
2 cowes.......... 0 0 10
22 acors of land..... 0 1 10
1 heade.......... 0 1 6

0 4 2

Elias Dawes
1 cowe............ 0 0 5
1 Mare 0 1 0
1 personn.......... 0 1 6

0 2 11

Jonathan Bayly...... 0 1 6
Yawcum Goijliffe 0 4 3
William Goulding.... 0 2 0

Per me
WᴹWILLIAMSON Constable.
Endorsed
Graues Ends
Estimation 1683

RATE LIST OF NEWTOWN 1683.

	Heads	Land	Horses	3 yeres	2 yeres	1 yere	Oxen	Cowes	3 yeres	2 yeres	1 yere	Sheepe	Swine
John Coe	2	30	1	0	0	0	1	4	0	0	0	6	6
John Smith	1	80	2	1	1	1	4	9	9	10	6	30	8
John Ramsden	2	30	2	0	0	0	2	9	0	3	4	6	7
Thomas Stevnson	1	40	1	0	1	1	4	8	5	5	4	20	7
Joseph Bourroughs	1	18	0	1	0	0	1	3	1	2	3	00	0
Samuel Kitsham	1	5	1	0	0	0	0	3	0	1	1	00	0
John Kitsham	1	80	3	0	0	1	4	8	4	2	8	20	3
phillip Kitsham	1	20	1	0	0	0	2	2	0	1	0	4	2
John Bourroughs	1	10	1	1	0	0	0	1	0	0	0	0	0
Joseph Reede	1	00	0	0	0	0	0	1	0	0	0	0	0
Edward Stevenson	1	40	1	0	1	0	3	6	1	2	1	12	1
Joshua Hazard	2	00	1	0	0	0	0	0	0	0	0	0	0
Thomas Robason	1	40	2	0	0	0	3	3	2	2	1	3	0
Jeremiah Reeder	1	10	0	0	0	0	2	3	0	1	0	3	3
Thomas Etherington	1	00	0	0	0	0	0	1	0	0	0	0	0
Joseph Reeder	1	10	1	0	0	0	1	1	3	2	0	0	0
Jacob Reeder	1	20	2	0	1	0	2	3	3	0	1	3	2
Content titus	1	18	2	0	0	0	2	6	1	2	0	16	3
Caleb Leveridg	1	24	1	0	0	0	2	4	0	1	1	15	1
Eleazor Leveridg	1	00	0	0	0	0	0	2	0	0	0	3	0

Joseph Lacit	1	8	2	2	2	3	0	0	0	0	1	20	1
daniell blomfield	3	12	2	2	0	3	3	0	0	0	1	15	1
John Reeder	1	10	3	0	1	6	2	0	1	0	1	10	1
Richard owin	0	0	1	0	2	3	1	0	0	0	2	10	1
Lambart Woodward	0	10	2	1	0	5	1	0	0	0	1	8	1
Samuell More	4	12	3	2	2	6	2	0	0	0	1	30	1
Benimin Cornish	0	00	0	0	0	2	0	0	0	0	1	2	1
Samuel fish	0	0	0	1	1	0	0	0	0	0	0	6	1
Stofoll fon Lawes	0	00	0	0	0	2	0	0	0	0	1	0	1
John pettit	2	6	1	0	1	4	2	0	0	0	1	8	1
Josiah forman juner	0	4	0	0	0	3	0	0	0	0	0	10	0
Robart feild juner	0	6	3	0	0	3	0	0	0	0	0	12	1
Robart feild sener	1	6	2	2	1	4	2	0	0	0	1	20	0
Jonath: Strickland	0	8	2	2	3	2	0	0	0	0	1	20	0
Jonathan farman	1	7	0	0	0	2	2	0	0	0	0	10	1
Josiah farman sener	0	0	0	3	0	3	2	0	0	0	1	20	0
Georg Wood	4	0	0	0	0	5	0	0	0	0	2	30	1
Nathaniell bayly	0	0	0	0	0	4	0	0	0	0	0	10	1
Richard fidoe	0	4	0	2	3	4	0	0	0	0	1	16	1
Gershom More	1	10	6	0	0	6	2	0	1	0	1	16	1
Nathan fish	2	0	1	0	1	2	0	0	0	0	0	10	2
Thomas Morrell	1	0	1	0	2	2	4	0	0	0	1	25	1
Gorg Cook	0	0	0	0	0	0	0	0	0	0	1	00	1
Gershom hazard	0	0	0	1	0	1	0	0	0	0	1	3	1
Jonathan hazard	1	8	0	2	0	5	2	0	0	0	1	20	1
Joseph phillips	1	0	1	1	1	2	2	0	0	0	2	10	1
Theophilus phillips	1	8	0	2	0	6	2	0	0	0	1	15	1

RATE LIST, &c.—(CONTINUED.)

	Heads	Lands	Horses	3 yeres	2 yeres	1 yere	Oxen	Cowes.	3 yeres	2 yeres	1 yere	Sheepe	Swine
Edward Hunt	2	30	2	0	0	1	2	5	1	2	4	5	1
Jerimiah bourroughs	1	20	1	0	0	0	2	4	2	2	3	6	2
John Copstafe	0	6	0	0	0	0	0	1	0	0	0	0	1
John Reed	1	6	1	0	0	0	2	3	0	0	0	4	0
John Rosell	1	2	1	0	0	0	0	1	0	0	0	0	0
Samuell Scudder	2	30	2	0	0	0	4	10	4	5	2	12	1
John Allburtis	1	30	2	0	0	0	2	4	1	1	3	6	2
Thomas Case	1	10	2	0	0	0	0	4	2	0	2	12	0
Thomas wandall	0	80	2	0	0	0	2	9	1	3	7	40	7
John Denman	1	15	1	0	2	0	0	4	0	0	1	8	0
Luck depaw	0	10	1	0	0	1	0	2	0	0	0	6	0
James way junr	1	10	1	0	0	0	2	5	1	1	2	4	0
James way sener	1	15	1	0	0	0	2	4	3	2	1	7	0
John way	1	15	1	0	0	0	2	4	2	2	2	12	0
Moses pettit	1	6	0	0	0	0	0	3	0	0	0	0	0
John farman	1	8	1	0	0	0	2	1	1	0	0	0	1
Thomas pettit	1	20	2	0	0	0	2	3	0	1	1	4	1
Nathaniell pettit	1	10	1	0	0	0	2	4	0	1	2	3	2
William hallett Senr	4	25	4	0	0	0	4	8	4	4	4	10	0
William hallett junr	1	20	0	0	0	1	2	7	4	4	3	8	0

Samuell hallit	0	15	0	0	0	1	2	5	3	2	2	2	0
Thomas Laurens	3	40	3	0	0	3	4	10	7	6	6	00	0
John Lawrens	0	10	0	0	0	0	0	4	3	0	0	8	0
Thomas skillman	1	10	1	0	0	0	0	6	3	0	2	0	0
Arnute webber	1	00	0	0	0	0	0	0	0	0	0	2	0
John Harrickson	1	22	5	0	0	2	0	7	4	5	3	0	0
Hendrick Smith	2	6	3	2	0	2	0	5	2	4	5	7	1
Nicolos Edds	1	10	1	0	0	0	2	3	0	1	1	4	0
Johanis Loroson	1	20	2	0	0	0	0	4	0	0	0	0	0
John woollton Croft	1	12	0	0	0	0	0	4	3	0	0	3	0
Andrew burd	1	4	2	0	0	0	0	2	0	0	1	0	1
Georg Stevenson	1	40	3	0	0	0	0	8	2	2	3	0	1
Steuen Georgson	1	8	2	0	0	0	0	2	1	0	0	8	1
John Parsell	1	6	1	0	0	0	2	3	0	2	0	0	0
widdow Parsell	1	30	0	0	0	0	0	3	4	2	0	0	3
Thomas Parsell	2	20	3	0	0	0	0	2	1	0	0	0	1
peter Johnson buckhood	2	25	2	0	0	0	2	4	0	0	4	0	0
John buckhood	1	12	0	0	0	0	0	2	2	2	2	4	1
Robart blackwell	1	20	2	0	0	0	0	3	0	2	2	4	2
Abram Reeck	1	14	2	0	0	0	1	3	0	0	2	0	1
hendrick martenson,	1	8	3	0	0	1	0	4	1	2	0	4	0
John Johnson fine	1	24	1	0	0	0	0	4	2	2	0	7	0
Roullof peterson	1	8	1	0	0	0	0	2	0	4	4	4	0
Riner Mill 100lb								2	0	4	4	0	0

Newtowne List of their Inhabitants Estates as they haue Giuen it in to the Clerke of ye towne

JONATHAN HAZARD.

Endorsed,   Newtowne Estimations 1683

FLUSHING ESTIMATIONS; 29ᵀᴴ SEPTᴿ. 1683.

Name	Males	Upland acres	Meadow acres	Horses	3 yere olds	2 yere olds	1 yere old	Oxen	Cowes	3 yere olds	2 yere olds	1 yere olds	Swine	Sheep	£ s d
Mr. John Laurence junior	4	60	30	8				6	14		2	10	5	10	01-13-11
Mr. Matthias Harvye	3	50	30	5			2	4	7	3	10	6	50	15	01-09-11
Widow Cartwright	4	30	50	2				14	3		4				01-03-09
Capt Wᵐ Laurence	2	20	50	4				2	5		5	4	10	20	00-19-09
Mr Elyas Doughty	3	30	20					4	10		8	6	20	40	00-19-06
John Hinchman	1	22	15	3				2	8	8	9	3	3	35	00-19-03
John Bowne	3	30	30	4	1	2	1	4	8	4	1	5	6	30	01-04-01
Nicholas parcell	1	12	20						8	3		4	2	20	00-10-06
Dauid Roe	1	20	15	1				4	6	5	3	7	2		00-15-03
Docter Taylor		20	15	2				2	8				2		00-10-11
Samuell Thorne	1	12	10	1				4	8	4	3	1	12	10	00-14-02
John Thorne		50	10					2	7		2	2		8	00-09-10
Morris Smith	1	30	20	2				4	6		2		3	10	00-13-09
Anthony Feild	1	30						2	4	4	3	3	4		00-12-08
James Whiticker	1	16	10	1				2	5	3		2	6	18	00-08-04
Edward Greffens	1	20	10	1				2	5	1	1	4	3		00-12-09
John Laurence	1	12		1					5		2	4	1		00-07-05
Richard Stockton	1	10	25	2	2			4	7	2	4	2	4	20	00-12-11
William Noble	1	28		2				2	5		3	2	2	30	00-14-04
John Adams	1	25		1		1		2	5	3	2	3	1	20	00-11-08

Wowter Gilbertson	00-11-04	25	6	4	3	3	3	2				2	10	18	
Charles Morgan	00-08-00		1	1			5	2				2		9	2
John Marston	00-08-08		3	2		2	6	2				2	3	3	
Margrett Styles	00-06-04		3	1	4		5	4					7	6	
Ffrancis Burtoe	00-09-03	8	1		2		3	2		1		3	5	12	
Jona Wright	00-07-05	0	2		2	1	5					2		12	
John Gelloe	00-06-08	10	3		3	1	3					2		6	
Thomas Ford	00-02-09	4	2			1	2					1		4	
John hopper	00-03-07	5	4	1	2		2						5	4	
Samuell Hoyt	00-08-09	18	1	1		1	3	1	1			2		4	
Madalin Lodew	00-02-10	00	1	2			2	4				1	4	16	
Hugh Coppethu	00-06-03	6	5		0		1	2		1		2	4	8	
James Clement	00-09-11		1	4	4	2	7							12	
Jasper Smith	00-04-04				3	1						1	5	12	
Edward Greffin	00-02-06	9	3		1		3							8	
Richd Wieday	00-05-04				2		3		1				0	12	
Jn°: Greffin	00-02-11		2	2		2		2			2	1	10	7	2
Rich^d. Tindalle	00-04-10	6		2	2		4	2					6		
John Embree	00-05-07	5			1		7	2					15	10	
Wm Heauiland	00-08-09						3						10	4	
Joseph Thorne	00-07-00		2		4	2	4					1		10	
Jn° Farrington	00-07-01	8					4					2	10	10	1
Dennis Holdron	00-03-02				2	0	3							5	
Tho: Farrington	00-04-11						2					1	10		
Aron Cornelius	00-06-00	8	1		2	1	2					2		6	
Harmanus King	00-04-03					1	3					1	5		
Jn°. Harrison	00-03-04						2					1			

RATE LIST, &c.—(CONTINUED.)

	Males	Upland acres	Meadows acres	Horses	3 yere olds	2 yere olds	1 yere old	Oxen	Cowes	3 yere olds	2 yere olds	1 yere olds	Swine	Sheep	£ s d
Ed: Farrington	—	—	10	1	—	—	—	—	2	—	—	—	—	—	00-04-02
Tho. Hedges	—	8	5	2	—	—	1	4	7	—	—	1	6	—	00-09-09
Jno. Terry	1	7	5	1	—	—	—	—	3	—	2	—	4	—	00-07-00
Francis Colley	—	5	—	1	—	—	—	—	3	—	3	—	—	—	00-04-02
Tho: Dauis	—	12	—	1	—	—	—	—	4	—	—	2	—	—	00-06-00
Tho: Kemsey	—	4	—	2	—	—	—	—	2	—	—	—	3	—	00-04-11
Daniell patri	—	6	—	1	—	—	—	—	1	—	2	2	2	—	00-03-09
Wm Warde	1	—	—	—	—	—	—	—	2	—	1	—	—	—	00-03-00
Richd. Chew	—	12	—	—	—	1	—	—	2	2	2	2	—	—	00-02-00
Jno. Feild	—	5	—	—	—	—	—	—	2	—	—	1	4	—	00-03-07
Joseph Hedges	—	—	—	3	—	—	—	—	2	—	—	—	3	—	00-03-00

£26-15-10

Errors Excepted
p J. C.

Endorsed.
ffushings
Estimations
1683

A LIST OF THE TOWNE ESTATE OF JEMAICA.

Anno 1683.	hors	3 ye	2 ye	1 ye	oxe	cowse	3 ye	2 ye	1 ye	swine	land	heads	estates
Capt. Carpentor	2	1	0	0	2	5	4	3	3	1	52	2	186-00-00
John Rodes sen	0	0	0	0	4	2	5	2	2	0	40	1	120-00-00
Thomas Smith sen	0	1	1	0	2	3	3	3	2	2	45	2	145-00-00
Jonathan Deine	1	0	0	0	0	2	0	0	0	0	18	1	58-00-00
John Everit	2	0	0	0	0	3	1	4	2	0	30	1	104-00-00
Joseph Smith	2	0	0	0	4	4	4	2	2	0	42	2	170-00-00
Thomas Bayles	1	0	0	0	4	5	0	2	1	1	33	1	119-00-00
Thomas Wigens iun	0	0	0	0	0	2	0	1	1	0	8	0	022-00-00
John Wigens	0	0	0	0	2	1	0	0	1	0	0	1	036-00-00
Girsham Wigens	1	0	0	0	1	1	0	0	0	0	0	1	041-00-00
Edward Higbee	1	0	0	0	0	3	2	2	2	1	30	1	092-00-00
Joseph Thurston	3	0	0	0	2	3	1	5	1	1	46	2	164-00-00
William Foster	2	0	0	0	0	4	2	2	4	0	35	1	116-00-00
Samuell Smith	2	0	0	0	6	6	2	3	3	0	50	3	204-00-00
Nicholas Everit	1	0	0	0	4	4	4	4	4	2	50	2	176-00-00
Daniel Whithed	2	0	0	0	0	6	2	3	1	2	45	0	118-00-00
Clem Salmon	0	0	0	0	0	1	0	0	0	0	10	1	033-00-00
William Creed	1	0	0	0	4	6	3	0	0	0	70	1	160-00-00
Peter Stringham	1	0	0	0	0	3	1	0	0	0	12	1	061-00-00
Beniamin Coe	1	0	0	0	0	4	1	1	1	0	27	1	085-00-00

RATE LIST, &c.—(CONTINUED.)

Anno 1683.	estates	heads	land	swine	1 ye	2 ye	3 ye	cowse	oxe	1 ye	2 ye	3 ye	hors
Samuell Messenger	080-00-00	1	10	0	2	0	1	3	1	0	0	0	2
Nathaniell Lynas	032-10-00	0	10	0	1	0	4	1	0	0	0	0	0
John Oldfield	124-00-00	2	36	0	2	2	0	4	4	0	0	0	0
George Woolsey iun	081-10-00	0	25	0	0	1	0	6	4	0	0	0	0
John Man	111-00-00	2	22	1	2	4	0	3	0	0	0	0	2
Sam Mathews	108-00-00	1	24	2	2	2	3	4	2	0	0	1	1
John Foster	047-00-00	1	8	0	0	0	2	1	0	0	0	0	0
Jane Foster	066-00-00	0	22	2	1	3	4	1	2	0	0	0	0
Richard Jones	037-00-00	1	14	0	0	0	0	1	0	0	0	0	0
Jonathan Mills	119-00-00	1	16	3	3	3	1	6	2	0	0	1	2
Jonathan Wood	018-00-00	1	0	0	0	0	0	0	0	0	0	0	0
Jonas Wood	051-00-00	1	5	0	0	4	0	2	0	0	0	0	1
John Wood	055-00-00	1	15	0	1	1	0	2	0	0	0	0	1
Elias Bayles	040-10-00	0	4	0	1	2	2	2	1	0	0	0	1
John Smithes	065-00-00	1	8	0	3	1	1	2	2	0	0	0	0
Samuell Denton	064-00-00	1	6	0	1	1	1	4	0	0	0	0	0
Alexander Smith	047-00-00	1	13	0	1	2	0	2	2	0	0	0	1
Zachariah Mills	083-00-00	1	19	0	1	1	2	2	2	0	0	0	2
Abell Galle	098-10-00	1	21	6	0	3	2	4	2	0	0	0	0
Fulke Davis	039-00-00	1	8	0	2	0	0	2	0	0	0	0	0

Samuell Davis	0	0	0	0	0	3	0	2	0	1	11	1	050–00–00
John Hindes	1	0	0	0	0	1	1	1	0	1	6	1	048–00–00
Richard Denton	2	0	0	0	0	0	0	0	0	0	0	1	042–00–00
Nehemiah Smith	1	0	0	0	4	4	3	2	1	0	22	1	116–00–00
Wait Smith	0	1	0	0	4	4	1	2	2	0	36	1	110–00–00
John Smithrows	1	1	0	0	0	3	0	2	1	1	26	1	086–00–00
John Jos. Ludly	1	0	0	0	6	3	2	3	1	0	30	2	154–00–00
John Carpenter	1	0	0	0	2	2	2	1	2	0	13	1	078–00–00
Samuell Mils	1	0	0	0	2	4	2	0	2	0	30	1	103–00–00
Nath Denton iu	1	0	0	0	2	3	2	1	3	0	15	1	087–00–00
Sam Deine Sen	2	0	0	0	4	6	0	2	3	0	34	1	139–00–00
Sam Deine Jun	0	0	0	0	0	0	0	0	0	0	4	1	022–00–00
John Deine	1	0	0	0	0	1	0	0	0	0	5	1	040–00–00
Nath Denton sen	2	0	0	0	4	6	0	1	0	1	55	1	153–00–00
George Mills	0	0	0	0	0	2	0	1	0	0	4	1	034–10–00
George Woolsey sen	2	0	0	0	4	6	2	4	0	0	36	2	168–00–00
Widow Ashman	1	0	0	0	4	3	0	0	2	0	21	0	075–00–00
John Rowlisson and Frederick	1	1	0	0	0	4	0	3	3	0	16	2	104–00–00
Thomas Wellin	0	0	0	0	0	05	0	3	2	0	30	0	065–10–00
John Bayles	2	0	0	0	0	3	0	3	8	0	22	1	098–10–00
Sam Ruscoe	0	0	0	0	0	2	0	0	0	0	16	1	044–00–00
John Hanson	0	0	0	0	0	8	2	6	3	1	14	2	118–00–00
Derick Powleson	2	0	0	0	0	6	0	3	4	0	22	1	107–10–00
Cornelius Barnson	1	0	0	0	0	2	0	0	0	0	10	1	050–00–00
Rich Everit	1	0	0	0	0	0	0	0	0	0	10	0	022–00–00
Hugh Forde	1	0	0	0	0	0	0	0	0	0	0	1	030–00–00

RATE LIST, &c.—(CONTINUED.)

Anno 1683.	estates.	heads	land	swine	1 ye	2 ye	3 ye	cowse	oxe	1 ye	2 ye	3 ye	hors
Thomas Smith iun	043-00-00	1	9	0	0	0	0	2	1	0	0	0	0
William Bringscel	044-10-00	1	3	0	1	0	0	2	0	0	0	0	1
Edw Burrows	032-00-00	1	5	0	1	1	0	1	0	0	0	0	0
Caleb Carman	198-00-00	2	19	0	0	4	0	5	6	0	0	0	1
John Rodes iun	079-00-00	1	9	1	1	1	2	3	0	0	0	0	2
Tho Foster	032-10-00	1	0	0	0	1	2	0	0	0	0	0	0
John Carman	028-00-00	1	0	0	0	0	0	2	0	0	0	0	0
Tho Woolsey	040-00-00	1	10	0	0	0	0	0	0	0	0	0	1
John Freeman	089-00-00	1	6	1	1	1	4	3	0	0	0	0	2
Beniamin Jones	058-00-00	1	6	2	0	0	0	1	0	0	1	0	1
William White	038-00-00	1	3	0	0	0	0	1	2	1	0	0	1
Hope Carpentor	055-00-00	1	4	0	1	1	0	1	0	0	0	0	1
Randolph Evans	009-00-00	0	9	0	0	0	0	0	2	0	0	0	0
Barnet Caterlin	018-00-00	1	0	0	0	0	0	0	0	0	0	0	0
John Foster	046-00-00	1	0	0	0	4	0	0	0	0	0	0	1
Jerein Hubard	034-00-00	1	6	0	0	0	1	2	0	0	0	0	0
Daniel Denton	056-00-00	1	0	0	0	0	1	2	0	0	0	0	2

AN ACCOUNT OF Yᴱ VALLVATION OF THE ESTATES OF THEE INHABITANTS OF Yᴱ TOWNE OF HAMPSTED ON LONG ISLAND : IS AS FOLLOWETH OCTOBER 11ᵀᴴ. 1683.

The Names of the Inhabitants	heads	Land and meadows Ackrs	Oxen	Cowes	three year oulds	two year oulds	year oulds	hoggs	sheep	Horses and mares majors	Ditto 3 years oulds	Ditto 2 year oulds	Ditto year oulds
John Smith blew	1	30	06	07	03	03	03	02	00	01	00	00	00
John Carman	2	80	10	15	07	07	07	08	00	02	00	00	00
Widdow Cearl	2	66	06	08	04	03	04	03	08	02	00	00	00
Richard Tottne	1	00	02	07	02	04	02	00	10	01	00	00	00
John Jackson	3	130	14	30	16	14	14	20	03	10	00	00	00
John Smith Showᵉⁿ	00	00	00	02	00	01	00	00	00	00	00	00	00
Capt. John Ceeman	02	266	14	16	07	08	05	12	70	07	00	02	03
John Ceemans Junior	01	28	04	04	02	04	02	00	00	01	00	00	00
Joseph Ballding	00	30	04	06	03	04	03	00	00	01	00	00	00
Thomas Ireland	01	18	00	02	00	01	01	00	00	01	00	00	00
Hendrick Dezbrough	02	50	02	05	00	01	00	00	00	04	00	00	00
John Ellisson: Senior	01	10	04	02	00	00	02	00	00	01	00	00	00
Thomas Ellisson Senior	01	30	02	04	03	03	02	01	00	01	00	00	00
John Carman Junior	01	00	02	04	01	02	02	00	00	00	00	00	00
Caleb Carman	01	00	02	04	00	01	00	00	00	00	00	00	00
Joseph Pettit	00	00	00	03	04	01	00	04	00	00	00	00	00
James Pine	03	40	08	08	02	03	05	04	20	02	00	00	00
William Thickstone	02	23	04	02	00	02	00	1	00	02	00	00	00
Daniel Beagle	01	9½	04	04	00	03	03	2	12	02	00	00	00

VALUATION OF THE ESTATES, &c.—(CONTINUED.)

The Names of the Inhabbitants	heads	Land and meadow	Oxen	Cowes	three year oulds	two year oulds	year oulds	hoggs	sheep	Horses and majors	Ditto 3 years oulds	Ditto 2 years oulds	Ditto year oulds
Josias Starr	01	00	04	05	00	02	04	01	00	02	00	00	00
Jeremiah Wood	01	36	03	05	03	02	04	00	00	01	00	00	00
Jonas Wood	01	00	01	00	02	01	00	00	10	01	00	00	00
Harmen fflower	01	00	04	03	03	02	04	00	00	01	01	00	00
James Mott	01	14	04	05	02	03	03	02	00	01	00	00	00
Richard Gvildersleiff Junr	00	12	02	02	01	00	02	02	00	02	00	00	00
Robert Beagle Senr	01	00	00	03	00	00	00	00	03	00	00	00	00
Rol ert Beagle Junr	01	23	04	03	02	00	01	00	03	01	00	00	00
Matiew Beagle	01	00	04	06	04	02	04	04	00	02	00	00	00
Richd. Guildersleiff Ser	02	50	08	07	05	09	02	00	13	03	00	01	00
George Hicks	01	00	00	00	00	00	00	00	00	00	00	00	00
Abraham ffrost	01	25	00	04	00	00	03	00	00	02	00	00	00
Petter Johnson	02	00	00	02	00	01	02	02	03	01	00	00	00
Jeremiah Wood jur	01	08	04	04	01	02	02	08	16	02	00	00	00
John Saring	01	05	08	08	05	02	03	07	12	00	00	01	00
Joseph Jennings	01	15	04	05	00	04	04	07	20	04	00	00	00
Thomas Suthard	02	25	06	08	02	05	03	07	00	03	00	00	00
Joseph Smith	01	01	04	07	06	05	05	02	00	02	00	01	00
Richd Vallentine Ser	01	34	06	08	02	02	04	01	12	02	00	00	00
Harman Johnson	01	02	00	02	01	00	01	00	00	00	00	00	00

Timothy Halsted	00	00	00	01	00	08	02	05	04	08	04	30	01
William Johnson	00	00	00	01	00	00	00	00	03	00	00	2½	01
George Heulitt	00	00	00	01	00	20	04	07	03	07	07	28	01
Jonathan Smith Rox	00	00	00	02	16	10	07	06	06	10	06	23	00
John Smith Rox: Ser	00	00	00	01	00	12	06	06	05	09	06	50	01
John Mott	00	00	00	02	00	03	03	05	04	03	02	00	01
Ellias & Jnº. Burling	00	00	01	01	04	00	00	00	00	01	00	00	02
William Smith	00	00	00	02	00	04	02	03	00	04	02	25	01
Hendrick Johnson	—	—	—	02	—	01	02	00	00	02	00	12	01
John Allin	—	—	—	—	—	02	00	00	00	02	00	05	01
Joseph Mott	00	00	00	01	20	—	01	02	01	02	—	—	01
Edmond Titus	01	02	00	01	00	00	04	03	02	08	04	29	01
Abraham Smith	00	00	00	04	00	04	06	02	00	05	02	14	00
Hope Williss	00	00	00	00	00	00	04	02	02	05	04	16	00
Thomas Cheessman	00	00	00	01	00	00	02	02	01	02	00	00	01
Jonas Vallentine	00	00	00	00	00	00	01	02	02	00	00	00	00
John Hauckins	00	00	00	01	00	00	00	00	00	05	00	12	01
Mordeika Bedient	00	00	00	02	00	00	00	00	00	01	00	04	01
Joseph Sutton	00	00	00	01	00	00	00	00	00	01	02	16	00
John Oackissam	00	00	00	00	00	00	03	00	00	02	02	25	00
John Bates	00	00	00	02	00	00	00	00	00	00	00	00	01
Jonathan Borge	00	00	00	00	00	00	00	02	00	02	00	00	01
Samuell Allin	00	00	00	02	00	00	02	02	00	03	02	10	01
Thomas Daniell	00	00	00	01	00	01	00	02	01	01	00	02	01
John Hubbs	00	00	00	01	00	01	01	00	00	04	04	10	00
Mr. John Inians	00	00	00	01	00	00	00	02	00	04	02	10	01
Thomass: Hutchinss	00	00	00	00	00	00	00	00	00	01	00	10	01

VALUATION OF THE ESTATES, &c.—(CONTINUED.)

The Names of the Inhabitants	heads	Land and meadow	Oxen	Cowes.	three year oulds	two year oulds	year oulds	hoggs	sheep	Horses and majors	Ditto 3 years ould	Ditto 2 years oulds	Ditto year oulds
Edward Avery	01	12	00	04	00	00	02	00	00	02	00	00	00
Samuel Pines	01	00	04	01	03	02	00	03	00	02	00	00	00
Rich^d. Vallentine Ju	00	06	03	03	02	05	01	00	00	00	00	00	00
Henry Willis	02	25	04	05	03	05	08	05	12	01	00	00	00
John Beedle	01	03	04	02	00	04	02	00	00	01	00	00	00
John Marvin	02	20	05	07	06	07	03	02	00	02	00	00	00
George Persson	01	15	04	03	03	02	02	00	04	01	00	00	00
Thomas Pearsson	01	15	04	03	02	02	02	03	04	01	00	00	00
William Lee	01	08	06	04	00	02	01	07	00	01	00	00	00
Robert Dingee	01	09	00	02	02	01	00	02	00	02	01	01	00
Nathaniell Pearssall	01	55	02	07	05	02	06	08	10	02	00	00	00
William Vallentine	00	02	00	05	02	01	03	02	00	01	00	00	00
Ellias Dorelant	01	22	04	08	06	03	04	02	20	02	00	00	00
Charles Abrahams	01	00	00	02	01	00	03	00	04	00	00	00	00
Rich Minthorne	01	00	04	05	01	02	01	00	00	02	00	00	00
John Pine	01	32	06	04	03	09	04	01	00	02	01	00	00
John Smith Rox: Ju^r	01	33	06	06	05	04	06	04	13	03	00	00	00
Rogger Pedly	01	14	00	01	02	03	02	00	00	01	00	00	00
Henery Linington	02	80	06	18	05	04	00	10	16	04	00	00	00
James Rylei	01	03	02	05	00	00	00	01	00	02	00	00	00

Joseph Langdon	01	32	04	05	00	02	02	00	00	01	00	00	00
Symon Saring	01	00	00	00	01	00	01	03	06	01	00	00	00
Thomass Walliss	01	04	00	02	00	00	01	03	00	01	00	00	00
Thomas Hedger	03	13	00	03	04	00	02	06	00	03	00	00	00
Richd Combes	01	13	02	04	00	02	03	06	00	01	00	00	00
Ralph Haull	01	07	00	03	00	03	00	01	00	01	00	00	01
Hannah Hudson	01	00	00	02	00	00	01	01	00	01	00	00	00
Robert Miller	01	06	02	00	—	—	—	—	—	—	—	—	—
Christopher Yeomans	01	15	02	03	00	02	00	05	00	02	00	00	00
William Thorne	01	16	02	04	03	02	04	03	00	02	00	00	00
William Wi: āte	00	03	00	01	—	—	—	—	—	03	—	—	—
Robert Hubbs Se	02	10	04	04	02	01	00	02	00	01	00	00	00
Robert Hubbs Junior	01	00	00	01	04	00	00	02	00	02	00	00	00
Joseph Williams	00	24	04	04	03	03	03	00	16	01	00	00	00
John Smith, Nan.	01	50	06	05	01	03	01	03	40	02	00	00	00
Jonathan Smith sen^r	00	24	06	05	05	06	03	12	04	01	00	01	00

These vnderwritten are ye Remaind^r of ye Inhabitants of ye said ' Towne which having not Brought in their valluations are Guest att by ye Cunstable and overseirs of ye Towne Afores^d—

	£ s. d.		
James Bates	054:13:04	Joshua Jaicoks	050:00:00
Solloman Cemans	164:13:04	Robert Williams	040:00:00
Samuel Emery	260:10:00	Richd Osbourn	176:00:00
John Champion	100:00:00	Moazes Emery	124:13:04
William Jones	064:10:00	Jeremiah Smith	130:00:00
Edward Cornwall	060:00:00	Jonathan fferman	030:00:00
John Cornwall	040:00:00	Samuell Raynor	080:00:00
Samuell Lancely	040:00:00	Barnat ye Taylor	100:00:00
William Jaicoks	104:13:04	Nathaniell Burcham	150:00:00
Richd Ellisson	190:00:00	Petter Totton	040:00:00
Benjamin Cemans	200:00:00	Jonathan Wood	018:00:00
John March	030:00:00	John Tredwell	250:00:00
Daniel Pearsall	125:10:00	Obediah Valentine	018:00:00
John Ellisson Ju^r	081:10:00	Frances Chappell	018:00:00
Mr Adam Mott Jun^ir	100:00:00	Mr Adam Mott	390:00:00
Samuel Denton	200:00:00		

Script^t as: as p^r ord^r by mee

FRANCIS CHAPPELL Clerke

Endorsed.

The List of y^e
Vallewations of the
Estates of ye inhabbitants
off Hampsted on:
Long: Island
1683.

A LIST OF THE ESTATES OF Y^E INHABITANTS OF OYSTER BAYE FOR A CONTRY RATE, THIS 29TE OF SEP^T 1683.

Imps	lb.		
Josias Latting	080	Henry Townsend: S^r	050
William Hudson	077	Joseph dickinson	038
Aron furman: J^r	080	John ffeexe	130
Tho: furman	039	John underhill	159
Simon Cooper	100	John Wright	073
Job Wright	040	John Townsend	082
Adam Wright	040	Georg douning	080
		John Wood	039

Jeams Townsend........ 090
Isack dotty.............. 066
Samuel dickinson........ 078
Caleb Wright............ 058
Abraham Aling........... 032
John Roger.............. 058
Jeams Cok.............. 100
Daniell harcutt.......... 079
nathanell Colles.......... 070
mary willits............. 220
Richard willits.......... 090
Edmund wright.......... 060
hope williams........... 100
John Townsend.......... 090
John williams.......... 050
Tho: willits............. 090
John Townsend: Jr....... 050
daniell Colles........... 100
Samuell Andrews........ 100
mathy prior. 100
John prior.............. 040
Joseph Carpenter........ 100
John ffrost.............. 030
John Robins............. 040
Aron furman: Sr......... 060
Samuell furman.......... 050
Richard harcutt.......... 080
Tho: youngs............. 040
Jeams weeks............. 050
franses weeks........... 040
Tho: weeks 050
Joseph Ludlam.......... 050

Georg Townsend 050
John weeks 040
william buttlar.......... 030
Gideon wright........... 040
Alce Crab.............. 100
Isack hornor 040
henry Townsend Jr 040
nathanell underhill 030
Ben: Birdsall............ 050
will: hoackshurst.......... 030
Samuel weeks........... 040
Joseph weeks 040
John Colles 020
Larance mott............ 018
william frost............ 100
Edward wright.......... 020
Samuell tilliar 030
John dauis 040
Joseph Eastland 040
Ephraim Carpenter 050
moses mudge............ 030
Robort Colles............ 080
nickolas Simkins......... 060
William willson.......... 020
John williams........... 040
Samuell pell............. 040
william Crafftt.......... 090
Richard Cirby 090
John ffry 040
Tho: Cok 040
Jeames Bleving.......... 020
John newman............ 020

The Inhabytants being at this time sikly and not sending in there lists, Acccording to order, the ouersears, ye Constable being Absent at roadislond did laye A valewation upon Euery mans Eastate to ye best of there vnderstanding According to law.

A true list p me   EDMUND WRIGHT, deputy Constable
Endorsed. "Oyster Baye Publique Rates. 1683."

A LIST OF THE RATABLE ESTATE OF Y^E TOWN OF HUNTINGTON TAKEN IN Y^E YEER 1683.

	£	s.	d.
Stephen Jarvice Ju^eir	031	00	00
John michall	026	10	00
Capt tho: ffleete	178	10	00
Stephen Jarvice Sein^r	123	00	00
Robert Cranfield	115	00	00
tho: Scudder	205	00	00
James Chichester se^ier	131	10	00
Nath: ffoster	088	00	00
Rob: Artor	039	00	00
Joseph Wood Cooper	076	00	00
tho: Higbe	032	10	00
Capt Joseph Baily	077	10	00
tho: whitton	111	10	00
John weeks	152	00	00
John wood	038	00	00
Isaac Platt	177	10	00
Joseph wood husband-man	158	10	00
Calleb wood	132	00	00
tho: Powell	233	00	00
Sam: wood	137	10	00
Jonathan miller	080	10	00
Robart Kellam	076	10	00
Jonathan Harnot	065	00	00
tho weeks	133	00	00
Jams Smith	087	00	00
John daucie	043	00	00
John Coxe	090	00	00
Richard daucie	033	00	00
Leu^tt Epenetus Platt	211	00	00
John Brush	082	00	00
tho: Brush	129	00	00
Richard brush	106	00	00
Jonas Wood Ju^eir	114	00	00
Joseph Whettman	145	00	00

Abiell tittus	092	00	00
Samuel tittus	127	00	00
Samuel Kicham	134	00	00
Richard Williams	159	00	00
dauid Scudder	086	00	00
Edward Kicham	056	00	00
John Kicham	084	00	00
Moses Scudder	054	00	00
Jonathan Scudder	122	00	00
John Jones	079	00	00
timothy Conklin	110	00	00
John Samons	133	00	00
Edward Higbe	034	00	00
John Betts	161	10	00
Jonathan Rodgers	204	00	00
James Chichester Ju^ier	073	00	00
Jeremiah Smith	066	00	00
George balldin	108	00	00
Edward Bunce	155	00	00
tho Scidmore	081	00	00
John Inkerson	154	00	00
tho: martin	057	00	00
John golldin	087	10	00
Phillip Bell	104	00	00
William Brodderton	095	00	00
John Green	084	00	00
Niccolas Smith	043	00	00
Edward Rutte	078	00	00
John Page	040	00	00
Jonathan Lewice	055	00	00
John Scidmore Ju^ier	026	00	00
John Scidmore Senier	030	00	00
John Aaddams	035	00	00
John Joanes	018	00	00
Samuell Griffin	018	00	00
tho: Bishop	018	00	00

This is A True Account as it is giuen to mee   ISAAC PLATT Constable

SMITH'S TOWNE ESTIMATIONS SEPT Yᴱ 28 1683.

	Heads	Lands	Oxen	Cowes	3 yr olds	2 yr old	1 yr old	horses	3 yr olds	2 yr olds	1 yr olds	Swine	Sheeps	
Richd Smith sen.........	00	60	00	09	02	00	00	07	00	00	00	20	20	201 13 4
Jonath. Smith........	02	25	06	07	07	06	05	04	00	01	00	80	04	304 06 08
Richd Smith Junʳ.....	03	33	06	08	07	03	07	06	00	00	00	30	06	306 00 00
Job Smith	01	13	04	04	01	00	00	00	00	00	00	14	00	092 00 00
Adam Smith......	01	09	06	03	00	00	01	05	00	00	00	08	00	147 10 00
Sam Smith......	01	15	04	02	04	01	03	04	00	00	00	25	00	158 10 00
Daniell Smith......	01	12	05	04	00	00	00	03	00	00	00	14	00	130 00 00
														1340

which at 1ᵈ p pound amounts to yᵉ sum of   05 10 08

Endorsed   " The Estimation off Smiths Towne."

VALUACON OF THE RATABLE ESTATE BELONGING TO BROOKEHAVEN ANNO 1683

Name	Heads	Lands and meadow	Horses	three yeare old	two yeare old	yearlings	Oxen & Bulls	Cowes	three yeare old	two yeare old	yearlings	Sheep	Swine
Petr Whitehaire	1	24	1	0	0	1	2	5	0	1	1	0	18
Saml Tyrell	1	3	1	0	0	0	0	1	0	0	0	0	3
Thomas Ward	0	12	1	0	0	0	2	3	2	2	2	0	6
Thomas Helme	1	7	4	0	0	0	0	0	0	0	0	0	5
John Thomas	1	4	1	0	0	1	0	0	0	0	0	0	1
Richard Hulse	2	2	1	0	0	0	2	2	0	2	2	0	0
Willm Sallyer	1	11	2	0	0	0	0	3	0	0	1	0	0
Tho: Biggs Junr	1	32	1	0	0	1	4	7	4	3	2	0	7
John Bennett	1	2	1	0	0	0	0	1	0	0	0	0	2
Jacob Longbottom	1	20	2	0	0	1	4	3	2	1	2	0	15
John Biggs	1	12	1	0	0	0	3	2	0	0	0	0	1
Obed Sayward	3	12	4	0	0	0	4	3	2	2	2	3	3
Saml Akerly	1	24	1	0	0	0	2	3	0	0	1	0	1
Antho Tompson	1	7	1	0	0	0	0	1	0	0	0	0	3
Willm Jayne	2	20	1	0	0	0	0	1	0	1	0	0	6
Jno Tooker Junr	1	5	1	1	0	0	0	3	2	1	0	0	1
Thomas Smith	1	14	3	0	0	0	2	4	0	2	2	0	6
Benja Smith	1	22	1	0	0	0	2	2	0	1	0	0	12
John Smith	1	7	1	0	0	0	0	1	0	0	0	0	6

Jnᵒ Besswick	0	0	0	1	0	4	0	0	0	0	1	0	1
Robᵗ Gouldsbury	1	0	0	0	0	0	0	0	0	0	4	8	1
John Roe	5	0	2	2	2	4	2	0	0	0	1	30	1
Andrew Gibb	0	0	1	0	0	2	2	0	0	1	2	6	1
Nat. Norton	5	0	2	3	3	4	2	1	0	0	2	20	1
Willᵐ Satterly	9	3	2	1	2	5	2	1	1	0	2	20	1
Samˡˡ Dayton	8	0	1	0	1	4	2	0	0	0	5	6	1
Andrew Miller	9	0	3	2	2	3	4	0	0	0	6	20	2
Zack: Hawkins	20	0	5	1	3	5	2	1	0	0	4	24	2
John Mosier	3	0	1	0	2	2	0	0	0	0	1	6	1
Michaell Lane	2	0	0	1	0	2	0	0	0	0	1	23	2
Walter Jones	0	0	0	0	0	0	0	0	0	0	1	3	1
Henry Rogers	1	0	0	2	0	2	2	0	0	0	1	13	0
John Wood	1	0	1	0	0	3	0	0	0	0	5	10	1
George Wood	0	0	1	0	0	1	0	0	0	0	0	10	1
Richᵈ Clarke	0	0	1	0	0	1	0	0	0	0	2	4	1
John Wade	0	0	0	0	0	0	4	0	0	0	0	1	1
John Toker senʳ	17	0	5	4	5	4	4	0	0	0	6	36	2
Tho: Briggs senʳ	6	0	2	0	0	3	0	0	0	0	3	13	0
Benjᵃ Gould	7	0	0	1	0	3	2	0	0	0	2	0	1
Abra Dayton	4	0	0	0	0	2	2	0	0	0	3	4	2
Jonat Rose	8	0	2	0	2	6	2	0	0	0	8	3	1
Joseph Davis	1	0	2	1	1	2	2	0	1	0	1	30	2
Richᵈ Waring	1	0	2	0	1	3	2	0	2	0	2	30	2
John Jennons	2	2	1	2	2	2	2	0	0	0	0	15	1
Thomas Jennons	0	0	0	0	0	1	0	0	0	0	0	0	1
Dennis Morphew	0	0	0	0	0	0	0	0	0	0	0	0	1

VALUATION OF THE RATABLE ESTATE, &c.—(CONTINUED.)

	Heads	Lands and meadow	Horses	three yeare old	two yeare old	yearlings	Oxen & Bulls	Cowes	three yeare old	two yeare old	yearlings	Sheep	Swine
Jnº Lawrence	1	0	0	0	0	0	0	0	0	0	0	0	0
Joseph Longbottome	1	36	4	0	0	0	4	5	0	0	0	0	20
Ralph Dayton	1	5	1	0	2	0	2	3	0	0	1	0	2
John Tomson	2	26	4	2	0	0	0	2	0	0	0	0	3
John Comes	1	06	1	0	0	0	0	4	2	1	1	0	0
Richard ffloyd	2	94	10	00	01	00	02	06	06	00	00	15	33
	62	742	112	04	8	07	75	133	46	38	51	23	264

£20: 19: 8d

THE ESTEMATION OF SOUTHOLD FOR Y^E YEAR 1683 STEPHEN BAILEY CCNSTABLE: THOMAS MOOR SIN^R BENJAMEN YOUNGS JONATHAN HORTON THOMAS MAPPS JUN^R OVERSEERS.

	£ s d		£ s d
Mr John Budd.....	350.00.00	John Reevs.......	076.00.00
Jarimiah Vaell Senr.	074.00.00	Daniell Terry......	141.00.00
John Paine Junr ...	040.00.00	Petter Dickeson....	121.00.00
Jasper Griffing.....	1ll.00.00	Thomas Dickeson...	083.00.00
Henry Case........	035.00.00	Joseph Reevs......	065.00.00
Lott Jonsone......	019.00.00	Nathaniell Ferry....	073.00.00
Simon Grouer......	073.00.00	Willm Wells......	085.00.00
Nathaniel moore....	046.00.00	Josiah Wells.......	081.00.00
Thomas moore Senr.	049.00.00	Samuell Winds.....	082.00.00
Joseph Youngs.....	098.00.00	Simion benjemen...	117.00.00
Samuell Youngs....	084.00.00	Garsham Terry.....	084.00.00
Petter Paine.......	056.00.00	John Goldsmith....	121.00.00
Christopher Youngs.	080.00.00	Thomas mapes Junr.	128.00.00
Stephen Bailey.....	103.00.00	Caleb Horton......	350.00.00
John Bailey.......	018.00.00	Benjamen Horton..	267.00.00
John Youngs mariner	058.00.00	Willm Colman.....	078.00.00
Benjamin Youngs...	123.00.00	Willm Reeves......	100.00.00
John Salmon.......	041.00.00	Thomas Tuston.....	066.00.00
Mr John Booth.....	131.00.00	Theophilus Curwin.	084.00.00
John Carwine......	131.06.0S	Thomas Mapps Senr.	244.00.00
Thomas Prickman..	042 00.00	James Reevs.......	228.00.00
Jonathan Horton....	440.13.04	Thomas Terrill.....	105.00.00
Richard Benjamen..	133.00.00	Petter Haldriag....	040.00.00
Benjamin Moore....	080.10.00	Thomas Osman....	228 00.00
Jarimiah Vaell Jeu^r.	103.00.00	John Osman	050.00.00
John Hallock......	080.00.00	Willm Haliock.....	236.00.00
Abraham Corey....	076.00.00	Thomas Haliock....	081.00.00
Ann Elton.........	077.00.00	John Swazey.......	202.00.00
Josuah Horton.....	173.00.00	Joseph Swazey.....	099.00.00
Isaac Ouenton.....	100.10.00	John Frankling.....	033.00.00
Barnibus Winds....	122.00.00	Thomas Ridder.....	166.00.00
Jacob Corey.......	092.00.00	Jacob Conkling....	101.00.00
Theopulos Case.....	109.00.00	John Hopson.......	083.00.00
Y^e Widdow Terry..	097.00.00	John Conkling.....	321.00.00

Willm Hopkins.... 046.00.00
John Rackett...... 057.00.00
Jonathan Moore.... 202.00.00
John Young Junr... 225.00.00
Christopher Youngs. 044.00.00
Timothy Martin.... 057.00.00
John Wiggins...... 068.00.00
Thomas Moore Junr. 137.00.00
Richard Brown Senr ⎫
Richard Brown Junr ⎬ 386.00.00
Jonathan Brown ⎭
John Tutoll Senr... 239.00.00
John Tutoll Junr... 099.00.00
Samuell King...... 150.00.00
Abraham Whitter... 180.00.00
Thomas terry...... 139.00.00
Gidion Youngs..... 173.00.00
John Paine Senr.... 94.00.00

Edward Peatty 062.00.00
John Lorring...... 076.00.00
Samuell Glouer.... 104.00.00
Calob Curtis....... 108.00.00
Cornilious Paine.... 081.00.00
Richard howell..... 098.00.00
Thomas booth...... 045.00.00
John Liman....... 018.00.00
Ebine Dauice...... 030.00.00
Richard Edgcomb.. 018.00.00
John Booth June^r... 018.00.00
Jonathan Reeves.... 030.00.00
Y^e totall Sume is.. 10819.00.00
   pr Stephen Bayley town clerk
Endorsed
   S^o hold the Esteemation for
ye year 1683

THE ESTEMATE OF THE TOWNE OF SOUTHAMPTON FOR THE YEAR 1683.

No. of Poles.

0 Widdow Hannah
   Howell 267 00 00
3 John Annings.... 088 10 00
3 Captn John Howell 442 10 00
2 Lief^t Joseph Ford-
   ham 459 10 00
3 Thomas Halsey .. 411 16 08
5 Edward Howell.. 400 00 00
2 Peregrine Stan-
   brough 320 16 08
2 Job Sayre....... 164 10 00
1 James Topping .. 249 06 08
1 Benjamin Palmer. 089 00 00
1 Josiah Stanbron... 130 00 00
3 John Davess..... 140 00 00
2 John Rose....... 133 00 00

No. of Poles.

1 Joseph Post...... 062 03 04
1 Simon Hillyard... 023 00 00
1 Benjamin Hand.. 086 00 00
1 Thomas Rose.... 047 10 00
1 John Burnett 056 06 08
1 Joseph More 083 00 00
2 Willm Hakelton.. 041 00 00
1 Thomas Burnett.. 119 06 08
1 Mr Phillips...... 164 06 08
0 Mrs Mary Taylor
   Widdow........ 064 13 04
2 Francis Sayre.... 178 00 00
2 Isaac Halsey..... 345 00 00
3 John Jessup...... 360 06 08
2 Henry Ludlam.... 203 13 04
1 Lott Burnett..... 100 00 00

1 James Hildreth... 030 00 00
1 Ezekiell Sandford. 060 00 00
1 Peter Norris...... 051 00 00
1 Robert Norriss.... 052 00 00
2 Joseph Marshall.. 058 00 00
1 John Rainor...... 094 00 00
1 John Jennings 129 10 00
1 Isaac Rainer...... 064 00 00
1 James White 092 16 08
1 John Lupton 067 00 00
1 Widdow   Mary
  Rainer.......... 166 00 00
1 Benony Newton.. 067 00 00
1 Samuell Mills.... 032 00 00
1 Samuell Lum 076 00 00
1 Edmond Clarke .. 056 10 00
2 Widdow   Sarah
  Cooper.......... 337 06 08
1 Obadiah   Roggers
  Junr 052 00 00
3 Tho: Travally.... 229 10 00
1 Mr Jonah Fordham 081 13 04
1 Josiah Halsey.... 125 13 04
1 Christopher Leam-
  ing 053 13 04
1 Jonathan Rainor.. 197 03 04
3 Daniell Sayre.... 207 03 04
0 Joseph Sayre 023 00 00
1 Benjamin Pierson. 051 06 08
1 John Laughton... 098 06 08
3 Charles Sturmey.. 198 10 00
2 Joseph Foster.... 138 03 04
1 Obadiah Roggers.. 200 16 08
1 Joseph Peirson.... 127 06 08
1 Isaac Mills 089 03 04
2 Samuell Whitehead 053 00 00
1 Robert Wooly 118 00 00
1 Thomas Cooper Junr 163 00 00

2 Joshua Barnes and
  Sam 232 13 04
2 John Jagger...... 289 10 00
2 Thomas Cooper .. 209 06 08
1 Widow   Martha
  Cooke........... 194 13 04
2 John Foster...... 178 06 08
1 John Lawrison ... 254 00 00
1 John Howell Junr. 121 10 00
1 John Earle...... 046 00 00
1 Christo: Foster ... 074 00 00
2 Richard Post 100 06 08
1 Abraham Howell. 043 00 00
1 John Post 169 13 04
1 David Brigs...... 040 00 00
1 Samuell   Clarke:
  old towne 059 10 00
1 David Howell.... 077 00 00
1 Josiah Laughton.. 024 00 00
1 Ben: Davess 107 06 08
1 Nathan^ll Short.... 030 00 00
1 Thomas Steephens 080 00 00
1 Gersham Culver.. 098 06 08
1 Thomas Goodwin. 030 00 00
1 Isaac Cory...... 148 03 04
2 John Bishop Junr. 055 13 04
2 Samuell Johnes.... 249 16 08
1 Abraham Willman 054 10 00
1 Henry Peirson.... 136 10 00
1 Samuell Clarke N^o:
  Sea............ 113 00 00
1 John Woodroufe.. 160 00 00
2 Elnathan Topping 275 00 00
3 John Bishop...... 214 10 00
1 Isaac Willman .. 187 10 00
1 Hanah   Topping
  widow.......... 180 00 00

No. of Poles

1 Humphrey Hughes 052 06 08
1 Thomas Reeves.. 101 00 00
1 John Cooke 169 00 00
1 John Mappein.... 112 13 04
1 Shamger Hand.... 089 13 04
1 John Else 030 06 08
1 Benony Flinte.... 060 00 00
1 Joseph Hiledreth. 100 00 00
1 John Carwithy f .. 040 00 00
2 Richard Howell.. 250 00 00
2 Thomas Shaw.... 060 00 00
1 Edmond Howell.. 240 00 00
3 Xtopher Lupton.. 200 00 00
1 George Harriss... 137 00 00
1 Richard   Howell
    Junʳ........... 050 00 00
1 John Morehouse.. 064 00 00
1 Willᵐ Mason.... 050 00 00
2 James Herrick... 180 00 00
1 William Herrike.. 059 00 00
3 Benjamin Foster.. 220 00 00
1 Aron Burnett.... 037 00 00
0 Widow Fowler... 027 00 00
1 Benjamin Haines. 140 00 00
1 Mathew Howell.. 070 00 00
1 Manassah Kompton 018 00 00
1 George Owen.... 023 00 00
1 Thirston Rainor .. 040 00 00
1 Mʳ William Barker 060 00 00
1 Willᵐ Simpkins.. 040 00 00
1 Mʳ Henry Goreing 018 00 00
1 John Gould 040 00 00

1 Joseph Whitehead. 030 00 00
1 Samuell Cooper.. 035 00 00
1 Josiah Barthallomew 018 00 00
1 Onesipherus Stand-
    ley 018 00 00
2 Abram Hauke.... 060 00 00
1 Zachary Laurance. 018 00 00
1 Callob Carwithy.. 018 00 00
1 John Petty...... 030 00 00
1 Thomas Shaw Junʳ 018 00 00
1 Isaac Willman Junʳ 030 00 00
0 Robert Kallem... 010 00 00
0 George Hethcote . 022 00 00
  John Sanders..... 012 00 00
1 John Wooley 018 00 00
1 Edward White... 030 00 00
1 Jonat Hildreth ... 030 00 00
1 John Mouberry .. 030 00 00
1 Mʳ Frencham 018 00 00

Sum totall is.. 16328 06 08
ZEROBABELL PYLLIPS Constable
JOHN JAGARR   ⎞
JOHN FOSTER   ⎟
JONᴼ HOWELL Junʳ   ⎬ Overseers
JOSEPH PEIRSON   ⎠
Southampton Septʳ yᵉ 1ˢᵗ 1683
    A true copy of yᵉ originall
by mee
    JOHN HOWELL Junʳ Clarke
Endorsed
    The Estemation of the Town
of Southampton   1683

SEPTEMBER Yᴇ 8ᵀᴴ 1683 THE ESTEMATE OF EASTHAMPTON.

	heads	Land	Oxen	Cowes	3	2	1	Horses	3	2	1	Swine	Sheep	lb s d
Capt Talmage	4	20	8	12	10	6	9	5	1	2	0	6	44	362– 3–4
Tho osborne	3	20	8	8	10	7	8	2	0	0	0	9	48	280–10–0
Wᵐ Mulforde	2	16	2	4	4	3	4	0	0	0	0	2	26	106– 3–4
Tho: Mulford	1	0	0	3	2	2	3	1	0	0	0	0	5	064– 3–4
Mr Baker	2	21	4	8	4	7	7	4	0	3	0	6	30	244– 0–0
Tho Edwards	1	10	2	5	3	1	2	2	0	0	0	5	0	117–10–0
John parsons Sen	1	12	0	2	2	0	2	2	0	0	2	0	12	079– 0–0
Jere: Conkling	3	28	4	8	8	7	8	2	0	0	0	4	35	247– 3–4
phillip Leek	1	4	0	3	2	0	1	0	0	0	0	4	12	057–10–0
Nath: Baker sᵉ	1	15	4	6	4	4	6	3	0	1	1	1	12	174– 0–0
Joshua garlick	1	9	4	3	3	0	2	2	0	0	2	1	14	110–13–4
capt Hoberts	2	10	0	4	1	0	0	1	0	0	0	1	3	095– 0–0
Nath donceny	1	13	2	2	0	1	0	1	1	1	1	1	0	73–10–0
John parsons	1	8	3	5	4	8	7	2	0	0	0	6	27	157–10–0
James Drinent	1	13	6	8	4	4	6	2	1	0	0	3	24	180– 0–0
Samu: parsons	2	13	2	5	3	4	6	5	0	1	0	0	15	158– 0–0
Wᵐ Bary	2	13	2	3	3	1	3	4	2	1	0	1	12	155– 0–0
John Whellen	1	13	2	5	2	6	2	3	0	1	1	2	25	144– 6–8
Enock fithian	1	6	1	4	2	2	3	0	0	1	0	2	10	072–16–8
John osborn	3	13	2	11	10	8	8	2	0	1	0	2	21	251– 0–0

ESTIMATE OF EASTHAMPTON, &c.—(CONTINUED.)

	heads	Land	Oxen	Cowes	3	2	1	Horses	3	2	1	Swine	Sheep	lb s d
James Hand	1	6	2	2	0	4	2	1	0	1	0	2	9	081– 0–0
Rich: Brook	2	15	2	5	0	3	3	1	0	0	1	1	12	120– 0–0
Mr Scellinger	3	16	6	7	2	2	6	5	0	1	0	0	54	246– 0–0
Benia: Conkling	1	12	0	5	3	6	4	2	1	3	1	5	17	148–13–4
John Miller se	1	13	4	4	4	4	4	1	1	1	0	0	28	140–13–4
Arthur Cresy	1	2	0	2	3	1	1	0	0	0	1	2	7	053– 6–8
Ben: Osborne	2	20	4	4	2	9	4	1	1	0	0	3	10	162–16–8
Wm Edwards	1	24	3	5	8	5	5	2	1	0	1	8	0	180– 0–0
Joseph Osborne	1	6	0	3	0	1	1	3	0	0	0	1	6	082– 0–0
John Squire	1	6	2	4	0	1	2	2	0	0	0	0	0	085–10–0
John Edwards	1	13	2	4	4	2	3	2	1	0	0	3	0	123–10–0
Ebene Leeke	1	2	0	2	0	0	1	2	0	1	1	0	0	063–10–0
James Looper	1	6	0	2	0	0	0	2	0	0	0	2	8	062–13–4
Wm Perkins	2	13	6	5	8	7	8	4	0	0	0	3	37	216–16–8
Stephen Hand	1	13	4	5	4	5	4	2	0	0	0	2	48	174–10–0
Tho diment	1	6	0	2	2	4	4	1	0	0	0	3	9	076– 0–0
John Miller Ju	1	6	2	3	3	2	2	2	0	0	0	4	15	104– 0–0
Jere: Miller	1	3	2	2	2	3	1	2	0	0	0	2	5	087–13–4
Edward Joans	1	3	0	3	1	0	2	1	0	0	0	0	0	055– 0–0

Name														£–s–d
James Bird	1	3	0	2	1	0	0	1	0	0	0	0	2	047–13–4
John Stretton	3	30	5	8	7	7	7	3	1	0	0	4	37	270– 6–8
John Stretton Ju.	1	10	2	5	5	6	5	2	1	0	0	4	35	154– 3–4
Joseph Stretton	1	0	0	6	3	3	7	1	0	0	0	1	15	100– 0–0
Samuell Mulford	1	20	2	6	3	4	4	2	0	1	1	3	15	148– 0–0
John Hoping	1	23	2	6	7	6	11	3	1	1	0	5	23	209– 3–4
John Feild	1	0	0	2	2	0	0	1	0	0	0	2	6	052– 0–0
Stephen Hodges	1	20	6	12	13	5	14	5	1	0	0	5	23	301– 3–4
Anthony Kelley	1	0	0	0	0	0	0	1	0	0	0	0	0	030– 0–0
Oliuer Noris	1	0	0	1	0	0	0	0	0	0	0	0	1	023– 6–8
Edward Hare	1	0	0	0	0	0	0	2	0	0	0	0	0	042– 0–0
Widow Shaw	2	0	2	2	2	1	1	0	0	0	0	1	6	073– 0–0
Rchard Shaw	1	8	0	1	2	0	0	3	0	1	0	1	0	081– 0–0
Tho Stretton	1	6	0	3	1	1	1	3	0	0	0	0	0	086– 0–0
Wm Hambleton	1	0	2	0	0	0	0	1	0	0	1	0	0	042– 0–0
Samuell Shery	1	7	2	4	0	2	0	3	1	0	0	3	0	102– 6–8
John Cerle	2	7	2	6	1	3	4	2	0	0	0	6	10	119–10–0
John Mulford	2	20	8	10	0	7	8	2	1	0	0	8	12	283–16–8
Thomas Chatfield	1	21	7	9	7	8	7	1	0	0	0	6	58	234–03–4
Nath Baker Ju.	2	4	2	4	1	3	3	3	1	0	0	0	44	118– 0–0
Robert Daiton	2	26	4	7	6	6	7	6	0	0	1	4	12	261– 3–4
Nath Bushup	1	13	4	7	4	3	5	3	0	0	0	2	32	189– 0–0
Rich: Stretton	1	6	0	3	1	4	2	1	0	0	1	0	30	070– 6–8
Tho Hand	1	8	4	5	2	2	2	2	0	0	1	2	4	121– 6–8
John Brook	1	16	0	3	2	3	3	1	0	0	0	4	16	087– 0–0
Tho Bee	1	3	0	2	1	2	2	3	0	0	0	4	6	081– 0–0
Wm Miller	1	8	2	4	4	6	5	2	0	2	2	7	17	148– 3–4

ESTIMATE OF EASTHAMPTON, &c.—(CONTINUED.)

	heads	Land	Oxen	Cowes	3	2	1	Horses	3	2	1	Swine	Sheep	lb s d
georg Miller	1	0	0	1	3	3	1	1	0	0	0	0	0	056– 0–0
Bewlick Osborne,	head and horse													030– 0–0
John Michell														030– 0–0
Tho Chatfield Ju														030– 0–0
Jacob Daiton														050– 0–0
The Totall is														9075– 6–8

Endorsed.

East hamptons
Estemation
168?

EARLY IMMIGRANTS TO NEW NETHERLAND; 1657 — 1664.

1657.

APRIL; *In the Draetvat.*

Arent Janssen; house carpenter, and Wife and daughter.
Marcus de Chousoy, and Wife, two workmen, and two boys.
Teunis Craey, from Venlo, and Wife and four children & two servants.
Heinrich Stoeff.
Jacob Hendricksen Haen; painter.
Adriaen Vincent.
Johannis Smetdes.
Dirk Buyskes.

DECEMBER; *In the Gilded Otter.*

Claes Pouwelson from Detmarsum; mason.
Jan Jansen van den Bos; mason, and his Brother.

DITTO; *In the Jan Baptiste.*

Jan Sudeich, and Wife and two Children.
Claes Sudeich.
Adam Breemen, from Aecken.
Douwe Claessen from Medemblick; mason.
Cornelis Barentsen Vande Kuyl.
Thys Jacobsen.

1658.

MAY; *In the Moesman.*

Jan Adriaensen van Duyvelant.
Christina Bleyers from Stoltenau.
Ursel Dircks from Holstein & 2 children.
Geertzen Buyers.

DITTO; *In the Gilded Beaver.*

Jan Barentsen house Carpenter, and Workman.
Anthony de Mis from Haerlem, and Wife and two children.
The Wife of Andries vander Sluys; Clerk in Fort Orange, and child.
Charel Fonteyn; a Frenchman, and Wife.
Peter Claessen, from Holstein; farmer & Wife and two children.
Gerrit Gerritsen van Gilthuys; Taylor.
Jan Jansen; house Carpenter, & Wife and four children.
Jan Gouwenberch, from Hoorn.
Adriaen van Laer, from Amsterdam, & servant.
Jan Gerretsen Buytenhuys; Baker, & Wife and sucking child.
Willem van Vredenburch.
Cornelis Andriessen Hoogland; Taylor.
Peter van Halen, from Utrecht, & Wife, two children, and boy.
Simon Bouché.
Cornelis Hendricksen van Ens.
Jan Evertsen van Gloockens.
Tryntje Pieters; Maiden.

JUNE; *In the Brownfish.*

Jannetje Volckertse Wife of Evert Luykese; Baker, and daughter.
Douwe Harmsen, from Friesland, & Wife and four children.
Adriaen Jansen, from Zea-land; fisherman.
Francois Abrahamsen, from Flissingen.
Joris Jansen, from Hoorn; House Carpenter.
Jan Aerensen van Kampen; Farmer.
Jan Isbrands; rope maker.
Huybert de Bruyn.
Machteld Stoffelsen; Widow, is acquainted with agriculture.
Dirck Smith, Ensign in the Company's Service 1, & a sucking child.
Jannetje Hermens; maiden, and her Brother Jan Harmensen.
Maria Claes; maiden.
Francisco de Gordosa from Davingen.
Charles Garet.
Jan Leynie, from Paris.
Dorigeman Jansen, from Dordrecht & his bride.
Claes Wolf, from the Elbe; Sailor.
Harmen Dircksen from Norway & Wife and child.
Adam van Santen, & Wife and two children.

1659.

FEBRUARY; *In the Faith.*

Jan Woutersen, from Ravesteyn; shoemaker, & Wife and daughter.
Catalyntje Cranenburg; maiden.
Jan van Coppenol, from Remsen; farmer, & Wife and 2 children.
Matthys Roelofs, from Denmark, & Wife and child.
Sophia Roeloffs.
Geertruy Jochems, from Hamburgh; Wife of Claes Claessen from Amersfoort, now in N. Netherland; and two children.
Peter Corneliss, from Holsteyn; Labourer.
Peter Jacobs, from Holsteyn.
Josyntje Verhagen, from Middelburg, & daughter.
Saertge Hendricks, from Delft.
Egbert Meynderts, from Amsterdam, & Wife and child and servant.
Jan Leurens Noorman & Wife.
Harmen Coerten, from Voorhuysen, & Wife and 5 Children.
Magalantje Teunis, from Voorhuysen.
Feytje Dircks.
Gillis Jansen van Garder, & Wife and four children.
Bastiaen Clement, from Doornick.
Adriaen Fournoi, from Valenciennes.
Jannetje Eyckers, from East Friesland.
Joris Jorissen Townsen, from Redfort; **mason.**
Nicholas Gillissen Marschal.
Wouter Gerritsen van Kootuyck.
Jan Jacobsen, from Utrecht; farmer, & Wife, mother and two children.
Arent Francken van Iperen.

1 Served in the Esopus war with great credit; he died Anno 1660 to the regret of the Director General and council. His widow thereupon returned to Holland. ED.

Dennys Isacksen, from Wyck by Daurstede.

Weyntje Martens van Gorehem.

Vroutje Gerrits, wife of Cosyn Gerritsen; Wheelwright.

Jan Dircksen, from Alckmaer, & Wife and three children.

Nettert Jansen, from Embden.

Epke Jacobs, from Harlingen; farmer, and wife and five sons.

Stoffiel Gerritsen from Laer.

Jan Meynderts, from Iperen; farmer, and Wife.

Jan Barents Ameshof, from Amsterdam.

Symon Drune from Henegouw.

Hendrick Harmensen, from Amsterdam.

Evert Cornellissen, from the vicinity of Amersfoort.

Laurens Jacobs van der Wielen.

Jannetje Theunis van Ysselstein.

Jan Roelofsen, van Naerden; farmer.

Jacob Hendricks, from the Highland, and maid servant.

Goossen van Twiller, from New-Kerk.

Lawrens Janssen, from Wormer.

Jan Harmens, from Amersfoort; Taylor, and Wife and four children.

Evert Marschal; glasier, from Amsterdam and Wife and daughter.

Boele Roelofsen, Joncker, and wife and four children, besides his Wife's sister and a boy.

DITTO; *In the Otter.*

Carel Bevois, from Leyden; and Wife and three children.

Marten Warnarts Stolten, from Swoll.

Cornelis Jansen vander veer; farmer.

Jan Luycas, from Oldenseel; shoemaker, and Wife and suckling.

Roelof Dircksen, from Sweden.

Sweris Dirxsz, from Sweden.

APRIL; *In the Beaver.*

Peter Arentsen Diesvelt; taylor.

Amadeas Fougie, Frenchman, farmer.

Jacques Reneau, Frenchman; Agriculturer.

Jacques Monier, Frenchman; Agriculturer.

Pierre Monier, Frenchman; Agriculturer.

Matthieu Savariau, Frenchman; Agriculturer.

Pierre Grissaut, Frenchman; Agriculturist.

Maintien Jans, from Amsterdam; maiden.

Peter Follenaer, from Hasselt.

Cornelis Michielsen, from Medemblick.

Grietje Christians, from Tonningen.

Claes Jansen, from Purmerend; wheelwright, and Wife, servant and child.

Marten van de Wert, from Utrecht; hatter.

Peter van Ecke; planter, from Leyden.

Jacobus vander Schelling, and his boy.

Albert Theunissen vermeulen, from Rotterdam, and Wife and four children.

Geertry van Meulen; maiden.

Hannetje Ruytenbeck, maiden.

Matthew Andriessen, from Peters-houck.

Hendrick Theunisz Hellinck and wife.

Lawrens van der Spiegel van Vlissingen.

DITTO; *In the Moesman.*

Lysbeth Arents, Wife of Corn: Barents, and daughter.

Aertje Leenders; widow, from Amsterdam.

Barent van Loo from Elburg.

Willem Jansen, from Rotterdam, Fisherman, and Wife and sucking child, and maid servant.

Peter Petersen, alias Pia, from Picardy, and Wife and daughter.

Dirch Belet, from Breda; cooper.

Louis Aertz, from Bruges; planter.

Gerrit Corn. van Niew-Kerk, and Wife and boy and sucking child.

Engelbrecht Sternhuysen, from Soest; Tailor.

Thys Jansen, from TerGouw; Agriculturist.

Albert Petersen; mason.

Geerty Claesen.

Gerrit Petersen.

Gillis Mandeville.

DECEMBER; *In the Faith.*

Christiaen de Lorie, from St. Malo.

Hendrick Jansen Spiers and Wife and two children.

Adriaen Huybertsen Sterrevelt; Agriculturist.

Harmen Stepfer, from the Dutchy of Cleef.

Joost Adriaensen Pynacker, from Delft.

Philip Langelens; Agriculturist, and Wife and two children.

Hendrick Bos, from Leyden, and Wife and two children.

Gerrit Gerritsen, from Wageningen, and Wife and one child.

William Aertsen, from Wagening.

Gerrit van Manen, from Wagening.

Albert Gerritsen, from Wagening.

Jan Gerritsen Hagel.

Hendrick Jansen, from Wagening.

Jan Aertsen, from Amersfoort.

Jacob Jansen, from Amersfoort.

Tys Jansen, from Amersfoort.

Wessel Wesselsen, from Munster.

Adolph Hardenbroeck, and Wife and Son.

Claes Theunissen, from Gorcum, and his servant, and boy.

Lubbert Harmensen, from Overyssel,

Lammert Huybertsen, from Wagening, and Wife and two children.

Jan Harmans and Wife and sucking child.

Roeloft Hendricks from Drenthe.

Femmetje Hendricksen, maiden.

Maria Mooris, from Arnhem, maiden.

Marten Abrahamsen, from Bloemendael, and Wife and two children.

The Wife of Hans Sodurat, Baker, and two children.

Leendert Arentsen Groenevelt, and Wife.

Aeltje Jacobsen; maiden.

Willem Petersen, from Amersfoort.

Claes Tysen; cooper, and two children.

1660.

MARCH; *In the Love.*

Wiggert Reinders, from Ter Gouw; Farmer.

Maritje Jansen maiden.

Bart Jansen, from Amsterdam; mason, and Wife and three children.

Cornelis Davitsen Schaets; wheel right.

Laurens Harmens, from Holstein and Wife.

Dirck Gerritsen vandien from Tricht; Agriculturer.

DITTO; *In the Moesman.*

Peter Lourens and Wife.

Hendrick Jansen, from Amersfoort, and Wife and four children.

DITTO; *In the Gilded Beaver.*

Annetje Abrahams; maiden.

Cornelis Niesen's Wife.

Jonas Bartesen, and Wife and two children.

Maria Jans; Orphan Daughter.

APRIL; *In the Spotted Cow.*

Jan Soubanich, from Byle in Drenthe.

Albert Janss; from Drenthe.

Peter Jacobs, from East Friesland.

Cornelis Bartels, from Drenthe.

Steven Koorts, from Drenthe and Wife and seven children.

Jan Kevers, from the Landscape Drenthe, and Wife.

Focke Jansen from Drenthe; Agriculturist, and Wife and seven children.

Claes Arentsen, from Drenthe, and Wife and three children, and boy.

Govert Egberts, from Meppelt, farmer's servant.

Evertje Dircks, from Drenthe; maiden.

Egbertje Dircks, from Drenthe; maiden.

Peter Jansen; shoemaker from Drenthe, and Wife and four children.

Coert Cartens, from Drenthe, farmer's servant.

Roeloft Swartwout; Agriculturist. [On his return to N. Netherland where he had previously resided.]

Cornelis Jacobs van Leeuwen; in the service of Swartwout.

Arent Meuwens, from Gelderland; in Swartwout's service.

Ariaen Huyberts, from Jena; in Swartwout's service.

Peter Hinham, from Nimwegen; Tailor.

Albert Heymans; Agriculturist, from Gelderland and Wife and eight children.

Jan Jacobsen Mol.

Annetje Harmens; maiden.

Beletje Foppe.

Elias Gyseling, from Zealand.

Roll of Soldiers embarked in the Ship Moesman, for New Netherland, 9th March, 1660.

Peter Gysen from Doornick Adelborst, with his wife.

Jan God-friend from Brussel.

Harmen Hendricks from Deventer.

Jan Jansen from Duynkerken.

William vander Beecke from Oudenaerde.

Pieter Beyard from Nieupoort.

Jacob Jansen from Muyden.

Andries Norman from Steenwyck.

Marten Petersen from Steenwyck.

Willem van Schure from Leuven.

Adrianus Forbiet from Brussel.

Johannis Verele from Antwerp.

Matthys Princen from Waltneel.

List of Soldiers embarked in the Ship the Spotted Cow, 15th April, 1660.

Claes Petersen, Adelborst from Detmarsum.

Claes Hayen from Bremen

Soldiers.

Jan Petersen from Detmarsen

Gerrit Manneel van Haen

Conraet Croos from Switserland

Hendrick Eyck from Srahuys

Christian Bartels Ruysh from Amsterdam

Hendrich Steveterinck from Osnasnigge

Peter Martens from Laens

John Hamelton of Hamelton.

Johan Verpronck from Bonn above Ceulen; a Smith and Baker.

Jan Wilekheresen from Bergen in Norway

Peter Petersen from Amsterdam, with his Wife & 2 children

Brant Kemenes from Dockum

Dirck Jansen from Rylevelt

Harman Jansen Engsinck from Oldenseel

Johannes Levelin from Bulhausen

Michiel Brouwnal from (Berg) Mont-eassel

List of Soldiers, embarked for New Netherland in the Ship Otter, 27th April 1660.

Jan Vresen, from Hamburg; Adelborst, and Wife and two children.

Jacob Loyseler, from Francfort.

Daniel Lengelgraast, from Amsterdam.

Thomas Vorstuyt, from Bremen.

Harmen Hellings, from Verda

Gysbert Dircksen, from Schans te voorn.

Teunis Warten, from Gorcum

Ferdinandus Willays, from Cortryck.

Reinier Cornelis, from Utrecht t be discharged whenever he request it, to follow his trade.

Joost Kockeiot, from Wrimigen.

Jan Vaex, from Nieustad.

Jan Vier, from Bon.

Jan Claesen, from Outserenter.

Paulus Mettermans, from L'Orient.

Peter Teunis, from Steenburg.

IMMIGRANTS; *In the Gilded Otter.*

Joost Huyberts, from Gelderland; Agriculturist, and Wife and two children.

Philip Cassier, from Calais; Agriculturist, and Wife and four children.

David Uplie, from Calais; Agriculturist, and Wife.

Matthews Blanchard, from Artois; Agriculturist, and Wife and 3 children.

Jan Adriaensen van Duyvelant's Wife.

Anthony Krypel, from Artois; Agriculturist, and Wife.

Canster Jacobs' Wife, from Hoesem and Daughter.

Willem Jacobsen, from Haerlem; Agriculturist.

Bastiaen Glissen, from Calemburg; Agriculturist, and Wife and five children.

Gerrit Jansz van Veen, from Calemburg; farmer's boy.

Gerrit Aartsen van Buren; Agriculturist.

Gerrit Cornelissen van Buren; Agriculturist.

Cornelis Abrahams, from Gelderland; Agriculturist.

1661.

JANUARY; *In the Golden Eagle.*

Cornelis Gerlossen, from East Friesland; Tailor.

Jannetje Barents, widow of Jan Quisthout.

Jacob Farments, wife and child.

MAY; *In the Beaver.*

Hugh Barentsen de Clein, and Wife and seven children.

Peter Marcelis van Beest, and Wife and four children and 2 servants.

Aert Pietersen Buys van Beest, and Wife and son.

Frans Jacobsen van Beest, and Wife and two children.

Widow Geertje Cornelis van Beest, and six children.

Widow Adriaentje Cornelis van Beest, and Daughter.

Goossen Jansen van Noort van Beest.

Hendrick Dries van Beest.

Neeltje Jans van Beest.

Geertruy Teunissen van Beest.

Geertje Willems, from Amsterdam.

Aert Teunissen Middagh.

Jacob Bastiaensen, from Heycop.

Estienne Genejoy, from Rochelle, and Wife and three children.

Jan Lammertsen, from Bremen.

Hendrickje Jochems.

Geertje Jochems.

Wouter Thysen, from Hilversom.

Gideon Jacobs.

The Son of Evert Peterson, Consoler of the sick.

DITTO; *In the St. Jean Baptist.*

Gerrit Gerritsen, from Besevenn.

Gommert Paulessen from Antwerp.

Aerent Teunissen, from Amsterdam, and Wife and two children.

Jan Theunissen, from Amsterdam, and Wife and two children.

Annetje van Genen, from Sinden.

Geertje Samsons, from Weesp.

Jan Willemsen, from the Loosdrecht, and Wife and two sons.

Peter Bielliou, from Pays de vaud, and Wife and four children.

Walraven Luten, from Flanders, and Wife and suckling.

Mynder Coerten, from Adighem.

Claes Jansen, from Uithoorn and Wife and child.

Andries Imans, from Leyden.

Jacob Abrahamsen Santvoort.

Gerrit Hendricksen, from Swoll.

Tys Barentsen, from Leirdam, and wife and three children.

Cornelis Dircksen Vos, from Leirdam, and Wife, mother and two children.

NOVEMBER: *In the Purmerland Church.*

Barent Cornelissen Slecht.

1662.

JANUARY; *In the Golden Eagle.*

Peter Jansen Cuyck, from Heusden, Agriculturist.

Peter Jansen, from Amsterdam; Agriculturist.

Teunis Dircksen Boer, and Wife and three children.

Seiwart Petersen, from Hoesem; Malster.

MARCH; *In the Faith.*

Lysbet Harmens, from the Traert.

Jan Gerrits, from Embden; labourer.

Jacob Wouters, from Amsterdam.

Barent Witten Hooft, from Munster, Tailor, and Wife and two children.

Stoffel Smet, from Keurlo; Agriculturist.

Adriaen Hendricks, from Borckelo; Agriculturist.

Precilla Homes, and her brother, and one suckling.

Thomas Harmensen Brouwers, from Sevenbergen; farmer.

Symon Cornie; farmer from France, and Wife.

Adriaen Gerritsen, from Utrecht; Agriculturist, and Wife and five children.

Albert Jansen, from Steenwyck; Tailor.

Reinier Petersen, from Steenwyck; Agriculturer.

Claes van Campen, from Oldenburg; farmer's boy.

Adriaen Aartsen from Thillerwarden in Guilderland.

Hendrick Arentsen, from the same place; labourer.

APRIL; *In the Hope.*

Annetje Hendricks, Wife of Jan Evertsen; shoemaker, and five children.

Cornelis Dircksen Hooglant; Agriculturer, and Wife, son and Daughter.

Jacob Jansen; N. Netherland; farmer, and Wife and three children.

Adriaen Vincian, from Tournay; Agriculturer.

Jochem Engelburgh, from Heusden.

Gerrit Hargerinck, from Newenhuys, and two sons.

Annetje Gillis van Beest; servant girl.

Jan Petersen, from Deventer; Tailor, and Wife and three children.

Jan Timmer, from Gorekum, and Wife.

Lúytje Gerrits; Agriculturist from Friesland.

Peckle Dircksen, from Friesland.

Willem Lubbertsen, from Meppel; Agriculturist, and Wife and six children.

Lubbert Lubbertsen, from Meppel; Agriculturist, and Wife and four children.

Jan Barentsen, from Meppel; Agriculturist, and Wife and five children.

Gerrit Jacobsen, from Meppel; Agriculturist.

Harmtje Barents, from Meppel; Maiden.

Willem Pietersen de Groot, and Wife and five children.

Abel Hardenbroeck, and Wife and child, and servant named Casper Ovencamp.

Balthaser de Vos, from Utrecht; farmer, and Wife.

Hendrick Aldertsen, from the Thillerwaerd; farmer, and two children.

Albert Buer, from Gulick.

Jan Spiegelaer, and Wife.

AUGUST ; *In the Fox.*

Jan de la Warde, from Antwerp.

Albert Saboriski, from Prussia.

Anthony Dircksen, from Brabant.

Pierre Martin, Pays de Vaud.

Gerardus Ive, from Pays de Vaud.

Joost Grand, from Pays de ·Vaud.

Jan Le chaire, from Valenciennes; Carpenter.

Jan Albantsen, from Steenwyck, and Wife and child.

Ammereus Claesen, maiden.

Hendrick Albertsen; Labourer

Jan Claesen; labourer.

Lysbet Hendricksen.
Jan Bossch, from Westphalen.
Roelof Hermansen, from Germany, and Wife.
Robbert de la Main, from Dieppe.
David Kraffort; Mason, and Wife and child.
Jacomyntje Jacobs, Daughter of Jacob Swart.
Juriaen Jansen, from Holstein.
Annetje Anthonis, wife of Gerrit Mannaet, and her child.
Souverain Ten Houte; Baker.
Albert Hendricksen, from Maersen; House Carpenter.
Symon Scholts, from Prussia.
Hendrick Tymensen, from Loodrecht.
David Ackerman, from the Mayory of Bosch, and Wife and six children.
Willem Symonsen, from Amsterdam.
Pierre de Mare, from Rouen; Shoemaker.
Dirck Storm, from the Mayory of Bosch, and Wife and three children.
David Davidsen, from Maestricht.
Jan Joosten, from the Thielerwaert, and wife and five children.
Claes Barents, from Dort.
Lendert Dircksen Van Venloo, of Rumunt.
Adreaen Lowrensen Van Loesren, carpenter.

OCTOBER; *In the Purmerland Church.*
Claus Paulus, from Detmarsum, and Wife.
Nicolas du Pui, from Artois, and Wife and three children.
Arnout du Tois, from Ryssel, (Lisle,) and Wife and one child.
Gideon Merlit, and Wife and four children.
Louis Louhman, and Wife and three children.
Jacques Cossaris, and Wife and two children.
Jan de Conchilier, (now, Consilyea) and Wife and five children.
Jacob Colff, from Leyden, and Wife and two children.
Judith Jans, from Leyden, maiden.
Carsten Jansen.
Ferdinandus de Mulder.
Isaac Verniel, and Wife and four children.
Abelis Setshoorn.
Claes Jansen van Heynengen.

1663.

MARCH; *In the Rosetree.*
Andries Pietersen van Bergen.
Dirck Everts, from Amersfoort, and Wife and three children.
Peter Jansen, from Amersfoort, and four children.
Fredrick Claesen, from Norway.
Jeremias Jansen, from Westerhoot.
Jan Jacobsen, from East Friesland, and Wife and two children.
Hendrick Hendricksen, from Westphalia.
Hendrick Lammerts, from Amersfoort.
Jan Jansen Verberck, from Buren, and Wife and five children.
Jannetje Willemsen.
Adrian Lammertsen, from Tielderveen, and Wife and six children.
Jacob Hendricks, his Nephew.

Theunis Jansen, from the country of Liege, and Wife and six children.
Thys Jansen, from the country of Liege, and four children.
Theunis Gerritsen; painter, from Buren.
Jan Petersen Buys van Beest.
Hendrick Hansen, from Germany.
Edward Smith, from Leyden.
Peter Martensen, from Ditmarsum, and child.
Bay Groesvelt, and Wife and sucking child.
Cornelis Claesen, from Amsterdam.
Hendrick Abels, from Leyden.
Barent Holst, from Hamburgh.
Hendrick Wessels, from Wishem.
Claes Wouters, from Amersfoort, and Wife and one child.
Grietje Hendricks, Wife of Jan Arentsen Smith in Esopus and daughter.
Jan Cornelisz van Limmigen.
Hendrick Jansen; painter.
Grietje Harmens, from Alckmaer.
Fredrick Claesen, from Mespelen.

DITTO; In the Eagle.

Willem Schot.
Elias Jansen, from Tiel.
Dirck Schiltman, from Tiel.
Andrees Petersen, from Tiel.
Maria Laurens.
Grietje Jaspers, from Tiel; maiden.
Dirck Lucas.
Clement Rosens.
Evert Dirksen, from Vianen, and two children.

APRIL; In the Spotted Cow.

Hendrick Corneliss, from New Netherland.
Staes de Groot, from Tricht.
Elje Barents, the Wife of Adam Bremen, and servant girl.
Jan Lourens, from Schoonder Woort, and Wife and two children.
Theunis Bastiaensen Cool, and child.
Jan Bastiaensen, from Leerdam, and Wife and four children.
Giel Bastiaensen, from Leerdam, and Wife and four children.
Gerrit Jans, from Arnhem, and Wife and Brother-in-Law, Arnoldus Willems.
Joris Adriaensen, from Leerdam.
Peter Matthysen, from Limborgh.
Jan Boerhans.
Lammert Jansen Dorlant.
Gerrit Verbeeck.
Grietje Gerrits, the Wife of Dirck Jansen, and two children.
Adriaen Jansen Honink from Well, and Wife and four children.
Hans Jacob Sardingh.
Juriaen Tomassen, from Rypen.
Jan Laurens, from Rypen.
Jan Otto van Teyl, and Wife and child.
Matthys Bastiaensen vander Peich, and daughter.
Marytje Theunis van Beest.
Jerome Bovie, from Pays de Vaud, and Wife and five children.

David de Marist, from Picardy, and Wife and four children.
Pierre Niu, from the Pays de Vaud, and Wife, sucking child and sister.
Jean Mesurole, from Picardy, and Wife and sucking child.
Jean Arien, from Monpellier, and Wife and child (removed to the Islands).
Martin Renare, from Picardy, and Wife and child.
Jacob Kerve, from Leyden, and Wife.
Pierre Parmentie, from Pays de Vaud, and Wife and son.
Joost Houpleine, from Flanders, and Wife and son.
Joost Houpleine, junior, and Wife and sucking child.
Guilliam Goffou, from Sweden.
Moillart Journay, from Pays de vaud.
Pierre Richard, from Paris.

JUNE; *In the Star*.

Peter Worster.
Vieu Pont, from Normandy.
Joan Paul de Rues.

DITTO; *In the St. Jacob*.

Geertje Huyberts, Wife of Jan Gerritsen, from Marken, and nephew.
Annetje Jacobs, from Gornichem.

SEPTEMBER; *In the Stetin*.

Schout Olferts, from Friesland, and Wife and child and servant Foppe Johannis.
Jacob Govertsen, and son.
Jan Jansen, the younger, and Wife and child.
Claes Jansen, from Amsterdam, and Wife and three children.
Anthoni Berghman, from Gorcum.
Hendrick Gerretsen, from Aernhem.
Willem Van Voorst, from Arnhem.
Grietje Jansen, from Weldorp.
Cornelis Teunissen, from Norway.
Peter Carstensen, from Holsteyn and son.
Jacob Bastiaensen, from Newerveen.
Jan Jansen, from Norway, and Wife.
Grietje Hargeringh, Jan Hargeringh, from Newenhuys.
Johannes Burger, from Geemen.
Gysbert Krynne Boelhont.
Beletje Jacobs, van Naerden.
Reinier Claesen, from Francken.
Hessel Megelis, from Friesland.
Jan Laurense, from New Netherland.
Albert Adriaense de Bruyn, from the Betawe.
Dirck Teunissen van Naerden.
Jan Vreesen, from Hamburg.
Jan Roelofsen, from Norway.
Susanna Verplanck, and child.
Lysbet ver Schuren.
Jan Brouwer, and Brother.
Annetje Hendricks, Wife of Fredrick Hendricks Cooper.
Douwe Aukes.
Merine Johannis, and Wife and four children, together with his Wife's sister and his servant.

OCTOBER; *In the St. Peter.*

Marritje Jans, from Amsterdam.
Boel Roelofs, from Friesland.
Peter Alberts, from Vlissingen, and Wife and two children.
Ariaen Peters Kume, from Flissingen.
Willem Luycass, from Maeslands-sluys.

1664.

JANUARY; *In the Faith.*

Marcelis Jansen van Bommel; farmer.
Evert Tack, from the Barony of Breda.
Lysbet Arens, from Amsterdam, and child.
Johannis Hardenbroeck, from Elberveld, and Wife and four children.
Janneken Juriaensen, from Gorcum.
Corneliss Cornelissen Vernoey, and Wife and sucking child.
Lysbet de Roode, from Dantzick, Wife of John Saline, and child.
Sara Teunis.

DITTO; *In the Broken Heart.*

Lysbeth Jansen van Wie, near Goch.
The Wife of Govert van Oy, and two children.
Jan Jansen, from Amsterdam.
Claes Gerritsen, son of Gerrit Lubbertsen, from Wesel.
S. Vander Wessels.
Jan Wouterse van Norden.

DITTO; *In the Beaver.*

Anietje Hendricks van der Briel.

APRIL; *In the Concord.*

Abigel Verplanck, and child.
Claes Mellis, from Great Schermer, and Wife and two children and servant.
Jan Taelman.
Hendrick Bartholomeus and five children.
Claes Gerritseu, and Wife and child.
Jentje Jeppes, and Wife and three children.
Bastiaen Corneliss, from Maersen.
Maes Willems, from Heyland.
The Wife of Jan Evertsen van Lier, and child.
Claes Andriessen, from Holsteyn.
Gerrit Gerritsen, from Swol.
Sicke Jans, from Amsterdam.
Seravia vander Hagen, and child.
Carel Enjoert, from Flanders, and Wife and three children.
Hendrick Wienrick, from Wesel.
Adriaentje Hendricks, and child.

CENSUS OF KINGS COUNTY; ABOUT 1698.

A LIST OF ALL THE FREEHOLDERS THEIR WIVES CHILDREN APPRENTICES AND SLAVES WITHIN THE KINGS COUNTY ON NASSAUW ISLAND.

[NOTE.—*E* affixed to the name, means *English; F French.*]

IN THE TOWN OF BROOKLAND.

	Men.	Wo.	Ch.	App.	Sla.
Adriaen Bennet	1	2	4	..	..
Jacob Bennet	1	1	..	..	..
Jan Bennet	1	1	2	1	..
Simon Aerson	1	1	12	..	2
Wouter van Pelt	1	1	4	2	1
Christopher Schaers	1	..	..	..	..
Claes van Dyck	1	2	5	..	1
Maria Van Dyck	..	1	..	..	..
Achias Van Dyck	1	1	7	1	..
Jan Pieterse	1	2	2	..	..
Volkert Bries	1	2	2	..	..
Geertie Bries	..	1	..	..	..
Jacobus Van DeWater	1	1	3	..	..
Cornelis Van DeWater	1	..	..	..	..
Jan Buys	1	2	1	..	..
Cornelis Poulisse	1	1	1	..	..
Cornelis Slegt	1	1	..	3	..
Joannes Slegt	1	..	..	..	..
Cornelis Van Duyn	1	2	3	0	..
Thomas Verdon	1	2	..	..	4
Jan Bennet	1	1	5	..	2
Willem Bennet	1	1	5	2	..
Willem Brouwer	1	1	2	2	..
Jacob Hansen Bergen	1	1	6	..	2
Cornelis Snebring	1	1	8	..	2
Catharina Hendrikse	..	1	..	..	..
Dirck Woertman	1	1	2	..	4
Jan Gerritz Couwenhoven	1	1	3	..	..
Robert Everden (*E*)	1	1	..	1	1
Jan Arison	1	1	3	..	7
Latitie Smith (*E*)	..	1	..	..	..
Stoffel Hooghlandt	1	1	..	..	..
Joris Jacobse	1	1	..	..	4
Harmen Jorisse	1	1	2	1	..
Jan Woertman	1	1	4	..	1
Juriaen Andriesse	1	..	..	..	..
Jurian Bries	1	1	4	..	..
Joannes Janse	1	3	3	..	..
Barent Sleght	1	1	2	1	..
Margaret Dolstan (*E*)	..	1	2	..	2
Elsie Sleght	..	1	2	..	..
Jacobis Beauvois	1	1	5	..	..
Thomas Knight (*E*)	1	1	1	..	..
Magdalena fardon	..	1	..	..	..
Joris Hansen Bergen	1	1	11	..	2

	Men.	Wo.	Ch.	App.	Sla.
Jan Fredrickse	1	1	7	..	..
Grietie Jansen	..	1	..	..	..
Griet Middag	1	1	3	..	2
Jan Janse Staast	1	1	8	..	..
Pieter Gerbrantse	1	1	..	1	..
Pieter Janse Staast	1	1	4	..	..
Cornelis Jorisse Bouman	1	1	1	..	..
Mighiel hanse Bergen	1	1	3	..	2
Jacob Brouwer	1	1	6	..	..
Adam Brouwer	1	1	4	..	..
Claes Vechten	1	1	..	..	..
Hendrick Vechten	1	1	4	..	3
Jan Cornelisse Damen	1	1	4	..	1
Gerret Middag	1	1	3	..	2
Samuel Berry	1	1	3	..	1
Gerrit Couwenhoven	1	1	3	1	..
Abraham Van Duyn	1	2	2	..	1
Judith Van Este	0	1	3	2	1
Annetie Rapaillé	..	1	..	..	..
Jeronimus Rapaillé	1	1	6	..	2
Teunis Rapaillé	1	1	1	..	..
Daniel Rapaillé	1	1	5	..	3
Jannetie Remse	..	2	2	..	..
Abraham Remse	1	1	2	..	1
Gysbert Bogaert	1	2	5	..	1
Teunis Bogaert	1	..	..	..	..
Neeltie Rapallé	..	2	1	..	1
Jacob Cousseau (F)	1	1	1	..	..
Jacob Buys	1	2	4	..	..
Matthys Cornelisse	1	1	5	..	..
Anthony Coesaer	1	1	1	1	..
Tys Lubbertz	1	1	4	..	..
Lysbeth Tysen	..	1	3	..	..
frans Abrahamse	1	..	2	1	..
Lambert Andriesse	1	2	1	..	..
Cornelis Vanderhoef	1	1	3	..	2
Thomas Lamberts	1	..	..	..	1
Dirck Tyssen	1	1	..	1	..
Isaac Mennist	1	1	1	..	..
Hendk Hendrickse	1	1	1	..	1
Jeronimus Remse	1	1	..	2	3
Jan Gerritz Dorlant	1	1	3	1	..
Gerret Sprong	1	1	5	..	..
Barbara Luycas	..	1	..	..	3
Clars Barentz Blom	1	2	4	..	..
Jan Bibon	1	1	6	1	..
Benja Van De Waeter	1	2	3	1	..
[Ought to be 78 Men & 102 Wo:]	77	101	240	26	65

IN THE TOWN OF BOSWICK.

	Men.	Wo.	Ch.	App.	Sla.
Pieter Janse Wit	1	..	1	..	5
Dorothea Verschuur	..	1	1	1	3
Joos Duré (F)	1	1	..	..	..
Albert Hendrickse	1	3	4	..	..
Hendrick Willemse	1	..	3	..	..
Abraham Detooy (F)	1	1	..	..	..
Jannetse Schamp	..	1	6	..	..
Jan Sevenhooven	1	..	2	..	..
David Sprong	1	1	2	..	..
Phillip Volkertsz	1	1	2	..	..
Pieter Willemse	1	1	2	..	..
Jacobus Looyse	1	1	1	2	..
Auke Reynierse	1	1	1	1	..
Jochem Verschuur	1	1	2	..	1
Willem West (E)	1	1	2	..	..
Nicholaes Brouwer	1	1	1	1	..

	Men.	Wo.	Chi.	App.	Sla.
Gabriel Sprong	1	1	3	..	..
Pieter Looyse	1	1	6	..	..
Lourens Hook	2	1	6	..	..
Joos Duré Senior (F)	1	1	6	..	2
Michiel Parmentier (F)	2	1	5	..	2
Pieter Usilla	1	1	4	..	..
ffredrick Symonse	1	1	3	..	2
nendk Jansz Van Amesfoort	1	1	3	..	..
Jan Muserol (F)	1	1	..	..	..
Cornelis Looyse	2	1	6	..	..
Jacob Bibon (F)	1	1	..	..	3
Jan Muserol Junior (F)	2	1	5	..	3
Thomas Baudé (F)	1	1	2	..	..
Anna fontain	..	1	4	..	3
Hendricus De Foreest	1	1	6	..	1
Theunis Woertman	1	1	2	..	3
Barent Gerritz Vlasbeek	1	1	..	..	..
Anna Volkertse	..	1	8	..	2
Dirck Volkertze	1	1	3	..	2
Pieter Pra	1	1	6	..	8
Humphry Clay (E)	1	2	1	..	6
Abraham Brouwer	1	1	2	2	..
Alexandre Coquer (F)	1	1	6	..	..
Jurian Coljer	2	2	3	..	..
Jean Lescuier (F)	3	2	1	..	..
Juriaen Nagel	1	1	5	..	5
Charles fontaine (F)	2	1	4	..	1
Catelyntie Cats	..	1	3	..	..
Hendrick Janse	2	1	6	1	..
Arent Andriesse	1	1	2	..	..
Dirck Andriesse	1	1	..	..	..
	51	49	141	8	52

IN THE TOWN OF NEW VTRECHT.

	Men.	Wo.	Chi.	App.	Sla.
Pieter Corteljau	1	1	4	..	3
Jacques Corteljau	1	1	6	..	2
Adriaen Lane	1	1	2	..	1
Jan Van Cleef	1	1	4	..	..
Gerret Coetten	1	1	4	..	..
Barent Joosten	1	1	1	..	1
Mynart Kourten	1	1	2	..	5
Aert Van Pelt	1	1	5	0	1
Hendk Matthyse	1	1	4	..	1
Joannes Smack	1	1	..	..	..
Cornelis Van Dyck	1	1	4	..	..
Jan Van Dyck	1	1	5	..	1
Gysbert Tysse	1	1	7	..	1
Jacob Verdon	1	1	7	..	..
Abraham Willemse	1	1	..	..	1
Pieter Tysse	1	1	5	..	..
Gerret Cornelisse	1	1	2	..	4
Cornelis Auke	1	1	7	..	..
Thomas Tierckse	1	1	4	..	..
Susanna —— ——	..	1	4	..	..
Harman Gerritse	1	1	..	..	..
Dirck Van Zutphen	1	1	8	..	3
Lawrens Jansen	1	1	3	..	2
Willem Berkeloo	1	1	1	..	..
Denys Teunisse	1	1	5	..	5
Cornelis Van Brunt	1	1	6	..	6
Andries Jansen	1	1	5	..	..
Hendrik Jansen	1	1	1	..	..
Cryn Jansen	1	1	4	..	..
Jan Verkerk	1	1	2	..	1
Joos De Bane	1	1	4	..	..
Rut Joos en Van Brunt	1	1	..	..	5

	Men.	Wo.	Chi.	App.	Sla.
Joost Van Brunt	1	1	1	..	4
Anthony Van Pelt	1	1	6	..	..
Teunis Van Pelt	1	1	..	..	2
Matthys Smack	1	..	..	..	..
Paulus Eigo	1	..	..	..	..
Joannes Swart	1	1	4	..	..
Joannes Eigo	1	1	3	..	..
Pieter Van Deventer	1	1	4	..	..
	39	38	134	..	48

IN THE TOWN OF FFLATLANDS als NEW AMESFOORT.

	Men.	Wo.	Chi.	App.	Sla.
Gerret Elbert Stoothof	1	1	7	..	4
Jan Teunisz Dykhuys	1	1	3	..	5
Roelof Martense	1	1	4	..	4
Coert Stevense	1	1	3	..	2
Gerret Wykhof	1	1	3	..	1
Hendk Wykhof	1	1	..	..	2
Dirk Jantz Ar:erman	1	1	7	..	..
Andriaen Kenne	5	1	2	..	..
Dirck Langestraet	1	1	3	..	..
Jan Kiersen	1	1	..	..	1
Alexandr Simson (E)	1	3	6	..	..
Jan Hansen	1	1	3	..	..
Pieter Nevius	1	1	7	..	1
Jacob Tysse Lane	1	1	4	..	..
Helena Aertsen	2	1	2	..	..
Simon Jantz Van Aersdaelen	2	3	..	..	1
Cornelis Simontz Van Aersdaelen	1	1	6	..	1
Willem Gerrittz Van Couvenhoven	1	1	6	..	..
Aernout Viele	1	1	..	..	2
Jan Alberttz ter heunen	1	1	6	..	2
Jan Brouwer	2	1	5	..	1
Thonis Jantz Amak	1	1	5	..	..
fferdinando Van Sigelen	1	1	5	.:	4
Claes Wykhof	1	1	6	..	..
Jan Wykhof	1	1	2	..	1
Willem Bruynen	1	..	..	..	..
Adriaen Langestraet	1	..	..	..	..
Lucas Stevense	3	2	7	..	4
Pieter Pieterse	1	..	..	..	..
Hendrick Brouwer	1	..	..	..	..
Albert Amerman	1	..	..	..	..
Pieter Van Couvenhoven	1	1	2	..	..
Marten Schenck	1	1	3	..	2
Jan Stevense	1	2	9	..	1
Pieter Monfoor	2	2	4	..	1
Steven Coerten	1	1	3	..	..
Rutgert Bruyn	1	1	7	..	..
	47	39	130	..	40

IN THE TOWN OF GRAVESEND.

	Men.	Wo.	Chi.	App.	Sla.
James Hubbard (E)	2	2	2	..	..
Cornelis Van Cleef	1	1	2	..	..
The Widow Strycker	..	1	8	..	1
Jochem Gulick	1	1	9	..	..
Willem Willemse	1	1	..	..	..
Nicholas Stilwill (E)	1	1	7	..	1
John Poland (E)	1	1	5	..	..
Isaac Haselbury (E)	1	1	3	..	..
Elias Stilwill (E)	1	1	..	..	..
Joseph Golder (E)	1	1	1	..	..
Abraham Emmans (E)	1	1	3	1	..
William Williamson	1	1	8	..	..
The Widdow Barentse	..	1	6	..	..

	Men.	Wo.	Chi.	App.	Sla.
Rymer Van Sigelen	1	1	4	1	1
Margaret Simson	..	1	..	..	..
Stoffel Romeyn	1	1	9	..	1
Barent Juriaense	1	1	6	1	..
Andrew Emmans	1	1	3	..	..
Cornelis Buys	1	1	3	..	..
Anthony Powland (E)	1	1	1	..	..
Thomas Craven (E)	1	1	4	..	..
John Emmans (E)	1	1	3	..	1
John Lake (E)	1	1	8	..	1
The Widdow Martentz	..	1	7	..	1
John Grigs Junir (E)	2	1	7	..	..
John Grigs Senior (E)	1	..	..	..	4
Anne Lake	..	1	..	..	..
Samuel Gerrittz	1	1	1	..	..
Jeremiah Stilwill (E)	1	1	4	..	3
Nicholas Stilwill (E)	1	1	4	1	2
John Simmons (E)	1	1	2	..	..
Albert Koerten	1	1	4	1	1
John Mash (E)	1	..	..	1	..
Lubbert Gerrittz	1	..	..	..	..
	31	**32**	**124**	**6**	**17**

IN THE TOWN OF FFLATBUSH als MIDWOUT.

	Men.	Wo.	Chi.	App.	Sla.
Henry ffilkin (E)	1	1	3	..	..
Joseph Hegeman	1	1	4	..	5
Stoffel Probascoe	1	1	6	..	2
Wilhelmus Lupardus *	1	1	7	..	..
Gerrardus Beekman	1	1	7	..	3
Jean Concess (F)	1	1	1	..	..
James Simson (E)	1	1	5	..	4
Engelbart Lott	1	1	6	1	5
Hendrick Ryke	1	1	3	..	3
Hendrick Vliet	1	2	2	..	..
Tobias Ten Eyck	1	1	7	1	3
Joannes Snebring	1	1	1	..	..
Cornelis Vanderveer	1	1	4	0	1
Jan Van Ditmarsen	1	1	1	..	4
Dirck Hooglant	1	1	6	..	..
Pieter Lott	1	2	..	..	..
Daniel Polhemius	1	2	6	..	4
Jan Benham (E)	1	1	1	..	..
Daniel Remse	1	1	..	..	1
Jacob Hendrikse	1	1	6	..	1
Ryk Hendrickse	1	1	1	..	1
Barent Volman	1	1	6	..	..
Henricus Kip	1	1	..	..	..
Denys Van Duyn	1	1	2	..	..
Gysbert Jantz	1	1	4	..	..
Cornelis Vanhougen	1	1	2	..	..
Denys hegeman	1	1	5	..	..
Benj hegeman	1	2	2	..	..
Jan Andriesse	1	1	2	..	..
Margareta Verschuur	..	1	4	..	..
Adriaen Ryerse	1	1	4	..	2
Cornelis Willemse	1	1	3	..	2
Leffert Pieterse	1	1	9	..	3
Abraham Hegeman	1	2	3	..	1
Aris Van de Bilt	1	1	10	..	5
Joannes Rees	1	1	8	..	..
Joannes Symonse	1	1	3	1	..
Lambert Sighels	1	1	5	..	1
Pieter Strycker	1	1	5	..	1

* Was D. Reformed Minister of Flatbush from 1695 to 1702. ED.

	Men.	Wo.	Chi.	App.	Sl.
John Richardson (*E*)	1	1	1	..	..
Matthys Pietertz Luyster	1	1	6	..	..
Symen Hansen	1	1	2	1	..
Aron Van Ooststrant	1	1	5	..	1
Andries Jansen	1	1	4	1	..
Ruth Albertsen	1	1	..	..	..
Joannes Van Eeckelen	1	1	6	..	2
Marten Andriesen	1	1	1	3	..
Jan Dehaen	1	1	1	..	..
Adrian hendrickse	1	1	2	..	..
Rymer Arentse	1	1	6	..	..
Evert Wikly	1	1	3	..	1
Jacobus Hegeman	1	1	3	..	1
Hendrik Willemse	1	1	4	..	..
Joannes Willemse	1	1	2	..	1
Cornelis Wickof	1	1	9	..	2
Elsie Teunisse	..	1	5	..	..
Daniel Martino	1	2	..	..	2
Rem Remse	1	1	8	..	..
Isaac Hegeman,	1	1	3	..	..
Gerret Strycker	1	1	4	..	2
Maritie Blom	..	1	9	..	1
Geertruy Van Boerum	..	1	3	..	..
Gerret Dorlandt	1	1	4	..	..
Jan Vliet	1	1	9	..	2
Joris Remse	1	1	7	..	2
Jan Vander Veer	1	1	2	..	..
	62	72	263	8	71

RECAPITULATION.

Total.		Men	Wo.	Ch.	App.	Sl.
509*	In the Town of Brookland	77	101	240	26	65
301	Boswick	51	49	141	8	52
259	New Vtrecht	39	38	134	..	48
256	Fflatlands	47	39	130	..	40
210	Gravesend	31	32	124	6	17
476	Fflatbush	62	72	263	8	71
	In all	307	331	1032	48	293

* (Ought to be 511)   Is together .... 2011 (ought to be 2013)

A TRUE LIST

OF THE RESPECTIVE OFFICERS AND SOULDIERS BELONGING TO THE REGIMENT OF MILITIA IN KINGS COUNTY; 1715.

RICD STILLWELL Coll.
Joust Van Brunt L. Coll.
Jeromas Remsin Major
Samuel Garrison agett

The Troop.

DANIEL REMSEN Captt
Rick Vansudam, Leff.
Johannis Sebring, Cortt
Marten Adrianse, Quartt
Gabrill Sprong
Daniel Rapelje
Klas ffolkerson
John Simasin
William Hogelantt
Jacob Nagell
John Rapelje
Hans Bargen
Jacob Martensin
John vankleeft
George Anderson
Joust debevoice
Cornelius Simason
Stephen Korten
Jacob Bennitt
Aartt Willemse
John vandervere
William van Nuess
Thomas Griggs
Abraham hegeman
Lawrence Ditmarse
Abraham Derje
hans Bargen
John Griggs
Joust Derje
Barent Bloom
Jacob debevoice
John Garrison
Nicholas Cowenhoven
John van kerk
Charles debevoice
Rem Joressin
Jaques Tunissin
Rem hegeman
Stephen Schenck
Charles derje
Barnadus Reide
Cornelius Wickhoff
Jacob bennitt
Jeromas vanderbilt
William fferdon
John van wickellen
Samuel Gronendick
Isaac Snediker
Peter Simson
Hendrick van Sudam
kort van Voierhuys
Jeromas Rapelje=== 52

II.

DEMENICAS VANDERVERE Captt
Philip Nagell Leff.
John Benham Ens
William Howard
Johannis Cornell
John Bennitt
hendrick keep
Jacob vander boog
Joseph hegeman
Johannis ditmarss
David Esubb
Cornelius pulhemus
Jacob pulhemus
Cornelius vandervere
John van der beltt
John Stryker
Johannis Janse
Abraham Loot
Johannis Ditmarss
Peter hagewoutt
Bartt vanderende
Adrejan hegeman
Class Simason
Simon Loise
Richard Beets
William van Borom
Charls van Borom
Elbartt hegeman
Evertt van wickellon
George Bloom
Jureen Probuscoo
Jacob Remson
Reinear reinearsee
Jacob Hagewoutt
Isaac hagewoutt
Aartt van derbilt
rem Adriaanse
Gerrett Adriaanse
John Lambertse
Harmanus Gisberse
Reinear ffollman
william vandune
Peter Luister
Peter Stryker=== 44

III.

AARTT VAN PELT Captt
Johannis Swartt Leff
Thomas fferdon Ens
Jacob van Sutfen
hindrick Janson
Andrew Emans
Barentt Bantt
Nicholas Lake
Benjamen Hulsart
Rutgartt van Bruntt
Tunis van peltt

John van peltt
hendrick Emans
Jaques Corteliau
Abraham van Sutfin
Johanis van Sutfin
Tiss Lane
Cherik van dick
John van peltt
Rutgart van Brunt
Jacob Swartt
Anthony Hulsartt
Okaa van nuies
John van nuies
Isaac van nues === 25

IV.

THOMAS STILLWELL Captt
Barent Johnson Leff.
ffer. van Sekelen Ens.
Cornelius Boyes
Samuel poling
Elias hubbard
Thomas Craven
Benjamen Griggs
Daniel Griggs
Jacobus Emans
Daniel Lake
Cornelius Stryker
ffer. van Sekellen
Tunis Gullyck
Nicholas williamson
Peter Willimse
Abraham morgan
Court Stevensin
John Ride
Johannis Emans
Samuel Griggs
Barnardus Verbrick
Simon van aarsdalen
Lauerence van Cleft
Stoffel van aarsdalen
Gerritt Verbrick
John Elbertson
Reinear van Sekellen
Gerritt Lambartse
John Walien === 30

V.

ROULIF TERHUNEN Capt
John Ameermon Leff.
Court van voorhies Ens.
John hanson
Marten Schenk
Oka van voorhies
William kowenhoven
Isaac amurmon
John van Sekellen
Jacob Amurmon
Daniel nortstrantt
Cornelius Monford
Jacob Monford
Evers van geldin
Roeluf Schenck
Roeluf van vourhies
Lucus van vourhies
Albart van vourhies
John van Aarsdalen
Meanu van vourhies
Albart van vourhies

Johannis Boyes
marten neves
Cornelius neves
Peter neves
hendrick van vourhies
Christofer Qubartus
John Brouwyer
Albartt terhunan
Peter van Voirhies === 30

VI.

FFRANCE TITUS Captt
ffredrik Simson Leff
Tunis wortman Ens.
Cornelius van Katt
John Missarole
Aren Anderson
Joras Isolius
Johannis Albertsin
Johannis van katt
Isaac Laquer
Peter Coljor
Peter Laquer
Isaac Loise
Abraham Laquer
David van katt
Charles Coenertt
Peter Conselje
Jacobus Cosine
Simon Derje
Andresse Andresin
Johannis Coljor
Garritt Sprong
John Sprong
Jacobus Coljor
Dirick Adrajanse
Johannis Bookhoutt === 26

VII.

DAVID AERSIN, Captt
Lambert van Sekols, Leff
Ewout Ewoutse, Ens.
Garritt proust
Lamburt Andresin
Jeromas Remsin
Hendrick Hendrickse
hendrick Vroom
Jacob Browyer
John midagh
William kowenhoven
Joseph hegeman
John Loran
Jacob Bennett
Isaec remsin
Jacob kason
John van Sekellen
Jacob van dewater
Simon Bogartt
John Johnsin
Isaac Johnsin
ffredrick Bargin
Isaac Sebring
ffredrick Blaw
haurey Blaw
Peter States
Garritt vanduine
William Vanduine
William fferdon
William Bennitt

Simon dehurtt
Christofer Johnson
Everadus Browyer
Tunis van Pelt
nicholas van dick
Thomas van dyck
John Petersin
Henry van dyck
Jacob van dyck
Samson Lafoy

Gerritt van ranss
Abraham Abramsin
George Bargin
George kowenhoven
Cornelius van dewater
Mathew van Dyck
Cornelius Ewoutse
Christofer Codellerse ===== 48

Totall 255.

LIST OF THE PALATINS REMAINING AT NEW YORK, 1710.

Name	Old	Y'ng
Hans Wm Stuckrath	37	
—Anna Margaretta	28	
—Anna Clara		10
—Catharine		4
—John Marcus		½
Anna Wormserin widdow	36	
Niclaus Jungens works in ye Govr gard	38	
—Anna Magdalena	25	
Frantz Lucas at New Rochelle at Mr. Chadden	38	
—Maria Eliz. his daughter	20	
—Frantz	13	
—Anna Maria		9
—Anne		7
—Anna Catharina		4
Matheis Bronck works in ye Govr Gard	50	
—Anna Christina his Daughter	22	
—John Hendrick his son	16	
Johannes Jung	32	
— — Anna	35	
Baltzar Wenerick	40	
— — Eliz	30	
— — Hans George	—	9
— — Johan Maltheis		6
— — Maria Eliz	17	
Benedictus Wenerich	32	
— — Christina	33	
— — Frantz		5
— — Johannes		½
Anna Apolona Sieknerin wid	44	
— — Johannes dead		9
— — Johan Jacob		7
Johannes Planck	43	
— — Maria Margt	32	
— — Johanna Eliz	14	
— — Ludwig Henrich		6
Hans Adam Zolner	52	
— — Maria: before Baumersin	40	
Andreas Richter	47	
— — Anna Maria	45	
— — Andreas	16	
— — Anna Barbara		9
Anna Maria Mengelsin wid	27	
— — John Carolus		3
— — Anna Maria		5
— — Juliana		1¼
Maria Margt Scherin wid	23	
Anna Eliz. Deitrich orph	20 A	
— — Anna Gertrude	12	
Peter Garlack	37	
— — Magdalena	39	
— — Margaretta	12	
Hironimus Klein	38	
— — Maria	38	
— — Amalia	12	
— — Anna Eva	14	
— — Anna Eliz		6
Anna Catharina Erbin wid	44	
— — Eliz Catha		9
Magdalena Baumin wid:	29	
— — Johan Niclaus	15	
Maria Cath: Bornwaserin wid:	26	
Maria Cath: Schutzin wid:	40	
— — Hans Valentine	17	
— — Maria Catherina	12	
— — John Henrich		3
Maria Niesin wid	38	
— — Maria Magdalena	15	
Frances Baschin wid	40	
— — Margaretha	20	
Susannah Beijerin wid:	30	
— Susannah Maria		1
Anna Maria Cramerin wid	38	
her eldest Sone ⋈	18	
— — Maria Eliz	12	
— — John Hendrich		7
— — Anna Catharina		5
— — Juliana Maria		1¼
Sittonia Melchlin wid	41	
— Anna Maria	11	
— Anna Eliz		8
Anna Cath Batzin	38	
— — John Ludwig		7
Anna Maria Reichin orph	17	
— — Anna Margt dead		8
Hans Thomas A	12	
Jeane Bruiere orph	18	
Jacque	15	

Susannah 6
Anna Eliz Rorbaalin Wid..... 34
— — Anna Morga 11
Anna Eliz. Schullzin wid 22
Conrad Frederich........ 52
— — Anna Maria.............. 45
— — John Peter.............. 14
— — John Conrad............. 13
Lucas Hauch, dead............. 44
   Anna Magda............... 45
   Maria Cathar 16
   Maria Margt............... 18
   John Jacob 13
   John George ⋈ 12
   Maria Eliz ⋈ 11
   Johannes.................
Johan Phillip Greisler.. 40
   Catharine 40
   John George............... 11
   Johannes 7
Ludwig Buers 32
   Maria Cath 28
   Catharine................. 3
George Ludwig Leicht 56
   Anna Margatta............. 58
Johan Henrich Newkirk....... 36
   Anna Maria............... 33
   Johannes.................. 11
   John Henrich dead........ 8
Anna Almerodrin wid.......... 67
Johan Henrich Leicht 24
   Anna Eliz 20
Johan Henrich Gossinger 31
   Anna Eliz................. 27
   Anna Margt............... 2
Conrad Hellich dead 30
   Anna Marie............... 26
   Johannes dead 1
Christopher Daunermarker 28
   Christina 28
   Cath: Eliz................ 8
Anna Margt Danemark wid.... 58
Christina Strüd................. 40
   Maria Ursula 28
   Catharine 13
   Anna Maria............... 11
   John Jacob 9
   Maria Catharine........... 13
Andreas Elich 37
   Anna Rosina.............. 23
   John George.............. 3

Johannes Engelle............. 31
   Anna Christina............. 12
   Anna Maria............... 8
   Anna Eliz................. 4
Michael Pseffer 32
   Anna Maria............... 28
Michael Storr........... 38
   Anna Marg 48
   Eliz: Catharine 12
Johan Deitrick Wannermacher. 28
Peter Jacob Kornman dead 51
   Anna Conigunda dead...... 52
   Anna Conig............... 24
   John Christopher.......... 12 A
Susannah Weisin.............. 36
Umbert Rosin 45
   Maria Barbara Onin............ 36
Conrad Lein.................. 56
   Maria Marga 46
   Juliana 18
   Margareta 14
   Anna Maria............... 12
   Abraham.................. 10
   Conrad................... 7
Peter Ableman................. 42
   Anna Margareta........... 32
Anna Maria Benderin wid...... 44
   Eva Catharina 12
   John Matheus.............. 8
Arnold Falck.................. 36
   Anna Eliz................. 35
   Johannes.................. 6
Anna Conegunda Rusin, wid... 44
   Anna Catharina............ 14
   Anna Margaretta.......... 10
   Maria Catharina 8
Johannes Kuatz................ 40
Maria Cath: Hebmannin, wid.. 40
   Anna Engel................ 21 A
   Gertraude................. 14
   Anna Magdalena........... 11
Anna Maria Sacksin, wid...... 30
John Matheus Keiser 23
Johannes Trilhauser ⋈ 23
Bernhard Lickard.............. 25
   Justina................... 32
Johan Wm Schneider ⋈ 28
Helena Brilmannin, orph ⋈ 17
Valtin: Bressler............... 41
   Christina 36
   Anna Eliz................. 14

* The poor widow's son whose name is found here among this crowd of obscure & helpless Immigrants became subsequently famous in New-York annals. He was apprenticed to Wm. Bradford the printer and became afterwards

Johannes 7
Anna Catharina 10
Anna Maria Gablin wid 34
Anna Maria 7
Benedictus Kuhner 36
Anna Felice 40
Jacob A 4
Eva Barbara 9
Anna Elizabetha Laukin 42
Margaretta Schmidtin, wid.... 27
Johan Daniel A 4
Daniel Teffa................... 30
Marianna 11
Abraham 7
Margaret Meserin, wid........ 50
Johannes 15
Susan Cath................. 10
Maria Galete wid.............. 38
Sarah Margaret 7
Jacob 4
Simon Vogdt 30
Christina 26
John Wm ffelton ⋈ 30
Christina................... 28
Anthoni 11
Anna Clara 17
Hermanus Hoffman ⋈ 30
Maria Gertrude ⋈ 30
These two remains at Hackensack at John Lotz's
Ludolf Korning................ 50
Otillia 50
Catharina 16
Anna Dorothea 15
Conrad..................... 7
☞ Johanna Eliz: Fucks frau.. 22
Bernhard Erkel................ 53

Anna Maria................. 43
Elizab. Salbachin.............. 15
Johannes Deible............... 38
Anna Catharina............. 7
Catharina Mullerin, wid....... 36
Hans George............... ½
Johan Jacob Starenburger 45
Catharina................... 33
Johan Langsert............. 14
Anna Cathar................ 12
John Jacob 11
John Adam 5
Johan Fred'ch Neff.... dead } 34
Johan............. 8
Johannes Dorner 36
dead Anna Margaretta......... 40
Anna Cath. Grauin............. 40
Anna Eliz................... 18
Anna Sophia............... 10
Johannes 11
Henrich Schmidt............... 54
Anna Eliz................... 54
Clements................... 24
Wilhelm............... 20
Hans George............... 13
John Niclaus............... 9
Anna Maria................. 18
Daniel Schumacher 30
Anna Maria................. 36
Hans Niclaus 8
Johan Lenhard................. 5
Eva Catharina 12
Phillip Petr Grauberger....... 29
Anna Barbara.............. 33
Johannes Roschman............ 33
Anna Eliz................... 30
Maria Cath................. 9

the proprietor and publisher of the N. Y. *Weekly Messenger*. In consequence of the boldness of its strictures on the government, this paper was ordered to be burnt by the Common hangman and Zenger the Palatine, was indicted for Libel in 1734. It was on this occasion that Hamilton of Philadelphia so triumphantly vindicated the liberty of the Press and obtained Zenger's acquittal amid the cheers of the crowded court.

NAMES OF THE PALATINE CHILDREN APPRENTICED BY GOV. HUNTER, 1710—1714.

DATE.	NAMES OF CHILDREN.	AGE.	PARENTS.	BOUND TO.	OF
1710. Aug. 31	John Philip Lepper	12	Orphan	John Hallock	Brookhaven
Sept 14	Justina Mona	13	"	H. Vanderhuil	N. Y.
"	George ffrederick	"	Conrad Weiser	S: Smith	Smithtown
21	Daniel Artopee	12	Orphan	Jno Johnston	N. Y.
"	Phillips Daniel	13	"		"
22	Anna Margt Lamberton	13	Elizth Lamberton	Jno Deane	"
"	Jno. Paul Denbig	7	Orphan	S. Phillips	"
"	Hans Jerick Coons	6	"	Saml Mulford	East Hampton
"	Hans ffellacoons	15	"	Caleb Heathcote	Scarsdale
25	Anna Harber	9	"	Rem Jorissen	NeartheFerry,Kings
"	Adam Creiner	13	Anna Maria Creiner	Jos: Hunt Jr	Westchester
26	Hans Jerick Paer	8	Johans Paer	Richd Smith	Smith town
"	Anna Cathrina	11	Magdalen Drum	Paul Droilhet	N. Y.
"	Johannes Lodowick Trorit	9	Orphan	Laur Van Hook	"
"	Susan Maria Harmin	7	"	Jasper Hool	"
"	Anna Maria Harmin	14	"	Laurce Van Hook	"
27	Hanna Catrina Laparing	16	"	Anlw Mead	"
28	Hendrik Porter	14	"	Garret van Horne	"
"	Mary Trum	15	Trum	Richd Willet	"
Oct 11	Anna Margt Wolfe	13	Orphan	John Garreau	"
16	Hans Bastian Gatian	12	Sara Catrin Bastian	Geo. Elsworth	"
17	Jno Barnard Ruropaw	10	Orphan	Jno Sebringh	at the Ferry Kings
"	Anna Sibella Shefering	10	Ann. Maria S.	Dr John Nerbury	ferry, L. I.
18	John Conearhart	9	Margt Otteene	Robt Walter	N. Y.
"	ffrederick Pather	7	"	Harman Rutghert	"
"	Anna Catrina Haver	10	"	Jacob Goelet	"
"	Maria Elizth Negilzin	11	"	Joseph Latham	"
19	Han Jerick Livisten	12	ffrawnick Swieter	Derk Phlips Conine	"
"	Peter Pyfrin	6	Orphan	John van Horne	"
"	Willm "	10	"		"
23	John Conrad Petre	12	"	Robt Livingston	Livingston Manr
"	Jerit Casinor	13	"	Michl Hawdon	N. Y.
"	Garrit Lamberton	12	Widw Lamberton		"
24	Magdelena Lizard	13	Widow Lizard	Wellm VandeWater	"

Oct 24	Catrina "	15		Isaac Stoutenburgh	N. Y.
"	Elizabeth "	13		James Leigh	"
"	Hans Gerit "	10		John Symons	"
26	John Peter Zenger	13	Widw: Hanah Zenger	Wm Bradford, Printer	Momereneck
Nov 1	Thoms Reich	12	Orphan	Saml Palmer	Flushing
6	ffrances Lamberton	10	Wdw Lamberton	John Hicks	N. Y.
15	Jacob Berliman	10	John Berliman	Henry Wileman	Rhode Island
20	Jno Paul Schmidt	12	Orphan	Nathl Kay	N. Y.
21	Magdalen Brilman	12	"	Lancaster Symes	N. Y.
23	Jerit Taylor	15	Taylor	Thos Noxon	Kingston
1711. Jan. 12	Johs Coenrt Matheis Horner	3	Orphan	Enoch ffreeland	N. Y.
"	Jacob Oyster-berk	7	"	John Williams	Fairfield, Con.
15	Margaret "	8	"	Hugh Nesbitt	Strafford "
"	Hans Hendrk Schilts	8	"	R. Livingston	Livingston Mass
"	Wyat Webber	10	"		"
"	Jonah Smith	12	Henry Smith		"
"	Anna Catha Rear Patchin	4	Orphan		"
Feb 16	Anna Christian "	10	"		"
19	Johannes Schilts	15	"		"
"	Mary Catharina Hendrick	12	"	Daniel Ebbetts	N. Y
Mar 6	Christian Angle	8	"	James Elmes	"
21	Anna Maria "	13	"	Mary Robinson	"
"	Arnout Sweet	14	"	Laur: VanGhulen	Communapong N. J.
Apr 23	James Bruere	9	"	Rip Van Dam	N. Y.
9	Peter Lonie	12	"	Abm Lackerman	Richmond
11	Ma-y Catha Schutsen	14	Mary Kathe Schutsen	Thos Bayeux	N. Y.
"	Nichs Telry	14	Jacob Tedry	Thos Wiggins	Jamaica L. I.
12	Katha Rose	10	Anna Rose	Thos ffell	N. Y.
17	Anna Margt Rosse	8	"	Alexr Moore	"
"	Elizth woolfe	7	Orphan	Wm Commons	"
19	Johannah Elizth Weizer	13	"	Albert Terhena	Flatlands
27	Peter De Mott	11	"	Cornelis Wyckoff	"
June 2	Jacob Berliman	13	John Berliman	Nathl Kay	R. Island
"	Elizabeth Rapell	14	Orphan	Arthur Knight	N. Y.
1712 May 2	Jno Willm Smith	12	"	Jacob Rutsen	Ulster
"	Simon Helm	8	Peter Helm	John Rutsen	Kingston
22	Maria Mangley	6	Anna Maria M.	Kathe Provost	N. Y.
"	Charles "	5	"	ffredk Seabringh	Kings
1714. May 5	Anna Elizth Angle	11	Orphan	ffrancis Salisbury	Kattskill
"	Mary Angell		"	Geo Willocks	Elizabethtown

Palatines Subsisted at New York vizt

	Days		Adults		Children
For ye Month of November..............	30	Each Day	286	&	113
For ye Month of December..............	30	Each day	272	&	112
For ye Month of January................	31	—— ——	273	—	112
For ye Month of February................	28	days	274	&	110
For ye Moneth of March to ye 25 day is 25 days			312	&	119

Palatines, Subsisted at New York, from ye 25th March, Exclusive to ye 24th June Inclusive, 1711.

	Days	Adults	Young
From ye 25th March Exclusive to ye 30th aprill Inclusive, is..	36	265	93
From ye first of May Inclusive to ye 1st June Exclusive,....	31	89	35
From ye first of June Inclusive to ye 24 of June Inclu:......	24	69	33

PETITION OF PETER WILLEMSE ROMERS.

To his Excellency ROBERT HUNTER Esqr Capt Gen^ll & Govern^or in chief in & over her Majesties Provinces of New York & New Jersey & the territories depending thereon in America & Vice Admirall of the same &c— in Councill.

The Petition of Peter Willemse Romers of the City of New York,

HUMBLY SHEWETH,

That yor Pet^r was the last summer Employed by Mr Secretary to make a number of coffins for the Palatines that dyed here in all two hundred and fivety, that yor Pet^r having brought in his accompt to the Secretary & upon some difference about the Prise yor Pet^r abated Twenty Pounds thereof So that there is due to yor Pet^r fivety nine Pounds Six Shill's for which he has not yet been able to obtain any Satisfaccon and being at this time greatly straigtened for money,

He humbly Prays yor Ex^cy to direct the Secretary to pay the said Sume to yor Pet^r

New York
the 5th Sept. 1711

And yor Pet^r as in Duty bound shall ever Pray &c.

STATEMENT of heads of Palaten famileys and number of
Persons in both Towns on ye west side of Hudsons River.
Winter, 1710.

	NAMES.	Men.	Lads from 9 to 15	Boys from 8 & under.	Women.	Maids fr'm 9 to 15	Girls from 8 & under.	Totall of Persons.
1	Jno. Christ. Gerlach Capt.....	1	2	—	1	—	1	5
2	Peter Maurer.................	1	—	—	2	—	—	3
3	Philip Muller.................	3	1		1	1	1	7
4	Jno. Georg Spanhimer........	1	—	—	1	2	1	5
5	Jno. ffrid : Caselman..........	1	1	—	2	—	—	4
6	Jno. Leher....................	1	1	—	1	1	1	5
7	Fred : Mirckle................	1	2	—	1	3	—	7
8	Georg Schaffer................	1	—	—	1	—	—	2
9	Jno. Adam Friedrich.........	1	—	—	1	—	—	2
10	Valinten Bendor	1	—	—	1	—	—	2
11	Brandau	1	1	—	1	—	—	3
12	Scheffer..............	1	1	—	1	—	—	3
13	Georg Helen.....	2	—	—	1	1	—	4
14	Arnold	1	—	—	2	—	—	3
15	Welhelmin...........	—	—	—	1	—	—	1
16	Hofman	1	—	—	1	—	—	2
17	Ana Maria Draberin..........	—	2	—	1	—	—	3
18	Henrich Scherman............	1	1	—	2	—	—	4
19	Valentin Wolleben............	1	—	—	1	—	—	2
20	Philip Wolleben..............	1	—	—	—	—	—	1
21	Peter Wagner.................	1	—	—	1	—	—	2
22	Jno. Hen : Krantz............	1	—	1	1	1	—	4
23	Jno. Straub...................	1	—	—	1	—	—	2
24	Frank Keller..................	1	—	1	1	—	—	3
25	Jno. Becker...................	1	1	—	—	—	—	2
26	Jno. ffred : Conterman.........	1	3	—	1	—	—	5
27	Philip Kelmer.................	2	2	1	1	2	—	8
28	Henrich Man..................	1	—	—	1	—	—	2
29	Thomas Ehman................	1	—	—	-	—	1	2
30	Alb : ffrid : Marterstork.......	1	—	—	1	—	—	2
31	Augustin Voschell............	2	2	—	1	—	—	5
32	Peter Voschell................	1	—	—	1	—	—	2
33	John Eberhard................	1	—	—	—	—	—	1
34	Peter Wohleben...............	1	1	1	1	1	—	5
35	Anthony Kremer..............	1	—	—	1	—	—	2
36	Herman Hastman..............	1	2	—	1	3	1	8
37	Stephan Frolich..............	1	—	—	1	2	1	5
38	Magde : Streiten..............	—	2	—	1	—	1	4
39	Jno. Franck	1	—	—	—	—	1	2
40	Andreas Ross.................	1	—	—	—	—	—	1
41	Gartrud Eikertin..............	—	1	—	1	—	1	3
42	Joseph Richart	1	—	—	—	—	—	1

NAMES	Men	Lads from 9 to 15	Boys from 8 & under	Women	Maids fr'm 9 to 15	Girls from 8 & under	Totall of psons
43 Agnus Lapin	—	—	—	2	—	—	2
44 Melch: Tousweber	1	—	—	2	—	—	3
45 Mr Kocherthales	1	—	—	—	—	—	1
46 Jacob Mand	1	—	—	2	2	—	5
47 Matheus Schlimer	1	—	—	2	—	—	3
48 George Wm Kiel	1	—	—	1	—	1	3
49 Peter Becker	1	—	—	1	—	—	2
50 Valin: ffaulkinberg	1	—	1	1	—	—	3
51 Wilheim Muller	1	—	—	1	—	—	2
52 Elisab: Jungin	1	1	—	1	—	1	4
53 Jho Ritzbacus	1	1	—	1	—	1	4
54 Elisab: Bayherin	—	—	1	1	—	—	2
55 Peter Keiseler	1	—	1	2	—	—	4
56 Jno Wm Keifer	1	1	—	2	2	—	6
57 Jno Henrich Schram	1	2	—	1	2	—	6
58 Peter Egner	1	—	—	1	—	—	2
59 Elizab: Sweden	—	—	—	1	1	—	2
60 Jho Michel Emrich	1	—	—	1	—	—	2
61 Georg Hen: Stubenrau	1	—	—	1	—	—	2
62 Peter Diebel	1	—	—	1	1	—	3
63 Catha: Schutzin	—	—	—	1	—	—	1
64 Christian Meyer	1	—	—	1	—	—	2
65 Peter Overbach	1	—	—	1	—	—	2
66 Henrich Moor	1	—	—	1	—	—	2
67 Conrad Merdin	2	1	—	1	—	—	4
68 Maria Highrin	—	—	1	1	—	—	2
69 Ana Mar: Emrichin	—	—	—	1	1	—	2
70 Adam Hardel	1	-	1	1	1	—	4
71 Godfrey Fidler	1	—	—	1	—	—	2
72 Jacob Dimouth	1	1	—	1	2	—	5
73 Godfrey Rigel	1	—	—	1	—	—	2
74 Hyron: Schib	1	—	—	1	—	—	2
75 Anna Maria Kuntz	—	—	—	1	—	—	1
76 Nicolaus Kerner	1	1	1	1	1	—	5
77 Dietrich	1	1	2	1	—	—	5
78 Mullerin	—	—	—	1	1	—	2
79	3			1			4
80 Weiden	—	1	—	1	1	1	4
81 ahl	1			1	1		3
82 Hyronimus Weller	1	—	1	1	—	—	3
Totall	77	36	13	84	33	14	257

. Where blanks occur in the above names, the MSS. is destroyed.

PALATINE VOLUNTEERS FOR THE EXPEDITION AGAINST CANADA; 1711.

QUEENSBURY

1	Johan Cond Wiser Capt	21	Niclaus Weber
2	Christian Haber	22	Wm George Lieut
3	Andreas Bergman	23	Fred Schaffer
4	Johannis Feeg	24	Antho: Ichard
5	Mattheus Kuntz	25	Jno: Pet. Sein
6	Mattheus Reinbolt	26	Jno. Jac. Munsinger
7	Jno Beter Dopff	26	Johan Leyer
8	Jno Jacob Reisch	28	Jacob Kuhn
9	Carl Nehr	29	Henr. Mathous
10	Henrich Jung	30	Nicklaus Eckard
11	Hen: Hoffman	31	Martin Dilleback
12	Werner Deichert	32	Niclaus Feller
13	Geo: Muller	33	Jacob Schnell
14	Fred Bellenger	34	Jacob Webber
15	Hen Widerwachs	35	William Nelles
16	Geo Mathias	36	Johannis Kisler
17	Cristo Hagedorn	37	Geo: Breigel
18	Frantz Finck	38	John Schaffer
19	Andreas Schurtz		George Dachstader
20	Peter Hagedorn		Johannes Zaysdorf

356 men, women & children in this Town.

A True Coppy from the Original
HENRY MAYER.

HAYSBURY.

1	John Christopher ffucks	10	Paulus Dientzer
2	John Wm Dales	11	Melch: Foltz
3	John Wm Schaff	12	John Segendorf
4	Christian Bauch	13	Phillip Laux
5	Peter Hayd	14	Abraham Langen
6	Henr. Hammer	15	Jno Jacob Schultz
7	Mich Ittich	16	Jno. Wm. Hambuch
8	Johan Kyser	17	Niclaus Laux
9	Jacob Cup	18	Niclaus Gottel

19 Paulus Reitchoff

243 men women & child:

ANNSBERG.

1	Hartman Winedecker Capt.	25	Valtin Kuhn
2	Jno Wm Dill	26	Henrich Winter
3	Peter Spies	27	Jno Geo. Reiffenberg
4	Herman Bitzer	28	Jno. Wm Linck
5	Johannes Schue	29	Jno. Mart. Netzbach
6	John Wm Schneider	30	Johannes Weis
7	Jacob Bast	31	Jno. Adn Walbourn
8	Johannes Blass	32	Jno. Hen. Arendorff
9	Johan Wm Kammer	33	Danl Busch
10	Johannes Bonroth	34	Jno. Hen. Conradt
11	Johannes Bernhard	35	Hen. Bellinger
12	Sebastian Fischer	36	Johan Schneider
13	Niclaus Hayd	37	Marcus Bellenger
14	Henrick Klein	38	Phill Schaffer
15	Hen. Balt. Stuper	39	Johan Kradt
16	Casper Rauch	40	Christ Sittenich
17	Hans Hen: Zeller	41	Jno. Hen. Schmidt
18	Johannes Zeller	42	Jno Phill Zerbe
19	Samuel Kuhn	43	Jno Phill Theis
20	Gerhard Schaffer	44	Martin Zerbe
21	Ulrich Bruckhart	45	Niclaus Ruhl
22	Jacob Ess	46	Adam Mic Schmidt
23	Ferdo Mentegen	47	Cond Maisinger
24	Conrad Kuhn	48	Thos Ruffener

Jacob Dings   Henrick Fehling   Joh Jost Petry   Lud. W. Schmit.

250 men women & children

a True Coppy from the Original

HEN: MAYER

Census of Slaves,

1755.

NOTE. The lists for the counties of Albany. New York and Suffolk, are missing.

SLAVES IN ULSTER CO. 1755.

KINGSTON.

A List of all the Names of all such Persons as have Given of their Negrous Slaves and their Number of Male and famale Unto me David Lametter: Capt of a Company Malitia In Kingstoun In Ulster County above the age of 14 Jaers Masters or oners Names.

	yr of male	yr of female		yr of male	yr of female
Abraham haesbrock	1	1	Adam Paorsen	1	-
Evert Wynkoop	3	3	Nickolas Bogardus	-	1
Charles Brodhad	5	2	Hans Kiersteden	2	1
John Croocke	3	1	Cornelis Elmondorph	1	1
Abraham Louw	-	2	William Dondij	-	1
Johannis Jansen	1	1	Abraham Van Keuren	3	2
David De Lametter	2	2	Wilhelmus hooghtelingh	3	3
Hendrickus Sleght	1	1	Johannis De Lametter	1	-
Jakop turck	1	-	Poulus Ploegh	1	1
Johannis Wynkoop	3	2	Petrus A louw	1	-
Cornelis De lametter	1	-	Hiskiea Du boois	1	1
Cornelis De lametter Jur.	-	1	Domyny Vas	1	1
Jakobus Eltinge	1	-	Ragel Du mont	1	3
Pieter tappen	-	1	Jakobus Elmendorph	1	1
Domyne Mansius	1	1	Hendrick oostrander	-	1
thomas Beeckman	1	1	Abraham Sleght	-	1
tjatie tappen	3	2	Petrus Smedus	3	1
Jakoba Wittiker	-	1	Abraham haesbroeck Jur.	1	-
Jan Eltinge	1	-			

DAVID DE LAMETTER.

By Capt Lawrence Salisbury a list of the Slaves Males and females and Their Names and the Names of their Masters as it Here Under Doth appear.

The Names of their Masters.		The Names of the Slaves. Males.		Females.
Coll Abrm Gaasbeck Chambers	4	Tom &Sam&Kellis &Robin&	2	Mary & Anna.
Coll John Tanbroeck	3	Sam & Tom & Bel	2	Bet & Anna
Capt Lawrence Salisbury.	2	Gif & Jack	1	Mary
Capt John Slegh			1	Catharien
Nicholas Demyer	5	John & frank & Jack & Smart & Quay	2	Dijaen & Deen
Wido Annaca Johnson	3	Trump & Frank & Penney..	3	Sare & Gen & Sue
Abrm Burhans	2	Dick & francis	3	Mary&Mary& Dien
Abrm post	1	Wil	1	Bat
Powlas Swart	1	Dick	0	
John Sneyden	2	Tom & Robin	0	
David Burhans	0		1	Bat.
Jacob Brink	2	Dick & Charles	1	peg
John Burhans Jur	1	Sam		
Lawrence Van Gaasbeck..	1	Ebo Roben	0	
Aaras Van Steenbergh	1	Prince		

The Names of their Masters		*The Names of the Slaves.*	
		Males.	Females.
Marta Snyder.............	0	 1	Bet
Phillip Vielle.............	0	 1	Dein
John Luyks.............	1	Tom....................... 1	Bet
John Burhans.............	2	frank & Robin.............. 1	Dijaen
Thomas Van Gaasbeck....	3	Heny & Jack & Sesar........ 2	Bet & Nan
WidoBlandienaTenbroeck	2	Bal & Dan.................. 1	Gen
Coenradt Tan Broeck.....	1	Sam 2	Regein & Regein
Abrm Van Gaasbeck.....	0	 1	Dijaen
Benjamin Tanbroeck.....	1	Titus 1	Gen
John Van Gaasbeck	1	Ben.........................	
Jacobus Delametter......	1	Bris 1	Sar
William Oosterhout......	2	George & Simon............ 2	Nen & Qussaba
Jacob Burhans...........	1	fort........................	
Wido Margareit Burhans	2	Tone & frank.............. 0	
David Burhans Jur.......	1	Robin 0	
Isaac Deccar.............	0	 1	Mat
Wid: Rachal Dumond....	1	Sam 3	Nan & Mary & Gin
Isaac pust................	1	fort.........................	
Peter Winne.............	1	Cato.......................	
Tuenes Ooesterhout......	1	Jack.......................	
Henderick Brink.........	2	Bern & Jack.............. 2	Mary & Dijaen

---

A True List Taken by Capt. Petrus Bogardus of All the Slaves Reported To him by Those Persons here under Written Both Male and female Above the Age of fourteen Years.

	Males.	Females.		Males.	Females.
Capt Petrus Bogardus......	3	2	Tjerck Dewitt.............	4	2
Petrus Ed Elmendorph.....	1	1	Waldron Dumon	1	2
Wid Cattrienna Croeck.....	1	0	Johanis Dubois	1	0
Thomas Beekman	1	1	Jacobus Dumon............	1	0
Christofel Kiersted	1	2	Nelle Oosterhoudt..........	2	1
Johanis Chris Thomas.....	1	0	Moses Contyn..............	1	1
Dirck Shepmoes	4	0	Wilhelmus Hooghteling ...	0	1
Cornelis Viele.............	0	1	Anthony Hofman...........	4	2
Tryntje Van Keuren	0	1	Hendrick freligh	1	1
Izack Dubois...............	2	1	Johanis Masten	0	1
Evert Bogardus...........	2	3	Barber Ploegh	0	2

SHAWANGUNCK.

A List of Slaves within the Precinct of Shawangunk Under the Command of Capt. Benjamin Smedes.

	Slaves upwards of fourteen years.	
Masters Names.	*Males.*	*Females.*
Jacobus Bruyn	Will, York, Cuff, Ball,Jo ...	Bett, Susan
Benjamen Smedes	Cesar, Will................	Jean
Cornelius Schoonmaker.......	Bass ....·.	Susan
Cornelius Schoonmaker Junr..	Tomma....................	Saar
Jacob Hoffman....	Bill, Charles	Dibb, Moll
Zacharias Hoffman............	Andries, Tam, Jack........	Bett, Derinda
Abraham Roosa	Tom.......................	Bett
Adriaen Newkerck...........	Maatt......................	
Isaac Hasbrouck........	Piet, Dick, Ephraim........	Luce
William Weeller.............	Wann.....................	
Cornelius Bruyn	Piet, Robin, Bristo	Diean, Jean
Robert Ken.................	Bristo	Dien
Hendrick Van Wyen..........	Herry	Dien, Abb
David Davis................	Patrick....................	

Masters Names.	Males.	Females.
James Phenix	Tom	
Burger Myndertse	Middletoun	Floor
David Windfield	Phillip	
Arie Terwillegen		Pegg
Jacob Decker	Jan, Charles	Floor, Grace
Marities Decker	Tom, Herry, Tone, Sopus, Jan	Saar
Thomas Jansen	Loudon, Cipio	Sivil, Nan
Jacobus Van Keuren	Lancaster, Tom	Bett
Benjamin Van Keuren	Jack, Mingo	
Johannis Jansen	Jack	

The above List is a full acct of all Slaves given up to me to be Enlisted
Untill this Seventh Day of May 1755 as witness my hand

BENJAMIN SMEDES Capt.

HURLEY ;

Masters } Names and Mistress }	Names of Negroes Male and	Female
Johannis Crispell	Herry	
Abraham delameter	prins	Izabel
Eva Suylandt	Will	
Johannis hardenberg	Leendert, tam: Jessewe. flink	Jane: bet
Abraham Van Wagenen	Mingo	Nane
Antonie Crispel	Awaan	Dien, Mary
Luycas Elmendorph	philip	Sare, Lane
Matthys Blanjan	James	Jane
Henderica Louw	Cubit, tamma, quack	Susan, Bet
Aldert Roosa		Dien, Sare
Cornelius Nukerck	piet, tam, Jack, toon.	Jane
Coenraat & Benyamen Nukerck	James	Jane, Eve, Rose
Cornelius Nukerk Jur	piet, Kof	Izabel, Jane
Derck Wynkoop	Sam.tam, herrie, Abram, maan	Sare, Luse
Cornelius Cool	Richard, Sezer, George	Lane, peg
Jacob Aarts Van Wagenen		hes, tryn
Gerrit Van Wagene	Dick	
petrus Crispell	herry	
Jan Crispell	Andrew	Cate
Johannis Van Wagene		fill
Matthys fever	Sem, tam	Sare
Johannis duboys	Kof, quas	Sare
Coenraat Elmendorp	hendrick, Sym	Mary
Jenneke ten Eyk	herry, Jack, tam	bet, Nane, bet
Gerardus hardenburgh	Sezer, Jem	bet
Jenneke Elmendorph	tam	Dien
Jan Vanduese		Susan
Lambert Brinck	Sezar	Mary, Susan

A true List of the Negroes Male and female above the Age of fourteen years;
of the touwnship of hurley In Ulsters County : Listed by me—Dated this 19th
Day of Aprill. 1755.

Capt. JOHANNES CRESPEL.

1755 *the 13 of April, By Cap^tn Edward Whittaker An account
of the Negro people males and females and their Names and The
Names of Their Masters as it Here under Doth appear*

The Names of Their Masters.	The Negro people or Slaves Males.	Females
Captn Edward Whittaker	1	Will	1	Gen
Widow: Elesabeth Whittak	1	Jack		
Widow Hillitie Whittaker	2	Jack, franck	2	gen, Deen

The Names of their Masters		The Negro people or Slaves		
		Males		Females
Widow Hannah Schoonmaker...	2	tom, trump...........	2	Dido, Jud
Widow Elsye Van Bunschoten..	2	Seas, Cof.............	2	gen Saar
Lutenent John Whittaker	2	Herry, Dick..........		
William Myer...........	1	Jack		
Luttenent Tobias Wynkoop....	2	Herry, tom...........	1	Dyan
Widow Antie Wynkoop........		....	1	Betty
Myndert Myndertse.....	2	toon, Jack...........	1	Dyan
Jacobus persen.........	4	Jack, Jack, piet, Joo.	2	pegg, floor
Samuel Dubois..........	1	piet..................	1	mar
Widow Elesabeth Oosterhout ..	1	Cof		
Johannes Troumbour...	2	tyen, Isac	1	Bet
Chrstiyan Myer	1	Cof..................	2	Bet, Jud
Richard Devenport.....		....	1	pegg
peak Dewit	1	gato		
Cornelis Langendyk....	1	Seazor	1	gen
Cronimus Valkenburgh.	1	Herry		
Nathan Dubois	1	Cof	1	gen
Daniel Whittaker.......	1	Ruben		
Insign William Legg..........	2	Seazor, Ruben	1	Dyan
John Legg Junier......	1	Sharp		
Hendrick Schoonmaker .	1	Cof		
Widow Tedotia Schoonmaker ..	1	Cof		
John Monk.............		....	1	Hester
peter Van Luven.......	1	Mingo		
Johannis Jury Elegh ...		....	1	Saar
Johannis Mourse	1	Jack		
Severyn Bruyn..........		....	1	gen

Capt Harmonse's List.

April yᵉ 2: 1755: then their Mersters first Give up their Slaves to me Capᵗ

Hendrick Heermans Negro man dirck is 63 jers old Negro wens Nen is 40 ys old Negro wens Bet is 51 yrs old.

Gerret van wagenen Negro man tam is 30 jers old Negro wens Dyaen is 40 jers old

Art van wagenen Negro man jo is 26 jers old

Evert van waganen Negro man ton is 66 jers old Negro wens yud is 23 jers old

Johen van wagenen Negro man ton is 18 jers old

Peter de wit Negro man jack is 30 jers old Negro wens anne is 50 jers old

peter de wit Negro man Abram is 18 jers old Negro wens bet is 35 jers old

Jogham raddely Negro man tam is 16 jers old Negro wens dyaen is 35 jers old

Matthew Sleght Negro man tobe is 26 jers old Negro wens belis 14 jers old

Hendrick Sleght Negro man pomp is 35 jers old

Jacobes van Ette yr.   Negro wens feb is 18 jers old

Col Hendrick beckman Negro man Prence is 60 jers old Negro wens Betty

hendrick beckman Negro man Cilkenney is 50 yrs Negro wens Marrian

hendrick beckman Negro man Jack is 16 yrs Negro wens mary

hendreck backmen Negro man Same is 50 yers old Negro wens Bekindo

Lea van waganen Negro man Jo is 66 jers old

Herry Hendrickse Negro man Herry is 30 jers old

William Traphage Negro man peet is 30 jers old

Jo Croffert   Negro wens Deen is 30 jers old

Arl Hendrickse Negro man pramis 65 jrs

Herry Hendrickse   Negro wens San is 33 yers old

Cherls Crock   Negro wens Nen is 25 jers old

Hendrikus Hermanse.

NEW PALTZ

A list of all the Slaves, Both Males and Females, that are above the age of Fourteen Years, in the Precinct of The New Paltz in Ulster County; Their number being Set down in the Columns opposite to their Masters or Mistresses names, To wit, The males in the first Column and the Females in the Second.

	Male	Female		Male	Female
Josiah Eltinge	3	1	Sarah Hasbrouck	2	3
Peter Doyo Junr.	1		Isaac Freer		1
Abraham Hardenbergh	4	3	Annetje van de merken		1
Benjamin Hasbrouck	3	2	Daniel Hasbrouck	2	2
Hendrikus Dubois	2	1	Petronella Lefever	1	1
Lewis Dubois	3	2	Samuel Bevier	2	1
Solomon Dubois	5	2	Simon Dubois	3	3
Abraham Bevier	1	1	Abraham Doyo	2	1
Jacobus Bevier	1		Jacob Hasbrouck	2	2
Benjamin Dubois	2	1	Nathaniel Lefever	1	1
Hugo Freer		1	Noah Eltinge	1	0
Chrtstiaan Doyo	2	1	Abraham Lefever	1	
Mary Lefever	1	1	Andrew Lefever	1	
Geesje Een	1		Philip Bevier	1	

JOSIAH ELTINGE, Captain.

MARBLETOWN

March ye 20th 1755.

A List of the Negro Slaves Which Are Given up to me (Fredk Davis) as Capt of the town of Marbletown pursuant to An Act of Generall Assembly made for that Purpose.

	Male	Female		Male	Female
Levi Pawling Esqr	5	3	John Crispell Junr	—	1
Levis Bevier	2	2	William Wood	1	—
Johannes Dewitt	3	2	Thomas Vendemerk	1	—
Gerret Dubois	2	2	Andrew Oliver	—	1
Matthew Newkerk	2	1	Peter Cantine	1	4
Johannes Jonson Jnnr	1	1	Ann Garting	4	3
Malgart Keater	—	1	Frederick Davis	1	—
Nathan Smades	3	2	Johannes Bogart	1	—
Jacob Hasbrouck	2	1	Wessel Brodhead	2	2
Isaack Hasbrouck	2	2	Cornelious Brink	1	—
John Newkerk	—	1	Hendrick Croom	4	3
Marten Delameter	3	2	Thomas Venkeuran	2	1
Marten Bogart	1	1	Solomon Vanwaganan	1	1
Stephen Nottingham	1	2	William Nottingham	1	—
Elesabeth Moures	—	1	faulintine Smith	—	1
Johannes Vanwaganan	—	1	frederick Schoonmaker	3	2
Samuel Mowris	1	—	Johannes Keater	1	1
Thomas Jonson	3	2	Matthew Cantine	1	—
Leonard Hardenbergh	1	1	Jannoche Elting	2	1
Daniel Brodhead	2	1		—	—
				61	50

SLAVES IN ORANGE CO. 1755.

Masters Names.	No: of males.	No: of females.
Benjamin Tusten	1	1
William Bull	1	1
Joshua Brown	1	0

Masters Names.	No: of males.	No: of females.
Solomon Tuthill..	1	0
Thomas Sayrs...	0	1
James Tuthill..	1	0
John Dain...	0	1
Yost Duryea	0	1
	5	5

The above is an Axact List of the Slaves both Mailes and Females within the District of my Company that Coms to my knowledge or information theyr being not more than two of them given in.

June ye 9: 1755.

pr BAY: TUSTEN.

---

the Number of all the Negro thats beloning Vnder Captain John Weesnor of floraday.

Nethanel Roo	two	a male & a famale
William Thompson.............	two	a male & a famale
Jeame Thompsone	one	a male
Dauid Shepeord.................	one	a male
Jonathan Elmor.................	one	a male
Hennery Weesner	one	a male
Josheph Alson...................	two	a male & a famale
Richard Alson...................	one	a male
Isrel Parshel....................	one	a male
Gorge Car	one	a male
Addem Weesner	one	a female
Mathew Howell.................	one	a female

JOHN WISNER

MAY IT PLEAS HIS EXCELLENCY

According to the act of your Assembly this is a true account of all the Slaues Belonging to my District.

to Cornel Dekay 1 neager Slaue
to Georg Dekay 1 neager slaue
to Richard Edsel 1 neager meal and 3 females slaues
to Beniaman Burt 1 neager slaue
to Thomas Welling 1 neager slaue
to Richard Edsel Juner 1 neager slaue
to John Allison 1 neager slaue
to Peter Clous 1 neager slaue

JACOBUS DEKAY.

NEW WINDSOR.

A List of the Negroes Male & female Above the age of fourteen Years in the Southern Division of the Precinct of New Windsor, otherwise Called the High Lands, Whereof Thos Ellison Jr is Captain Vizt

Number of males	Number of females	To whom Belonging
4	2	To Thomas Ellison
..	1	To James McClogery
1	..	To James Edmondstone
4	2	To the Estate of Evan Jones,

Number of males	Number of females	To whom Belonging
1	1	To Charles Clinton
2	..	To Christian Hartel
..	1	To Joseph Sacket Tert:
..	1	To John Moffet
..		To Frances Nicolls
..		To James Jackson Junr
1	1	To the Honble John Chambers
13	11	New Windsor Octobr ye 23 : 1755
		THOS ELLISON Junr

SLAVES IN DUTCHESS COUNTY. 1755.

A true List of all the Negroes that are in my District above the Age of fourteen according to the Act of Assembly for that purpose made and provided

Masters and Mistress Names	Negroes Names Males	Negroes Names Females
Collo: Martin Hoffman...	Jack Fortune Frank Francis Toby Jo:.................	Sarah Dean Susan Bet
Capt Zacharias Hoffman...	Bristoll, Will	Jenny Peggy
Vullard Widbeck.........	Jack......................	Diana
Harman Knickerbacker..	Tom	
John Van Benthouse	Pompey, Cuffy..............	Hannah, Jenny
Barrent Van Benthouse...	Bastian,Andrew,Cuffy,Peter, Simon,prince Adam Mathew	
Anthony Hoffman.........	Jo:.......................	
John Vosburgh...........	Jo Tom....................	Phillis
Capt Evert Knickerbacker		Maria
Adam Pitzer..............		Kate
Peter Pitzer..............	Fortune	
Rier Schemerhorn........		Diana
Peter Heermanse.........	Quash	
Garrett Heermanse.......	Ned	

The above List was taken by me this 12th Day of May 1755

ZACHARIAS HOFFMAN Captain

RYNEBECK PRECINCT, March 22 Day.

A List Taken of the Slaves or Negroes In my Distract According to the Act of the Generall Assembly

Masters or Mistres	Male	Famale
Mr Jacob Siemon..............	Antony...................	0
Margerit Bennin...............	Tam......................	0
Symon Kool	Pamp.....................	Bette
Nicholas Stickel..............	Frank....................	0
Johannes Feller	Piet.	0
Petrus Ten Brock.............	Tam, Cornelis, Jack	Sara Bette
Ms Catherine Palling...........	Robben	Deen
Andries Heremanse............	Go	Mary

Taken up by me EVERT

KNEKERBACKER Capt

RHYNEBECK PRECINCT, March yᵉ 22 Day.

A list taken of the Slaves or Negroes In my District according to the act of the General Assembly.

Masters or Mistres.	Male.	Famels.
Mrs. Aleda Rutsen............	Thom, Robin, Coffie........	Filis, Riet, Dean
Mrs. Rachel Van Steenbergen	Lou, Pieter	
Lauwrence Tiel..............	Tam	
Henry Tiel....................	Jack	
Philip Veller.................	Lou.........................	Betty
Johannes Lambert...........		Bett
Jack Keip....................	Tom, Pieter..............	Jan, fillis
Roelof Keip..................	Tom....................	Keet
Abraham Keip...............		Betty,Mary,Bess
Gerrit Van Benthuysen......	Herry....................	floor, Dill
George Toevelt..............		febe
George Adam Toevelt........		Dien
Susan Angenes Sheeferen....		Kinno
Corneles Ostevanter.........		Wench fillis
Mrs.Cathlynje V : fretenborg..		Yud

Taken op by me, FRANS NEHER Capt.

SLAVES IN WESTCHESTER COUNTY. 1755.

NORTH PART OF THE MANOR OF PHILIPSBURGH.

A List of the Negro Slaves In the Mannor of Philips Burgh In the upper Part where William Hamman is Capt

Masters	Males	Females
Josiah Martin Esqr his Slaves	Caser, Tom, Argile, Oxfoot, Jeffery	Mally
Joseph hitchcock his slaves..	Harry	Abigal Lue
Joseph Paldon his slaves	Harry	fillis
harmon Yurcksea his slave..	Jno Sharp	
Moses Sherwood his slaves..	Ned	flora
William Brett his slaves....	Ceaser.....................	gine
John Anten his slaves.......	Charls, Ben	Marcy
Thos Champenois his slaves.	tom	fillis
Samuel devenport his slaves.	Harry Jack.................	dine
Jno Smith his slaves.........	Stephen	flora
Richard devenport his slaves	tom	
Beniamen Kipp his slave....	franck.....................	
Elbert Artsea his slave	Philip.....................	
Barth Cornell his slave......	Petter.....................	
Anthony woodhouse his slave	....	Mally

Here is in the Upper part of this mannor twenty negro man.

Here is in the sd Upper part Eleven negrois Women whereof Wm hammand is Capt

WILLIAM HAMMAN.

MORRISANIA.

An Account of the Negroes above fourteen years of Age belonging to Lewis Morris, at Morrisania. m

Mens Names	their Ages	Womens Names	Their Ages
Samson, Blind..................	96	Old Hanch	82
Mulatto Harry	82	Ambo........................	67
Mandos Hary	68	Betty	52
Pawby........................	65	little Hanch..................	52
Robin........................	63	Hager	42
Old Peter.....................	59	Long Betty..................	31

Mens Names	their Ages	Womens Names	Their Ages
Joseph	50	Zibia	27
Yaff.........................	47	Hannah	25
George.....................	45	Abigail.......................	24
Long Peter.	41		
John	32		
Daniell	29		
Benjamin......	28		
Sam Cooper..............	28		
Simon.....................	27		
Sam.......................	20		
Ando	25		
Peter Short..............	18		
Ocumah...................	63		
Demmy....................	41		

BOROUGH OF WESTCHESTER.

A List of Negros Males & Females In Joshua Hunt Capt. of West-Chester foot Companys Districts According to a Act of Assembly.

	Males.	*Famales.*
Peter Delancey Esqr	Honnyball, Tom, Tim, Sam, Lew, Jupiter, Class	Susanah, Nan, Dafne, Flore, Grace
Isaac Willitt Eqr.	James, Fait, Jacob, Herculus, George	Ginne, Ginne, Tammes, Hester, Abigall
Theophilus Barto	Ben, Moses	Lille
Anthony Barto	Johne, Jeck	Nell
Bassill Barto...	Abram	
Edward Stevenson.	Will, Tite, Luke	Ginne
Phillip Palmer	Robin, .	bess
Ester Palmer		Lue
John Hunt	Tobe .	Hannah
Benjaman Palmer	Tonney	
Nathaniell Lewis		Ginne
John Pugsly	Jack	fillis, Ginne
Walter Brigs	Newport	Nanney
Lewis Palmer	Ceaser	Hannah
John Williams	Charls	
Nathaniel Underhill	Peter Pinna	Easter
Israeli Honneywell Jur	Indian Will Fell Imdus	bell
Arron Quinby	Tom	
Israel Honneywell Ser	James, Tom	Margett
John Oakley	York, Lew	Ginne, Mary
Thomas Uail	Lew, James	Hannah
Stephen Hunt		Nan
Stephanus Hunt	Robin	Agness
Thomas Hunt	Abram, Titus, Tobe	Lille, Gin
David Hunt	Dick	Luce, Ginne
Jacob Hunt	Cuffe, Lew	
Thomas Willitt	Abram, Harry	Ginne, Gin
Augustin Baxter	Dick	
John ferris	Arron	
Bartholomew Hadden	Jerre, Will.	
Thos: Palmer	Tiss	
Thos: Hadden		Sue
John Ganter	Job, Tittus.	
James ferris	Jo & Abram	
Richard Cussens	Charls	Rose

		Males.	
Caleb Hunt	Geffery................		1
			54
Caleb Hunts aded......	....		55
		Famales	35
Cousens Rose aded.....	....		1
			36
Hezekiah Fergusons			
Cate aded...........	....		37

This is a True List Taken by me   JOHN HITCHCOCK Clerk.

by order of   JOSHUA HUNT Capt

of Westchester foot Company.

recd from Mayor Aprill 9, 1755.

		Males.		*Jeamals.*
Vndrill Barns	1	Bohaneo		
phebey Turner	1	Luk	2	Nell, Gene

MANOR OF PELHAM.

A True List of all the Slaves Both Male & Female in the mannour of Pelham above the Age of Fourteen Years according to Report to me made in Submission to the present Malitia Act of General Assembly of this province

	Numb,
Joshua Pells numbr males 2	2
Caleb Pells numbr males two Femals two.................................	4
Philip Pells numb males two Femals two.................................	4
Samll Rodmans number Males two Femals two.........................	4
Bernard Rylanders males two Femals one...............................	3
Phebe Pell wd Jos. pell Decd one male one Femal.....................	2
Executrs of Isaac Contine Decd males one...............................	1
for my own possession males three, Female 1...........................	4

number of the Whole.   24

From your Honnours Most Humble Servant

Aprill the 12th 1755   JOHN PELL, Captain

of the Mannor of pelham.

MAMARONECK & SCARSDALE.

A List of the Indian Negro and Malatto Slaves Within and Belonging to the Township of Mamaroneck and Mannor of Scarsdale taken Aprill ye 5th 1755 by Joseph Sutton Capt.

Owners Names.	Males.	Females.	Owners Names.	Males.	Females.
Joseph Sutton...............	one		Jonathan Griffin...............	one	one
Vnderhill Bridd...............	two	two	RichardCornell	two	one
John Stevanson...............	two	one	Richard Cornell Junr.........	one	one
Hanah disbrow...............	one	one	William Barker...............	one	one
Nehemiah Palmer.............	two	one	Benjamin Griffen	0	one
Nehemiah Palmer Junr......	one	one	William Griffen.	one	—
Reuben Bloomer.............	0	one	Anthony Hill Junr.............	one	one
Daniel Barker.................	one	0	John Tounsend................	0	one
Benjamin Palmer............	0	one	Nicolas Baylie..	one	one
John Roads....................	one	0	Edward Merrit................	one	0
Joseph Ccrnell...............	one	one	Elizabeth Allair...............	five	one
John Gidney	one	one	Thomas Hading	one	one

RYE.

A List Taken of the Negros to the Est of Blind Brook in Rye Within the Milintary Command of Captn Solomon Purdy, March ye 26: 1755

	Male	Female		Male	Female
Thomas Lyon	1	1	Adam Seamans	1	—
Gilbert Lyon	1	0	Roger park Jun	2	1
Joseph Merit	1	—	Anne Disbro	1	1
Jonethan Brown	1	1	Daniel Strang	1	2
Major Hasechiah Brown	1	1	John Thomas Junr	1	1
Widow Hannah Brown	—	1	Hannah Lyon Widow	1	2
Benjaman brown	1	—	Calab Kniffin	0	1
Lievt Samll Wilson	1	1	Mr James Wetmore	2	1
Samll Brown	2	0	Ralph Jacobs	0	1
David Kniffin	1	—	Abreham Theat	0	1
Thomas Brown	1	—	Cornelus fleman	—	1
Benjaman Brown Junr	—	1	Joseph Brundig	0	1
Abreham bust	—	2	Richard Wilis	0	1

A list of all the Slaues taken within my Limets In the year 1755 by me James Horton Captain of a Company of Militia a foot in West Chester County.

Persons Names	Negroes Male	Female	Persons Names	Male	Female
Colinel William Willit	3	2	Joseph Haviland	1	0
Mr John Thomas	2	2	Caleb Purdy	1	0
Crestepher Eisenhart	2	1	Henry Griffen	0	1
Job Hadden	1	1	Gilbert Blomer	0	1
Andrew Cannon	—	1	Thomas Carpender	0	1
Thomas Haviland	1	2	Thomas Carpender Junr	2	0
Jeremiah Fowler	1	1	William Anderson	0	1
Thomas Stars Tredwell	—	1	James Gedney	0	1
Anthony Field	—	1	Nathan Field	1	1
Joseph Lyon	1	1	James Pine	0	1
Samuel Tredwell	2	1	Peter Jay	3	5
William Duesenberry	1	—	David Hay Junr	0	1
Benjamin Birdsell	1	1	Rodger Park	1	1
Benjamin Haviland	1	—	Just Daniel Purdy	3	0
William Haviland	1	—	Joshua Purdy	1	1
David Holsted	2	1	Joseph Thield	1	0
Thomas Holsted	1	1	John Crawford	1	0
Joshua Barns	1	1	Charles Thield	1	2
James Horton	1	1	Total	38	35

CHARLES HAIGHT.

NORTH CASTLE May 4: 1755

this Comes to let you know that Aron Forman has one Negro man Named franses and George Knifin has two Negro men one named pomp and the other Cuffe and Thomas Golding has one wench Named Elizabeth and Antoni Trip has one Negro fellow Named Ned and a wench Named francis and Roger Lyon has one wench Named Mereum and Samuel Banks has one wench Named Marget and Timothy Carpenter has one wench Named Susanah this from your friend to serve

AARON FORMAN Capt

NORTH CASTLE.

A list of yᵉ Nagros in Captine Dusenber Compyny for yᵉ year 1755

Robert Dikensen	1 man................	Dick
Nathaniel Carpenter...........	1 wench.............	Dinah
Able Weeks	1 man...............	Lewis
Joseph Sutton	2 a man and woman..	Roger and Dorrity
Peter Toten...................	1 man...............	prins
Elias Clap....................	1 man...............	Narow
Caleb Fowler..................	1 wench.............	peg
Elisabeth Fowler..............	1 wench	Teen

SLAVES ON LONG ISLAND. 1755.

BUSHWICK.

A List Taken by Capᵗ Francis Titus of Bushwyck in Kings County of the Slaves Belonging to the Inhabitants of his District Vizᵗ

Owners Names	Males	Females	Owners Names	Males	Females
John Misroll................	1	1	David Van Cots..........	1	—
John Liequare	—	1	Theodorus Polhemus.....	1	1
George Durje................	1	1	Daniel Burdett...........	2	2
Abraham Liequere..........	1	—	Jacob Durye..............	1	1
Folkert Folkertsen	2	2	Peter Lot.................	—	1
William Bramebosch	2	1	Abraham Schenck........	4	1
John Roseveldt	1	—	Evert Van Gelder........,	—	1
Jacob Misroll..............	—	1	Neclos Folkertsen	1	1
Nicholas Lefferts...........	1	—	Andris Stucholm	—	1
Catherine Lefferts..........			Peter Conselye	—	1
Abraham Miller	—	1	Capt Francis Titus.......	1	2
Marritje Woertman........	—	1			
				21	22

Capt FRANS TITUS.

BROOKLYN.

A List taken from the Negro's belonging to the Inhabitance, under the Command of Saml Hopson Captn of the West Company of Brookland in Kings County

Negroes Names	To Whom Belonging
One Negro Man cald Francis	
Do Sambo.........................	Isaac Sebring
One Do Wench Judy.........................	
One Negro Man Cald Roger...........................	
Do Harry...........................	
Do Peter...........................	
Do Josey...........................	John Bargay
Do Esquire.......................	
One Negro Wench cald Mary.........................	
Do pegg.............................	
One Negro Man cald Will.............................	Derk Bargay
Do Cezer...................................	
One Negro Man cald prince...........................	Simon Booram
One Negro Man cald Ceser...........................	Cornel Sebring
One Negro Man cald Dick.............................	
Do Prince............................	Saml Hopson
One Do Wench Dine..................................	
One Negro Man cald Robin	Peter Van Pelt
One Negro Man cald Tight............................	Micael Bargan
One Do Wench Dine.................................	

Negroes Names	To Whom Belonging
One Negro Man cald Thom......................	
Do Jack..........................	Chrispr Seehar
Do Wench Bett..............................	
One Negro Man cald Toney	
Do Wench cald Mary	John Carpenter
Do Tracey........................	
One Negro Man cald Tobey......................	Whitead Cornwell
Do Wench cald Flora	
One Negro Man cald Ceaser	John Middagh
Do Wench Jane...............................	
One Negro Man cald James	John Vandike
Do Wench Bett	
One Negro Man cald Sam	
Do Thom	Clos Vanvaughty
Do Wench Jane..............................	
One Negro man cald Clos........................	John Griggs
One Negro Man cald Chalsey.....................	Israel Hosfield Junr
One Negro Man cald Thom	
Do Wench Jane...............................	Peter Stots
One Negro Man cald Harry	
Do Wench Libe	Sam: De Bevoice
One Negro Man cald Frank......................	
Do Thom	Mr Van Doune
Do Wench Anne	
One Negro Man cald Harry......................	
Do Wench Phillis	Jacob Sebring
One Negro Man cald Coffe......................	
Do Wench Judy...............................	Abrm Brewer
One Negro Man cald Tight	Israel Hosfield
One Negro Man cald Willing	Jacob De Bevoice
One Negro Man cald France.....................	
Do Wench Elizabeth.........................	Jacob Bennet
One Negro Man cald Sam	
Do Wench Dine............................	Jery Bruer
Do Deyon.........................	
One Negro Man cald prime	George De Bevoice
One Negro Man cald Ceaser	
Do Wench Lil..............................	Jury Bloue
One Negro Man cald Isaac.......................	Winant Bennet
One Negro Man cald Jo	
Do Wench Jane...............................	Mrs Vandike
One Negro Wench Cald Jane......................	Earsh Middagh
One Negro Man Cald Harry......................	
Do Nease..........................	
Do Dick	Jacob Bruington
Do Charles	
Do Wench Peg..............................	

43 Negro Men
21 Do Women
—
Total   67

The above is a just account of Negroes to the Best of my knowledge belonging to the Inhabitants of the West Company of Brookland

Saml Hopson.

The list of the Negroes both male and female Who Reside In the District of Capt John Lott In Kings County in brucklen To Every Person belonging by name as foloing

Christopher Codwise	2 male..............	2 female
John Cowenhoven	4 male..............	1 female
Marten Reyerse....................	1 male..............	..
Jeremias Remse...................	2 male..............	2 female
Lammert Sudam	1 male..............	1 female
John Lott........................	....	2 female

Jacobus Degraew	1 male............	1 female
Barent Jansen................	1 male............	1 female
Jan Ryerse	1 male............	
Rem Remsen	1 male............	
Hendrik Sudam...............	....	1 female
Abram Remsen	1 male............	
Tuenes Bogaert...............	1 male............	
DW Sara Rapelie.............	1 male............	
Benjamin Waldron............	1 male............	
Joost Debavois	1 male............	1 female
Jakes Durje.....	2 male............	2 female
Jan Noorstrant...............	1 male........,....	
Gerritt Noorstrant	1 male............	1 female
Jeronemus Rapelie	2 male............	1 female
Jacobus Lefferse.............	1 male............	2 female
Jacob bergen	1 male............	1 female
Pieter V D Voort.............	....	1 female
Karel Debavois	1 male............	2 female
Johanis Debavois	....	1 female
Jacobus Debavois............	1 male............	1 female
Cornelis V D hoef.............	2 male............	
Arsus Remsen	1 male............	2 female
Adriaen Hegeman.............	1 male............	
DW Dina Rapalje	1 male............	1 female
John Rapalje...............	3 male............	2 female

1755 April 11.   A true Leist of the negroes male and female by me

Capt JOHN LOTT.

FLATBUSH.

A true List of all the Slaves Both male and female of fourteen years old and above in the township of flatbush in Kings County on Nassaw Island in the Province of New Yorke this Eighteenth Day of April anoq Dom 1755.

Owners Names	Males	their names	females	their names
Dominie Van Sindere	—	....	1	Isabel
Peter Stryker.......	1	Jack	1	Syne
John Stryker........	2	Minck & tom..........	1	Dyne
Johannes V:Sickelen	1	Sambo		
John Waldron	—	....	1	Lies
Doctor V: beuren...	—	....	1	Roos
Barent V: Defenter.	3	Jack: henck & Ben....	1	Saar
Barent Andriese	—	....	1	Graes
Widdow Clarkson...	3	Jafta Jacob & herry...	2	Bass. and Saar
hendrick Suydam ...	—	....	1	Isabel
David Sprong.......	—	....	1	Mary
henry Cruger.	3	Isack: John & hammell	1	Catleen
Engelbart Lott......	2	Jan and Batt	2	Syne & Bett
Jacobus Lott........	2	Sam & Jafta...........	1	Wyne
Cornelis Van D:Veer	1	Roos	2	flllis & Saar
Johannes Ditmarss..	2	frank and frans........	1	Syne
Laurens Ditmars....	1	Claes.................	3	Eva: Bett & Wyntje
Adriaen Voorhees...	—	....	1	Dyane
Rem Martense	2	Sam & herry	2	Emme & Susan
Phillip Nagel.......	1	Doll	—	
Phillip Nagel Junr..	1	Libb	1	Bett
Seytje V: D Bilt	1	Sam	1	Bett
Leffert Martense....	1	Sam	1	Pagg
Rem Hegeman......	2	Dick & herry..........	1	Syne
Evert hegeman......	1	Sesor.................	—	
Peter Lefferts.......	1	Ben	2	Dyne & Isabel
John Lefferts........	1	herry	—	
Jeremyes V: D: bilt	1	Minck	1	Kea

Owners Names	Males	their names	females	their names
Adriaen Martense...	2	Nienus & Lans	1	Isabel
Antje Ver Kerck....	3	Adam: Jack & Jafta ...	4	Jane: Kouba: Mare & Diane
Cornelis V: Duyn...	—	....	1	Bett
John V.: Der Veer ..	1	herry	1	Isabel
Gerret Cozyn	1	herry	—	
Jeromus V: D: Veer	—	....	1	Jude
Steven Williamse. ..	1	....	1	Sale
Johannes Lott Junr.	1	Andrew	1	Bett
Isaac Snediker	—	....	1	Mary
Jacob Snediker......	1	toon....................	—	
Gerret boerem......	1	Commenie.............	1	Lybe
Cornelis Wykhoff...	1	Sesor..................	1	Dyane
Abraham Bloom	1	Claes..................	1	Bett
Jan boerem.........	1	Will	—	
Karel boerem.......	—	....	1	Susan
Maurits Lott........	1	Minck.................	1	Bett
Douwe Ditmarss....	1	Primus................	1	Dyne
Johannes Elderts....	—	....	1	filles
thomas Batts........	1	Yorke.................	2	Moryn & Lill
hendrick Lott.......	1	tom	1	Eva
Joseph howard	—	....	1	Isabel
harmpje Lefferts....	1	Prins..................	1	Rachel
Rem V: D: bilt......	1	Julus	1	Jane
	53		55	

the total number 108

PETER STRYKER Captn of flatbush.

FLATLANDS.

A true list of all the Slaves both male and female from fourteen Years and upwards according to an act of assembly.

	Male.	male.		Male.	Female.
John Schenck Captain of the said town...................	1	1	Willem Kouwenhoven Esqr..	1	1
John V. Der Bilt.............	1	1	Gerrit Kouwenhoven	0	1
Wilhelmus Stoothof Jur.....	1	1	John Amerman	2	1
harmanis hooglant...........	1	0	Gerrit Wykof...........	1	1
Roelif Van Voorhees Esqr...	0	1	Marten M. Schenck..........	0	1
Wilhelmus Stoothof..........	0	1	Johannis Lott...............	2	2
Abraham Voorhees	1	1	Dirrick Remsen.............	1	0
Cornelis Voorhees	1	1	Johannis W. Wykof.........	2	1
Steve Schenck................	1	0	Pieter Wykof...............	1	1
John Ditmars................	0	1	Joost Vannuis	0	1
				17	18

JAN SCHENCK Capt.

New Utrecht.

A true List of all the Slaves of the Township of Newuytreght in Kings County.

Names of the Masters.	The No. of each Man.	Male Sex.	Female male Sex.	Names of the Masters	The No. of each Man	Male Sex	Female male Sex
Petrus Van Pelt	3	2	1	Willem Van Nuys	3	2	1
Jacobus Van Nuys	2	1	1	Willem Van Nuys Junr..	1	0	1
Hendrick Johnsen	1	1	0	Rutgert Van Brunt Junior	10	6	4
Haert Van foerhees	3	2	1	Evert Suydam	1	0	1
Jaques Cortelyou	2	1	1	John Johnson	1	1	0
Jaques Cortelyou Junior	2	1	1	Rutgert Van Brunt	3	1	2
Pieter Cortelyou	4	2	2	Andries Emans	2	I	1
Deneys Deneys	8	4	4	Wilhelmis Van Brunt	1	1	0
Saartje Barkeloo	2	1	1	Thomas Pollock	3	2	1
Thomas Van Dyck	1	0	1	Roelof Van Brunt	1	1	0
John Laan	1	1	0	Joris Lot	4	2	2
Casper Crapster	2	1	1	Neeltye Pietersen	1	1	0
Gerrit Kounover	2	1	1	Rebecca Emans	1	0	2
Gerrit Van Duyn	2	1	1				
					67	37	30
					the whole number		

PETRUS VAN PELT Captn.

Gravesend.

A List of the Negroes In the township of Gravesend Male and Female from the age of fourteen years and upward May 1. 1755.

	Males.	Females.		Males.	Females.
Richard Stillwell	2	2	James Hubbard	0	1
John Grigg	2	1	Daniel Lake	2	1
John Voahears	2	1	Cornelious Stryker	0	1
Nicholas Stillwell	1	2	Fernandus van Sicklen	1	0
Roeliff terhunen	1	1	William Johnson	0	1
Isaac Denyce	1	2	Peter Williamson	0	1
Samuel Garritson	1	0	Bengaman Steimets	0	1
Neeltye Voorhears	1	0	Cort Johnson	1	0
Farnandus Van Sicklen	1	1		—	—
Nicholas Williamsen	1	1		17	17

The totle Number of Males Seuenteen
The totle Number of Females Seuenteen

HEMPSTEAD.

Hemsted in Queens County on Nissaw Island and in the province of New-Yorck. accompt of the slaves brought in to George Everit Capt. within his Districts. April ye 28—anno. 1755.

Georg Rierson	3 mals Seasor adom. Jack	1 famale, Diannah
Cornelius Rierson	-	1 famale—bet
Beniamin Dvsenbere	1 male—mike	2 famals, bess, pen
William Corneil	3 mals been. Charls. Sam.	1 famale—nan
Hendrick Hendricksen	1 male savl	1 famale—Gin
Thomas hendricksen	-	1 famale—Jvde
John ffoster	-	1 famale—Gin
John: Montonye	1 male Jack	
Jacob Vollintine	-	1 famale Greech
Beniamin Downing	-	1 famale elly
William Lines	3 mals Dick. prince Eliiah	1 famale peg
Thomas Seamons	1 male—Jack	
Jonathan Vollintine	-	1 famale Sarah
Samvel Searing	1 male franck	1 famale Cate
Daniel Searing	1 male tie	
Jacob Searing	2 males—Stephen—Lew	
Jeams Smith	1 male Yorck	
Timothy Smith	1 male Robbin	1 famale—nan
Ellixander Davorson	2 mals—tom—robbin	
John Cornell	1 male Lew	2 famals, hannah, Diannah
David Allgoe	3 mals, David, pero Jack.	2 famals Janna nanot
Sarah Seamons	2 mals Jack—peter	2 famals—Dinah post
Robbard Marvil	3 mals Ciah lonnon, hithro	1 famale Dosh
John Smith	-	1 famale mander
peter titvs	3 mals will Jefroy—bob..	2 famals sib pendor
John Combs	-	1 famale—nan
beniamin Smith Jeams Smith and Richard Smith	3 mals Corso oxford John	1 famale pendor
Richard Titvs	1 male Jeffre	1 famale—bet
Vriah plat	1 male waterford	1 famale Gin
John Townsand	2 mals Jack ned	1 famale Gin
Richard townsand	1 male Lew	
phebe mot	1 male Ciah	1 famale pendor
John Petors	1 male York	
Epenetos plat	1 male Lve	
Ambros fish	2 mals Jack—bendo	1 famale—ame
Samvel willis	1 male tie	1 famale—hagor
Richard Williams	1 male sam	1 famale
John Williams	1 male savl	
William titvs	1 male Jeams	1 famale—francis
mary titvs	1 male Cato	1 famale Nancy
Stephan titvs	1 male—ben	1 famale Gin
Josiah Martin	3 mals-papav Jack sackoe above 60 years old	3 famals present, Jemina and nab
George hvlit	1 male Jacob	1 famale Jvde
John Smith	2 mals Dick—Stephen	1 famale—hannah
John Searing	-	1 famale Chat
Samvel Rowland	1 male harre	
John hicks	1 male Charls	1 famale—Gin
Jacob Smith	2 mals—will—tom	2 famals, biblor—bet
Isaac Smith	1 male seasor	1 famale—peg
Ephraim Vollingtine	1 male petor	
Elisabath titvs	1 male Gem	1 famale—Sarah
Charls petors	2 mals petor—tie	1 famale—rose

A List of the Negro Indian and Mullata Slaves within the District whereof Benjamin Smith is Captain at Hempstead in Queens County taken the first Day of April 1755.

Owner	Male	Female	Owner	Male	Female
Jacob Hicks Esqr	1	2	Richard Cornell	1	1
Jacob Hicks Junr	1	1	Benja Lewes	—	1
Thomas Hicks	—	1	Henry Mott	1	—
Phebe Hicks	—	1	Vall: Hewlet peters	1	1
James Mott	—	1	Elias Durlun	1	1
Daniel Hewlet Junr	1	1	Eldard Lucas	1	1
John Cornell	2	2	Jacobus Lawrence	—	1
Joseph Scidmore	—	1	Elias Durlun ye 3d	—	1
Thos Cornell Esqr	1	2	Abraham Bond	—	1
Capt Brown	6	1			
				17	21

P : BENIAMIN SMITH Capt

A List of the Slaves Male and Female above 14 *years of Age An Account of which has been bro^t in to Capt John Birdsall, for his District in the Township of Hempstead in Queen's County, according to the late Act of Assembly.*

Owners Names	Males	Females	Owners Names	Males	Females
The Revd Mr Seabury	1	1	Jacob Seaman Esqr	2	2
Benjn Lester	2	0	Cornell Smith	1	0
Jerm Bedell	1	1	Patrick Mott	1	0
Benjn Hewlett	1	1	Danl Hewlett	0	1
Josh: Birdsall	1	1	Thos Carman	2	1
Soln Seaman	2	1	Jno Jackson	1	1
James Pine	1	1	James Seaman	1	1
Benjn Smith	3	1	Jno Hall	1	0
Leffurt Haugewout	1	0	James Smih Junr	1	0
Wid: Lininton	1	0	Danl Smith	1	1
Elias Durland Junr	1	0	Daniel Smith	1	0
Richard Jackson	3	2	John Grissman	1	0
Joseph Petit Junr	1	1	Anthony Semans	1	0
Thos Tredwell	2	1	Daniel Pine	1	0
Jno Carman	1	1	Benj: Carmon	0	1
Saml Jackson	3	2	Richard Suthard	1	1
John Rowland	1	0	Males	43	
Thos Seaman	0	1	Females	26	
Thos Seaman Junr	0	1		—	
James Smith	1	1		69	

May it please yr Honr

This is a true Account of what has been brout. in to me

Sr yr most humble & obedient Servt

JOHN BIRDSALL.

Hempstead
April 5th 1755

CENSUS OF SLAVES.

NEWTOWN.

Newtown May 1st 1755.

A List of Negroes Male and Female According to the Act of Assembly of the Province of New York taken by me

JEROMES RAPELYE.

	Males	Females		Males	Females
Jeromes Rapelye............	0	1	Nathaniel Baily.............	0	1
Cornelius Rapelye Esqr.....	1	1	Abraham Rapelye..........	1	2
Jacobus Lent	1	1	Samuel Fish Senr	2	4
John Rapelye...............	1	1	Abraham Polhemus	0	1
John De Bevoyce	1	3	Gabriel Furman.............	1	0
Jacob Rapelye	1	1	Revd Simon Horton.........	2	1
Daniel Rapelye Senr........	1	1	John White.................	2	1
Joseph Moore Esqr	0	1	Widow Titus................	1	0
Bernardis Bloom............	1	0	William Sackett Esqr	1	1
Daniel Rapelye Junr........	1	1	Joseph Woodard............	2	0
Nathaniel Fish..............	2	1	Samuel Moore Esqr	1	1
John Levirich	1	0	Samuel Moore Lieut	1	0
William Furman............	1	1	John Moore.................	1	0
Samuel Waldron	1	1	Samuel Moore son of Joseph		
Philip Edsal	2	3	Moore Esqr.	1	0
Elizabeth Pumroy	2	1	Benjamin Waters............	1	2
Robert Coo	1	1	Sarah Burrows	1	1
Robert Field Senr...........	0	1	Cornelius Berrian Esqr......	0	2
Abraham Brinkerhoff.......	2	1	Jeromes Ramsen.............	1	1
Hendrick Brinkerhoff.......	1	0	Rem Ramsen	1	1
Samuel Fish Junr	2	1		—	—
Dow Sidam..................	0	1	Total 44		43
Joseph Morrel..............	1	0	Males 44 Total		
Edward Titus	0	1	Females 43 —		

26th May 1755.

List of Negroes in Queens County sent by Jacob Blackwell.

Jacob Blackwell	2 Male	1 female	Richard Alsup	3 Male	3 female
Joseph Sacket........	3 Det	2 Det	Beniaman Skilman...	1 Det	——
Samwell Hallett......	2 Det	1 Det	Abraham Skilman....	1 Det	——
George Vannolst.....	1 Deto	——	Isack Lott	1 Det	1 Det
Nathon More.........	1 Det	——	Samwell Allburtes ...	1 Det	——
Samwell More	1 Det	1 Det	Samwell Goslen......	1 Det	——
Richard Hallett......	1 Det	——	Dannel Bets..........	1 Det	——
Richard Hallett Jen..	1 Det	——	Richard penfold	2 Det	——
Jacob Hallett	1 Det	1 Det	Jacob Bennet	——	1 Det
Robort Hallett.......	1 Det	——	Samwell Scuder......	1 Det	——
Necolos parsel	2 Det	1 Det	Johnnathon Hont....	1 Det	1 Det
John parsel	1 Det	——	Whillem Bets........	1 Det	1 Det
Samwell Hallett Jen..	1 Det	——	Samwell Way........	1 Det	2 Det
Tunus Brinkkerhouf.	1 Det	——	Tunus Skank.........	1 Det	2 Det
Georg Brinkkerhouf..	——	1 Det	Richard Bets.........	2 Det	3 Det
Samwell Hallett minor	1 Det	——	Jeams Way	2 Det	1 Det
Peter Borgow........	——	1 Det	Joseph Bets..........	2 Det	——
Isack Borgow........	1 Det	3 Det	Andros Reiker.......	2 Det	1 Dt
Isack Borgow jen....	2 Det	1 Det			

OYSTERBAY.

A List of ye Slaves Delivered unto me, of the Eastern District of Oisterbay, Pursuant to the Direction of an act of his Honour the Lieutenant Govenour the Council and General Assembly of the Colony of New York.

Oisterbay April 24th 1755—   JACOB TOWNSEND

Masters & Mistresses Names	Nom males	Nom females	Masters & Mistressess Names	Nom males	Nom females
George Townsend	1	1	Silas Carman	1	—
Obediah Seaman	—	1	Thomas Youngs	2	1
Thomas Seaman	1	—	Daniel Birdsall	1	—
John Powell	1	1	John Schank	—	1
James Tillott	1	—	William Jones	2	2
Melanthon Taylor Woolsey	1	2	Isaac Powell	1	1
Benjamin Birdsall	1	—	Isaac Doty	—	1
Metice Lane	1	—	Nathaniel Townsend Estate	1	1
George Weekes	1	1	Richard Willits	—	1
Samuel MacCoune	1	—	Samuel Waters	—	1
William Hawxhurst	—	1	Samuel Willis	2	1
Simon Cooper	2	2	Minard Vansyckley	1	—
Henry Whitson	1	1	Wright Coles	1	1
John Cock	—	2	Charles Ludlam	—	1
Cornelius Hogland	1	1	Richard Alsop	1	1
Daniel Duryea	—	1	Zuroiah Wright	1	—
Joseph Cooper	3	1	William Moyles	2	—
George Youngs	1	1	Henry Townsend	1	3
John Woatman	—	1	Sarah Wright	1	—
Thomas Smith	3	1	John Robbins	1	—
Sarah Ludlam	1	—	David Jones Esqr	6	4
Ezekel Shadbolt	—	1	Henry Lloyd Esqr of Queens		
John Townsend	1	1	Village	5	3
Samuel Townsend	1	1			
			Total	53	44

Capt: Wright Frost's List of Slaves in Oysterbay.

Wright Frost	1 male	1 Female	Derick Alderson	1 male	......
Micajah Townsend	2 males	2 Females	John Striker	1 Male	......
Amos Underhill	......	1 Female	Joseph Hagaman	1 Male	1 Female
Henry Cock	1 Male	1 Female	Joseph Coles	......	1 Female
Thoms Rushmore	1 Male	2 Females	Joseph Lattin	1 male	......
Daniel Underhill	2 males	1 Female	Willm Walton	5 Males	2 Females
James Sands	3 Males	1 Female	Peter Hagaman	1 Male	......
Thomas Bound	1 Male	......	Abraham Underhill	1 male	1 Female
Jacob Bound	......	1 Female	Samll Underhill	1 male	1 Female
Thoms Kirbe	1 male	......	Thoms Underhill	1 male	1 Female
George Townsend	1 Male	......	Henry Dickenson	1 male	1 Female
Silvenus Townsend	1 Male	1 Female	TownsendDickensen	1 male	1 Female
Hezekias Cock	1 male	......	Jacob Volingtine	1 male	1 Female
Adrian Hagaman	1 Male	1 Female	Thoms Parsall	2 Males	1 Female
Willm Frost	1 Male	1 Female	Joseph Wood	1 Male	......
Meribah Townsend	1 Male	1 Female	BenjaminWolseyJunr	3 Males	1 Female
John Semicon	......	1 Female	Jean Caverly	1 male	......
Willm Larence	1 Male	......	William Kerby	......	1 Female
Benjamin Wolsey	2 Males	2 Females	Daniel Coles	1 Male	......
Daniel Cock	2 males	.....	John Anderson	......	1 Female
Jacob Frost	2 males	1 Female	Timothy Townsend	2 Males	1 Female
Joseph Frost	1 Male	1 Female	Hannah Frost	1 Male	......
Deborah Cock	1 Male	1 Female			

may it please your Honnourin Compliance with an act of the Generall Assembly & in obedience to your Honnours Command I transmit an accompt of ye negroes in that part of ye Town that is Aderest to me I wait your Honnours further Commands and shall with the utmost pleasure obey & I remain your Honnours most Humble and obedient servant

WRIGHT FROST

Oysterbay Aprill 29
1775

A List of the Slaves Delivered in unto me by Virtue of An Act of ye Legislature of the Province of New York By the persons hereafter named (viz:)

	Male.	male.
David Seaman at Jericho within ye Township of Oyster bay.......	—	2
Obediah Vallentine at ye North Side In ye Township of Hempsted.	2	—
Samuel Seaman at Westbury In Oyster Bay	—	1
William Crooker at Wheatly in Oyster bay........................	1	—
William Willis at Cederswamp In Oyster Bay	2	—
Jonathan Seaman at Jericho in Oyster Bay.........................	—	1
Sarah Titus at Wheatly in Oyster Bay	1	—
Phebe Townsend at Jericho in Oyster Bay.........................	—	1
James Townsend at Jericho in Oyster bay	2	—
Jacob Titus at Wheatly in Oyster Bay............................	1	1
Silas Rushmore near Jericho in Oyster Bay	1	—
Daniel Youngs near Oysterbay	1	—
Thomas Vallentine Junr at ye East Woods In Oyster Bay..........	—	1
Robert Seaman at Jericho In Oyster bay	1	1
Zebulun Seaman at Jericho in Oyster Bay	1	1
William Seaman at Jericho in Oyster bay.........................	1	1
Thomas Jackson at Jericho in Oyster Bay	1	—
John Hagewout at Jericho in Oyster Bay	1	—
John Hewlet at ye East Woods in Oysterbay	—	1
John Hewlet Jur at ye East Woods in Oysterbay	—	1
Robert Crooker at Wheatly in Oysterbay	—	1

Jericho in Oysterbay April ye 25th 1755.

To the Honorable James Delancee Esqr his Majesties Lievtenant Governour and Comander in Chief In and Over ye province of New York and Teritorys Thereon Depending In America &c:

MAY IT PLEASE YOUR HONOUR

Whereas there is Sundry free Negroes Melattoes and Mustees Resideing within ye Township of Oysterbay that may probably Be Likely In case of Insurrections To be as Mischevious as ye Slaves, Therefore I Thought it my Duty to Acquaint Your Honour Therewith; The following is a List of them Resideing in and about ye Village of Jericho, and I Do Expect that ye Other Captains in Oysterbay will acquaint Your Honour of those Resideing in ye Other parts of ye Township; from Your Very Humble Servant

ZEBULUN SEAMAN.

April ye 25th 1755.

A List of ye Free Negroes Mustees &c: Resideing at ye Severall places hereafter Discribed (viz)

	Male.	Female.
David Seaman at Jericho In Oyster Bay	1	—
Obediah Vallentine at ye North Side in Hempsted	1	1
John Willis Junr at Westbury in Hempsted	1	—
Elizabeth Titus at Westbury In Hempsted	1	—
John Williams at North Side In Hempsted	—	1
Richard Willets at Jericho in Oyster bay	1	—
Jeremiah Robbins at Jericho In Oyster bay	1	—
Totall	6	2

HUNTINGTON.

Aprill the 12th 1755 Negroes Belonging to Huntington male & female.

Capt Isaac Platt		one female
Capt Platt Conklin	one male and	one female
Doctor Zopher Platt	four males and	two females
Mr Ebenezer Prime	two males and	one female
Justice Eliphilet Wickes	two males and	two females
Just Jonas Williams		
Lievt thomas Jervis		one female
Nathan Volentine		one female
Solomon Ketcham	one male	
Thomas Brush	one male and	one female
David Rogers	one male	
Widow hanah Wood		one female
Nathaniel Ketcham	one male	
Philip Ketcham	one male	
Samuel Brush	one male	
Joseph Rigway	one male and	one female
Denis Right	one male and	two females
Benijah Jervis	one male and	one female
Doctor Gilbert Potter	one male	
Nathll Williams	one male and	one female
azariah Wickes	one male and	one female
thomas Bunce	one male	
Joseph Freland	one male	
Benjamin Right	one male	
Philip Vdle	one male	
Josiah Smith		one female
Just Moses Scudder		one female
John Samis		one female
Israel Wood		one female
Robert Brush	one male	
Epenetus Conklin	one male and	one female
John Wood Levth	one male	
Capt Alexander Briant Jr	one male	
Epenetus Platt		one female
Timothy Scudder	one male and	one female
Joseph Smith	one male and	one female
Isaac Ketcham	one male	
James Smith	two males	
Philip Wickes	one male and	one female
Alexander Smith	one male	
timothy Carl Jr		one female
Daniel Blackly	one male	
Jesse Carl	two males and	one female
thomas Rogers	one male and	one female
Bridget Scudder	one male	
Timothy Carle Sen	one male &	one female
Zopher Rogers	one male	
Augustin Bryan	one male	
Macy Lewis		one female

Mary Platt..............................   .... two females
Simon fleet............................   one male
William Hawxhurst....................   one male.................. one female
Cap John Davis ....   one male
Livt Joseph Luis......................   one male.................. one female
Thomas Denis.........................   .... one female
     A True List &c.   ISAAC PLATT
                                        PLATT CONCKLIN
                                        ALEXR BRYANT.

SMITH TOWN & ISLIP.

A List of the Slaves Within the District of Captain Job Smith or In the Townships of Smith Town and Islip.

	Male	Females			Males	Females
George Norton......	one 1	0	Richard Blidenburge	two	1	1
John Mobrey........	one 0	1	Stephen Smith........	one	0	1
Charles Floyd.......	five 4	1	George Phillips......	....	0	1
Obadiah Smith Junr.	one 1	0	Job Smith............	six	3	3
Edmund Smith.......	six 4	2	Joseph Vondel.......	two	1	1
Richard Smith.......	seven 4	3	Andrew Tid..........	one	0	1
Obadiah Smith sener.	three 2	1	Thomas Smith	three	2	1
Lemuel Smith.......	one 1	0	Anna Willis..........	two	1	1
Richard Smith Stone-			Rebeckah Willis.....	two	1	1
brook	one 1	0	Richard Willis	two	1	1
Otheniel Smith	one 1	0	Obadiah Smith.......	two	1	1
Isaac Mills..........	one 1	0	Daniel Smith Juner...	one	0	1
Jonas Platt..........	one 1	0	Daniel Smith	four	2	2
Zephaniah Platt.....	four 1	3	Epenetus Smith	one	1	0
Jonas Mills..........	one 1	0	David Bruester.......	one	1	0
William Saxton	one 0	1	Wiliam Nicols	six	5	1
Solomon Smith......	five 3	2	Elnathan Wicks......	one	0	1
Floyd Smith........	three 2	1	Caleb Smith..........	one	1	0
Mary Tredwell.....	six 5	1	Jonathan Mills.......	two	1	1
Robert Arter........	one 1	0				

The Aboue Account Is a true List of all the Slaves as Came to my knowledge
                                          JOB SMITH Captain.

STATEN ISLAND; NORTH DIVISION.

A List of The Names Male and Female belonging to

Males.	Females.
Thomas Dongan	
1st Thomas Tice	1st Philis
2d Ceaser	2. Peg
3d Jack	3. Hanna
4th Jack Mollato	
5th Joe	
6th Robbin	
7th Parris	
Jacob Corssen Ceneor	
1: Japhory...............................	1: Mary
2: Sam...................................	2: Nanne
3: Jupeter	
Jacob Corssen Juner	1 Rose
	2: Nans
John Vegte	
1: Tom....................................	1: Bette
2: Primes	2: Jean
Gerardus Beekman	
1 Bristo..................................	1 June
In the Care of G. Beekman and Belong-	
ing to John Beekman In New York.	
1: One Negro Na. Sam	
2: One Negro Na. Jo.....................	
3: One Negro Na. Warwick	
Antony Watters	
1: One Negro Na, Sam....................	1: One W Leana
2: One Negro Na, Will....................	2: One W Phillis

Males.

　　　Henry Cruse
1　One negro Na Charles

　　　Cornelius Cruse
　　　Simon Simonson
1:　One Negro Na Napten ..
　　　Johanis de Groet
1:　One negro Na Jack
　　　Joseph Rolf
1:　One negro Na, sam

　　-　Cristeiaen Corssen
1:　One Negro Na, Jack
2:　One Negro Na Nenes
　　　Josuah Merseral
1:　One Negro Na Flip
　　　John Deceer
1:　One Negro named Jem
　　　Garret Crussen

　　　Garrit Post
1:　one Negro Na Bos.
　　　John Roll Junr
1　one, Na Jaek
　　　Barent marteling
1.　one Na. forten.
　　　Richard merrill
1.　one Na Sam
　　　one na Bink
　　　Otto Van turyl
1　Negor N harry
2　Dto N John ..
　　　Bastian Ellis
1　Negro Tom
　　　John Veltmon
1　Negro Na Quam......
　　　Abraham Prall
1　Negro Na Jack
2　Dto Na Tom...

　　　Charles Meeleen
1　Negro Na Ben
　　　Margret Simonson
1　Negro Na kof......
　　　Joseph Lake
1　Negro Na Kinck.
　　　John Roll
1　Negro Na Tom..
2　Dto Na Cornelias.
3　Dto Na harry
　　　Elenor haughwout
　　　Abraham Crocheron
1　Negro Na Lue
　　　Barnit De Pue
1　Negro Na Tom .
　　　John Crocheron
1　Negro Na Sambo
　　　David Cannon
　　　Aron Prall
1　Negro Na harry
　　　Charyty Merrill
1　Negro Na frank
　　　Joseph Begel
1　Negro Na Harry
　　　Cornelias Korsan.

Females.

1:　One W Na lade
2:.　One W na Dina
3:.　One W na Sary
1:　One W. na Dina

1:　One W. Na Susanna

1:　One W, Na Jude
1:　One W, Na Sary

1:　One W, Na Darkis

1:　One W, Na Jane
1:　One W, Na mat
1: *One W, Na bet

1:　One W, Na flore

1:　One W Na Sary

　　One W Na Tittie
　　One W Na Sary
　　........ M
1 W Na Jane
2 W, Na Jude

1 Wench Na Hage
2 Dto Na Jane
3 Dto Na Bet

1 Wench Na floar

1 Wench Na Peg

1 Wench Na Sary

1 Wench Na Bet

1 Wench Na Mary

1 Wench febe

1 Wench Na Bet

1 Wench Na Philis
1 Wench Na Susanna

A list of the Neagroes of my division in the North
　　　Compeny of Staten Island　　　JACOB CORSSEN Jur.

THE LIST OF THE TOWNE OF NEW ROCHELLE &c. XB^R 9TH 1710.

	Aged		Aged		Aged
William Le Conte	52	Anne Morcye	16	John Sycar	3
Mary Le Conte	42	ffrancis Le Conte	45	Elizabeth Sycar	10
William Le Conte Jr.	16	Mary Le Conte	55	Mary Sycar	06
Hester Le Conte	17	Josiah Le Conte	13	Sussanna Sycar	03
Jean Le Conte	06	Mary Le Conte	18	Robert Bloomer	76
Alexander Allear	50	John Teast	54	Sarah Bloomer	68
Jane Allear	45	Susanna Teast	54	Margett Bloomer	35
Peter Allear	15	John Lambert	52	James Mott	15
Philip Allear	08	Katherine Lambert	49	Thomas Mott	09
Jean Allear	03	Isaiah Baddo	46	Hecter Mott	14
Isaace Allear	01	Hester Baddo	44	Fredk Bolt	36
Katherine Allear	20	Isaiah Baddo	12	Allida Bolt	36
Aritus Allear	12	Andrew Baddo	10	Peter La Roue	12
Peter Vallow	46	Mary Baddo	80	Alida La Roue	17
Susanna Vallow	45	Andris Barrett	63	Mary La Roue	15
Josiah Le Villien	48	Mary Barrett	56	Johanna La Roue	10
Peter Le Veillien	09	John Barrett	25	Anne La Roue	05
John Le Vellien	04	Barnabas Barrett	16	Mary ffrederick	01
Hannah Le Vellien	06	Andris Barrett	13	Daniel Sycar	40
Peter Martine	45	Sussanna Barrett	19	Sussanna Sycar	30
Maria Martine	22	Peter Angevine	44	James Sycar Senr	75
Maria Martine	01	Deborah Angevine	42	Daniel Sycar Junr	12
Andrew Nodden Senr	73	Lewis Angevine	08	John Sycar	11
Mary Nodden	50	Marget Angevine	10	Peter Sycar	09
Andrew Nodden Junr	34	Susanna Angevine	50	Andrew Sycar	03
Sussanna Nodden	26	John Barrett	50	Mary Sycar	06
Andrew Nodden	02	John Barrett Junr	07	Peter percout	47
Anne Nodden	03	Gabriel Barrett	06	Katherine parcout	37
John Rannoo	46	Peter Barrett	50	John Parcout	15
Susanna Rannoo	45	Peter Brittain	28	Andrew Parcout	09
Stephen Rannoo	22	Judy Brittain	25	Sarah Parcout	12
Jacob Rannoo	13	Peter Brittain Junr	03	Judy Parcout	06
John Rannoo	03	Anthony Leppener	24	Hester Parcout	12
Mary Rannoo	11	Sussanna Leppener	23	John Couton	52
Andrew Jarro	45	Marget Leppener	66	Sussanna Couton	50
Mary Jarro	43	Mary Chance	24	John Couton Jur	15
John Jarro	13	John Chance	01	Peter Couton	12
Andrew Jarro Junr	11	John Neffveile	69	Judy Couton	11
James Jarro	03	Katherine Neffvile	55	Hester Couton	09
John Mannion	45	Josiah Neffveile	18	Frederick Scurman	80
Sussanna Mannion	50	Johanna Neffveile	26	Mary Scurman	70
Hannah Mannion	12	Susanna Neffveile	23	Marget Scurman	50
Peter Fruteer	25	Mary Neffveile	20	Jacob Scurman	40
Marget Fruteer	22	Sarah Neffvile	15	Altia Scurman	38
Isaiah Vallow Senr	72	Grace Neffvile	14	Jacob Scurman Junr	11
Peter Vallow	10	Lewis Guion Senr	56	Miles Scurman	6
Daniel Bondett	58	Mary Guion	54	Alexander Scurman	3
Jane Bondett	56	Ammon Guion	20	Anne Scurman	10
William Landering	13	Issaace Guion	25	Sarah Scurman	5
Magdalen ffortyer	7	Sussanna Guion	25	Peter Symon	47
Zachariah Angevine	46	John Lammon	28	Hester Symon	50
Mary Angevine	31	Hester Lammon	23	Peter Symon Junr	12
Zachariah Angevine	06	James fflanders	46	Marget Symon	15
Daniel Angevine	02	Katherine fflanders	27	Anne Symon	10
Margett Angevine	18	James fflandrs Junr	4	Sussanna Symon	8
Mary Angevine	12	Peter fflanders	01	Katherine Symon	5
Mary Angevine Jur	04	Betty fflanders	6	Charles fruttye	56
James Morcye	55	Paul Pillon	40	Mary frutye	36
Mary Morcye	45	Katherin Pillon	46	Oliver Bayley	52
Daniel Morcye	09	Paull Pillon Junr	14	Judy Bayley	56
Susanna Morcye	20	James Sycar	34	Mary Tovett	72
Mary Morcye	19	Mary Sycar	20	Peter Le Doof	46

	Aged		Aged		Aged
Mary Le Doof	36	Hannah Garrien	43	Johanna Bonnett	11
Daniel Le Doof	14	Mary Garrien	13	Sussanna Bonnett	08
Peter Le Doof Junr.	08	John Murro	46	Josiah Hunt	43
John Le doof	05	Sussanna Murro	38	Sussanna Hunt	43
Andrew Le doof	04	Peter Murro	09	Josiah Hunt Junr	15
Hannah Le doof	18	John Murro	13	Anne Hunt	13
Mary Le doof	12	Marget Murro	12	Mary Hunt...,	09
Anne Le doof	10	John Martine	25	Sussanna Hunt	06
Sussanna Le doof	06	Hannah Martine	22	Elias Bon Repo	54
Judy Le doof	02	Peter Frederick	68	Jane Bon Repo	47
ffrancis Geenar	45	Isabel Frederick	44	John Bon Repo	11
Anne Geenar	45	Johanna Frederick	14	Hester Bon Repo	17
Mary Geenar	09	Mary Frederick	13	Blanch Bon Repo	13
ffrederick Scurman	43	Peter Sluce	18	Mary Bon Repo	05
Judy Scurman	37	Peter Frederick Junr	26	Gregory Guyion	44
Marget Scurman	18	Judy Frederick	23	Mary Guyion	40
Sussanna Scurman	15	Katherine Frederick..	01	Gregory Guyion	07
Elizabeth Scurman	13	John Boullie	35	Judy Guyion	11
Isabell Scurman	04	Katherine Boullie	43	Hester Guyion	08
Daniel Rennoe	55	John Boullie Junr	05	Johannah Guyion	05
Anne Rennoe	55	Daniel Bonnett	45	Hannah Guyion	12
Theophlus ffurtye	68	Judy Bonnett	40	Peter Dais.	48
Anne ffurtye	61	Daniel Bonnett Junr.	17	Johanna Dais	40
John Sarrineer	25	John Bonnett	15	Sussanna Dais	14
Hannah Sarrineer	19	Peter Bonnett	05	Mary Dais	10
Stephen Garrien	46	Mary Bonnett	13	Judy Dais	06

In the Town of New Rochell & Itts Districts : are Male Christians—67 female do 137 : Male Slaves 23—female do 34.

EAST CHESTER.

In the Town of Est Chester & Its Districts are Male Christians 153—female do 136: Male Slaves 17—female do 8—and men from 16 year old to 60 as followeth, viz

	Aged		Aged		Aged
Capt. John Drake	55	John ffowler	17	John Uaile	24
Michial Chadderton	52	Thomas Pinkney	48	William White	26
Joseph Thompkins	32	Isaac Oadale	35	Edward fitz giarral	28
Nathaniel Tompkias	32	Mathias Ualantine	40	Isaac Terhill	56
Joseph Drake Senr	47	John Ualentine	19	John Thompkins Junr	26
John Bloomer	28	Richard Osburn	34	Lewis Guyon	24
John Hyat	32	Thomas Astin	26	Jonathan Oadale	35
Thomas Shute	40	Joseph Drake Junr	24	Moses Hoit Junr....,	40
Jeremiah Fowler	37	Isaac Taylor Senr	45	Eluzar Hoit	16
Isaac Lawrence Senr	44	John Haddon Senr.	47	Edmond Thompkins..	34
Isaac Laurence Jur	18	John Haddon Junr	27	Abraham Hiat	29
Roger Barton Senr	44	John Stanton malatto	32	Henry ffowler Junr	31
Roger Barton Junr	17	John Lancastor	43	John Ward	25
John Shute	39	Joseph Taylor	24	John Lawrence	40
william ffowler	50	Mosis Taylor	21	Samuel Causten Junr..	21
William Pinkney	29	John Taylor	17	Jeremiah Looper	38
Thomas Pinkney	27	Joseph Gee	34	Thomas Chadderton..	28
Edmond Ward	39	Arthur Uaile	19	Edward Aury	39
Samuel Ferris	34	Richard Curry	30	Benjamin Chipp	21
Henry ffowler Senr	52	Robert Stiuers	19	Mosis ffowler	26
William ffowler	23				

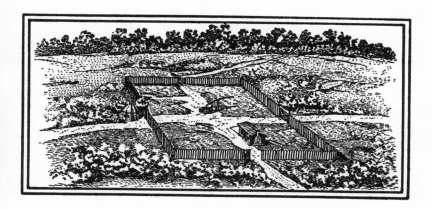

A LIST OF THE FFREEHOLDERS WITHIN THE COUNTY OF ULSTER, 1728.

*The ffreeholders for the Town of Kingston, Viz*ᵗ

William Schepmoes
Coenraet Elmendorp Esqr
Doct Jacobus Elmendorp
Simon Van Wagenen
Tjerik De Witt
Walran Du Mond
Gerrit Van Wagenen
John Sleght
Nicholas Hofman
Mattys Sleght
Petrus Bogardus
Samuel Nights
William Eltinge
William Herris
Hendrick Pruyn
Major Johannis Wynkoop
Mattys Persen
William Doughty
Phillip Viely
Lewis Dubois Junr
Thomas Beekman

Jacob Ten Brook Esqr
Johannis Ten Brook
Jonas De Lange
William Ploegh
John Crook Junr
Hendrik Oosterhout
John Oosterhout Junr
Mattys Van Steenberge
Anthony Sleght
Nathaniel Devenpoort
Johannis Low
Maj Johannis Hardenbergh
Peter Tappen
Tjerik Van kueren
Samuel Burhans
Aldert Kiersteeden
Evert Roosa
Solomon Bunschooten
Hendrik H: Schoonmaker
Eghbert Schoonmaker
Edward Whittaker Esqr

James Whitaker
William Legg
Peter Oosterhout
Cryn Oosterhout
John Peterse Oosterhout
Jacobus Du Bois
Arie Kuyckendall
Jacobus A Van Etten
Hiskiagh Du Bois
Nicolas De Myer
Hendrick Brinck
Cornelius Langendyck
Barent Burhans
Evert Wynkoop Esqr
John Persen
Arie Newkerk
Johannis Snyder
Johannis Wm Snyder
Harmanus Hommel
Frederik Merkel
William Keel

Jeronomus Klyn
Nicolas Dromboer
Christyaen Myer
Peter Mouerse
Jurya Overpagh
Juryan Snyder
Felter Fier
Peter Wynnen
Lowrens Merkell
Jacob Rutsen Junr
Coll Wessel Ten Brook
Johannis V. Steenberge
Abraham V. Steenberge
Johannis Swartt
Philip Moore
Johannis Jansen
John Makleyn
Doct Hans Kiersteeden
Cornelius Delametre
Johannis Delametre
Coll Abraham Gaasbeck
     Chambers
Christophell Tappen
Mattys Van Keuren
Abraham De Lametre
Gisbert Van Denbergh
Johannis Tappen
Abraham Low
Thomas Van Steenberge

Aris Van Steenberge
Lowrens Hendrik
Andries Heermans
Johannis Turck
Stephen Gasharie
Cornelius Van kueren
Cornelius Swartt
Teunis adamse Swart
John Davenpoort
Basteyaen De Witt
Tobias Van Bueren
Teunis Swartt
John Wels
Johannis Masten
Adam Swartt
William Swartt
Jacobus De Lametre
Lowrens Swart
Cornelius Elmendorp
Johannis Schoonmaker
Hendrik Jansen
John Oosterhout
John Ploegh
John Wood Senr
John Wood Junr
Edward Wood
John Legg
Peter Luyks
Peter Peele

Andries Hoff
Gysbert Peele
Peter Van Leuven
Moses Cantyn
Mattys Du Bois
Wilhelmus Hooghtelingh
Peter Van Acken
Boudwyn Lacount
Manuel Gonsalisduck
Manuel Gonsalisduck Junr
William Traphagen
Peek De Witt
Arie Van Vliet
John Freer
Johannis Hd Schoonmaker
Aldert Ariese Roosa
Charles Brodhead
Dedrick Foets
John Wolf
Christopher Wanbomel
David De Lametre
Hendrick Frelingh
William Smith
Hendrick Ruyter
Hiskiag Schoonmaker
Jacob Middagh
Coenraet Rightmyer
Tjerik Schoonmaker

The ffreeholders of Wagaghkemek:

Harme barentse Van Emweegen
Peter Gomar
John Van Vliet Junr

Samuel Swartwout
Barnardus Swartwout Junr
Jacob Kuddebeck

The ffreeholders of the Towne of Hurly:

Coll Jacob Rutsen
William West
Aldert Roosa
Mattys Ten Eyck
Peter Oostrander
Arien Gerretsen
John Roosa Senr
Cornelius Cool
Jacob Du Bois
Eghbert Constable
Huyber Suylandt
Johannes Schepmoes
John Crispell
Albert Janse Roosa

Cornelius Wynkoop Esq
Anthony Crispell
John Roosa Junr
Salomon Ter Willige
Eghbert Brinck
Teunis Oostrander
Garret Constable
Symon helm
Aert Van Wagenen
John Van Etten
Johannis Crispell
William Sluyter
Gerret Newkerk
Evert Roosa

John Van Duersen
Marynis Chambers
Arent Oostrander
Abraham Van Wagenen
Jacob Van Wagenen
Nicolas Blanjan
Isaak Van Wagenen
Hendrek Oostrander
Mattys Blanjan
Gerardus Hardenbergh
Abraham Ten Eyck
Jacob Freer
Teunis Teerpening

The ffreeholders of the Towne of Marble-Towne:

Cornelius Eltinge Esqr
Richard Brodhead
William Nottingham
Cornelius Tack
George Middagh
Jacobus De Lametre
Huybert Lambertse
Daniel Brodhead Senr
Wessel Brodhead
Thomas Cock
William Cock
Samuel Cock
Jeremie Kitle
Nicolas Keator

Arie Van De Merke
Jacob Van De Merke
Frederick Van De Merke
Thomas Jansen
Jacob Keyser
John Van Kampen
Nicolas De Pew Esqr
Gysbert Roosa
Jacobus Boss
Andries Van Leuven
Lambert Dolderbrinck
Martte Boogert
Hendrick Crom
Hartman Hyne

Roelof Dolderbrinck
Benjamen De Pew
Richard Pick
Cornelius Cortreght
Teunis Claerwater
Robert Beatty
Cornelius De Pew
Lewis Bovie
John Newkerk
Valentyne Smitt
Johns De Witt
Thomas Van De Merke
William Beatty
Mathew Aleger

Peter Contyne
Johannis Van Leuven
John Gysbertse Roosa

Fredrick Davis
John Beatty
Jury Best

Benjamen Aleger
James Aleger

The ffreeholders for the Towne of Rochester:

Dirik Crom
Teunis Oosterhout Esqr
David Du Bois
Moses De Pew Senr
Isaak Van Acken
Jochem Schoonmaker
Jacobus Schoonmaker
Lodewick Hoorenbeek
Cornelius Switts
Jacob De Witt
Hendrik Roosecrans
John Cortreght
Peter Low

Dirik Westbrook
Alexander Roosekrans
Johannis Vernoy
Cornelius Vernoy
John Bovie
Fredrick Schoonmaker
Mattys Low
Philip Du Bois
Moses De Pew Junr
Johannis Hornebeek
Tjerik De Witt Junr
Benjamen Schoonmaker
Arie Oosterhout

Lowrens Cortreght
Kryn Oosterhout
Abraham Bovie
Matthewes Vande Willige
Tobias Hornebeek
Symon Van Wagenen
Benjamen van Wagenen
Albert Pawling Esqr
Jacobus Quick
Josephat Du Bois
Cornelius Hoornebeek
John Oosterhout Junr
Johannis De Pew

The ffreeholders for the Towne of New Paltz :

Christian Du jou
Hendrik Du jou
Solomon Hasbrook
Daniel Hasbrook
Jacob Hasbrook
Andries Lafeever
Hugo Freer
Jacob Freer
Petrus Low

Solomon Du Bois
Lewis Du Bois
John Teerpening
Hugo Freer Junr
Abraham Du Bois
John Lafefer
Daniel Du Bois
Samuel Bovie

Agustinus Van de Merke
Roeleff Eltinge Esqr
Nicolas Roosa
Peter Du jou
Isaak Lafever
Isaak Freer
Dirik Teerpening
Gerret Keeteltass

The ffreeholders for Shawengongh :—

Capt Jacobus Bruyn
Capt Zagharias Hofman
Benjamen Smedes
Abraham Schutt
Jacob Decker
Evert ter Willige
Josua Smedes
Cornelius Schoonmaker
John ter Willige
Hendrik Decker
Mattys Slimmer
Hendrik Newkerk

Hendrik Krans
Edward Gatehouse
        Galatie
Jeronimus Weller
Johannis Decker
John howard
James Spennik
Cornelius Cool
Henry Wileman Attorney
    at Law
John North
George Andrew

John Mackneel
Jeronimus Mingus
Thomas Mackolm
Christoffel Moul
Samuel Neely
Israel Rogers
John Neely
John Williams
Caleb Knap Senr
Caleb Knap Junr
Alexander Neely
Coll Cortlandt

The ffreeholders of the high Lands :

William Chambers Esqr
Phineas Mackentosh Esqr
Thomas Ellis
James Elsworth
Jurie Quick
William Bond
Burger Mynderse
John Alsop Esqr
William Ward
John Haskell
John Van Tien
George Wayagont*

Burger Mynderse Junr
William Sanders
Doct Goldent Esqr
George Ebina
Tobias Wayagont*
Robert Kirkland
John Umphry
Peter Long
David Suthrland
John Davis
Melger Gilli
Henry Hasell

Benjamen Elsworth
Nathaniel foster
Francis Harrison Esqr
John Mackneel Junr
James Gamwell
Stephan Bedford
Thomas Shaw
Joseph Gale
George Spedwell
John Moute
Christian Chervis

Pursuant by & order to Me Directed out the Supreme Court Requiring Me to make a Generall List of the ffreeholders within my Bayliwick Soe that a Special Jury be struck there out to trey the Cause between Major Hardenbergh and the Corporation

* Qu. Weygand ?   † Qu. Colden ?

of Kingston wherefor I have accordingly taken all the Care to Not forgitt aney of the ffreeholders to the best of my Nollege, and here of I Doe make my returne this 7th Day of July 1728.

JACOBUS VAN DYCK Sherriff.

———————◆———————

A LEST OF THE COMMANDING OFFICERS AS WELL MILLETERY AND SIVEL.

| Collo Jacob Rutsen | Levt Collo Abram Gasbeek Chammers |
| Major Jno hardenburgh | Adgedent Geysebert Van Denbergh |

JUSTICES.

Collo Henry Beekman	Mr Corneles Coll	Mr Josef hasbrok
Cap : Dereck Schepmoies	Mr George Medaegh	Mr Jacobes Bruyn
Mr Arie Gerese	Mr Lodwyck horenbeek	Mr Mattyse Janse
Mr Eghbert Schonmaker		

OLD OFESERS AND OLD MEN

Capt Mattys Mattyse	Mr Geysebert Van Garden	Levt Sallomon Duboys
Levt Jno heremans		Levt Beniamen Smedes
Mr Jno Wynkoop	Capt Tomes Gerten	Levt Nicolas meyer
Mr. Ja Artsen	Capt Cherels Brodhed	Mr Mattys Sleght
	Capt Richert Brodhed	
Capt Joqem Schonmaker	Mr Geysebert Crooem	Capt Conraet Elvendorp
Mr Moses Dupue	Mr Jno Coock	Mr Evert Bogardus
Mr Tuenes Osterhout		Mr Tuenes tapen
Mr Jacob De Witt	Capt Abram hasbroiek	Capt Wessel tenbrok
Mr Sander Roosekrans	Mr Lawies Bovie	Mr Albert Roosa
Mr Cornels Swets		

———————◆———————

ENROLMENT OF THE PEOPLE CALLED QUAKERS

Pursuant an act of Generall Assembly of this province passed the 19th of ffebruary 1755, Entituled an Act for Regulating the militia of the Colony of New York. Those for Dutchess County are as follows vizt

1755. Aprill 22.

Joshua Shearman of Beekmans precinct......................Shoemaker
Moses Shearman of the Same place........................Labourer
Daniel Shearman of the Same place........................Labourer
Joseph Doty of the same place...............................Blacksmith
John Wing of the same place..............................ffarmer
Zebulon Ferris of the oblong in Beekmans precinct.........ffarmer
Joseph Smith Son of Richard Smith of the same place......Labourer
Robert Whitely of the Oblong..............................farmer
Elijah Doty of the Oblong House.................... .....Carpenter
Philip Allen of the Oblong.................................Weaver
Richard Smith of the Oblong................................ffarmer
James Aiken of the Oblong................. ....Blacksmith
Abraham Chase Son of Henry Chase of the Oblong...........ffarmer
David Hoeg of the Oblong
John Hoeg of the Oblong....................................ffarmer

Jonathan Hoeg of the Oblong..................................Blacksmith
Amos Hoeg Son of John Hoeg of the Oblong...............Labourer
William Hoeg Son of David Hoeg of Oblong...............Farmer
John Hoeg Son of John Hoeg of Oblong
Ezekiel Hoeg of the Oblong..................................Labourer
Judah Smith of Oblong......................................Taylor
Mathew Wing of Oblong
Timothy Dakin of Oblong.....................................ffarmer
Jonathan Akin of Oblong......................................Labourer
Samuell Russell of Oblong....................................Labourer
John Fish of Oblong..... ....Farmer
Reed fferris of Oblong.......................................Shoemaker
Benjamin Ferris Junr of Oblong..............................Labourer
Josiah Akin of Oblong..Blacksmith
Israel Howland of Oblong....................................ffarmer
Elisha Akin of Oblong.......................................ffarmer
Isaac Haviland of Oblong....................................Blacksmith
Nathan Soule Son of George Soule of Oblong...............ffarmer
James Birdsall of Oblong....................................Labourer
Daniel Chase of Oblong......................................ffarmer
Silas Mossher of Oswego in Beekmans precinct.............ffarmer
William Mosher of the Same place...........................ffarmer
Silvester Richmond of the Same place.......................ffarmer
Jesse Irish of the same place...............................ffarmer
David Irish of the Same place...............................ffarmer
William Irish of the Same place............................ffarmer

23d

Josiah Bull of the Same place...... ....ffarmer
Josiah Bull Junr of the Same place..........................ffarmer
Allen Moore of the Same place..............................ffarmer
Andrew Moore of the Same place.... ....ffarmer
William Gifford of the Same place..........................ffarmer

25th

Nathaniel Yeomans of the Same place.......................ffarmer
Eliab Yeomans of the Same place............................ffarmer

26th

William Parks of Oswego in Beekmans precinct............farmer

DUTCHESS COUNTY ss: The aforegoing are all the Quakers Enroled in my office
to this 1st day of July 1755

Per HENRY LIVINGSTON Clerk

A LIST OF THE NAMES OF QUAKERS

Enrolled in the office of Town Clerk, of and in the City of New York, in Lib: No. 1 of Quakers, &c: Pursuant to an Act of Assembly, Entitled an Act, for Regulating the Militia of the Colony of New York; made & Published the 19th day of February Last, vizt:

Thomas Dobson of the City of ....New York		Merchant
Samuel Brown of...........................	Do	Do
Henry Haydock of	Do	Do
James Burling of	Do	Distiller
John Laurence of	Do	Boalter
Caleb Laurence of	Do	Merchant
William Palmer of..........................	Do	Joiner
Hugh Ryder of.............................	Do	Shopkeeper
Walter Frankling of	Do	Do
Isaac Martin of............................	Do	Tallow Chandler
Thomas Frankling of.......................	Do	Merchant
John Frankling of	Do	Shopkeeper
Thomas Frankling Junr of	Do	Hatter

William Field of	Do	Shopkeeper
John Burling of...........................	Do	Merchant
John Burling Junr of.....................	Do	Miller
Robert Murray of.....................	Do	Shopkeeper

To the 19th of May 1755.

AUGT V. CORTLAND Clk Co.

A LIST OF THE NAMES OF SUCH MORAVIANS

Who have Enrolled their names pursuant to the Directions of an act to continue an Act Entituled an act for Regulating the Militia of the Colony of New York with Some Additions thereto published the 1st of April 1756. *Vizt:*

1756.

May ye	5th	James Arden of the City of............	N. Y.	Joiner
		Christian Trocklick of................	Do	Sugar Baker
	6th	William Nixon of	Do	Cooper
		Daniel Miller of.....................	Do	Potter
	11th	Henry Van Vlack of	Do	Mercht
		Garrase Roebuck of..................	Do	Corck Cutter
		John Kingston of....................	Do	Blacksmith
		William Pearson of..................	Do	Butcher
		John Runcy of.......................	Do	Tobacconist

Names of Quakers who have Enrolled their names:

May the 10th	Nathll Pearsall of..........	N. Y.	Storekeeper
	Thomas Pearsall of........	Do	Do
	Samuel Franklin of	Do	Do

Enrolled.

pr AUGT V. CORTLANDT Clk.

Decr ye 1st 1756   A LIST of *all the Money Taken from the* QUAKERS *in* QUEENS COUNTY *Persuant to two Acts of General Assembly of the Province of New York.*

Town of fflushing

	£	s
John Thorn...................	2	—
James Burling...............	2	—
James Bowne.................	2	—
Benj Doughty................	2	—
Stephen Hedger..............	2	—
Danll Bowne.................	2	—
James Persons...............	2	—
Danll Lathum	2	—
Samll Thorn.................	2	—
Caleb Field..................	2	—
John Thorn..................	1	—

New Town

	£	s
John Vanwick	2	—
John Way	2	—
Samll Way...................	2	—
Robert Alsop	2	—
William Betts	2	—
James Way..................	2	—
Richard Hollet..............	2	—
Samll Burling	2	—

Jamaica Town

	£	s
Robert Doughty..............	2	—

Town of Hempstead

	£	s
Stephen Lines	2	—
Thomas Seaman..............	1	10
William Lines	2	—
Joseph Clements.............	2	—
Adam Mott...................	2	—
Stephen Mott................	2	—
William Mott.	2	—
Nathaniel Pierceall..........	2	—
Samuel Titus................	2	—
William Titus................	2	—
Stephen Titus...............	2	—
James Mott..................	2	—
James Titus	2	—
Samuel Willis Jur...........	2	—
Francis Nash	1	—
Thomas Alsop	1	—

Oysterbay Town

	£ s		£ s
Joseph Wood	2 —	Jacob Cock	2 —
Israel Pierceal	2 —	Clark Cock	2 —
Isaac Doty	2 —	Samll Cock	2 —
Abraham Underhill	2 —	Henry Cock	2 —
Joseph Underhill	2 —	Reese Cock	2 —
John Powel	2 —	John Mott	2 —
John Witson	2 —	Henry Titus	2 —
John Witson Jr.	2 —	Obadiah Seaman	2 —
Richard Alsop	2 —		£102 10

John Willett late Treasurer of Queens County Came before me Francis Filkin—and made oath that this is a true list as aforesaid according to the best of his knowledge

JOHN WILLETT.

Sworne in New York Decr 16: 1756 before me

FRA^s FILKIN Justice.

———

Suffolk ⎱ ss   A LIST OF *the Names of the People called* QUAKERS
County ⎰   *who have entered their Certificates in the Clerke's*
               office in the County aforesaid.

Edward Hallock of Brookhaven

Richard Willets ⎫
Jacob Willets   ⎪
Samuel Willets ⎬ of Islip   John Whitson Junr ⎱ of Huntington
Joseph Willets ⎪   Jeremiah Wood   ⎰
Isaac Willetts ⎪
Thomas Willets ⎭

The above are entered in Suffolk County's Book of Records Vol: B: Fol^s 34. 36.

p W. NICOLL Junr Clk.

A LIST OF THE NUMBER OF INHABITANTS
WHITE AND BLACK ABOVE AND UNDER THE AGE OF TEN YEARS IN
THE CITY AND COUNTY OF ALBANY.

Whites males above ten years...................... 3209
Dtto Fameles above ten........................... 2995
Dtto males under ten............................. 1463
Dtto Fameles under ten........................... 1384
   Totall of White 9051
Black's males above ten.......................... 714
Dtto Fameles above ten........................... 496
Dtto males under ten............................. 223
Dtto Fameles under ten........................... 197
   Totall of Blacks.............................. 1630

The whole No of White & Black above & under ten 10681
P^r. JOHN LINDESAY, *Sheriff*

A LIST OF THE NUMBER OF INHABITANTS
BOTH WHITES AND BLACKS MALES AND FEMALES EACH SORT ABOVE
AND UNDER THE AGE OF TEN YEARS IN THE COUNTY OF DUTCHESS.

Whites Males above Ten years old.................. 940
Whites females above 10 years old................. 860
Whites males under 10............................ 710
White females under 10........................... 646
   Total of Whites............................... 3156
Blacks Males above 10............................ 161
Blacks ffemales above 10......................... 42
Blacks males under 10............................ 37
Blacks ffemales under 10......................... 22
   Total of Blacks 262

The number of the Whole in the county Except the
High Lands...................................... 3086

A LIST OF THE NUMBER OF INHABITANTS

BOTH WHITES AND BLACKS MALES AND FEMALES EACH SORT ABOVE
AND UNDER THE AGE OF TEN YEARS IN THE COUNTY OF ULSTER
ANNO, 1738.
.....

Whites Males above ten years old................... 1175

Whites Females above 10 years..................... 1681

Whites Males under 10............................ 541

Whites Females under 10.......................... 601

Totall of whites................................ 4398

Blacks Males above 10 378

Blacks ffemales above 10.......................... 260

Blacks males under 10............................ 124

Blacks ffemales under 10.......................... 110

Total of Blacks 872

The number of the whole in the County Except ye ——
high Lands................................ 5270
....

A LIST OF THE NUMBER OF INHABITANTS

BOTH WHITES AND BLACKS MALES AND FEMALES OF EACH SORT
ABOVE AND UNDER THE AGE OF TEN YEARS IN THE COUNTY OF
ORANGE 1738.

Ye fovre presincts of Orange County	Whites males above ten years old.	Whites females above the age of ten years old	White males under ten years old	White females under ten years old	Black males above ten years old	Black females above ten years old	Black males under ten years old	Black females under ten years old
Orangetown...............	00238	000231	000113	000108	00053	00048	00022	00017
Goshan	00319	000249	000183	000191	00034	00023	00007	00011
Haverstraw	00205	000176	000144	000072	00029	00019	00005	00004
Minnisinck	00098	000097	000061	000062	00009	00005	00004	00003
	860	753	501	433	125	95	38	The to-tall of Blacks 283
	753			The to-tall of whites 2547				
	501							
	433							
	2547							
	283							
	2830							

The above is a true acount of the numbers of the Whites and Blacks in the County of
Orange This 20 day of June 1738.   W. DUNING, Sheriff.

LIST OF INHABITANTS IN THE COUNTY OF NEW-YORK
1738.

City and county of New-York William Cosby Sheriffe	White males above 10 years old	White females above 10	White males under 10	White females under 10	Black males above 10	Black females above 10	Black males under 10	Black females under 10	Totall of Whites	Totall of Blacks
East Ward	558	610	246	229	213	203	76	69	7943	1719
West Ward	298	396	144	136	65	48	7	8		
South Ward	305	414	221	111	66	96	20	21		
North Ward	357	312	111	168	88	43	47	38		
Dock Ward.........	274	292	161	167	117	126	36	35		
Mountgomry Ward..	235	323	136	147	60	41	19	14		
Bowry Ward	150	134	47	54	44	30	15	10		
Harlem Ward	76	87	22	26	21	22	9	12		
	3253	3568	1088	1036	674	609	229	207		
	3568				609					
	1088				229					
	1036				207					
	8945 total of whites				1719		totall of both....			9662

Return'd p WILL: COSBY vid: com:

NOTE.—There are several errors in the footings of the above which are left uncorrected.—ED.

A LIST OF THE NUMBER OF INHABITANTS
BOTH WHITES AND BLACKS MALES AND FEMALES OF EACH SORT ABOVE AND UNDER THE AGE OF TEN YEARS IN KINGS COUNTY, 1738.

the names of the towns	Whites males above 10 years old	Whites females above 10 years old	Whites males under 10	Whites females under 10	Blacks males above 10	Blacks females above 10	Black males under 10	Black females under 10	The number of the whole in the County
flatlands	83	76	32	27	19	19	7	5	268
gravezand.............	75	70	22	25	15	16	6	6	235
Bruckland.	191	196	66	84	74	49	31	30	721
flatbush.	148	138	56	64	44	41	18	31	540
New-uytrick.	72	65	26	32	36	23	17	11	282
Bushwick..............	85	86	33	32	22	21	5	18	302
	654	631	235	264	210	169	84	101	2348
Totall of Whites..........				1784	Total of Blacks...			564	

PETER STRYCKER, JUNR. Sheriff.

A LIST OF THE NUMBER OF INHABITANTS

BOTH WHITES AND BLACKS MALES AND FEMALES EACH SORT ABOVE
AND UNDER THE AGE OF TEN YEARS IN QUEENS COUNTY ; VIZ

Whites males above ten years old...................... 2407
Whites females above ten years old................... 2290
White males under ten............................. 1395
Whites females under ten........................... 1656
  Totall of whites.................................. 7388
blacks males above ten 460
blacks females above ten........................... 370
blacks males under ten............................. 254
blacks females under ten........................... 227
  Total of Blacks................................. 1311

the number of the whole in the County 8699
ye 26th of June 1738   Adm LAWRENCE, Sheriff.

A LIST OF THE NUMBER OF INHABITANTS

BOTH WHITES AND BLACKS MALES AND FEMALES EACH SORT ABOVE
AND UNDER THE AGE OF TEN YEARS IN THE COUNTY OF SUFFOLK.

1. Whites males above ten years old 2297
2. Whites females above ten years old.............. 2353
3. Whites males under ten......................... 1175
4. Whites females under ten....................... 1008
  The totall of whites.............................. 6833
5. blacks males above ten.......................... 393
6. blacks males under ten.......................... 307
7. blacks males above ten......................... 203
8. black females under ten........................ 187
  The Totall of blacks 1090

The number of the whole in the county of Suffolk 7923

A LIST OF THE NUMBER OF INHABITANTS

BOTH WHITE AND BLACKS MALES AND FEMALES OF EACH SORT, ABOVE
AND UNDER THE AGE OF TEN YEARS IN THE COUNTY OF RICHMOND
TAKEN IN MARCH 1738.

White Males above 10 years old	488
White Females above 10 years old	497
White males under 10.............................	289
White Females under 10	266
Total of White	1540
Black Males above 10	132
Black Females above 10	112
Black Males under 10	52
Black Females under 10	53
Total of Black	349

The Number of the whole in the County &c....... 1889

PAUL MICHAUX

Sheriff

₊ For the Table showing the total population of the Province in 1738, see *Doc. Hist. of N. Y.*, Vol. I, Art. XXIII.

A LIST OFF ALL THE INHABITANTS

OFF THE TOWNSHIP OFF FLATTBUSH BOTH OF WHITES AND BLACKS,
MALES AND FEMALES.

The names off the masters off the the house or mistresses &c.	White males above 10 years.	Males under 10 years.	Whites females above 10 years	females under 10 years.	Blacks males above 10 years.	under 10 years.	Blacks females above 10 years.	under 10 years.
Jus polhmvs	2	1	1	3	1			
Lamert bennet	2₄	..	3	..				
William Boerrom.......	3	2	1	..				
Carl boerrom...........	2	2	1	1	..	..	1	
Isaac hegeman	2	..	1	..	..			
John blom.............	1	..	1	3	..			
William bennett........	1	3	1	1	..			

The names off the masters off the house or mistresses &c.	Whites males above 10 years	Males under 10 years.	Whites females above 10 years.	females above 10 years.	Blacks males under 10 years.	under 10 years.	Blacks females above 10 years.	under 10 years.
Garritt Snedeker	1	1	1	1				
Hendrick wickhot	1	..	1	2	..	..	1	
Cornelius wickhof	2	..	..	..	1	..	1	
Nicklas wickhof	1	3	1	2	..	..	2	
Nicklas andrissen,	2	..	..	..	..	..	..	
Johannis Cornel	2	..	1	..	..	..	1	
Isack Snedeker	3	1	..	1	..	..	..	
Jurey perbasko	1	1	2	2	1	..	2	
Elbert hegeman,	3	..	5	..	..	..	..	
John Van wicklen,	1	..	2	2	..	..	1	
Garrit Cosine	1	..	1	..	..	..	..	1
Joseph hegeman	3	1	3	3	0	0	0	0
John lot	1	1	1	2	1	..	2	
John Striker	3	1	3	1	1	..	1	
Laraîce detmas	1	1	2	..	1	1	1	1
Denijs Hegeman	1	..	2	..	..	..	..	
John detmas	4	2	2	2	1	2	2	3
John uanderuer	3	..	3	..	1	..		
Abraham lott	3	1	3	..	2	..	2	1
inder freeman	1	..	1	..	1	..	1	2
Jus Sadam	2	1	4	..	2	..	1	
Jacob Sadam	2	..	2	..	..	..	1	2
Daniel Ramson	2	..	1	..	2	..	1	..
Pieter Stry ker junr.	1	1	1	2	..	..	1	..
Corneallas bennum	1	..	..	1	..	..	..	
William hogaland	3	..	3	..	..	..	..	
Cattren uanderveer	..	..	3	..	..	..	..	
Cornealas Sadam	2	..	1	1	..	..	..	
John Sadam	3	2	3	1	..	..	..	
John Vanderwort	1	2	1					
Adrayonn Hageman	3	2	1	1	..	..	..	
Martin Simson	1	..	1					

The names off the masters off the house or mistresses &c.	Whites males above 10 years	Males under 10 years.	Whites females above 10 years.	females under 10 years.	Blacks males above 10 years.	under 10 years.	Blacks females above 10 years.	under 10 years.
Johanas Johnson.........	3	..	3	2	1	..	1	1
Isaac Okey	1	1	1	1	..	..		..
Born Vande Vandan, ...	2	..	2	2	1	..	1	2
Dom Antonadus	1	..	1	..	..	1	1	1
Adn Hegeman	2	..	2	1	..	..	..	..
John Waldron..........	4	..	3	0	..	..	..	..
Coll Peter Stryker	1	0	1	0	0	0	1	0
Tryntje [s]olleman......	0	0	2	0	0	0	0	0
John Renham	2	0	0	0	0	0	0	0
Joseph Renham	1	0	1	2	0	0	0	0
John Van Bueren.......	1	1	1	1	0	1	1	0
Giljan Cornel...........	4	[5]	2	..	1	..	..	..
Cartryna filkin.........	1	..	2	..	1	..	..	..
Marten Adriaansz.......	1	..	1	..	..	..	..	..
Rein Martense	1	1	2	..	1	1	1	..
Adriaan Martense.......	1	..	1	4	1	2	1	1
Phillippus Nagel........	2	..	3	2	1	4	1	1
Ari Van der Bilt........	2	..	4	3	2	2	1	2
Abraham hegeman......	2	..	2	..	1	..	..	..
Cornelius Cornel........	3	1	2	..	..	2	1	1
Isaac Leffertze..........	1	2	2	..	2	..	1	..
Jan Van der Bilt........	5	..	1	..	1	..	1	..
Rem hegeman..........	4	1	2	1	1	,.	1	..
Peter Leffertz..........	4	..	2	4	1	1	1	3
Dominicus V D Veer....	2	3	5	3	..	..	..	..
Gerrit Van Duyn........	1	0	2	0	0	0	0	0
John Verkerck..........	1	1	3	3	1	3	1	1
Rolef Verkerck.........	1	0	2	0	3	1	2	3
Peter Lyster............	1	2	1	3	1	0	0	0
William houerd.....:...	2	..	2	..	..	0	0	0
Josef houerd...........	1	1	1	1	..	0	0	0
Jus Bloum.............	3	..	2	..	..	0	0	0

The names off the masters off the house or mistresses &c.	Whites males above 10 years.	males under 10 years.	Whites females above 10 years.	females under 10 years.	Black males above 10 years.	under 10 years.	Blacks females above 10 years.	under 10 years
Cattrin Lot.............	..	..	1	..	1	0	1	0
Sarah Lot....	2	1	2	2	1	1	1	0
Thomas betts...........	1	..	2	1	..	0	1	1
Jacob Ramsen..........	2	3	2	..	0	0	0	0
Robert betts............	1	1	2	..	1	0		
	141	59	144	66	39	19	44	27

A LIST OFF ALL THE INHABITANTS

OFF THE TOWNSHIP OFF FLATT LANDS, BOTH OF WHITES AND BLACKS, MALES AND FEMALES.

The names off the masters off the houses or mistresses &c.	Whites males above 10 years.	Males under 10 years.	Whites females above 10 years.	females under 10 years.	Blacks males above 10 years.	under 10 years.	Blacks females above 10 years.	under 10 years.
Johannes Lott..........	03	03	02	01	02	00	01	02
Marten Schenck........	02	00	02	01	01	00	01	00
hendrick wickof........	02	00	01	00	02	00	01	00
Jacobus Amerman.......	03	00	02	00	00	00	00	00
yan Amerman..........	04	00	02	00	01	00	00	00
pieter nevyus..........	02	00	01	00	00	00	00	00
pieter Wickof jur.......	01	01	01	00	01	00	00	00
ijan Stevensen..........	04	00	03	00	01	00	01	00
wijllem kovwenoven.....	04	01	04	03	02	00	01	00
Steven Schenk..........	02	00	03	03	01	00	00	00
gerret hansen...........	01	00	01	00	01	00	00	00
pijeter monfoor.........	02	02	02	01	00	00	00	00
wijllem van gelden......	05	00	03	00	00	00	00	00

The names off the masters off the house or mistresses &c.	White males above 10 years.	males under 10 years.	Whites females above 10 years.	females under 10 years.	Blacks males above 10 years.	under 10 years.	Blacks females above 10 years.	under 10 years.
Cornelvs van voorhees...	03	00	02	01	02	00	01	00
marten Schenck.........	02	00	02	00	02	00	00	00
koert van voorhees......	01	02	01	01	00	00	00	00
Lvijcas Stevensen.......	01	00	01	00	02	00	01	00
cornlvs van arsdalen.....	04	00	04	00	00	00	00	00
ijan van voorhees.......	05	02	02	03	00	00	01	00
auken van voorhees.....	04	00	02	00	00	00	00	01
tevnys rijennesen.......	02	00	01	00	00	00	00	00
cornelys nefevs....	02	02	01	02	00	00	00	00
ijzaack van voorhees.....	02	01	01	02	00	00	00	00
ijan elbersen.......... ...	02	01	04	02	01	00	01	00
pijeter wycoff..........	04	00	02	00	01	00	00	00
pijter wijcoff...........	01	01	01	01	00	00	00	00
abraham westervelt	01	00	02	00	00	00	00	00
ijohannes van sijggelen ..	01	00	02	00	00	00	00	00
ijan ouken.............	03	01	03	00	00	06	00	00
ijan terhvnen	01	00	02	00	01	01	01	02
wijlhelmus Stothof......	01	01	03	00	02	00	01	01
cornelvs Stevensen......	02	01	01	00	00	00	00	00
harmanus hoogelant.....	04	02	04	01	01	00	00	00
roelof van voorhees	02	00	02	01	00	00	00	00
	81	21	70	23	24	1	11	6

A LIST OFF ALL THE INHABITANTS

OFF THE TOWNSHIP OFF GRAVESEND, BOTH OFF WHITES AND BLACKS, MALES AND FEMALES.

The names off the masters off the house or mistresses.	Whites males above 10 years.	Males under 10 years.	Whites females above 10 years.	females under 10 years.	Blacks males above 10 yrs.	under 10 years.	Blacks females above 16 years.	under 10 years.
S: Gerritsen	5	..	2	1	..	..	..	..
Bernardus Reyder	3	..	1	1	1	1	1	1
Roeloff Ter hunen	2	1	5	2	..	..	..	..
Richd Stillwell	4	0	2	1	1			
Jacobus Strycker	1	1	3	1	1	1		
Nicklas willams	2	4	2	2				
Samuell Hubbard	2	..	2	1	1			
Garret lambertson	2	2	3	1	..	..	..	..
Andro Emmans	1	1	..	1	1	..	..	..
weedaw Emans	1		1	1	..	..	..	..
farnandus: U: sicklen	3	..	2	..	..	..	..	..
Widdeu Courten	1	..	2	..	1	..	..	..
John Boys	2	..	2	..	..	..	..	..
Willem bouil	1	..	1					
Nicklas Stilwill	1	1	1					
Cournelas Strikar	1	1	4	..	1			
John Griggs	1	2	5	1	1	..	1	
Elizabeth Griggs	..	..	1	..	..	..	..	
Elias Hubbard	3	1	1	4	..	..	1	..
Garret Dorland	1	..	2	..	..	..	..	..
farnandus. V Sicklen	3	3	2	1	1		1	
Jacobus Emans	5	2	3	2	..	..	..	..
barnt Jonson	4	1	2	1	..	..	..	..
Daniel Lake	2	3	1	2	1	2	2	..
John Rider	3	3	4	1				
Kourten V. fores	2	1	2	4	1		1	..
Peter Willamsen	2	..	1	4				
Pheby Van Clift	1	1	1	..				
John Van Clift	2	3	2	4				
	61	31	60	36	11	4	7	1

A LIST OFF ALL THE INHABITANTS

OFF THE TOWNSHIP OFF NEWUTRECHT, BOTH OFF WHITES AND BLACKS, MALES AND FEMALES.

The names of the master of the house or mistresses &c.	Whites males above 10 years.	Males under 10 years.	Whites females above 10 years.	females under 10 years.	Blacks males above 10 years.	under 10 years.	Blacks females above 10 years.	under 10 years.
Samuel Groenen Dyck ...	5	2	1	2	1	4	1	0
Cornelis Van brunt......	2	1	3	0	3	0	3	1
grijete bant	1	0	3	0	0	0	0	0
rubecha eemans	2	0	3	0	2	0	2	1
Sarels berrij	1	2	2	2	0	0	0	0
yoost van brunt	1	0	1	0	7	1	2	2
elisabet gewout.........	0	0	1	1	0	0	0	0
myndert ijansen	1	1	1	0	0	0	0	0
henderick ijaensen	5	0	2	0	1	0	1	0
rutgert van brunt.......	3	3	2	1	2	0	1	1
edword dryncwater......	1	1	1	1	0	0	0	0
aert van Pelt....	2	0	0	0	1	0	1	1
albert koerte...........	2	0	3	0	3	0	1	1
ijan van pelt.	2	1	2	3	1	0	0	0
pijeter kartelijou........	1	0	3	0	2	0	1	0
ailte karteloijou.........	3	0	2	0	1	0	1	0
Jaques Denyes..........	1	2	1	1	4	0	2	0
William Barkelo........	2	0	3	0	1	3	1	1
William Ver Done	2	3	1	0	1	0	1	2
Thomas Stillwell........	4	5	4	0	0	0	0	0
John piterse............	3	0	4	1	1	0	0	0
Thomas Van Dick	2	1	1	0	0	0	0	0
Cherck Van Dick	3	0	5	0	0	0	0	0
gerret Van Dyck........	1	0	1	0	0	1	0	0
hendrik Suydam........	2	1	1	3	1	0	1	2
Rutgert Van Brunt......	2	2	3	1	3	2	3	3
Joseph Ditmars.........	1	0	1	0	0	0	0	0
machijel vanderver......	1	2	2	2	0	0	0	0

The names of the master of the house or mistresses &c.	Whites males above 10 years.	males under 10 years.	Whites females above 10 years.	females under 10 years.	Blacks males above 10 years.	under 10 years.	Blacks females above 10 years.	under 10 years
gerrijt van duijn........	1	1	1	1	1	0	0	0
marija van nuijs........	0	0	2	0	0	0	0	0
ouken van nuijs	1	5	4	1	0	0	0	0
ijacobus van nuijs.......	2	0	1	0	0	0	0	0
Wyllem van nuijs.......	3	1	2	0	0	0	0	0
ijan van dijck	1	0	0	0	0	0	0	0
	64	34	67	20	36	11	22	15

A LIST OF ALL THE INHABITANTS

OFF THE TOWNSHIP OFF BROOKLAND, BOTH OFF WHITES, AND BLACKS, MALES AND FEMALES &c.

The names of ye masters of the house or mistresses &c.	White males above 10 years.	White males under 10 years.	White females above ten years.	White females under 10 years.	Blacks males above 10 years.	under 10 years.	Black females above 10 years.	under 10 years.
Jeronymus Rapalje......	1	1	3	0	1	0	2	3
George Rapalje...,......	2	1	2	1	2	0	2	0
Isaac Johnson..........	3	2	3	1	0	0	0	0
Jacob Ryerson	4	1	0	2	0	0	1	0
Hans Bergen...........	2	2	3	0	0	0	0	0
Jacob Bergen	2	0	2	1	1	0	1	0
Jeremias Remsen	1	0	2	4	0	1	0	1
Gizbart Bogaert	2	0	2	0	0	0	0	0
Gizbart Bogaert Junr	2	2	1	2	0	0	0	0
Cornelius Bogard	1	1	2	1	1	1	0	1
Nicasius Couwenhoven ..	3	0	1	0	1	1	0	1
Marten Vanderhoeven...	4	1	2	1	0	0	0	0

The names of ye masters of the house or mistresses &c.	White males above 10 years.	White males under 10 years.	White females above 10 years.	White females under 10 years.	Black males above 10 years.	under 10 years.	Black female above 10 years.	under 10years.
Gerrit Adriaanse	2	1	2	1	1	0	0	0
Nicholas Vechten	1	0	2	2	1	0	0	0
Fredrick Blaeuw	2	1	1	0	0	0	0	0
John Blaeuw	1	0	1	1	0	0	0	0
Juryen Blaeuw	1	0	1	1	0	0	0	0
Peter Staets	4	0	3	2	0	0	1	0
Adrian Bennet	3	0	1	0	0	0	0	1
Cornelius Van Duyn,	2	0	2	1	1	0	1	0
Johannes Holst	2	2	3	0	0	0	0	0
John Bennet	3	0	3	1	1	0	0	0
Jacob Bennet	2	0	2	0	0	0	0	0
Thomas Van Dyck,	2	0	1	1	1	0	0	0
Samuel Stellingwerg	1	0	2	1	2	0	0	0
Simon D' Hart	2	0	3	2	6	2	3	2
Wouter Van Pelt,	4	0	3	0	3	0	1	0
Joseph Hegeman	1	3	3	2	0	0	1	1
Hendrick Van Dyck,	1	1	2	0	1	0	3	1
Elizabeth Garner	0	1	1	1	0	0	0	0
George Remsen	1	1	1	0	1	0	1	0
Rem Remsen	2	0	2	1	0	1	1	0
Isaac Sebering	4	2	2	1	1	2	1	2
Aeltje Sebering	2	0	2	0	2	0	1	1
Israell Horsfield	3	1	1	2	3	0	0	0
John Thompson	1	1	1	0	0	0	0	0
Mally Burwouter	0	2	1	0	0	0	0	0
Theophilus Elsworth	4	1	4	1	5	3	2	1
Petrus Ewetse	1	1	1	2	2	0	0	0
John Rhyn	2	1	2	1	0	0	0	1
Gabriall Cox	3	4	2	4	0	0	1	0
John Rapalje	2	0	1	0	2	1	2	0
Thomas Browne	1	1	1	3	0	0	0	0
Billy Nicbin	1	1	1	1	0	0	0	0

The names of ye masters of the house or mistresses &c.	White males above 10 years.	White males under 10 years.	White females above 10 years.	White females under 10 years.	Black males under 10 years.	under 10 years.	Black males above 10 years.	under 10 years
Daniell Bontecoue	1	0	2	2	1	1	0	0
Aert Middagh	1	0	1	0		1	0	0
Breghje Glieiff	0	1	1	0	0	0	1	0
Hendrick Stryker	2	0	1	3	1	0	1	0
Cornelius filkin	1	1	2	0	0	0	0	0
Aeltje Provoost	1	0	2	1	1	0	0	0
John Middagh	1	1	1	1	1	0	1	0
Christopher Codwise	12	2	5	2	2	0	2	0
Cornelius Ewetse.......	7	0	1	2	0	0	1	0
John Ewetse...........	2	2	2	1	0	0	0	0
James Harding.........	1	1	5	0	1	0	0	0
Jacob Deklyn..........	1	0	2	1	0	0	0	0
Rem Remsen..........	7	0	4	3	2	1	1	1
Everardus Brouwer.. ...	2	2	2	2	0	0	0	0
Johannes Johnson.......	3	0	0	0	0	0	1	1
Albertje Johnson	0	0	1	0	0	0	0	0
George Bergen..........	1	2	2	2	0	1	0	0
Jacob Hanse Bergen.....	1	0	1	0	1	0	0	0
Cornelius Webbers......	1	2	2	0	0	0	0	0
Isaac D'Graw...........	2	2	2	1	0	0	1	0
Joost D'Beavois.........	2	0	5	1	0	0	0	0
Jacobus Beavois.........	3	0	1	0	1	0	0	0
John Ellen.............	1	0	0	0	0	0	0	0
Hans Bergen...........	4	1	6	0	1	0	1	0
Jacobus Vandewater.....	3	1	1	2	0	0	0	0
Benjamin V. D. Water...	3	0	3	0	0	0	0	0
Styntje Vander Voort....	0	0	1	0	0	0	0	0
Lambert Andriesen......	3	0	2	0	0	0	0	0
Jacobus Leffertze........	2	1	3	0	1	2	1	0
George Rapalje.........	2	3	2	0	0	1	1	0
Barent Blom	2	2	4	3	1	0	0	0
Rem V. D. Beeck.......	2	2	1	1	0	1	0	0

The names of ye masters of the house or mistresses &c	White males above 10 years	White males under 10 years	White females above 10 years	White females under 10 years	Black males above 10 years	under 10 years	Black females above 10 years	under 10 years
John Dorland...........	1	1	1	2	1	0	0	0
Hendrick Suydam.......	3	0	2	0	1	0	0	0
Cornelius V. D. hoven...	1	0	1	0	1	0	1	1
Cornelius V. D. hoeven Ju^r.	2	2	1	2	1	0	0	0
Peter V.. D. Voort.......	1	2	1	2	1	0	0	1
Paulus V. D. Voort......	1	0	1	2	0	0	0	0
John V. D. Voort	5	1	5	0	0	0	0	0
John Van Noortstrant....	2	1	2	2	2	1	1	2
Dirck Rapalji..'.	1	0	1	0	1	0	0	0
Sara Rapalje...........	0	0	1	0	1	0	1	0
Jacob Cossauw..........	5	3	0	1	0	0	0	0
Isaac Remsen...........	7	1	2	2	2	0	1	0
Jacob Durrie........	3	3	2	0	1	1	1	0
Mathys Van Dyck.	2	2	2	2	2	1	1	1
Abraham Brewer........	2	1	2	2	2	0	0	0
Juryen Brewer..........	1	2	2	2	0	0	0	0
	199	81	175	92	69	23	43	23

A LIST OFF ALL THE INHABITANTS

OFF THE TOWNSHIP OFF BUSHWYCK, BOTH OF WHITES AND BLACKS, MALES AND FEMALES.

The names of the masters of the house or mistress &c	Whites males above 10 years	under 10 years	Whites females above 10 years	under 10 years	Blacks males above 10 years	under 10 years	Black females above 10 years	under 10 years
Johannes Schenck.......	1	00	1	00	1	00	2	00
David Sprongh.........	3	1	3	00	00	00	00	00

The names of the masters of the house or mistress &c	Whites males above 10 years	under 10 years	Whites females above 10 years	under 10 years	Blacks males above 10 years	under 10 years	Black females above 10 years	under 10 years
Marijtie Schenck	4	3	00	1	1	00	1	1
Jannitie Van Ende	6	1	00	1	2	00	1	00
Symon Dorijie	3	00	2	1	00	00	1	00
Charel Dorijie	2	4	2	1	1	2	2	00
folkert folkertse	1	1	1	00	1	00	00	00
Necklaas folkertse	1	00	4	00	1	00	00	00
Jacobus Cozyn	2	00	2	00	2	00	1	00
Pieter Fonck	4	1	2	1	00	1	00	00
Geertruy Wortman	2	02	1	00	00	00	00	00
Abraham Coeck	1	1	1	2	00	00	00	00
Joost Dorijie	1	00	1	00	00	00	00	00
Jacob Pieterse	2	00	2	2	00	00	00	00
Arent Stockholum	2	00	5	00	1	00	00	00
Daniel bodet	2	2	2	1	1	00	00	00
Jurijen Nagel	2	00	2	00	1	1	2	00
Hendrick Vande W^{tr}	1	3	1	00	00	00	00	00
femmetie anders	2	00	2	00	00	00	00	00
abraham Liquir.	4	00	4	2	00	00	00	00
Tryntie Calijer	2	00	2	00	00	00	00	00
Jacobus Calijer	1	00	1	1	00	00	00	00
Pieter wit	3	1	4	3	1	0	1	00
Johannis pieter	1	00	2	00	00	00	00	00
David Cats	1	00	2	3	00	00	00	00
Alexander berd	2	00	2	00	1	1	1	00
Pieter praa	1	00	1	00	4	2	3	00
Derck Wortman	2	00	1	00	2	1	2	1
frans Tijtus	2	1	1	2	3	00	2	00
Thomas fardon	5	00	2	2	1	00	2	2
Jams Bobijn	1	00	1	00	1	1	4	5
Andris Stockholum	2	1	2	3	1	00	00	00
Johannis Calijer	3	00	4	1	00	00	00	00
Jacobus Calijer	2	00	3	00	00	00	00	00

The names of the masters of the house or mistress &c.	Whites males above 10 years.	under 10 years.	Whites females above 10 years.	under 10 years.	Blacks males above 10 years.	under 10 years.	Blacks females above 10 years.	under 10 years.
Johannis boechout......	3	00	5	1	1	00	00	00
tuenes Rapellie.........	1	00	1	2	01	00	00	00
Abraham dorijie........	4	2	3	2	00	00	00	00
Leffeert Leffertse........	1	00	1	3	01	00	00	00
Jan mesrol.............	4	1	4	2	1	1	1	00
Pieter Consellie.........	2	2	5	00	00	00	00	00
Johannis aberse.........	3	00	6	1	1	00	1	00
	92	27	91	39	31	11	27	9

Comp^t : 325 Ziele.

A LIST OF FREEHOLDERS
IN SUFFOLK COUNTY 27 FFEBRUARY 1737

James Beebe
Willam King: Ju^r
Joshua Curtis
Charles Glover
Thomas terry
John King: Ju^r
Gideon Youngs
Jonathan Youngs
Richard Shaw
Richard Brown
Joseph Brown
Samuel Crook
Samuel Emmons
David Youngs
John Racket
Henry tuttle: Junr
Henry Conklin

David Moore
Walter Brown
Samuel Conklin
John Conklin
Joseph Conklin
Joseph Conklin Junr
John Conklin Junr
peter pain
John Budd
John vail
Alsup pain
Samuel Landon
Sylvester Lhummidué
Isreal Moore
Samuel Griffing
Ebbenezer Johnson
John Youngs

Thomas Reeve
James Landon
John peck
Jonathan Horton
John Salmon
Thomas Conklin
Joseph Horton
Isaac Hubbard
Samuel Reeve
Samuel terry
Joshua Budd
Benjamin Reeve
peter Halliock
John Dickinson
Nathaniel Youngs
Samuel Case
John Goldsmith
Daniel tuttle: Ju^r
William Salmon
Hazekiah Reeve
Joshua Horton: Junr
Samuel Curwin
Sylvenus Davis
Benjamin Case
Zebulon Hallick
David Reeve
William Reeve
Henry Wells
Uriah terry
Thomas Goldsmith
Jonathan Horton Junr
Solomon Wells
William Benjamin
Joshua Wells: Junr
Richard terry
Thomas Booth
Gideon Wickham
Daniel Osmon

Constant king
Barnebus Winds
John Reeve
David Horton
John hudson
Samuel Clark Junr
Caleb Horton
David Curwin
Gersham terry
Daniel Reeve
James Reeve
Timothy Hudson
Thomas Reeve Junr
John Howel
Isaac Howel
Thomas Clark
Aaron Howel
John Cleaves
David Cleaves
Daniel Curwin
Ezekiel pette
James terry
Josiah Youngs
Daniel Youngs
Samuel Wells
Daniel Wells
Nathaniel Wells
Richard Howel
Stephen Sweasay
Joseph Mapes
David Howel
peter Hallick
Richard Swasey
Elezer luce: Ju^r
Daniel terry
Christipher Youngs
Hezekiah howell
Jonah Bower

Obadiah Rogers
Ichabod Seayr
Ichabud Cooper
Thomas Stephens
Henry person
Josiah howel
John foster
James hearick
Narthan hearick
Benjamin hains
Samuel Jenings
Thomas lupton
Job Seayr
Hugh gilson
Jonathan peirle
Stephen herrick
Gershem Culver
Jeremiah Culver
Samuel Ludle
John Mitchel
Joseph Rodgers
Henry Holsey
David phithin
Samuel hains
Daniel Moore
Thomas Sandford
Ezekiel Sandford
Abraham peirson
Josiah peirson
Stephen tapping
Josiah tapping
Job peirson
Henry wick
James Cooper
John lupton
Thomas Cooper Jur
Elisha howel
Elias pette

Elnathan white
John moorehouse
John norris
Daniel hedges
Theopple howel
Thomas holsey
Constant heavins
Joseph howel
Abraham holsey
Nathaniel holsey
David burnit
John Seayr
James White
Aaron burnit
John tapping
Benjamin howell
Henry howell
Zechariah sandford
Joshua hildreth
Elias Cook
Abraham howell
John peirson
Benjamin Woodruph
Stephen bower
Nathaniel Jesup
Artter howell
John Cook
Jonathan Cook
Isaac hildreth
Timothy mulford
Jeremiah mulford
William hedges
Narthan dayton
William osman
Elisha Conklin
Mathew mulford
Edward Jones
Daniel miller

Eleazer miller
Samuel persons
John merry
Thomas talmage
John talmage
Lion gardner
Samuel hedges
Ephraim burnet
Samuel hudson
John mulford
Josiah miller
Henry hudson
Thomas osmon
John hunting
Robert moore
Jonathan wick
Ezekiel hubard
James chittester
David Kitcham
Samuel Smith
Daniel Keeley
James Keeley
Obediah Rogers
David Rogers
Joseph lewes
William Jerves
Nathaniel Kacham
philip plat
John Rogers
Job smith
Arron Smith
David Carey
William row
Jonathan Jones
Jacob Munsel
Platt Smith
Solomon Smith
Zephaniah plat

John hockins
Moses Acerly
Josiah wicks
John Scidmore
Robert Arter
Joshua Arter
Timothy tredwell
Obadiah Smith
Benjamin Gold
Daniel Smith
Richard Smith
Job Smith
Ebenezer Smith
Shubel Marchant
Timothy Smith
Joseph Smith
Edmond Smith
Richard Smith
Isaack Mills
Timothy Mills
Richard Blidenberg
James Dickonson
John Dickonson
Jonathan Dayton
John Arter
William Green
William phillips
Amos willis
Richard willis
Richard floyd
Nichols floyd
Nathaniel Woodhull
William Smith
James tutthil
Danniel Brewster
James Smith
Israel Smith
James Sell

Joseph roberson
John robberson
Hezekiah Dayton
Nathaniel Dayton
Noah hallock
Thomas Green
William Miller
Richard Miller
Andrew Miller
Robert robinson
Thomas robinson
Moses burnett
Joseph phillips
Joseph dauis
Samuel dauis
Daniel dauis
Beniamin dauis
John tucker
George Norton
John Mosier
Henry Dayton
Hugh Mosier
Thomas Strong
George tucker
John row
Nathaniel row
Henry robbins
Nathaniel brewster
John wood
Samuel D'henuar
William Jean
Stephen Jean

Matthews Jean
Josep brewster
Nathaniel Liscom
Nathaniel Sattirly
George Owen
Samuel Smith
Arter Smith
John hellock
Beniamin hallock
John tucker
Samuel thompson
Jonathan Owen
Nathaniel bigss
William helms
Eleazer hockins
Amos Dickenson
Henry Smith Esq
Thomas Chatfield
Joshua Youngs
Joseph wickham
Nathaniel warner
Mathias burnett
Daniel Sayr
William Jenings
Nathanil Smith
George phillips
Richard Woodhull
Obadiah Smith
Charles Saxton
John wicks
Dauid Corey Sherriff
The whole amounts to—328

LIST OF THE FFREEHOLDERS
OF DUTCHESS COUNTY VIZT.

Henry Beekman
Lowrence Knickerbacker
Nicholas Hoffman
Martinus Hoffman
Barent Van Benthuysen
Philip Londen
Hendrick Kip
Nicholas Row
Jury Soefelt
Zacharias Haber
Fredricke Sipperly
Johannis Spaller
Jury Feder
William Cole
Hans Heyner
Johannis P : Snyder
Johannis Backus
Hans felte Wollever
Hans Lambert
Joseph Rykert
Hendrick Sheffer
Peter Oostrander
Benjamin Van Steenbergh
Hans felte Sheffer
Willem Freer
Teunis Freer
Jury Ackert
Evert Knickerbacker
Nicholas Bonesteel
Jacobus Van Etten Junr.
Basteaan Trever
Coenradt Berringer
Wendell polver
Peter Van Etten
William Simon

William Scott
Michaell Sipperly
David Richart
Jacob Mowl
Mathys Earnest
Adam Oostrander
Simon Kool
Godfreed Hendrick
Wendel Yager
Jacob Drom
Martinus Shoe
Jury Adam Soefelt
Philip foelandt
Andries Widerwox
Fran Neker
Christophell Snyder
Marten Tiel
Arnout Viele
Lowrence Tiel
Jacob Cool
Philip More
Jan Van Benthuysen
Zacharias Smith
Josias Ross
Gysbert Westfall
Andries Hermans
Michael Polver
Johannis Weaver
William Van Vreedinburga
Johannis Kip
Arie Hendrickse
Willem Van Vreedinburgh Junr
Isaac Kip
Roeloff Kip
Jacob Kip

Abraham Kip
Mathys Sleght
Evert Van Wagenen
Goese Van Wagenen
Hendrickus Heermans
Lowrence Oosterhout
Peter Tippell
Albartus Shriver
Stephen Frelick
Arent Oostrander
Philip Feller
Henry Filkin
Francis Hagaman
John Gay
Isaac Filkin
Jan Ostrom
Roeloff Ostrom
Simon Flegelaer
Augustine Creed
Jacob Hoff
Lowrence Hoff
Isaac Germain
Isaac Germain Jun[1]
Josias Crego
Isaac Tietsort
Richard Sackett
Gerret E : Van Wagenen
Isaac Runnells
Isaac Runnells Jun[r]
Frans Van Dyck
Nehemiah Runnells
Nicholas Van Wagenen
Peter Palmer
Nathaniell Marshall
Joseph Palmer
Jacob Van Campen
John Runnells
Samuell Palmer

Joshua Palmer
Manuell Gonselesduck
William Palmer
Peter Lassing
Isaac Lassing
William Lassing
Christophell Van Bomell
Jacob Van Wagenen
Lewis Du Bois
Mathys Du Bois
Marcus Van Bomell
Rudolphus Swartwoudt
Mathewis Van Keuren
Hendrick Willsie
Elias Van Buntschoten
Jacobus Van Bomell
Thomas Lewis
Henry Vandenburgh
John Concklin
Jacob Low
Johannis Van Kleek
Simon Freer
Mosis De Graaff
Barnardus Swartwoudt
Johannis Tappon
Myndert Vandenbogart
Hendrick Ostrom
Barent Van Kleek
Frans La Roy
Lowrence Van Kleek
Jacobus van Den Bogart
Frans Filkin
Bowdewine La Count
Lowrence Gerbrantz
Robert Kidney
Peter Viele
John Emŏns
Magiel Pells

Abraham Freer Junr
Peter Parmatier
Gybsert Peelen
Arie Van Vliet
Johannis Van Benthuysen
William Syfer
William Smith Secundus
Alexander Griggs
Jacobus De Yeo
James Auchmoty
Samuell Mathews
George Ellsworth
Johannis Dollson
Jacob De Witt
David De Dutcher
John Cook
John Carman
Nicholas Koens
Nicholas Emigh
Hendrick Ow'
Mosis Nauthrup
Stephen Crego
Peter Simpson
John Gamble
William Humphreys
Francis Nellson
Thomas Davinport
Isaac Van Amburgh
Peter Du Bois Junr
Cornelis Bogardus
Jacobus De Peyster
John Calkin Junr
Johannis Van Voorhees
Coert Van Voorhees
Johannis Van Voorhees Junr
Hendrick Philip
Johannis Middellaer
John Lossee

Johannis Willsie
Johannis Ter Boss
Isaac Dollson
Teunis Van Vliet
Hendrick Van Tessell
Hendrick Ter Boss
Robert Britt
Jacobus Ter Boss
Cornelis Van Wyck
Francis Britt
Hendrick Rosekrans
Thomas Langdon
John Baily
Christiaan Du Bois
Jacobus Swartwout
Theodorus Van Wyck
Benjamin Hasbrook
Willem Schutt
George Brinckerhoff
Daniell Boss
Ephraime Bloome
John Brinckerhoff
Cornelis Lossee
Lowrence Lossee
Jonathan Du Bois
Jacob Du Bois
John Montross
Peter Mufford
John flewellen
William Drake
Joshua Griffen
William Ver Planck
Samuell Hallstead
Daniell Yeomans
John Rosekrans
Cornelis Willsie
Maes Oostrander
Abraham Swartwoudt

Isaac Brinckerhoff

Baltus J Van kleek

Baltus B Van kleek

Simon La Roy

Ahaswarus Van kleek

Teunis Van Buntskoten

Gideon Ver Veelen

Peter Outwater

Jacob Brinckerhoff

Hendrick Mufford

Marten Shenk

Mathew Du Bois Jun[r]

Abraham De Graeff

Dutchess ss August 28: 1740

The Aforegoing is a True List of the ffreeholders of said County To the best of my knowledge.

JA. WILSON Sheriff

A LIST OF THE OFFICERS AND SOLDERS

BELONGING TO THE REGIMENT OF FFOOT MILITIA IN THE COUNTY OF ORANGE IN THE PROVINCE OF NEW YORK CONSISTING OF EIGHT COMPANYS OF FFOOT WHEREOF VINCENT MATHEWS IS COLL[o].

Vincent Mathews Coll

Soll[o] Carpenter Let[t] Coll:

George Ramsen Major

Michael Jacson Adej[t]

James Tompson Quart[s]

first Company

Ram Remsen Cap[t]

Cornelius Smith Liv[t]

Eb Smith Ensine

Three Sarjents

Three Corporalls

One Drumer

Sixty Three private men—in all 73

2 Company

Sam[ll] Odel Cap[t]

Henry Cuyper Liv[t]

Benjam: Allison Ensine

Three Sarjents

Three Corporalls

one Drumer

fifty Eight private men—in all 68

3 Company

John Holly Cap[t]

Mich Duning Liv[t]

Solomon Carpenter Jun[r] Ensine

Three Sargents

Three Corporalls

one Drumer

one Hundred & Eleven private men—in all 121

4 Company

Jacobus Swartwoot Cap[t]

Johan[s] West Brook Liu[t]

Johan[s] West Brook Jun[r] Ensine

Three Sarjents

Three Corporalls
one Drumer
fifty five private men—in all 65
5 Company
Nathaniel Dubois Capt
David Sovtherlon Leut
Isaac Hennion Ensine
Three Shargents
Three Corporalls
one Drumer
Sixty three private men—in all 73
6 Company
Abra Hearing Ju^r Capt
Garret Blawvelt Liv^t
John Hearing Ensine
Three Sargents
Three Corporalls
one Drumer
Sixty two private men—In all 72

7 Company
Jacob Vander Bilt Capt
Andrew Underdonk Liv^t
Aron Smith Ensine
Three Sargents
Three Corporalls
one Drumer
fifty private men—In all 60 =
Troop of Hors
Henry Youngs Capt
Wm Mapes Liv^t •
Michael Jacson Corn^t
Two Shargents
Two Corporalls
One Trumpeter
fifty two private men—In all 60
The totall 595
officers & Soldiers
Sub officers   56 ffoot

The above is a Trew Account of the numbers of y^e Officers &
Soldiers boath of Hors & foot under my Command in the County
of Orange according the Respective Roles I have Received from
each Respective Capt

This 20 Day of June 1738   VIN^T MATHEWS

LIST OF THE QUEEN'S COUNTY COMPANY
COMMANDED BY CAP^{tn} JACOB HICKES

Cap Ja^{co} Hicks
Lef. Sam^m Seman
In^{si} Jos^{he} Barns
Sa : John Carle
Sa : John Sovthword
Sa : Solo^{mo} Seman
Sa : Will^{ia} Pine
Tho Carman
Tho Spragg

Calip Carman
Nath^{an} Vollintine
Ben^{ia} vallintine
Tho Lee
Jo^{se} Lee
Ric^{ha} Townsend
Sim^{an} Searing
George Gildersleeve
John Mott

Sam Williams

Elias Dorlon

Rob^a Williams

John Bedle

Sam Bedle

Jere^m Bedle

John Jonson

Will^i Langdon

Josep Langdon

Sam^v Langdon

Sam^v Carman

Der^{ic} Brevar

Tho Manering

Barns Cornelos

Da^{vi} Pine

Edw^{ar} Spragg

Jon^{at} Smith

Sam^{ve} Rainer

Ben^{ia} Wood

Ben^{ia} Wood

Sam^{ve} Bertsel

Will : Totton

Ben^{ia} Britsel

Jeams Wood

Abra^h Sovthward

Char^{ls} Abrahams

John Abrahams

Jes^{pe} Totton

Robart Lee

Tho Gildersleeve Drummer

John Smith

Mordeca Lester

Rich Bedle

Sam^{ve} Seman J

Dani^{el} Smith

Tho Seaman

Josep Carman

Hen Seman

Jos^{ep} Seman

Gar^{sh} Smith

Josep Pettet

George Boldin

Dan^{il} Bedle

Jea^{ms} Smith

Isaac Jarman

Jeams Bedle

Joseph Wood

John Carle : J

Ben^{ia} Pine

Ric^{ha} Gildersleeve

Ben^{ia} Bedle

Jose^h Bedle

Adam Mott

Sam^{ve} Carman

Ric^{ha} Maniring

John Seman

Jacob Seman

Jonas fflower

Rich^a Totton

Will. Verity

John Sovthword. J.

Daniel Hevlet

Mat^{ha} Totten

Sam^{ve} Totten

Robart Marvin

John Smith J.

John Rainer

Jeams Pine

Ben^{ia} Smith

Jeams Seman

Jeams Mott

Sam^{ve} Seman

This is a tru Copy taken out of ye Original Roll by me
CAP^N JACOB HICKES

LIST OF THE NEW YORK COMPANIES 1738.

A LIST OF THE BLUE ARTILLERY COMPANY UNDER JOHN WALDRON.

John Brown Capt Lietenant

Peter Low first ditto

Wm Harmersly second ditto

Henry Rew third ditto

Willillam Carr

William Hillton

Vicktor Beekers

Zebadiah Hunt

Henry Ricke

John Tebout

William-Floyde

John Turner

Frances Siluester

Andrew Law Junr

Beniaman Thomas

John Braser

John Golett

Isreal Chadwick

John Morschalick

Tharnett Basley

Alexander Aliar

Jacob Golett

Thomas Hill

William Smith

John Pintard

James Spencer

Andrew Bristed

Phillip Jacob Bomper

Jeremiah Lattouch

Thomas Niblett

Hasewell van Cure

Abraham Pells

John Walker

Moses Gamboa

Allbartus Tebout

John Byuank

Danel Bonett

William Carr

John Lewis

Dauid Griffis

Robert Prouoost

Peter Pantynier

Ahasuars Ellsnorth

Joseph Lidle

John Turman

Richard Baker

James Sauers

Samuel Lawrance

Isaak Johnson

Thomas Hunt

Nicholas Carmer

Jacob Sarly

Mathew Woollfe

Robert Bennett

Edmond Peers

Robert Wood

John Hunt

Henry Williams

Peter Demett

John Lush

Andrew Mansfild

Alexander Phinix

Samuel Bourdett

James Tucker

Linthorn Ratsey

Jacob Phinix

Daniel Bloom

Robert Ratsey

Jaob Kip

Henry Tucknep

James Hill
John Bell
Phillip Brown
Thomas Tateke
Richard Barker
James Skellton
Richard Jeffers
William Deen

William Boyde
Dauid Goodwine
Samuel Payton
Jespar Bush
Vincent Bodine
James Fauear
William Bryant

LIST OF THE COMPANY OF MILITIA
UNDER THE COMMAND OF GERARD BEEKMAN.

first Lieutenant & Second Ditto
Richd Van Dam & Jacob Miller
both Dec^d.
Meyer Insign non resident

Gerard^s Comford ⎫
Wm Gilbert   ⎬ Sargants
Ger^t Harsen   ⎪
Dan^{ll} Gotier ⎭

Jacobus Quick
Thos Howard
Abraham Ten Eyck
Aron Smith
John King
Lewis Nordyn
Daniel Meker
James Young
John Quick
John Van Gylder
John Williams
John Bassett
Jacob Haraw
Arie Bogaert
Peter Marschalk

John Delamontanje
John Lashly Junr
David Gallation
Lucas Kierstead
John Nicholls
Richard Bocas
William Eagles
John Beekman
James Davie
Jacob Wessells
John Van Deursen
Jacob De Lamontanje
Jacob Slover
David Van Gelder
David Provoost
Barent Coerten
Jacob Trimper
Collin Bursey
. ... Swaen
John Tiljew
Walter Heyer
Charles Missebagh
Jeremia Sherdewyn
Peter Rusten
39 men

A LIST OF THE COMPANY

BELONGING UNDER THE COMMAND OF CAPT. CHARLES LAROEXS.

Gul^n Ver Plank, first Lut^n
Tobias Stoutenburgh second Lut^n
David Abeel Insigne

Andrew Hunter
Henry Carmer
John Dewint
Joseph Hayse
Gilbert Rotery
Seth Smith
Samuel Burling
John Man
William Freedenburgh
William Seatly
John Freedenburgh
Hannes Snoek
Lucas Van Veghte
John Burges
John Roberson
George Ellman
John Tennor
William Snyder
Daniel Dyke
William Dyke
Abraham Persel
John Casanie
Phillip Shaljoth
Jacob Shareman
John Grig
Israel Shadick
William Roose
Daniel Revoe
Joseph Annow
Standly Homes
Cornelius Quackenbosh

John Killmaster
James Harding
Dirk Amerman
Cohan Jurry Mitter
Johan france Waldron
Thomas Wood
William Brown
William Strong
William Hoppe
William Horne
Abraham Van Aram
Phillip Soper
Thomas Montanjea
Abraham Poalin
Petrus Montanjea
John Ackerson
Edward Anderson
Richard Green
Isaac Van Gelder
Phillip Young
Jones Wright
William Van Syce
Symon Van Syce
William Moor
Joseph Montanjea
James Louwe
John Van Wyke
Theopheles Elswort
Mathew Redit
Andrew Redit
Fredrick Sebrant
John Coxs
Baran Juda
Peter Smith
Fredrick Becker

James Simson
John Meserol
Marta Bont
Hendrick Orders
Tunes Tebout
John Coxs
Isaac Demilt
Martinus Bogaart
John Balden
Henry Jenkings
Aron Magerson
John Magerson
Robert Carter
Frank Moany

George Arter
Samuel Pell
John Lawrence
John Kingston
Peter Degrot
Patrick Smith
Joseph Doty
John Montanjea
Esias Smith
Peter Wyth
Isaac Borea
Thomas Wallace
Peter Panebaker
Simon Breasted—**94**

CAPT. STUYVESANT'S COMPANY.

G^r Stuyvesant Asq^r Capt
Lif^t Jacobus Kip
Insine Phillip Minthorne
    Sariants
John Horn
Marten Van Evera
Dirrick Benson
William Waldron

Christian Hartman
William low
Jacob Tinne
Fransis Child
John Minthorne
Chernalus Child
Fradrick Webbers
John Harson
Charls Dosson
Jacob Horn

Arnovt Horn
John Kip
Isack De Lamantanya
Andris Anderson
David De Voor Se^r
David De Voor Ju^r
Abraham Anderson
Johnthon Hardmon
Arron Buse
William Richson
John Bas Se^r
John Bas Ju^r
Abraham De Lamarten
Mathan Megure
Burger Van Evera
John Sprong
John De Voor
Robert Greage
John Waldron Van Hornshoke

Benjamin Waldron
John Waldron
Arron Kortreght
John Benson
Abraham Van Bramen
Isack Mier
John Sickels
Omfre Patoo
Abraham Myer Ju^r
Arron Myer
John Luis
David De Voor
Peter Waldron
Adovlf Benson
Adovlf Myer Ju^r
John Myer Ju^r
Sammual Waldron J^r
John Waldron Van hogt
Jocom Cardener
Jacob Cardener
John Dyckman
Lowrance Low
Abraham Van Braman
John Karsse
Abraham Karsse
Ressolvert Waldron
John Van Oblenes
Jacob Dyckmen
Jacob Dyckmen Ju^r

John Nagel Ju^r
Harman Van Dewater
Addrian Hogland
John Anderson
Chernalus Dyckman
Edde Van Evera
Handrick Van Flackra
Tunnes Van Flackra
William Dickre
John Dyckman
Nicklus Dyckman
John Fox
John Wabbers
Jacob Van Ourda
Abraham Van Flackra
Isack Wabbers
Chornalus Wabbers
John Hoppah
Andris Hoppah
John Cownoven
Foulkert Somerindiek
Isack De Lamter
William Algalt.
Fradrick Allgalt
John Duffeback
John Mandevele
Jelyes Mandevele
Choranlus Wabbers—86 men

CAPT RICHARDS COMPANY

A MALITIA COMPANY UNDER YE ESPECIALL COMMAND OF

Paul Richards Esqr
Cornelius Sandford First Lef^t
Abell Hardenbroock 2^d Lef^t

Joseph Coutey Insigne
Moses Gomer Clarke

Henry Meyer ⎫
John Vangelaer ⎪ Serjeants
Abraham Vangelder ⎬
Nicholas anthony ⎭
Cornelius Myer
William Varnall
James Weyley
Joseph Waldron
John Bealy
Isaac Twentymen
William Hyer
Burtoll miller
James Best
Andrew Clappar
John Roerbeck
Cornelius seabrean
Wandle Horn
Richard Anlay
Samuell Hazard
William Procter
John Wright
Thomas Brown
John basett
James Budselott
Henriques Wessells
Petter vandick
Richard vandick
Daniell Yow
John Rynders
John Taylor
Jacobus Montanie
Seidney Briess
Potter Fressneau
Nathaniell Hazard
Alexander Weyley
Cornelius Turk

Jacob morris
Hendrikes Bulen
John Ellsworth
Anthony Lamb
William Guest
Albartus Bush
John Coae
Henry bedlow
James Brown
John Horse
Joseph Read
Herry King
Lawrence Fresst
Arculas Windfford
John Fordham
James Favier
William Stone
Mathias Gonear
Gerrett & andrew Abrahams
Ephffriam Braiser
Jacob Abraham
Alexander Oglesby
John Myer
Isaac Revara
David Van horne
Isaac Blanck
Petter Coake
Daniell Dunscum
Curoth Covernover
Thomas Picketh
Petter Prawboneth
John Steward
Denis Hicks
Andrew barhead Senior
Andrew barhead Junior
John Masiay

William McDovall   Petter A Voatts
Ellias Mambrewtt   Stephen Burdet—h73 Men
John Flasher

CAPT. BOELEN'S COMPANY.

AN EXACT LIST OR MUSTER ROUL OF THE COMPANY WHEREOF IS

Capt Abrah Boelen

Lut^t Abrah Van Wyk

Sec. Lut. Henry Beekman

Insign William de Peyster

Sargiants

1	Victoor Heyer	24	Jn° Couzyn
2	Kasper Burger	25	Jn° Hatton
3	Jn° Roome	26	Phillip Boiles
4	Jn° Meyer	27	Joseph de Vou
	Coarprals	28	Thomas Windover
5	Walter Hèyer	29	Samuel Berry
6	William Beek	30	Henry George
7	Isack Van Deurse	31	Harman Bensin
		32	Gerrit Hyer
		33	Jn° Demmok
8	William Baldwin	34	Harman Linch
9	Jn° Coo	35	Jn° Van Horne
10	Jn° Parmijter	36	Peter Hebon
11	Edward Hiter	37	Joshua Slyder
12	Jn° Ten Brouk	38	Jacobus Berry
13	Arond Heyer	39	Jn° Walker
14	William Heyer	40	Vincent Montanie
15	William Oglesbey	41	Walter Hyer
16	Oliver Sioert	42	Cornelius Bussing
17	Cornelius Van Den Berg	43	Jeptah Smith
18	Johannes Aelstyn	44	Gerret Cozyn
19	Samuel Bell	45	Adriaen Hogeland
20	Jn° Barlow	46	Henry Slyk
21	Abrah Aeylstyn Junr	47	Thomas Welsh
22	Sampson Bensin	48	James Turner
23	Abrah Finsher	49	William Roome
		50	Peter Roome
		51	Thomas Lawrence
		52	Jn° Barker
		53	Daniel Van Deurse

54 Samuel Dunscomb
55 Thomos Sanders
56 William Welsh
57 Jno James
58 Robberd Sickles
59 William Lattim
60 Jno Johnson
61 Jno Exeen
62 George Willis

63 Machiel Cornelisse
64 Roberd Troop
65 Jno Montayne
66 Jacob Roome
67 George Van Horne
68 Fredrik Bloom
69 Herman Johnson
70 Cornelius Van Hook—74

New York Feb^r 8 A^o 1737 | 8.

A LIST OF THE COMPANY
OF CAPT. CORNELUS VAN HORNE.

Capt Cornelus Van Horne
Lev^t Jacob Walton
2 Lev^t David Provoost
Insign Henry Rutgers

Serjeants { Arie King
Jacob Kip
Henry Benson
Aernout Rome

  5 Samson Benson Sam^s Son
James Hyde
Abraham Sanders
Samson Benson Thewes Son
James Clerck
10 Samuel Maghee
Alexander Maghee
John Stephens
John Evvets
Thomas Perdou
15 John Waddell
Lodewyck kraan
John White

David Michell
Benjamen Loory
20 Phillip Lewis
John Christian
Samuel Barnhart
Marthen Myer
Isack Brazier
25 Abraham Peltrou
Johannes Pool
John Van Pelt
Charles Sprangier
Robbert Provoost
30 Joshua Laplaine
Samuell Weever
Jonathan Peasley
Peter Vergeroa
Edward Killey
35 Nicolas Murfey
John Bogert John Son
Jacobus Quick
Samuell Couwenoven
John Robins

40 Pieter pontenier
    aswerus Elzewaart
    Cap Nathaniel Hinson
    Wynant van Gelder
    Jonathan Right
45 James Burlin
    Richard Gill
    William Hauckshurst
    Lodewyck Bemper
    Daniell Bountekoe
50 Abraham Hyat
    Isack Bokee
    James Bussy
    Aarent Gilbord
    John fine
55 George Joung
    James Codden Junr
    George Marschalk
    Henry Van de Water
    Daniell Bonett
60 Jacob Senjoor
    Wiliam Eckson
    Hugh Wentwort
    Phillip Cetchim
    Gilbord Hyatt
65 John Chappell
    Isack Varian
    Nathaniell Sackett
    Isack Gardner
    Mozes Tayler
70 Thomas Fealds

    John Walless
    John Suttin
    Richard Durham
    Cornelus Van Gelder
75 John Saunders
    Jeremia Sherdevine
    Alexander Mackdou
    Robberd Marrell
    Thomas Bradberry
80 Peter De Groof
    Wiliam Bartled
    Thomas Grant
    Edward Hix
    Orstin Hix
85 Walter Achter de Long
    Charles Smith
    Thomas Sickels Junr
    Richard Waldron
    Hendrick Header
90 Daniell Vaun
    Joseph North
    John Dunscum
    Joseph Collett
    David Schot
95 Wiliam Boyd
    John Lake
    Mathew Woodford
    Wiliam Cerlijal
    Abraham Bokee
100 Caleb Farley
101 Daniell Van Vleck—105

A LIST OF THE COMPANY.
OF MALITIA WHEREOF IS CAPTN. HENRY CUYLER.

James Searle 1st ⎫ Leiv^{ts}
Wil^m Walton 2^d ⎭

John Vanderspegle Ensign

Thos Hall ⎫ Sergeants.
Ja^s Creighton ⎭

Wm Colegrove
Martin Clock
Sam^{ll} Sage
Sam^{ll} Lewis
John Hamans
Hutchin Marshal
Benjamin Moore
Humphry Jones
Sam^{ll} Babington
John Stout
Hendrick Cregeer
Martinus Cregeer Junr
Abraham Bargeau
John Smith
Benjamin Shoot
James Wallbritten
Francis Wessels
Henry Holt
Thos Peirce
James Jarret
Sam^{ll} Levy
David Robinson
John Pintard
Thos Duncan
Tobias Ten Eyck
John Hastier
George Burnett
Charles Hume
Joris Brinckerhoff

Jacob Franks
Moses Franks
David Franks
Thos Willit
Joseph Leddel
Joseph Leddel Junr
Stephen Calas
Robt Crook
Thos Oaks
James Bayley
Thos Tyte
Sam^{ll} Pell
Gerardus Duyckinck
John McMullen
Richd Ray
Wm Shermur
John Swilivan
Wm Orsban
Wm Gale
Barant Bush
John Wright
Elijah Heaviland
George Lamb
Joseph Watkins
Charles Sleigh
John Williams
Sam^{ll} Myers Cohen
Andries Ten Eyck
Richd Ten Eyck
Peter Telyew
Henry Demire
Robt Richardson
Richd Evits
John Ganter
Nicholas Ganter

Thomas Griggs
Thomas Griggs Jun[r]
William Colwill
Isaac Shurdavine
Rice Williams
John Lundlakin
Jacobus Fork
Richard Fork
Elias Burger
Jacob Vandergrift
Peter Praw Vinsant
John Gasharee
Henry Patterson
Peter Galatian

Sam[ll] Brown
John Dewitt
John Buckanover
Franciss Worner
Rineer Burger
Daniel Lynsen
David Walker
Tho[s] Picks
Tho[s] Rigby
Rich[d] Byfield
Joseph Scott
Lashare
Charles Hanley—91 Men
97 (officers omitted.)

A LIST OF A FOOT COMPANY

UNDER THE COMMAND OF CAPT. JOSEPH ROBINSON TAKEN IN NEW
YORK THE 21 DAY OF JANUARY 1737 | 8

Isaac De peyster Leuff
N W grant Second Leuff
gaul Du Bous Insine
Jacobes Stoutenburgh Clarck

harme Bussingh
Benjamen Quackenbos
Christeaen Stuiver
John Blanck Ser[d]
John Monthanye Drummer

1	John Eeuwets	8	John oblyne
2	franses Barrea	9	John Stoutenburgh
3	Richard hopper	10	Tobias Stoutenburgh
4	Isaac Stoutenburgh	11	Albàrtus Van de Water
5	John Vredenburgh	12	henderyckas Van de Water
6	odreen Deppye	13	frerick heyr
7	Walter De Graau	14	Richard Warner
		15	John Bond
		16	Adward Linter
		17	John Nicholds
		18	Adam Van de Bergh
		19	Willm Spoor
		20	Aswerus turck
		21	Zacharejas Ziggelse
		22	Richard Baker
		23	Willm Louwdeth
		24	Peter Pruar
		25	Peter Lott

26	thomas Ellon	58	John Bogert
27	Pieter Losie	59	henry Van Ness
28	Corneles Van Vechten	60	Richard Kip
29	Willm poppelstorf	61	Isaac Bussingh
30	Alexander Willsen	62	Aron Bussingh
31	gerrit Van gelder	63	Caspares Blanck
32	Evert pels	64	John van orden
33	Samuel pels	65	John Davis
34	Marchus Peffer	66	Jacob Bruar
35	Corneles Cozeijn	67	John Bruar
36	John Whiler	68	Abram Bruar
37	adward kimmel	69	Nicolas tomas
38	Wilm Croleus	70	Daniel Burger
39	Peter Corsieleus	71	Nicholas Rosevelt
40	henderickas oth	72	Adam king
41	Johannes Remie	73	Willm fisser
42	Johannes Staat	74	John Post
43	Johannes pieter Kimpel	75	Peter Carbie
44	gerret de freest	76	henry Stanton
45	Baltus hejr	77	John monthanye
46	John Cure	78	Jacob Monthanye
47	Robbert Cure	79	Anthony Boutser
48	Ducke arrell	80	Barnaba Saruch
49	Jacob Wickenbergh	81	Corneles Magielse
50	Wilm Acklye	82	Benjamen Watchen
51	John Acklye	83	amus Willckenson
52	Pieter Andriesse	84	Willm Burneth
53	geysbert gerritse	85	John hughsten
54	Samuel oths	86	henry hennejon
55	Wilm persell	87	Isaac hennejon
56	Anthony hem	88	Michall Louwerier
57	John Dubs	89	Everardus Bruar—95 Men

New York ye 10th Aprill 1738.

A LIST OF YE INHABITANTS

OF Y^E SOUTH WARD IN Y^E BEAT OF CAP^T MATHEW CLARKSON.

Capt Mathew Clarkson		27	David Cox
Simon Johnson first Leutenant		28	Isaac Maddox
Cornelius Wynkoop 2nd Leuten^t		29	Justis Witfeald
John Dyer Ensigne		30	Henry Witfeald
John Heyer	Sarg^t	31	Daniel Effets
John Lesher		32	Gedion Lynsen
John De Foreest Corp^r		33	John De Mercor
1	Cornelus Bruckman	34	Henry Carmor
2	James Symes	35	William Lewis
3	Adam Dobbs	36	James Manna
4	Samuel Johnson	37	Stheven Smith
5	James Cammel	38	Andrew Breasted
6	Daniel Masters	39	William Holton
7	John Richard	40	William Dobbs
8	Peter Wessells	41	Anthony Yerrenton
9	William Brown	42	Francis Harding
10	Abraham Isaac	43	Dennes Andersin
11	Henry Breasted	44	Nicholas Anthony
12	James De Hart	45	Joseph Simson
13	John Dunlop	46	Thomas Edwards
14	Edward Nickolds	47	Henry Biffins
15	John Cregier	48	John Bloom
16	Harmanis Schuyler	49	Abrahan Van Deursen
17	Richard Nauwood	50	Jassa De Foreest
18	Francis Bratt	51	Adam Beeckman
19	Solomon Myers	52	John Blage
20	John Ten Eyck	53	Benjamin Blage
21	Thomas Routh	54	Henry Peek
22	Jarvis Routh	55	James Mecerty
23	Abraham Marchalk	56	John Nickolds
24	John De Foreest	57	William English
25	Isaac De Foreest	58	Garret Heyer—65 with of-
26	Nicholas De Foreest		ficers

LIST OF THE COMPANY OF MILITIA
FORMERLY COMMANDED BY JOHN MOORE.

David Schuyler 1st Lieutent

St George Talbot Ensine

      but since removed

Isaac Blanck   } Sergeants

Tunis Devour   }

Tunis Van Wort Corporal

      Private Centinels

1	Cornelius Van De Water	27	Thomas De Waite
2	Wm Hitchcock	28	John Brasier
3	Jacob Van Deursen	29	John Norris
4	Matthew Bell Senr	30	Robert Griffith
5	Matthew Bell Junr	31	Wm Griffith
6	Wm Ellsworth	32	Wm Pritch
7	John Claude	33	David Griffith
8	John Alwin	34	John Thompson
9	Peter Armant	35	Wm Lyell
10	Jeremiah Reading	36	Wm Pearsley
11	John Johnson	37	Aron Van Hook·
12	Wm Millerin	38	John Meckilsa
13	Cornelis Brower	39	Elias Stanbury
14	Benjamin Killmaster	40	David Goodwin
15	James Bodin	41	John Steinobuck
16	Joseph De Lorne	42	Jacob Peek
17	John Johnson	43	David Smith
18	John Morin	44	John Peterskyder
19	Benja Appleby	45	Yost Palden
20	George Witts	46	Gisbert Vytden Bogert
21	Anthony Rutgers	47	Jacob Pitt
22	Robert Benson	48	Abraham Pitt
23	Richard Bradburne	49	Peter Lamerse
23	Henry Beckman	50	Robert Harris
24	Matthew Allstine	51	Peter Cobusnyder
25	Samuel Goodness	52	Saunders Rutson
26	Peter Petersen	53	Surt Olivers
		54	Adam King
		55	Henry Cavalier
		56	Paulus Speder
		57	Paulus Berger
		58	Jacob Bush
		59	Peter Plowman
		60	Gisbert Van Deursen

61	Surfus Fleerinboome	77	Hendrick Anthony
62	George Prior	78	William Cansaly
63	Peter Lesser	79	John Dennis
64	Jacob King	80	Gisbert Van Vlecq
65	Samuel Browne	81	Barent Barhite-
66	Gisbert Uytden Bogert	82	William Morgan
67	Cornelius Roomer Senr	83	Dirrick Cook Junr
68	Cornelius Roomer Junr	84	Peter Van Norden
69	Cornelius Thorp	85	John Elnor
70	John Clarke	86	William Peick
71	John French	87	Abraham Blanck
72	Abraham Wheeler	88	Jacob Bennet
73	William Cook	89	Garret Defreest
74	Lawrence Lamerse	90	Thomas Maybourn
75	Elbert Hommerman	91	Roger McCornet—with of-
76	Abraham Florentine		ficers 98

LIST OF OFFICERS ISSUED FOR NEW YORK
WITH THE DATES OF THEIR COMMISSIONS.

No. Charles Le Roux Esqr Major - - - 1738, Augt 15
1 Abram Vanwyck Captain in the room of Captn Le Roux   16
2 Guilian Verplanck Capt in the room of Coll Moore - - 17
3 Isaac De Peyster Capt in the room of Coll Robinson - 18

First Lieutenants.

1 Henry Beekman -	- To Capt. Abram Boelen -	-	19
2 Jacob kip - - -	to Capt. Gerard^s Stivesant -		21
3 David Provoost -	- to Capt. Paul Richards -	-	22
4 William Walton Junr -	to Capt Abram Vanwyck -		23
5 Abel Hardenbrook	- to Capt Gerardus Beekman	-	24
6 Tobias Stoutenburgh -	to Capt Isaac Depeyster	-	25
7 Walter Dubois -	- to Capt Gulian Verplank	-	26

Second Lieutenants.

1 Philip Minthorne	- to Capt Gerardus Stivesant		28
2 David Abeel	- - to Capt Henry Cuyler -	-	29
3 John Dyer	- - to Capt Mathew Clarkson	-	30

4	William Depeyster	-	to Capt Abram Boelen -	-	31
5	John vanderspiegle	-	to Capt Cornel's Vanhorne Sept^r		1
6	Henry Rutgers	-	- to Capt Abram Vanwyck	-	2
7	John Pinhorne	-	to Capt Guilian Verplank	-	4
8	John Dewit	-	- to Capt Gerardus Beekman		5
9	Edward Hicks	-	to Capt Paul Richards -	-	6
10	Thomas Duncan -	-	to Capt. Isaac Depeyster	-	9

Ensigns.

1	Thos Willet -	-	to Capt Guilian Verplank	-	9
2	Barent Rynders -	-	to Capt Henry Cuyler	-	11
3	Humphry Jones	-	to Capt Abram Vanwyck	-	12
4	And^w Clopper	-	to Capt Isaac Depeyster	-	13
5	Barth^w Lereaux	-	to Capt Cornelius Vanhorne	-	14
6	Robert Bensen -	-	to Capt Gerardus Beekman		15
7	John Barberie -	-	to Capt Paul Richards -	-	16
8	Abram Cortlandt	-	to Capt Math^w Clarkson	-	18
9	Gerardus Beekman Junr		to Capt Abram Boelen -	-	19
10	John Bensen -	-	to Capt Gerardus Stivesant -		20

ULSTER COUNTY MILITIA 1738.

FIELD OFFICERS.

Coll^o A. Gaasbeek Chambers.
Le^t Coll^o Wessel Ten Broeck.
Mayor Coenradt Elmendorp.
Quarter Master Cornelis Elmendorp.

ULSTER SS: *A List of the Troopers Under the Command of*

Capt Johannis Ten Broeck   3rd Corpor^l Arie Van Vliet
Lieut^t Wessel Ten Broeck Junr 4th Corpor^l Martie Lamatre
Corn^t Tho's Gaasbeek Chambers 5 Corpor^l Ffrederick Schoon-
1st Qr. Mas. Hendrickus Krom   maker
2nd Qr. M. Johannis De Lamatre 6 Corpor^l Solomon Haasbrock
Trump^r Abraham Constapell   Solomon Van Bunschoten
1st Corpor^l Richard Wells   Jacob Haasbrock
2nd Corpor^l Gerrit Elmendorph Cornelis Depue

Samuel Bovie
Benjamin Depue
Egbert Brinck
Jan Ffreer
Cornelis Ten Broeck
Johannis Wynkoope Junr
Daniel De Bois
Danill Haasbrock
Arent Ploegh
Samuel Schoonmaker
Tjerck Schoonmaker
Arie Oosterhout
Wessel Broadhead
Simon Jacob^s Van Wagenen
Simon Van Wagenen
Jacob Van Wagenen
Egbert De Witt
David Burhance
Edward Whittaker Junr
Jacobus Schoonmaker
Thomas Nottingham
Abraham Van Wagenen
Cornelis De Witt

Cornelis New Kerck
Petrus Ten Broeck
Abraham de Lamatre
Wilhelmus Van Hooghtyling J^r
Joghem Schoonmaker Junr
Wessel Jacob^s Ten Broeck
Jan Tuenis Oosterhout
Martie Middagh
Johannis Dubois
Petrus Tappen
Coenraedt Elmendorph Junr
Abraham Hardenbergh
Gysbert Hend^k Krom
Leonard Hardenbergh
Cornelis New Kerck
Jacob Rutsen Junr
Harma Rosekrans
Philip Dumon
Lucius Elmendorph
Abraham Kiersted
James Scott
William Krom Junr
tot^{ll} 60

ULSTER } *A list of the foot Company of Militia of the Corpora-*
COUNTY } *ration of Kingston Under the Command of*

Capt John Persen
Lievte. Peter Oosterhout
Ensign Edward Whittaker
Sarj^a Aarey Newkerk
Sarj^a Ned Devenport
Sarj^a Jacobus Van Dyck
Corp^o Samuel Nights
Corp^o Nathan Dubois
Corp^o Solomon Freer
Dromer Andries Van Leven

Christian Myre
William Legg
Jacobus Debois Jn^r
Samuel Debois
William Whittaker
Jacobus Whittaker
John Davenport Jn^r
Johanes Schram
Corn^e Longing Dyck
Abr^a Hardenberge

Samuel Wood
Jacobus Roosa
Coenradt Elmendorp
Jacobus Persen
Peter Van Leven
Nemiah Debois
Ricard Davenport
Andris Hoof
Phillip Hoof
Hendricus Oosterhout
Daniel Whittaker
Samuel Davenport
Cornelus Persen
William Myre

Anthony Sleght
John Legg Jn^r
Humphy Devenport
Mosas Youman
Brure Decker
John Decker
Tobias Winekoop
Johanes Humble
Godfrey Woolf Jn^r
Fredrick Row
Michel Planck
Jurian Tappen
Robert Bever
Totall 47

ULSTER COUNTY } *A list of the foot Company of Militia of the Corporation Kinston Under the Command of Capt. Tjrck Van Keuren.*

Capt Tjrck Van Keuren
Lievten^t Abraham Low
Ensign Dirck Winekoop
Serg^t William Swart
Serg^t Tobias Van Bueren
Corp^l Petrus Smedes
Corp^l Ephraim Dubois
Corp^l Marynis Van Aken
Drom^r Corn^l Jansen
Willem Eltinge
Peter Van Aken
Thomas Beekman
Cornelis Van Kueren
Cornelis Sleght
David De Lametter
Evert Bogardus
Nicolas Bogardus
Jan Heermans

Teunis Van Steenbergh
Abr^a Van Steenbergh
Hendrikus Slegh
Johannis Dubois
Abr^a De Lametter
Johan^s Ba : De Witt
Hiskiah Dubois
Evert Winekoop Ju^r
Tobias Van Steenbergh
Jan Van Aken
Johannis Chonsalisduck
Jan Perse Ju^r
Petrus Low
Isaac Van Wagenen
Abr^a Van Kueren
Gerett Freer
Corn^l Perse
Robert Beever

Mooses Jorck

Giedeon Van Aken

Frans Hendrick

Joseph Chonsalisduck

Thimoteos Van Steenbergh

Jacobus De Ioo

Dirck Teerpen

Maas Bloemendal

Jacob Turck

Jacobus Eltinge

Jan Lome

Johannis Felter

Jame Letsin

Peter Vanderline

Petrus Eltinge

Corn^l De Lametter Ju^r

Abr^a Lome Ju^r

Jacobus Van Kueren

Willem Krom

Petrus Van Aken

William Deen

Dirck Van Vleet Ju^r

Benjamin Van Vleet

Johannis Van Vleet—tot^{ll} 60.

ULSTER COUNTY *A List of the foot Company of Militia of the Corporation of Kingston under the Command of*

Capt Tjrck Dewitt

Left Petrus Bogardus

Ins^i Igenas Dumont

Serj^t Jury Snyder

Serj^t William Wells

Serj^t Petrus Viele

Corp^o Lukas Dewitt

Corp^o Peter Dumont

Corp^o Wilhelmus Hoghteling

Clark Jarman Pick

Phillip Viele Ju^r

Sam^{ll} Wells

Corn^e Viele

Corn^e Marston

John Masten

Gerritt Viele

Jacobus Dumond

Benj^a Marten

John Maclene

Antony Hoffman

Hend^r Vankuren

Teunis Ploegh

Zacryas Hoffman Ju^r

Petrus Edmundus Elmendorp

Lenard Hardenbergh

Jacob Hardenbergh

Peter Leebonte

Dirck Shepmoes

Johanes Viele

Gerritt Van Steenbergh

Corn^e Van Kuren Ju^r

Johanis Masten

John Waters

Henry Ellis

Jacob Mauris

Isaac Wheeler

Hump^h Davenport

Peter Burgar

Isaac Dubois

Johan^s Shepmoes

Gerrett Davenport

Art Masten

Coenr^a Vanburen

Albert Beein

Dirck Teerpening
Jacobus Deyoe
Johan[s] Degrave
Corn[e] Vankuren
Jacobus Vanetten
Mattys Merkell
Hendrick Vreligh
Coenrad Rechtmire
Heskia Winekoop
Christan Derick
Fredrick Row
Tobias Winekoop
William Bell
Arie Delonga
Corn[e] Vandenbergh
Johan[s] Hoghteling
Jacob Dubois Ju[r]
Tot[ll] 61.

ULSTER COUNTY *A List of the foot Company of Militia of the Corporation of Kingston under the Command of*

Capt Hendrick H. Schoonmaker
Leut: John Sleght
Insjn Lawrens Van Gaasbeck
Sarj: Edward Wood
Sarj: Dirck Van Vleet
Sarj: Jacobus De Lametter
Corp[o] Teunis Swart
Corp[o] Johanas Snyder
Corp[o] William Oosterhout
Clark Benjamin Sleght
John Ploegh
Peter Winne
Heskiah Schoonmaker
Teunis A. Swar
Aarent Ploegh
John Wittaker
Abr[a] Burhans
Cryn Oosterhout
Jan Peterse Oosterhout
Aares Van Steenbergh
Teunis Oosterhout
Jan Krinse Oosterhout
Hendrick Brinck
Jacob Brinck
Lawrens Swart
Abr[a] Post
Abr[a] Oosterhout
Jan Woolf
Johannis Burhans
Marta Snyder
Zachary Backer
Lawrence Salisbury
Johannis Burhans Jn[r]
Poules Pelen
Bowdewine Vanderlip
Teunis Van Bunschote
Wilhelmus Demyer
Jacobus Van Steenbergh
Hendricus Ploegh Jn[r]
Hend[r] Krynse Oosterhout
Petrus Krynse Oosterhout
Hendricus Ploegh
Abr[a] Davenport
Petrus Oosterhout
Corn[r] Swart
Grieg Magriegere—tot[ll] 46.

ULSTER COUNTY. *A List of the foot Company of Militia of marbletown under the Command of Capt. Daniel Brodhead.*

Capt Daniel Brodhead
Liev^t John Dewitt
Ensign John Brodhead
Serjeant Martin Bogart
Serjeant Jacobus Bush
Serjeant Thomas Keator
Corporal Cornelius Van Kampen
Corporal Christopher Davis
Corporal Jacob Keator
Drummer Seter Vandenbergh
Clerke Ric^d Pick

Lambert Brinck
Johannes Van Luven
Andreas Van Luven
Frederick Davis
Gysb^t Roosa
Jan Roosa
Jacob Keyser
Valentine Smith
Tuenis Klarwater
Johannes Bush
James Robinson
Mathew Algar
James Algar
Hartman Hine
Arien Vandermarke
Jacob Vandermarke
Jacob Middagh
Jacobus Tack
Isaac Tack
Johannes Jansen
Dirck Bush

Melgart Ketor
Thos Vandermark
Augustinus Ketor
Hendrick Roosa
Hend^r Vandermarke
Dirck Keyser
Samuel Davis
Samuel Cock
Benj^a Davis
Alexander Ennis
Andrew Kernith
Isaac Van Kampe
Samuel Mourits
Johan^s Thomas
Moses Cantien
Nicholas Keyser
William Hine
John Wood
Johannes Elting
Anthony Gerrits
Corn^e Tack Jn^r
Henry Jansen
Thos Bush
Fred^r Keator
Hend^r Bush
John Price
Lambert Bush
Moses Depuy
Johan^s Vandermarke
Thom^s Vandermarke
Nicholas Vandermarke
Arie Ketor
Thom^s More

John Krom
Henry Krom Jn[r]
Robert Maginnis
Lewis Bevier
Johanas Kool
Andreas Conterman
Henry Conterman
Adam Hoffman
Hendricus Van Steenburgh
Abr[a] Constapie
Richard Lonsberry
William Ennis

Augu[s] Vandemarke
Ephaim Chambers
Dirck Keyser Jn[r]
Jacob Keyser Jn[r]
Jacob Sleyter
Nicholas Sleyter
Nich[a] Sloyter Jn[r]
Johannes Depuy
Fred[r] Schoomker
Power Easel
Edward Robason
John Smith—tot[ll] 89

A LIST OF THE COMPANY OF MILITIA

OF THE WALL A KILL UNDER THE COMMAND OF CAPT JOHN BYARD

Cap[t] John Byard
Liev[t] William Berland
Ensign William Keils
Serj[t] John Newkerk
Corp[o] John Miller
Lendert Coll
Cornelius Coll
Barnat Coll
John Robeson
James Glispy
Thomas Glispy
John Willkine
William Wilkins
Andraw Graham
George Olloms
John North
John North Ju[r]
Samuel North
James Young
Robert Young

Mathew Young
John Andraws
James M[c]Neill
John M[c]Neill
Andraw borland
John borland
John M[c]Neill Ju[r]
James Craford
John Craford
Alexander Milligan
Nathaneill Hill
Alix[d] kid
Archabald Hunter
James Hunter
John Wharrey
Benj[a] Hins
John M[c] Neill Senior
Mathew Prea
William Craford
Robert hunter

James Munall
Gors Monull
John Munall
William Monall
Thomas Neils
Robert Neils
John Neils
Mathew Neils
Nathaneill jojter
John Neily Ju^r
Joseph butteltown
Thomas Colman
Joseph Shaw
pathrick broodrick
William Soutter
John butfield
John M^{c}ve
John Jones
Joseph knap
Isakiah Gaill
Celab knep
Robert McCord
William fallkne
Ezrail Rodgr
Jaremiah Rodgr
James Rodgr
James Whit
John Manly
francius walls
Robert Hughy
Robert banhanan
James Egar
Thomas McCollom
Sojornars Her
John Haves
M kam Clein
Jury burger

Hugh flenign
Benj^a benot
Patrick M^c peick
John Eldoris
Patrick Galasby
John Lowry
Samuel mith
Jopth Teall
James Craford
Joseph Sutter
David Cree
Edward Andrews
Samuel Crayford
Endrew Doell
Phillip Milsbugh
Cronamas Mingus
Stuffel Moll
Hannas Crane
John Yong
Hendrick Newkerk
Frederick Sanzabus
Cornelius walls
Hendrick Crist
Hunas Crist
Lowrance Crist
Mattys Milsbigh
and his son
John Mings
Stevanis Crist
Jacob bush
Cronamas falter
Richard Gatehouse
John boyls
Richard boyls
John Jameson
John McDonall
James Davis—tot^{ll} 114

ULSTER } *A list of the foot Company of Militia of hurly under*
COUNTY }   *the Command of Capt. Cornelis Wine Coop.*

Capt Cornelis Wine Coop
Lef^t Antonie Crispel
Insin Abraham Ten Eyck
Serj^e Hendrick Konstaple
Corp^l Solomon ter Willege
Corp^l Jacob Vanwagene
Drom^r Marynis Chambers
Jan Van Duese Clarke

Nicolas Blansjan
Lambert Brinck
Tuenis Oostrander
Jan Roosa
Hendrick Oostrander
Gerret Konstapel
Johannis Crispel
Johannis Suylandt
Arie Van Etten
Harmanus Oostrander
Antonie Crispel Ju^r
Johan^s Konstaple
Andries Van Vliet
Heyman Roosa
Jan A Roosa
Gysbert Roosa Ju^r
Jan Crispel Ju^r
Dirck Roosa
Gerret Je^o Freer
Ned Wieler
Edvart Chammers
Daniel potter

Robert Wieler
Wouter Sluyter
Evert Sluyter
Willem Smit
Gerret Van Wagenen
Johan^s Van Wagenen
Aert Van Wagenen
Matys Blansyan Ju^r
Simon Helm
Adam Sjeever
Jefta De Lange
Chrisstoffel Brosie
Mattheus Nieukerck
Benj^a Nieukerck
Petrus Crispel
Jan Ja : Roosa
Abr^a Roosa
Nicolas Roosa
Benj^a Claerwater
Jan ter Willege Ju^r
Jan Van Deuse Ju^r
Jan Brinck
Johannis Oostrander Ju^r
Willem Sluyter Ju^r
Hendrick Ja : Freer
Jan Waters
Albert Ja : Roosa
Willem Burhans
Jacop Clyn
Jacop Oostrander
            Tot^{ll} 60.

ULSTER } *A list of the foot Company of Militia of Rocester*
COUNTY } *under the Command of Capt. Cornelius Hoornbeck.*

Cäpt Cornelius Hoornbeck
Lieut phillip Dubois
Ensign Cornelius B : Low
Serja Johannis Hoornbeck
Serja John Wesbroeck
Serja Harmanis Rosekrans
Corpo Samuel Swarthout
Corpo Tuenis Middagh
Corpo Manuel Gonsalis

Arien Van Vliet
John Schoonmaker
Benja van wagenen
John Robeson
John Hillmen
Frans Kelder
Jacob Kelder
William Kelder
Felter Kelder
Jacobus Quick
Jacobus Depue
Joha Hendreickson
Joha Krom
Hendrick Krom
Daniel Schoonmaker
Jocham Fra : Schoonmaker
Johannis Miller
Josaphat Dubois
Jacob Vernoy
Tuenis Oosterhout Jur
Kryn Oosterhout
Nicholas Ketor
Petrus Oosterhout
Hende Oosterhout

Jonathan Westbroeck
Johannis Westbroeck
Matheus Terwillige
Nicklas Low
Abra Low
Cornelius Low
Jacobus Low
Johannis Oosterhout
Jeremia Van Dermerke
Jacob Dewitt Jur
John Dewitt
Cornelius Winekoop
Jacobus Terwillige
John Terwillige
Benja Hoornbeck
Dirck Hoornbeck
Peter Westbroeck
Tobias Hoornbeek
Jacobus Hoornbeck
Lowrence Cortreght
Mathew Cortreght
Peter Cortreght
Hendrick Cortreght
Johannis Ketor
Isaac Van Aken
Charles Danneson
Richard Kittle
Benja Roggers
Wessel Vernoy
Coenradt Vernoy
Michel Helm
Petrus Low
Lawies Bovier Jur
Cornelius Bovier

Samuel Bovier Ju^r
Jacob Bovier
Manuel Gonsalis Ju^r
Jacob Middagh
Abr^a Middagh
Isaac Middagh
Johannis Middagh

Janies Simson
Jacob Vandermarke
Geradus Van Inwegen
Benj^a Coddebeck
William Coddebeck
Abr^a Coddebeck
Peter Jemare—totall 81.

ULSTER } *A list of the foot Company of Militia of the Pals*
COUNTY }   *under the Command of Capt. Zacharias Hoffman.*

Capt Zacharias Hoffman
Liev^t Benjamin Smedes Ju^r
Ensign Zacharias Hoffman Ju^r
Serj^s John teer penning
Serj^s John Freer
Serj^s Evert Terwillege
Corp^o Christian Dujo
Corp^o Hendrick Dujo
Corp^o Isaac Lefever
Isaac freer
Tuenis Terpening
Jan Une
Jonas freer
James Agmodi
Simon Lefever
Petrus Low
Johannis Low
Josia Elting
Abr^a Dujo
Cornelius Dubois
Jonathan Dubois
Hend^r Dubois
Mosis Dujo
August^e Van Dermerke
Jacob Ge: Decker
James Pinnick

Daniel Winfiel
Manewel ter Willige
Johannes Terwilige
Hendrick Decker
Petrus Terwillige
Thom^s Janson Ju^r
William Rosekrans
Josua Smedes
Gerett Ja: Decker
Stevanis Swart
John Robertse
Andrew Grames
Rober Greams
John Blake
James Jonston
Salamon Isrel
Samuel Sampson
Roger blamles
Richard Davis
Lawrence Eldorp
Tomas Maccoun
John Andrew
Arie Terwillege
William Schoot
Cornelius bruyn
William Ja: Decker

Jacob Ja: Decker
Abrᵃ Ja: Decker
Isaac Ja: Decker
Benjᵃ Ja: Decker
Jacob He: Decker
Abrᵃ He: Decker
Abrᵃ Terwillige
Isaac Terwillige
Evert Terwillige Juʳ
Cornˢ Schoonmaker Juʳ
Cornˢ Cool
Johannis Cool
Lowis Pontenere
John Gream
William Weller
Hendrick Weller
Isaac Haasbroeck
Jacob Haasbroeck Ju
Benjᵃ Haasbroock Juʳ
Zacharias klarwater
Abrᵃ Bovier

Mathues Bovier
Jacobus Bovier
Isaac Bovier
Abrᵃ Lefever
Nathael Lefever
Benjᵃ Haasbroeck
Symon Dubois
Isaac Lefever Juʳ
Peter De: jo
Huge Freer Juʳ
Hendrick Van Wijak
Abrᵃ Vandermerke
Lewis Sa: Bovier
William Armstrong
Robert Jong
Mathew Jong
Robert Cain
Robert Hanne
John Magdonel
John Jemson
Johannes Masseker—totˡˡ 94

———

ULSTER COUNTY } *A list of the foot Company of Militia of the present of the Higland Under the Command of Capt. Thos. Ellison.*

Capᵗ Thomas Ellison
Lievᵗ George Harrison
Ensign John Young
Serjent David Davis
Serjent Patrick McCloghry
Serjent Mosas Garitson
Corpᵒ Jacobus Bruyn Jnʳ
Corpᵒ James Stringham
Corpᵒ Jonathan Hazzard
Clark Charles Clinton
John Umphrey

Jame Gamble
John Gamble
Cornelius McClean
John Umphry Jnᵗ
James Umphry
Peter Mulinder
Robert Burnet
Archibald Beaty
Arthar Beaty
David Olliver
Mathew Davis

Alexander. Falls
David Bedford
William Coleman
Joseph Sweezer
Thomas Coleman
John McVey
John Jones
Patrick Broderick
Joseph Shaw
Calab Curtis
William Sutten
Jeremiah Foster
Charles Beaty
Amas Foster
Alexander Denniston
James Young
James Nealy
Robert Feef
Joseph Butterton
Samuell Luekey
John Markham
John Read
Jeseph McMikhill
David Umphrey
Johannis George
Jeremiah Tomkins
Isaac Tomkins
William Watts
Josiah Elsworth
James Elsworth
Anthony Preslaer
Jonathan Tomkins

John Nicoll Jnr
Alexander McKey
Robert Sparks
Jevriah Quick
Thomas Quick
Jacob Gillis
Joseph Simson
James Clark
John Clark
Lodewick Miller
Peter Miller
George Waygant
William Ward
William Ward Jnr
John Mattys Kimbergh
William Smith Jnr
James Edmeston
Tobias Waygate
Jerry Mause
Thomas Johnston
Casparis Stymas
John Monger
James Luekey
Thomas Williams
Robert Banker
Thomas Fear
Frederick Painter
Mosas Elsworth
John Marie
Jonathan Owens
Andrew McDowell
Daniel Coleman—Tot. 86

LIST OF OFFICERS

CIVIL AND MILITARY FOR RICHMOND COUNTY.

Judges of the Court of Common Pleas.

John Le Conte *Judge*
Christian Corsen *Second Judge*
Gozen Adrianz *Third Judge*

Justices of the Peace.

* Nicholas Britton
* Richard Stilwell
* Joseph Bedell
* John Veghte
* Rem Vander Beek
* John La Tourrette
* Thomas Billopp
Corneillius Corsen
Joshua Mersereau
Abraham Cole
Barent Martling
Those marked thus (*) are of the Quorum.

Nicholas Larzelere *Sheriff*
John Hillyer *Coroner*
Daniel Corsen *Clarke*

Military Officers.

Jacob Corsen Colonel
Christian Corsen Lieut. Col
Thomas Billopp Major

For the North Division.

John Veghte Captain
Frederick Berge Lieut^t
Jacob Corsen Jn^r Ensign

For the S'th Division.

Corneillius Stouthoff Capt
Jacob Berge Lieutenant
Aris Rvertse Ensign

For the West Division.

Nathaniel Britten Capt
Matthias Johnson Lieut^t
Abraham Maney Ensign

For the Troop.

Peter Perrin Captain
Gerrett Crosse Lieut
Wynant Wynants Cornet
Daniel Wynants Quarter Master

A LIST OF THE HEADS OF THE FAMILIES

IN THE SEVERAL TOWNS HEREAFTER MENTIONED IN THE COUNTY
OF GLOUCESTER, 1771.

NEWBURY
Robert Johnston
Err Chamberlin
Thos Chamberlin
Danl Tillotson
Jacob Bayley
David Weeks
Jonathan Fowler
Ephraim Bayley
Peter Powers
Thomas Johnson
Samuel Hale
Ephraim Spafford
Moses Thursten
Frye Bayley
Gideon Smith
Elisha Johnson
Uriah Chamberlin
John Foremon
Abial Chamberlin
Venice Heath
Nathaniel Chamberlin
Stephen McConnall
Saml Barnett
Hagness Johnson
Jonathan Butterfield
Jon'n Goodwin
John Mills
John Hasletine
Joseph White
Jacob Kent
Robt Hunkins
Ebenezer White
Simeon Stephens
Ezekial Colboy
Abner Fowler
Abner Fowler Junr
John Nutting
Levy Sylvester
Nehemiah Lovewell
Josh: Chamberlin
Richd Chamberlin
Enoch Hall
Danl Hall

John Taplin Junr
Robt Hasletine
Jacob Fowler

MOORE TOWN.
Robt Kennady
James Horner
David Thompson
William Thompson
William Bell
Ebenezer Martin
John Martin
Obededam Saunders
Noah White
Ephraim Martin
Nathl Martin
John Peters
Saml Miller
James Miller
Matthew Miller
James Aikin
Jesse McFarlin
Saml Galt
Saml McDuffie
Hezikiah Sillaway
Amos Davis
Benj Jenkins
Ephraim Collins
Hugh Miller
John Sawyer
Benoni Wright
Widdow Hannah Sleeper
Samuel Davis

BARNETT, RYEGATE LUN-
ENBURGH & GUILDHALL.
Aaron Hosmir
Jacob Hall
Elijah Hall
Uriah Moss
Ruben Powers
Timothy Nash
Ebenezer Richardson
John Sawyer

Enoch Hall

THETFORD
Samuel Gillett
Jonn Howard
Noah Sweetlon
John Colson
Joseph Downer
Joseph Horseford
Benj Colborn
Raben Strong
John Strong
William Moore
Israel Smith
Saml Wise
Saml Osborne
Ebenezer Green
Abner Chamberlin
David Chamberlin
Elijah Howard
Edwd Howard
Thos Chumley.
Bnj. Chamberlin
Timothy Bartholomew
Jon: Sumney
Abner Howard
Peter Grant
Edwd Howard Junr
John Chamberlin
Richd Baxter
Amos Chamberlin
Elihu Horseford

STAFFORD.
James Pinnock
Wm Chamberlin
Wm Pinnock
Ezekiel Parish
Isaac Baldwin
Danl West
Aaron Pinnock
Saml Pinnock
Jesse Pinnock

LIST OF VERMONT SUFFERERS

WHO OBTAINED LAND IN THE TOWNSHIP OF CLINTON,
(NOW BAINBRIDGE) CHENANGO COUNTY N. Y.

Persons Deemed by the Commissioners of the Land Office,
Sufferers in Opposing the Government of the pretended State of
Vermont with the proportion of Land adjudged to each set

Opposite to their respective names together with the Number of the Lots Ballotted to them respectively by the Secretary in the presence of the Board.

[From Land Papers endorsed Petitions of Vermont Sufferers]

	Names	Acres	
6	Timothy Church	3840	N°. 47.35.60.90.71.84
5	William Shattuck	3200	N°. 36.53.65.82.78
2	Francis Prouty	1180 }	for Prouty N°. 52
	Isaac Kendell	100 }	for do & Kendell N°. 86
1	William White	640	N°. 83
1	Joseph Peck	640	N°. 68
1	Daniel Ashcroft	640	N°. 88
	Thos. Baker	260 }	N°. 81
1	Saml. Bixby	380 }	
	Hezekiah Stowell	840 }	for Stowell No. 37
2	Orlanda Bridgman	260 }	for do. Bridgm & Clark N°.73
	Samuel Clark	180 }	
	Ephraim Knapp	100 }	
	Artems. How	200 }	N°. 58
1	David How	170 }	
	Reuben Smith	170 }	
	Samuel Meldy	420 }	N°. 98
1	Jonath. S. Alexander	220 }	
	James Davidson	500 }	N°. 39
1	James Wallace	140 }	
	David Lamb	300 }	
1	Jacob Stoddard	170 }	N°. 89
	Samuel Earl	170 }	
	Elisha Pierce	200 }	
1	Eleazer Church	260 }	N°. 97
	R B Church	180 }	
	Joseph Chamberlin	380 }	N°. 66
1	Oliver Teal	260 }	
	John Adams	160 }	
	Charles Packer	160 }	N°. 64
1	Jonathan Stoddard jun	160 }	
	Benjamin Ballow	160 }	
	Joseph Wells	360 }	N°. 38
1	Asa Packer	280 }	
	Caleb Nurse	240 }	
1	David Thurber junr.	200 }	N°. 94
	Jonath. Stoddard	200 }	
	Amos Yeaw	210 }	
1	Eleazer Tobe	210 }	N°. 92
	David Culver	220 }	
	Josiah Price	200 }	
1	Newel Earl	200 }	N°. 55
	Joseph Coleman	240 }	
1	David Thurber	640	N°. 40
	David Thurber	200 }	
1	Asa Stowell	220 }	N°. 56
	Edmund Beamos	200 }	
	Abraham Avery	430 }	N°. 87
1	William Gault	210 }	
	Seth Clark	160 }	
1	John Alden	160 }	N°. 48
	James Packer	320 }	
3	Henry Evens	1920	N°. 73.79.80
	John Alexander	280 }	
1	Isaac Crosby	180 }	N°. 77
	Reuben Church	180 }	

	Names	Acres	
	Noah Shepherdson	90	
1	Joel Bigelow	350	N°. 74
	Joshua Nurse	200	
	Nathl. Carpenter	280	
1	Samuel Colefax	180	N°. 96
	Jothan Bigelow	180	
	Charles Phelps	508	
1	Nathan Avery	132	N°. 42
	Timothy Phelps	280	
1	Samuel Cutworth	180	N°. 70
	John Burrows	180	
	Daniel Shepherdson	280	
1	Moses Yeaw	180	N°. 95
	Israel Field	180	
	Elijah Prouty	465	
1	Jonathan Dunkly	175	N°. 44
	Hezekiah Broad	350	
	Benjan Baker	97	
1	Ephraim Rice	97	N°. 100
	Joseph Garsey	96	
	Joseph Shepherdson	263	
1	Jonathan Church	217	N°. 67
	John Collins	160	
	Samuel Noble	214	
1	Thos. Whipple	214	N°. 91
	Adonijah Putnam	212	
	Icabod Parker	214	
1	Amos York junr	214	N°. 62
	Nathan Culver	212	
	Elisha Clark	100	
	Caleb Ellis	180	
	Elijah Curtis	180	N°. 93
	Isaac Slatter	180	
	Daniel Whitney	180	
	Artemus Goodenough	180	
1	Joseph Whipple	180	N°. 57
	Dean Chace	100	
	John Gault	280	
1	Hal Salsbury	180	N°. 59
	Samuel Curtis	180	
	Aseph Carpenter	350	
	Matthew Ellis	97	
1	Asa Clark	97	N°. 69
	Ithamer Goodenough	96	
	Cyrryl Carpenter	220	
	Henry Evens	100	
1	Paul Nicolls	140	N°. 41
	Daniel Wilkins	90	
	Shabal Bullock	90	
	David Goodenough	340	
	Edward Carpenter	300	N°. 49

Lots not drawn N°· 43.45.46.54.61.72.75.76.85.99.

Philip Frisbee	Samuel Frisbee	Philip Frisbee junr
Ephraim Guthrie	Eben Landers,	Seth Stone
Goold Bacon	Heman Stone	Nathl Benton jr.
Joseph Landers	Roderick Moore	and their Associates.

By Act of the 20th March 1788 are to have grants for the Lots N° 45 & 61 in Clinton Township on their applying for the same.

The following persons also had grants, viz :—Isaac Crosby ; Israel Smith ; Henry Morgan ; Col. Seth Smith—780 acres ; James Comins, William Pierce, Francis Comins, James Cummins Junr. 500 acres.   Obadiah Wells, Capt Joseph Elliot 450a. ; Joshua Lindes, Samuel Lindes, Judathan Roberts, Giles Roberts, John Sherburn, Ensign Rutherford Hays, Amariah Parks, Zephaniah Shepardson.

SETTLEMENT OF THE VERMONT DIFFICULTIES.

" To facilitate this business and to get Vermont into the Union the Legislature of the State of New York passed a law in the year one thousand seven hundred and ninety appointing Commissiners on the part of the State of New York to settle a boundary Line with the Commissioners appointed on the part of Vermont.

That the Commissioners on both sides met in the City of New York in the month of October of that year, when a Treaty was entered into and executed by the New York Commissioners whereby they ceded to the state of Vermont all the lands together with the Islands in Lake Champlain Lying to the Eastward of the following bounds to witt, Beginning at the North west corner of the State of Massachusetts thence westward along the south boundary of the township of Pownall to the southwest corner thereof thence northerly along the western boundaries of the Township of Pownall Bennington Shaftsbury Arlington Sandgate Rupert Pawlet Wells and Poultney as the said Townships are now held or possessed to the river commonly called Poultney River thence down the same through the middle of the deepest Channel of East Bay and the waters thereof to where the same communicate with Lake Champlain thence through the middle of the deepest channel of Lake Champlain to the Eastward of the Islands called the Four Brothers and the westward of the Islands called Grand Isle and Long Isle or the two Heroes and to the westward of the Isle La Motte to the forty fifth degree of North Latitude in the consideration of Vermont paying to the State of New York Thirty Thousand dollars within a time therein limited which sum of Thirty thousand dollars it is matter of notoriety bears no proportion to the value of private property so ceded."—*Petition of Theophylack Bache & others.*

DIVISION OF THE $30,000.

Names of the Claimants, who are entitled to compensation with the sums (in the third column) to which they are respec tively entitled.　April 23, 1799.

[Minutes of the Comrs. on Vermont Claims.]

Numbers of the several claims	Names of Claimants	Sums to which each of the Claimants in the 2d column is entitled.
		Dollars Cents
Number 1.	Samuel Avery	2655　03
2.	James Abcel	548　93
3.	Goldsbrow Banyar	7218　94
4.	John Bowles	745　26
5.	Catharine Bowles	49　91
6.	James Beeckman	72　56
7.	William Banyar	309　42
8.	Thomas B. Bridgen	162　65
9.	Samuel Bard	149　72
10.	Robert Bowne	49　91
11.	William Cockburne	1495　95
12.	Ebenezer Clark	37　42
13.	James McCarra	24　93
14.	Alexander Cruikshank	37　00
15.	Cadwallader Colden, Thomas Colden, Alexander Colden and Josiah Ogden Hoffman surviving Executors of Cadwallader Colden deceased	449　15
16.	Richard Carey and Ann his Wife	122　92
17.	Henry Cruger	149　72
18.	Thomas Clark	237　05
19.	Archibald Campbell	49　91
20.	Archibald Currie	9　98
21.	William McDougall	37　42
22.	James Chatham Duane, William North and Mary his Wife, Sarah Duane, Catharine Livingston Duane and Adelia Duane.	2621　29
23.	Gerardus Duycking junior	49　91
24.	John De Lancey	49　91
25.	Obadiah Dickenson	49　91
26.	Alexander McDougall	34　93
27.	George Etherington	98　32
28.	Thomas Etherington	74　11
29.	James Farquhar	99　81
30.	Jellis. A. Fonda	49　90
31.	John Galbreath	99　81
32.	James Guthrie	37　42
33.	William Giles	5　49
34.	Joseph Griswold	147　73
35.	John Goodrich	199　63
36.	Charles Hutchins	9　98
37.	Jonathan Hunt	948　23
38.	John Hensdale	49　91
39.	John Johnston	124　77
40.	Luke Knowlton	249　53
41.	Peter Kemble	199　63
42.	Abraham Lot	698　69
43.	John Lawrence	49　91
44.	Robert Lewis	119　78
45.	Joel Lyman	49　91

Numbers of the several claims	Names of Claimants	Sums to which each of the Claimants in the 2d column are entitled. Dollars Cents
46.	Elijah Lyman	49 91
47.	Catherine Metcalf Executrix of Simon Metcalf deceased	1417 47
48.	Catharine Metcalf	99 81
49,	Thomas Norman & Elizabeth Martha his wife	718 60
50.	Jane Nesbit	12 48
51.	Elias Nixon	24 95
52.	Barbara Ortley	134 75
53.	Eleazar Porter	49 91
54.	John McPherson	99 81
55.	Isaac Rosevelt	399 25
56.	Peter Sim	37 42
57.	Samuel Stevens	653 63
58.	William Smith	1181 69
59.	Jacob Shefflin	97 32
60.	Francis Stevens	199 63
61.	Diana Smith	49 91
62.	Mary, Elizabeth, Esther and Rachel Schlatter Surviving Executors of Michael Schlatter deceased.	99 81
63.	John M. Scott	49 91
64.	John Titts	9 98
65.	Samuel Thatcher	149 71
66.	Peter Van Schaack	199 63
67.	William Wickham	149 72
68.	Brooke Watson	1197 76
69.	Gerard Walton	49 91
70.	John Watts	99 82
71.	William Walton	199 63
72.	George Wray	39 92
73.	Staltham Williams	199 63
74.	John Bard	449 15
75.	John Plenderleaf	1096 68
76.	Samuel Partridge	49 91

Total   -   -   -   30,000 Dolr.

*** Whoever is disposed to investigate this subject further, can consult with advantage the following works. They are in the State Library.

A State of the Right of the Colony of New York with respect to its eastern boundary on Connecticut river; so far as concerns the late encroachments under the Government of New Hampshire.

[This paper was principally drawn up by Hon. James Duane, who purchased soldiers rights and claims in the above district, to the amount (according to John Adams) of $100,000. It was agreed to by the New York Provincial Assembly on the 8th March 1773, and ordered to be sent to England.]

Narrative of the Proceedings subsequent to the Royal Adjudication concerning the Lands to the Westward of Connecticut River, lately usurped by New Hampshire, with remarks on the claim, behaviour and misrepresentation of the Intruders under that Government. New York; printed by John Holt, 1773. With an Appendix.

A Brief Narrative of the proceedings of the Government of New York relative to their obtaining the jurisdiction of that large District of Land to the westward from Connecticut River, which antecedent thereto had been patented by his Majesty's Gov. and Council of the Government of New Hampshire. And also, of the Monopolizing conduct of the Government of New York, in their subsequently patenting part of the same land, and oppressing the Grantees and Settlers under New Hampshire, Together with arguments demonstrating that the property of those Lands was conveyed from the Crown to the New Hampshire Grantees, by virtue of their respective Charters; with Remarks on a Pamphlet entitled, " A state of the Right of the Colony of New York," &c. By Ethan Allen, Bennington 23d September, 1774. Hartford, printed by Eben. Watson, near the Great Bridge.

A Public Defence of the right of the New Hampshire Grants (so called) on both sides Connecticut River to associate together, and form themselves into an Independent State, containing remarks on sundry paragraphs of Letters from the President of the Council of New Hampshire, to His Excellency Governor Chittenden, and the New Hampshire Delegates at Congress. Dresden: printed by Alden Spooner, 1779.

A Concise Refutation of the Claims of New Hampshire and Massachusetts Bay to the Territory of Vermont; with Occasional Remarks on the long disputed claim of New York to the same. Written by Ethan Allen and Jonas Fay Esqrs. and published by Order of the Governor and Council of Vermont. Bennington, the first day of January, 1780. Hartford, printed by Hudson and Goodwin.

The Present State of the Controversy between the States of New York and New Hampshire on the one part, and the State of Vermont on the other. Hartford: printed by Hudson & Goodwin, 1782.

Vermont State Papers, Records and Documents relative to the Assumption and Establishment of a Government by the People of Vermont; the Journal of the Council of Safety; the first Constitution &c. compiled by William Slade, Secretary of State. Middlebury, 1823.

ALSO:

The Evidence and arguments in support of the Territorial rights and Jurisdiction of the State of New York against New Hampshire as a Government; against the Claimants under it; both in respect to the right of Soil and an Independent Jurisdiction; and against the Claims of the Commonwealth of Massachusetts; stated by JAMES DUANE, one of the Agents and Commissioners appointed by acts of the Legislature of the State of New York to manage those important controversies.

[This is a MS. vol. of 189 pp. It is to be found in the Library of the New York Historical Society.]

Memoirs of Thomas Chittenden, first Governor of Vermont, with a history of the constitution during his administration. By Daniel Chipman, 1849.

Memoirs of Seth Warner, By the same. Also the several Histories of New York, New Hampshire and Vermont.

NOTE.—All the Documents regarding the controversy with New Hampshire and Vermont published in this Vol. are from the Records and MSS. in the Secretary of State's office, Albany, N. Y., except when otherwise noted.

INDEX

Croeck/Croocke/Crock,
  Cattrienna 197
  Cherls 199
  John 196
Croes/Croos/Crosse/
  Crussen, Conraet 168
  Garret/Gerrit/Gerrett
  101,219,287
Croft, John Woollton 135
Croleus, Wilm. 270
Crom/Croom/Crooem/Crum
  (see Krom)
Cromlin, ____ (Mr) 24
Crook, John (Jr) 223
  Joseph 49
  Robt. 268
  Samuel 49,248
  Sussannah 49
Crooker, Robert 216
  William 216
Crosby, Isaac 290,292
Crosson, Ely 54
Crow, Hugh 34
Cruger, Henry 209,294
Cruikshank, Alexander 294
Cruse, Cornelius 219
  Henry 219
Cuinst, Barrant 3
Culver, David 43,290
  Gersham/Gershem/
  Gershum 43,157,250
  Jeremiah/Jerimiah 43,
  250
  Jonathan 43
  Mary 45
  Mary (Jr) 45
  Moses 43
  Nathan 291
  Nahum 43
Cummins/Comins, Francis
  292
  James 292
  James (Jr) 292
Cup, Jacob 193
Cure, John 31,270
  Robbert 270
Curry/Currie, Archibald
  294
  Richard 221
Curtis/Curtjes, Caleb/
  Calab/Calob 49,67,156,
  286
  Elijah 291
  Eliza 49
  Hannah 49
  Joshua 49,248
  Mary 49
  Richard 49
  Samuel 49,291
  Sarah 49
Cutworth, Samuel 291
Cuyck, Peter Jansen 169
Cuyler/Cuylar/Coyler,
  ____ (Mrs) 33
  Abrahm./Abram./Abra.
  12,18,60
  Henry 54,268,273,274
  Johannes/Johannis 18,56
Cuyper, Cornelis Claessen
  58
  Henry 256

        -D-

Dachstader, George 193
Dain/Daines, John 51,201
Dais, Johanna 221
  Judy 221
  Mary 221
  Peter 221
  Sussanna 221
Daivedes, Andreis 16
Dakin, Timothy 228
Dales, John Wm. 193
Damen, Jan 37
  Jan Cornelis/Jan
  Cornelise/Jan
  Cornelisse 104,118,
  123,176
Danemark/Daunermarker,
  Anna Margt. 185
  Cath. Eliz. 185
  Christina 185
  Christopher 185
Danfard, William 79
Daniel/Danielse/Daniell/
  Daniels/Danilse,
  Arent 19
  Daniell 19
  Jan 19
  Peter/Pieter 19,38
  Phillips 188
  Simon 21
  Thomas 36, 145
Danneson, Charles 283
Danswick, William. 1
Danton,Daniel 55
Darkins, Robt. 30
Daucie/Dauice, Ebine 156
  John 150
  Richard 150
Dauly, Nicholas 23
Dausweber, Anna Maria 186
  Maria Christina 186
  Melchior 186
Davenport/Devenport/
  Davinport/Davenpoort/
  Devenpoort, ____ (Mr) 26
  Abra. 278
  Gerrett 277
  Humphrey/Humphy/Humph.
  59,276,277
  John 224
  John (Jr) 275
  Nathaniel/Ned 223,275
  Richard/Ricard 199,203,
  276
  Samuel 203,276
  Thomas 255
David, John 3
  Joshuah 24
Davidson/Davidsen,
  David 171
  James 290
Davidts, William 117
Davie/Davi, James 260
  John 24
Davis/Daves/Davies/Dauis/
  Davess, Abiell 43
  Agnes 31
  Amos 288
  Anthony 32
  Arther 43
  Balhariah 43
  Beniamin/Benja./Ben.
  157,252,279
  Christopher 279
  Daniel/Daniell 43,252
  David 197,285
  Eldad 43
  Elizabeth 45
  Euan 50

Davis (cont)
  Frederick/Fredrick/
  Fredk. 200,225,279
  Fulke 140
  James 281
  John 34,43,88,149,156,
  218,225,270
  John (Jr) 43
  Joseph 89,153,252
  Mahitable 45
  Martha 45
  Mary 45,50
  Mathew 285
  Philip 36
  Richard 284
  Samuel/Samuell 141,252,
  279,288
  Sylvenus 249
  Tho. 138
  Willem 39
Davorson, Ellixander 212
Dawes, Elias 131
Dayton/Daiton, Abra./Abr.
  89,153
  Henry 252
  Hezekiah 252
  Jacob 162
  Jonathan 251
  Narthan 250
  Nathaniel 252
  Ralph 154
  Robert 61,161
  Saml./Samll. 88,153
Deane/Deen/Deine,
  John/Jno. 141,188
  Jonathan 139
  Sam (Jr) 141
  Sam (Sr) 141
  William 260,277
De Bane/Debaene, Joost/
  Joos 38,177
D'Beauvois/D'Beavois/
  De Bevoice/De Bevoyce/
  Debavois/Beauvois/
  Beavois, Charles 181
  George 208
  Jacob/Jacobus/Jacobis
  37,175,181,208,209,245
  Johanis 209
  John 214
  Joost/Joust 181,209,245
  Sam. 208
D'Boise, Walter 31
De Boogh, Gerret 27
  Isaac 30
Debross, James 24
Debrouts, ____ (Capt) 26
De Bruyn/De Browne,
  Albert Adriaense 173
  Huybert 164
  John 54
  Jon. Henry/Jan Hendrix
  9,60
De Camp, Laurens Janse 38
Deceer, John 219
De Chousoy, Marcus 163
Decker/Deccar, Abra. Ja.
  285
  Abra. He. 285
  Benja. Ja. 285
  Broer 20
  Bruce 276
  Corn. 11
  Gerritt Jansa/Gerrett
  Ja. 2,284
  Hendrick/Hendrik 225,
  284
  Isaac 197

De Witt (cont)
  John/Johns 2,224,269,
    274,279,283
  Lukas 277
  Peck/Peak/Peek 17,199,
    224
  Peter 199
  Pieter Janse 38
  Terrick Claes 4
  Tjerik/Tjrck/Tierck
    197,223,277
  Tjerik (Jr) 225
De Yeo/Deyeo/De Ioo (see
  also Du Jou),
  Jacobus 255,277,278
Dezbrough,Hendrick 143
D'Fries, Ariantje 15
  John. 15
D'Henuar, Samuel 252
Diamond, Thomas 45
Dicken, Evert 25
Dickenson/Dickinson/
  Dickonson/Dikensen,
  Amos 252
  Henry 215
  James 251
  John 251,249
  Joseph 148
  Obadiah 294
  Robert 207
  Samuel 149
  Townsend 215
Dickerson, John 48
  Mary 48
  Mary (Jr) 48
  Naomy 48
  Peter 48
  Philemon 48
  Thomas 48
Dickeson/Dicisson,
  Petter/Peeter 73,155
  Thomas 155
Dickre, William 263
Dickter, Jo. 28
Diebel, Peter 192
Dientzer, Paulus 193
Diesvelt, Peter Arentsen
  165
Dietrich/Deitrich, ____
  192
  Anna Eliz. 184
  Anna Gertrude 184
Dill, Jno. Wm. 194
Dilleback, Martin 193
Dimouth, Jacob 192
Dinell, Isaac 25
Dingee, Robert 146
Dingmans, Gerrit 20
Dings, Jacob 194
Dircksen/Dircks/Dirckse/
  Dirckx/Dirksen/Dierckse/
  Dirxsz, Anthony 170
  Egbertje 167
  Evert/Evertje 167,172
  Feytje 164
  Gysbert 168
  Harmen 164
  Jacob/Jabecq 103,114
  Jan 165
  Paulus/Poulus 38,99,119
  Peckle 170
  Roelof 165
  Stoffel 39
  Sweris 165
  Ursel 163
  Volkert/Volckert 38,
    102,114
Disbrow/Disbro, Anne 206

Disbrow (cont)
  Hanah 205
Ditmars/Ditmarss/
  Ditmarse/Detmas,
  Douwe 210
  Johannis/Johannes 181,
    209
  John 210,237
  Joseph 242
  Laurens/Lawrence/
    Larance 181,209,237
D'Lanoy, Peter 55
D'Le Fountaine, Jno. 31
D'Markeys, Isaac 33
Do, Conradus 32
  Peter 32
Dobbs/Dubs, Adam 271
  John 270
  William 271
Dobson, Thomas 228
Doell, Endrew 281
Dohneare, Johanes 24
Dolderbrinck, Lambert
  224
  Roelof 224
Doley, Phill. 31
Dollson, Isaac 255
  Johannis 255
Dolsie, ...ies 32
Dolstan, Margaret 175
Domskon, Danl. 27
Donceny, Nath. 159
Dondij, William 196
Dongan, Thomas 218
Doorn, Artt Martenson 3
Dopff, Jno. Beter 193
Dorijie, Abraham 248
  Charel 247
  Joost 247
  Symon 247
Dorlandt/Dorlant/
  Dorland/Dortlant/
  Dorelant/Dorlon/
  Durland/Durlun,
  Elias/Ellias 146,213,
    258
  Elias (Jr) 213
  Elias (Ter) 213
  Gerret/Gerrit/Garret
    37,38,180,241
  Jan Gerritse/Jan
    Gerrise/Jan Ger(r?)itz
    38,121,176
  John 246
  Lambert Jansen/Lammert
    Jansen 96,172
Dorner, Anna Margaretta
  187
  Johannes 187
Dorrony, Natha. 62
Dose, William 36
Dosson, Charls 262
Doughty/Doty/Douty/Dotty,
  Benjamin/Benj. 40,229
  Charles/Charely 40,41
  Elias/Elyas/Alias 40,
    41,79,136
  Elijah 227
  Elizabeth/Elizabth/
    Eliz. 41
  Francis 40
  Isaac/Isack 149,215,
    230
  John 41
  Joseph 226,262
  Mary 40
  Obadiah 40
  Palmer 40

Doughty (cont)
  Robert 229
  Sarah 40,41
  Thomas 41
  William 40,223
Douw/Douwe/Dow,
  Andris/Andrew 12,28
  Folcort 21
  Hendr. 21
  Jonas 12,21
  Theunis 58
Doweher, ____ (Wid) 27
Downer,Joseph 288
Downing/Douning,
  Beniamin 212
  Georg 148
Downs, Abigall 49
  Abijah (Jr) 49
  William 49
Doxie, Saml. 21
Doyo/Dovo
  Abraham 200
  Chrtstiaan 200
  Pettr. 1
  Peter (Jr) 200
Draben, Ana Maria 191
Drake, John 10,221
  Joseph 10
  Joseph (Jr) 221
  Joseph (Sr) 221
  William 255
Dregz, Jesies 121
Dreths, Josias 38
Drimiez, Henderick 28
Drinent, James 159
Drk, Cornelius 35
D'Roblus, ____ (Wid) 33
Drom, Jacob 252
Dromboer, Nicolas 224
Druelef, Benj. 23
Drulett/Droilhet, Paul
  33,188
Drum, Anna Cathrina 188
  Magdalen 188
Drune, Symon 165
Dryncwater, Edword 242
Duane, Adelia 294
  Catharine Livingston
    294
  James 295,296
  James Chatham 294
  Sarah 294
Dubels, Susanne 99
Dublett, John 30
Du Bois/Dubois/De Bois/
  Debois/Duboise/Duboys/
  Du Boois/Dibois/Deboijs/
  Du Bous/Deboyes/
  De Boyes, ____ (Madam)
    26
  Abraham 1
  Benjamin 200
  Christiaan 255
  Cornelius 284
  Daniel 225,275
  David 3,225
  Ephraim 276
  Gaul 269
  Gerret 200
  Hendrikus/Hendr. 200,
    284
  Hiskiah/Hiskiagh/
    Hiskiea 196,223,276
  Isaac/Isack/Izack 1,3,
    197,277
  Jacob/Jacobus 3,223,224,
    255
  Jacob/Jacobus (Jr) 275,

Howell (cont)
  Israell 44
  Jacob 48
  James 43
  Jerusha/Zerusah 46
  Johanah 45
  John/Jno. 44,49,53,55,
    156,249
  John (Jr) 157,158
  Jonah 44
  Jonathan/Jonnathan 44,
    48
  Jonathan (Jr) 44
  Jono. (Jr) 158
  Joseph 43,250
  Joseph (Jr) 43
  Josiah 44,250
  Judith 46
  Lemuell 44
  Lidia 45
  Mahite 46
  Martha 46
  Mary 45,46
  Mathew/Matthew 5,47,54,
    158,201
  Nathaniell/Nathan 44
  Nehemiah 44
  Obadia 44
  Penellopie 46
  Phebee 46
  Philip 44
  Prudence 46
  Ralph 147
  Richard 44,48,75,156,
    158,249
  Richard (Jr) 44,48,158
  Ruth 51
  Samuell 44
  Sarah 45,46
  Sary 45
  Sibell 45
  Susanah 46
  Theophilus/Theopple 45,
    250
  Theoph. (Jr) 45
  Tho. 44
  Zebulon 43
Howland, Israel 228
Hoyt/Hoit, Eluzar 221
  Joseph 36
  Moses (Jr) 221
  Samuell 137
Hubbard/Hubard, Elias 182,
  241
  Ezekiel 251
  Isaac 249
  James 178,211
  Jerem. 142
  Samuell 241
Hubssen, Elbert 36
Huck, Thoms 25
Huddleston, ____ (Mr) 25
Hudson/Hutson,
  Goodwin & 296
  Hannah 147
  Henry 251
  John 51,249
  Margrett 31
  Mary 51
  Samuel 251
  Timothy 249
  William 148
Hughes/Huse, Abner 44
  Humphrey 44,158
  Jedadia 44
  John 44
  Martha 46
  Wriah 44

Hughsten, John 270
Hughy, Robert 281
Huijbrechtz, Gerritt 15
Huijcken,Willem 37
Huker, John 42
Hukes, Benjamin 39
  Charles/Charely 39
  Isaac 39
  Mary 39
  Stephen 39
  Tho. 39
  Wm. 39
Hulsart/Hulsartt,
  Anthony 182
  Benjamen 181
Humble, Johanes 276
Hume, Charles 268
Humphreys, William 255
Hun, Johannis 18
Hunkins, Robt. 288
Hunksman, Robert 58
Hunt/Hunts/Hont,
  Anne 221
  Caleb 205
  David 204
  Edward 134
  Jacob 204
  John 204,259
  Jonathan/Johnnathan
    214,294
  Jos. (Jr) 188
  Joshua 204,205
  Josiah 221
  Josiah (Jr) 221
  Mary 221
  Ralph 87
  Stephen/Stephanus 204
  Sussanna 221
  Thomas 204,259
  Zebadiah 259
Hunter, Andrew 261
  Archabald 280
  Eliza 50
  Eliza (Jr) 50
  Hannah 50
  James 280
  Robert 190,280
  Thomas 50
  Zervia 50
Hunting, John 251
Husey/Huse, Abner 44
  Humphrey 44
  James 16
  Jedadia 44
  John 44
  Martha 46
  Uriah 44
Husyele, Peter 21
Hutcheson, Elizabeth 50
  Martha 50
  Martha (Jr) 50
  Mathias 50
  Samuel 50
  Samuel (Jr) 50
  Thomas 50
Hutchins/Hutchinss,
  Charles 294
  John 31
  Thomass 145
Huyberts, Ariaen 167
  Geertje 173
  Joost 168
Huybertsen/Heybertsin,
  Lambert/Lammert 3,166
Huyck/Huicke, Andries 21
  Burger 20
  Cornelis 20
  Johannis 20

Huyck (cont)
  Lamert 20
  Willm. 118
Hyatt/Hyat/Hiat,
  Abraham 221,267
  Gilbord 267
  John 221
Hyde, James 266
Hyne, Hartman 224

-I-

Ichard, Antho. 193
Imans, Andries 169
Inians, John 145
Inkerson, John/Jno. 65,
  150
Ireland, Thomas 36,143
Irish, David 228
  Jesse 228
  William 228
Isaac/Isaack, Abraham
  271
  Aerent 99
Isacks, Joseph 23
Isacksen, Dennys 165
Isbrands, Jan 164
Isolius, Joras 182
Isrel, Salamon 284
Ittich, Mich. 193
Ive, Gerardus 170
Ives, Thomas/Tho. 10,26

-J-

Jackson/Jacson,
  James (Jr) 202
  John/Jno. 7,36,143,213
  Michael 256,257
  Richard 213
  Robert 36
  Samuel/Saml. 36,213
  Thomas 216
  William 26
Jacobs/Jacobse/Jacobsen/
  Jacops/Jacopsen,
  Aeltje 166
  Annetje 173
  Arrent 3
  Barrant 3
  Beletje (see Van
    Naerden) 173
  Canster 168
  Cornelius 33
  Epke 165
  Gerrit 170
  Gideon 169
  Herpert 18
  Jacomyntje 171
  Jan 164,171
  Joris/Jores 101,120,175
  Leury 2
  Pieter/Peter/Pietter/
    Pettr. 2,107,114,164,
    167
  Ralph 206
  Reyner 56
  Thys 163
  Tunis 2
  Tylman 127
  Vrolphert 36
  William/Willem/Wm. 2,

326

Matthyse (cont)
  Hendrick (cont) 193
  John 3
  Matthys/Matthis 1,56
  Peter 172
Mattyse/Matyssen/Mattyson
  (see also Matthyse),
  Henderyck 127
  Matthias/Mattys 11,226
Maul, Anna Catharina 186
  Anna Eliz. 186
  Anna Maria 186
  Anna Ursula 186
  Catharina 186
  Frederick 186
  John Jacob 186
Maurer, Peter 191
Maurice/Mauris, Jacob 27,
  277
Mause, Jerry 286
Mavein, John 36
Maybourn, Thomas 273
Mayer/Maer/Mayr (see also
  De Myer and Myer),
  Andreas 26
  Henry/Hendrick/Hen. 22,
  193,194
Mayhew, Mary 48
  Patience 49
Maynard/Mynard, Danl. 24
  Georg 23
Mead, Andw. 188
Mecerty, James 271
Meckilsa, John 272
Meebe, Abram. 19
  Jan 19
Meet, Pieter Jansen 113
  Yan 29
Megelis, Hessel 173
Mek, Edward 15
Meker, Daniel 260
Melchl, Anna Eliz. 184
  Anna Maria 184
  Sittonia 184
Meldy, Samuel 290
Melgertssen, Jeurian 15
Mellis, Claes 174
Melvine, Hanah 46
Mengels, Anna Maria 184
  John Carolus 184
  Juliana 184
Mennist, Isaac 176
Mentegen, Ferdo. 194
Merdin, Conrad 192
Merier, Isaac 10
Merkell/Merkel/Mirckle,
  Frederik/Fred. 191,223
  Lowrens 224
  Mattys 278
Merlit, Gideon 171
Merrick, Christopher 50
  Hannah 51
Merrill, Charyty 219
  Richard 219
Merritt/Merrit/Merrett/
  Merett/Merit,
  Edward 205
  Joseph 206
  Margry 14
  Meyer 23
  William/Will. 14,15
Merry, John 251
Mersereau, Joshua 287
Mervet, Wm. 9
Meser, Johannes 187
  Margaret 187
  Susan Cath. 187

Messcher, Adam Machielse
  39
Messenger, Samuell/Saml.
  65,140
Mester, Hendrick 27
Metcalf, Catherine/
  Catharine 295
  Simon 295
Mettelares, Abrahm 34
Mettermans, Paulus 168
Meueson, Jno. 4
Meuwens, Arent 167
Mey, Anna Eliz. 186
  Maria Meyir 186
Meyer/Meijer (see also
  Mayer and Myer),
  ___ (Ensign) 260
  Antje 15
  Christian 192
  Henry 264
  John/Jno. 15,265
  Nicolas 226
Meynderts/Myndertse/
  Mynderse/Mindertsen/
  Mijnerssen/Miadsron,
  Burger/Burgar 1,198,225
  Burger (Jr) 225
  Egbert 164
  Fred. 18
  Jan 165
  Johannis 19
  Mary 14
  Myndert 199
  Reyner/Reijnier 14,18
Michaux, Paul 236
Michell/Michill/Michall,
  ___ 24
  David 266
  John 44,150,162
  John (Jr) 44
Michielsen/Michaelson,
  Cornelis 165
  Johannus 130
Middagh/Middag/Midagh/
  Medaegh, Abra. 284
  Aert 245
  Aert Teunissen 169
  Earsh 208
  George 11,224,226
  Gerret 176
  Gerrit Aerts 37
  Griet 176
  Isaac 284
  Jacob 224,279,284
  Johannis 284
  John 2, 182,208,245
  Martie 275
  Tuenis 283
Middellaer, Johannis 255
Miles, Jonathan 44
Mill, Riner 135
Miller, Abraham 207
  Andrew/Andr. 51,88,153,
  252
  Burtoll 264
  Daniel 229,250
  David 51
  Eleazer 251
  Eliza 51
  Georg 162
  Hannah 51
  Hugh 288
  Jacob 260
  James 288
  Jere. 160
  Johannis 283
  John 61,280
  John (Jr) 62,160

Miller (cont)
  John (Sr) 160
  Jonathan 150
  Josiah 251
  Lodewick 286
  Margarett 51
  Margarett (Jr) 51
  Peter 286
  Richard 252
  Robert 147
  Saml. 288
  William/Wm. 61,161,252
Millerin, Wm. 272
Milligan, Alexander 280
Mills/Mils, George 141
  Isaac/Isaack 44,157,218,
  251
  Isaac (Jr) 44
  John 288
  Jonas 218
  Jonathan 140,218
  Samuell 141,157
  Timothy 251
  Zachariah 140
Milre, Robt. 28
Milsbigh, Mattys 281
Milsbugh, Phillip 281
Mimelay, Albert 15
  Meenske 15
Mingaell, Johannis 18
Mings, John 281
Mingus, Cronamas 281
  Jeronimus 225
Minthorne/Minthorn,
  John 262
  Philip/Phillip 35,262,
  273
  Richard/Rich. 146
  Sarah 46
Minvel/Monvel/Munvill,
  ___ (Mrs) 30
  David 35
  Peter 30
Miseroll/Miserol/Misroll/
  Missarole/Mesurole/
  Meserol/Mesrol/
  Merseral/Muserol,
  Jacob 207
  Jan 115,177,248
  Jan (Jr) 115,177
  Jean 108,173
  Jean (Jr) 38
  John 182,207,262
  Josuah 219
Missebagh, Charles 260
Mitchel, John 250
Mith, Samuel 281
Mitter, Cohan Jurry 261
Modge, Moses 58
Moffet, John 202
Mogon, ___ (Mrs) 32
Moll/Moul/Mol/, Abraham
  25
  Christoffel 225
  Engletre 29
  Jan Jacobsen 167
  Stuffel 281
Molts, Abraham 23
Mona, Justina 188
Monall/Monull, Gors 281
  William 281
Monen, John Phillips 186
  Maria 186
Money/Moany, Frank 262
  Henry 34
Monfortt/Monffoort/
  Monford/Monfoor,
  Cornelius 182